UNFELT

UNFELT

THE LANGUAGE OF AFFECT IN THE BRITISH ENLIGHTENMENT

JAMES NOGGLE

CORNELL UNIVERSITY PRESS
Ithaca and London

Open access edition funded by the National Endowment for the Humanities.

Copyright © 2020 by Cornell University

The text of this book is licensed under a Creative Commons Attribution-NonCommercial-NoDerivatives 4.0 International License: https://creativecommons.org/licenses/by-nc-nd/4.0/. To use this book, or parts of this book, in any way not covered by the license, please contact Cornell University Press, Sage House, 512 East State Street, Ithaca, New York 14850. Visit our website at cornellpress.cornell.edu.

First published 2020 by Cornell University Press

Library of Congress Cataloging-in-Publication Data

Names: Noggle, James, author.
Title: Unfelt : the language of affect in the British Enlightenment / James Noggle.
Description: Ithaca : Cornell University Press, 2020. | Includes bibliographical references and index.
Identifiers: LCCN 2019017311 (print) | LCCN 2019018072 (ebook) | ISBN 1501747134 (pdf) | ISBN 1501747142 (epub/mobi) | ISBN 1501747126 | ISBN 1501747126 (cloth)
Subjects: LCSH: English prose literature—18th century—History and criticism. | Emotions in literature. | Enlightenment—Great Britain.
Classification: LCC PR448.E46 (ebook) | LCC PR448.E46 N64 2020 (print) | DDC 820.9/353—dc23
LC record available at https://lccn.loc.gov/2019017311

Cover photograph courtesy of Tate Images/Digital Image, Tate, London 2014. *The Strode Family*, by William Hogarth, ca. 1738. Oil on canvas, 870 × 915 (34 1/4 × 36 in).

To Ferrell Mackey

Contents

Acknowledgments   ix

Introduction: Unfelt Affect   1

Chapter I. Philosophy: Affective Nonconsciousness   25

   1. The Insensible Parts of Locke's *Essay*   28

   2. David Hartley's Ghost Matter   42

   3. Vivacity and Insensible Association: Condillac and Hume   50

   4. Sentiment and Secret Consciousness: Haywood and Smith   59

Chapter II. Fiction: Unfelt Engagement   69

   1. Unfeeling before Sensibility   73

   2. External and Invisible   81

   3. Insensible against Involuntary in Burney   95

   4. Austen as Coda   108

Chapter III. Historiography: Insensible Revolutions   113

   1. The Force of the Thing: Unfelt Moeurs in French Historiography   117

   2. The Insensible Revolution and Scottish Historiography   126

   3. Gibbon in History   137

   4. The Embrace of Unfeeling   145

CHAPTER IV. POLITICAL ECONOMY:
MOVING WITH MONEY   155

1. Mandeville and the Other Happiness   159
2. Feeling Untaxed   169
3. The Money Flow   175
4. Invisible versus Insensible   183

EPILOGUE: INSENSIBLE EMERGENCE
OF IDEOLOGY   191

Notes   197
Bibliography   241
Index   259

Acknowledgments

A number of people and organizations helped me in my work on this book since I began it in 2011, and I want to express my gratitude to them. A fellowship from the National Endowment for the Humanities during the academic year 2014–15 gave a much appreciated vote of confidence to the project as it was finding its final shape, and allowed me to do a significant amount of research and writing. (The views, findings, and conclusions expressed in this book do not necessarily represent those of the National Endowment for the Humanities.) Wellesley College also generously supported my work during this leave year, and well beyond. I also thank Bucknell University Press for allowing me use material in this book from my essay, "Unfelt Affect," which appeared in *Beyond Sense and Sensibility: Moral Formation and the Literary Imagination from Johnson to Wordsworth*, edited by Peggy Thompson (Lewisburg, PA: Bucknell University Press, 2015). I add a particular thanks to Mahinder Kingra, editor in chief at Cornell University Press and my acquisitions editor, whose intellectual engagement with the book's ideas and presentation helped me along a sometimes winding road toward its acceptance for publication. I am grateful too to Brian Bendlin, who copyedited the manuscript with precision and insight, regularizing what I thought was my regular system of citation and fixing many errors. All mistakes that remain are, of course, my doing. And I thank Karen Laun, Mary Ribesky, and the rest of the production team for their care in bringing the manuscript into print.

I have presented parts of the book's argument at colloquiums and panel discussions over the last six years. Several of these presentations occurred at annual meetings of the American Society for Eighteenth-Century Studies (ASECS). I first described the project's principal ideas on a panel put together by Martine Brownley titled "Beyond Sense and Sensibility" at the ASECS Annual Meeting in San Antonio, in 2012; my work on David Hartley found a place on the panel "Quantifying the Enlightenment," chaired by Corrinne Harol in Pittsburgh in 2016; and I presented on affect and the economic writing of Hume and Adam Smith in Minneapolis on a panel titled "Affect Theory and the Literature of Sensibility," convened by Stephen Ahern in 2017. I am grateful to the panel chairs, my copanelists, and audience members at these ASECS gatherings for thought-provoking discussion and their questions in response to my work. I especially want to thank Peggy Thompson, whom I met on the "Beyond Sense and Sensibility" panel and who edited the collection of that title for Bucknell University Press. Her incisive and insightful editorial comments and criticisms helped me bring my essay, which resulted from the panel, to its final form. I am also grateful to Martin Cohen, who invited me to speak about my project at the Philosophy, Poetry, and Religion Seminar at the Mahindra Humanities Center at Harvard University in 2014; we had a lively and fruitful discussion there about affect, felt and unfelt.

My work has also been supported in less direct but considerable ways by communities at Wellesley College. I am grateful to participants, from many disciplines, in our Long Eighteenth Century Working Group—particularly Simon Grote, whose zeal for our collective intellectual life here has been both inspiring and practically effective, and Hélène Bilis, whose generous and expert help with some of the French quoted in this book makes me wish, as I look again over passages I didn't want to bother her with, that I'd consulted with her more. I am also grateful to the Wellesley English Department, the most collegial and mutually supportive department I've ever encountered or even heard of. Our daily lunches, with Margery Sabin, Tim Peltason, Marilyn Sides, Vernon Shetley, Kate Brogan, Bill Cain, Lisa Rodensky, Susan Meyer, Dan Chiasson, and Larry Rosenwald among the most devoted participants, represent somebody's idealized fantasy of intellectual and workplace friendship and support. Lucky for me, it's real.

As I think about the people I am closest to, the main idea of this book gains a depth and fullness that has the power, even after all the time I've spent writing about it, to take me by surprise. The strongest feelings I have are like the surface of an unfelt ocean of intimacy and passing time that buoys them. During the years this book was written, Clara Noggle was always funny, always critically acute, and always loving, yet these traits lived in the spontaneity of her performances of them, each of which burst forth as if unprecedented. Dexter Noggle's warmth of love, creativity, and skeptical humor came to light both in striking expressions and in his gentle way of being in a room, as the two modes continuously heightened each other. Barbara Noggle's loving presence in my life continues to extend, uninterrupted and vital, from a time before *presence* and *love* were words I knew. And T. Mackey mixed affection with a genius for physical comedy in ways that always felt surprising and yet, in immediate retrospect, predictable. Finally, the happiness I get from reflecting that this is the third book I have dedicated to Ferrell Mackey wells up from the years, the apartments and a house, the plans and accidents, we have shared together. Everything unexpected, fun, difficult, odd, and exciting in our lives is held together in a hugeness of tacit, passing time that, however unrecoverable, is always ours.

UNFELT

Introduction
Unfelt Affect

The word *insensibly* recurs with strange persistence in British prose of the age of sensibility. "A thousand occasional meetings," says Frances Burney's heroine in *Evelina* (1778) of her growing feelings for Orville, "could not have brought us to that degree of social freedom, which four days spent under the same roof have, insensibly, been productive of."[1] In this book, I consider the meanings and uses of these recurrences and related idioms in Enlightenment prose. The word has struck me as suggestive from the time I started reading a lot of eighteenth-century literature in graduate school. It seemed "poetic," even romantic, somehow—evoking (to use Burney's word) a *productive* movement of feeling that cannot itself be felt, attended to, or defined while it is happening. Such resonances put me on alert, and I noticed the term wherever it came up, in eighteenth-century literature or not. Any version I happened on, for instance, of the popular French ballad "Insensiblement," written by Paul Misraki during World War II, caught my ear: "Insensiblement vous vous êtes glissée dans ma vie, / Insensiblement vous vous êtes logée dans mon cœur" ("Insensibly you have glided into my life, / Insensibly you have lodged in my heart . . ."—though I first heard Django Reinhardt's wordless rendition recorded in 1953).

This peculiar combination—the unfelt emergence and motions of strongly felt feelings—appears all over eighteenth-century writing. "But, above all, in conversing with her," writes Henry Brooke in his novel *The Fool of Quality* (1765–70), "the Music of her Accents, and the Elegance of her Sentiments fell insensibly on his Soul that drank them up, as a dry Ground drinks up the invisible Dew of the Evening."[2] As I began to think about such locutions in a more deliberate way, I observed their occurrence in contexts well beyond novelists' depictions of falling in love unawares. Philosophy, historiography, and political economy all make copious if discreet use of such terms, though in a way quite different from how some "keyword" or "complex word" would be deployed.[3] The usages express something deep but inexplicit about how affect was understood in the eighteenth century, how feeling, passions, the emotions, and even perception itself were seen subtly to come into existence and move people. Instead of drawing attention to itself as an especially significant, well-defined concept or idea, a word like *insensibly* occurs almost in passing in the period's writing. But this unstudied casualness, far from rendering its meaning insignificant, holds a key to its power. A scarcely noticed but crucial and consistent set of gestures to an affect that cannot be felt: that is the terrain this book explores.

The adverbial character of these terms, their association with action and change, specifies the idiom that interests me in this volume. Instead of indicating a mere lack of feeling—an affective blockage, impassivity, stupefaction—insensibly unfolding processes initiate and build strong feeling or make it possible. The adjectival form can evoke that too. Writers refer to the "insensible (or imperceptible) degrees" by which a feeling or perception intensifies and alters, an additive sense with an essentially temporal dimension. (In Samuel Johnson's *Dictionary of the English Language*, 1755, *insensibly* is said to mean "by slow degrees.")[4] But the adjective also often *does* refer to a mere lack of feeling, numbness, insensitivity. Brooke's *Fool of Quality* again: "Hannah stooped, in Haste, and applied Hartshorn to the Nose of the Woman, who appeared wholly insensible."[5] Here the term is strictly privative, describing someone who does not feel anything, and the heavy noun *insensibility* tends to do the same. (I will say more about the grammar of these usages below.) Samuel Richardson's Clarissa Harlowe, for instance, declaims against the "barbarous insensibility" of any man unaffected by compassion on "*proper* occasions."[6] The privative dimension of such language—feeling muted or dampened—has been treated in a few scholarly accounts, in eighteenth-century studies and beyond.[7] (And Fredric Jameson's notion of the "waning of affect" in postmodern times has endured as a point of reference.)[8] This book explores something like the opposite. Literature of the long eighteenth century consistently appeals to the insensible as a covertly burgeoning, narrative force, a movement from which sensibility emerges.

This introduction will outline the critical approach needed to understand this group of stylistic functions—the term *ideas* would reify them too much—in eighteenth-century writing. The insensible allows writers in widely different areas of prose to describe feeling as involved in physical systems, temporal frameworks, and collectivities of movement that human beings subject to them do not feel. This subtle, secret layer of unfeeling could seem like an eighteenth-century analogue of the unconscious mind, before that concept had even begun to be invented. The unfelt undercurrent makes our felt lives the way they are. This study will, however, indicate more consistently the limitations of this analogy than its strengths. More helpful to me will be ideas from affect theory, and especially the strand initiated by Gilles Deleuze, which defines the "nonconscious" dimensions of affect as different from the workings of the Freudian unconscious.[9] (Freud's exegetes, including Jacques Lacan, stress that Freud rejects the very possibility of unconscious affects, insisting that only mental contents—ideational representations, *Vorstellungen*—can properly be called unconscious.)[10] Affect theory's accounts of affective flows and feedback, the "subtlest of intensities," the "miniscule or molecular events of the unnoticed,"[11] will help clarify what eighteenth-century appeals to the insensible have to say. But differences between the two will also emerge. Not a theory, not a set of names for isolatable states, forces, or even processes, the language of the insensible spreads unselfconsciously throughout writing in the period to designate an open variety of unfelt changes to feeling. But this variety has a shape.

The Logic of an Idiom

My sense as a reader of the distinctive prevalence of terms like *insensibly* in eighteenth-century prose turns out to be quantifiably verifiable. A Google Ngram search shows that usage of the word rose steeply and steadily (after some earlier spikes) from 1686 to a peak around 1786, then dropped off precipitously to where it is now (see figure 1).[12] This is the roughly one-hundred-year period explored in this book. In parallel, my four chapters each attend to examples from early in this span—from philosophy, fiction, historiography, and political economy—and then focus on the rising peak during the age of sensibility, roughly 1745–90, and then point to what happened afterward.

The French case, relevant here because of the French influences on English writing that I discuss throughout, shows *insensiblement* on a slightly more jagged Ngram course, with peaks in the seventeenth and early eighteenth centuries and a final one around 1795. But Misraki's song notwithstanding, the decline in French matches the one in English, as usage in both falls steeply through the nineteenth and twentieth centuries. These graphs seem to present something in need of explanation. Written representations of the phenomenon of unfelt change themselves changed in some way in the 1780s or 1790s. Words like *insensibly* stopped being useful, and a different vocabulary emerged, with different emphases and implications, to take its place.

The root error that such basic word searches promote, however, is viewing a vast multitude of distinct, possibly incompatible facts—discrete instances

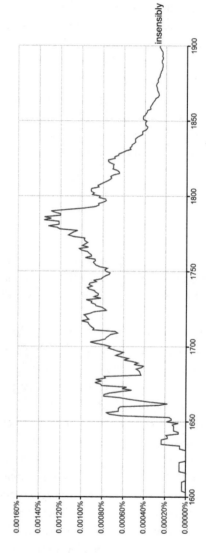

Figure 1. Jean-Baptiste Michel et al. "Quantitative Analysis of Culture Using Millions of Digitized Books," *Science* 331.6014 (2011): 176–82.

of usage—as if they were just one fact, a single, meaningful line sloping upward and then falling. In that form, they sometimes encourage those looking at them to propose a cause of the line's shape, its rise and fall, perhaps in this case to identify some important event around 1790 that changed usage. As Matthew L. Jockers, a promoter of more sophisticated quantitative methods in the humanities, bluntly cautions, "when we examine a word, or an n-gram, out of the context in which it appears, we inevitably lose information about how that word is being employed."[13] And context is everything with a word like the adjectival form *insensible* because it has two opposite meanings, unfeeling (privative) and unfelt (additive).

The history shown in lossy Ngram pictures, then, can be only a rough starting point. This book will explain the meaning of this pattern of usage by examining a sequence of examples in detail across disparate kinds of prose. The examples are related not only because they have a specific set of words in common but also because together they shape these words into an idiom, a common style of expression and thought put to certain uses. Though a philosophical account of a particle's effect on the senses obviously differs from a novelistic description of a heroine's insensibly changing feelings, these verbal gestures project a complex and consistent meaning across the period's prose. Collectively the texts I survey will demonstrate not just that *insensibly* and like terms are words of the eighteenth century, as Ngram charts show. They will also reveal why. Far from an unintelligible spread of disconnected uses, this terminology specifically and concretely serves the period's understanding of feeling.

It is important to recognize the unusualness of this claim at the outset. I am arguing that a seemingly casual idiom, which may at first glance seem like little more than a tic in Enlightenment prose style, acts like a concept, with specific content. The writing of the period does not consider or elaborate on the idiom's semantic significance very fully, which is instead manifested in the way it acquires meanings in usage, especially in discourses centered on sensations, passions, and feelings. The idiom is an inconspicuous but load-bearing element of these discourses, allowing them to function as they do and solve the problems they set out to solve without drawing much attention to itself. The depth and consistency of its meaning—its logic—across the kinds of writing I treat in this book partly derive from three of its quasi-semantic features.

First, the close association between the insensible and the senses, throughout the different contexts that this book surveys, is striking. The structure of the word itself helps ensure this. By including the idea of sensation in its negation of it, the term remains in close proximity to feeling (unlike more neutral expressions such as "by slow degrees"). To call a process insensible is to say two things about it, in a strongly ironic tension with each other: It cannot be felt, and it exists. Its existence presses, so to speak, its unfelt status into a position especially pertinent to what we eventually do come to feel. Instead of offering criticism of or a retreat from the era's obsession with the passions and the sensing mind, the unfelt proves, again and again, to be that discourse's enabling element. If a principal project of the age of sensibility is narrating the civilization of the appetites and passions, whether in individual cases (barbarous men in novels acquiring tender feelings) or in collective ones (rude peoples becoming polite), the insensible nature of the transformation consistently plays an indispensable part.

So Edward Gibbon writes of the Huns in *The History of the Decline and Fall of the Roman Empire* (1776–89): "Their manners were softened, and even their features were insensibly improved, by the mildness of the climate, and their long residence in a flourishing province."[14] Here sociable and physical softenings emerge, by unfelt degrees, together. Modern society also arrives at its peak of sensibility due to processes set in motion in preceding eras that cannot be sensed as they occur. David Hume, in the first published volumes of *The History of England* (1754–61), describes the climate of feeling at the turn of the seventeenth century: "about this period, the minds of men, throughout Europe, especially in England, seem to have undergone a general, but insensible revolution."[15] And again, the process he describes entwines material changes (in industry, commerce, navigation) with a refinement of feelings and manners. The insensible is used to mark the unseen point of the emergence of sensibility or permit the change from one order of feeling to another.

This mediating function of unfeeling is a second commonality among its occurrences in the long eighteenth century. Writers repeatedly use these terms as a kind of lubricant in narration, a way of getting from one state or situation to another that seems incompatible with it: indifference to love, barbarity to politeness. In chapter IV of this book I discuss how political economists portray the link, itself unfelt, between two affective states: the strong, often rather sordid passions (greed, envy, "self-liking," vanity) that drive commerce, and their fortunate affective outcome, what Adam Smith in *The Wealth of Nations* (1776) calls "the publick happiness."[16] The "silent and insensible operation" of international trade for Smith destroys feudalism and creates the more or less happy system of modern European commercial states. Similar idioms perform the role of mediator in quite different contexts.[17] As chapter I describes, John Locke in his *Essay concerning Human Understanding* (1689) postulates the existence of "insensible parts" of matter to mediate between the two halves of his most famous distinction: primary and secondary qualities. And in section 2 of chapter I, I show how the notion of a fantasy substance in the brain radically unavailable to sense helps David Hartley mediate between what feels and what is felt, spirit and matter, the ultimate divide. Finally, what motivates the turn to *insensibly* is the need for a term to bridge personal, intense feeling to some opposite: the material body, a social collective, a historical pattern—in an era in which detailed scrutiny of all three of those things intensifies. The logic of the idiom, its reference to a potent but blank affect, movement, or power, makes it consistently useful to writers who seek to join states or conditions of being that otherwise seem incompatible.

A third widely evident aspect of the idiom, also built into its semantic structure, is its tendency to refer to a prepersonal component of affect. The adverb *insensibly* very often modifies the actions of slow processes that no one deliberately or otherwise personally performs. *Things* happen insensibly, *to* people. The idiom portrays people as objects of insensible processes rather than subjects of "insensible emotions." So in the passage from Burney quoted at the beginning of this introduction, it is the "four days" that have been insensibly productive, not Evelina or Orville. In the one from Brooke, "Music" and "Elegance" act insensibly, and though the alluring Panthea performs these, she does not perform their insensible effect. They are insensible not because of the special way she does them but because of how such things work affectively in time. They produce profound effects on personal feelings precisely because they impersonally precede them. For this reason, we do not encounter personalities or literary characters distinguished by a tendency to act in an especially insensible way. When applied in adjectival form directly to a person, in fact, the term simply flips to its privative sense: "He was insensible to the music of her accents and the elegance of her sentiments."[18] He would then be understood merely as lacking sensibility, not as affected unawares by it (and so would join the class of notably impassive characters called "insensibles" by Wendy Anne Lee in her book *Failures of Feeling*, 2018).

These three elements of meaning are not deliberately worked up by any eighteenth-century novelist or philosopher into an elaborate concept. They instead arise naturally, we might say, from the idiom's ordinary but complex grammar in usage. This most basically appears in the function of terms like *insensible* as what grammarians call noninherent adjectives, as opposed to inherent ones. An insensible man, again, does not feel, is in a stupor or is unable to sympathize with the sufferings of others. The adjective in that case is inherent because it applies to what he is himself. But this book focuses on the potential of the word as a noninherent adjective. In phrases like "a safe neighborhood" or "a melancholy necessity," the adjective does not describe the noun inherently. The neighborhood itself is not safe from flood or fire, the necessity does not itself feel sad. Such adjectives point away, so to speak, from the words they seem to modify. The necessity is melancholy because it affects somebody that way, and the streets are safe because of how a person—anybody—might feel walking on them. Describing a process as insensible likewise does not mean that the process itself does not feel. It means someone—but who?—does not feel it, even as it also indicates that something *is* happening. It is additive, not merely privative and, applying to the process, does not personalize itself, again, to the person who does not feel it.

If it seems simpler just to say that the adjective has two distinct meanings, in a tension with each other—unfeeling and unfelt—it is still evident that the second leaves the insensible profoundly unspecified in application. It is open, as it were, to the world. And the adverb expresses this openness even better. When, in one of the broad-brush, "philosophical" chapters of *The Decline and Fall*, Gibbon declares that "the progress of manufactures and commerce insensibly collects a large multitude within the walls of a city,"[19] we may ask, Insensibly to whom? And the answer could include the people gathering in the city, or the people still outside looking in, or anybody else—tax collectors, social commentators—in a position not to notice. Finally the answer could be, well, to nobody—not insensibly to anybody in particular, just insensibly in general. This indeterminacy, especially evident in the work of historians, expands human time beyond a reductive understanding of it as a sequence of events consciously experienced by particular people. The idiom's pre- or nonpersonal character, its openness to the world, sentient and insentient, ensures that it works in ways resembling affect as described in certain theoretical discussions, as we shall see.

All this semantic richness makes the word useful to writers about feeling, but it attracts nothing like the self-conscious philosophical attention that the passions, sentiments, and sensibility do in the eighteenth century. Generally speaking, adverbs and adverbial phrases tend to be less theorized than nouns or classifying adjectives (such as *sentimental*). A *how* can seem less susceptible to systematic treatment than a *what* or a *what kind*. Often an abstract noun works in a theory to put a wide array of adverbs in order. So all the ways that things move through space—quickly, erratically, steadily, slowly—call forth a unified theory of gravity or "universal attraction." There are no treatises in the period (that I know of) on "how things happen insensibly." It is instructive in this respect to contrast the insensible with concrete cognitive phenomena like attention and distraction, which have been treated in studies of eighteenth-century literature and thought.[20] A person can be distracted from or attentive to something, and mocked or praised for being so, but the insensible offers no such options. Its essence lies in its gestures to what is beyond notice, something "not discoverable by the senses," as the definition of *insen-*

sible in Johnson's *Dictionary* has it. The word characterizes any unfolding and enfolding process, and only its privative sense refers to individuals' cognitive states. (So references to the four days that affect Evelina and Orville, and to the progress that collects people in a city, are not meant to raise questions, satirical or otherwise, about their powers of attention, but rather comment on the peculiar way that passing time affects sensibility.) These features make the idiom resist scholarly attempts at conceptual history, the kind of *Begriffsgeschichte* in the style of Reinhart Koselleck.[21] What I offer here is something like a conceptual history without a concept.

This lack, however, also provides an opportunity. Ordinary idioms and elements of style sometimes do profound work. Everyday talk, about ourselves and our feelings, reveals commitments to ways we look at ourselves in the world. It is wrong, I think, to call these commitments philosophical.[22] But it is also wrong not to read ordinary language with care to help it tell us what we think. The relation of elements of common prose style to theoretical understanding or philosophy in any period takes many forms. In the eighteenth century, some fashionable terms first get elaborated in philosophy and criticism—*sublime*, for instance—and then find their way into common usage. A diary or poem will refer to a sublime scene or a sublime thought, and the relation of such utterances to authoritative critical definitions and elaborations can be discerned. In other cases—*taste*, for instance—a word appears first in common conversation, then undergoes a kind of discipline in periodical essays, literary criticism, philosophical treatises, and the like. So Joseph Addison begins his *Spectator* essay on taste, typically seen as an inaugural statement in the aesthetic tradition: "As this Word arises very often in Conversation, I shall endeavor to give some Account of it."[23] But then any reference to taste in the literature of the eighteenth century, no matter how casual, can be plotted against such painstaking accounts.

As my work on this study advanced, I realized that even if I discovered some extended commentary on insensible processes written in the period, it could not have served as the source or headwater of the examples and contexts that the term makes interesting. Even Locke's account of an insensibly formed personal identity does not look like such a source, supremely influential though his *Essay* is. When Gibbon—the only author treated in this study whose addiction to the term *insensibly* has been widely remarked on by commentators—says early on in the *Decline and Fall* that "education and study insensibly inspired the natives of those countries [of the western barbarians] with the sentiments of Romans,"[24] he does not "allude" to Locke or anybody else but rather employs a favorite stylistic device. In contrast, when a letter, a poem, or a periodical essay refers to "secondary qualities," or mental "ideas," we hear a distinct and perhaps deliberately sounded Lockean note. The usage of the insensible, though consistently meaningful, is promiscuous and "horizontal"— heedless of evident disciplinary hierarchy and available to anybody who wants to talk about the effect that unfelt change has on something felt. It is more a fashionable idiom than a term of art.

I will show throughout this book how this idiom gets taken up in and enables diverse, sometimes incompatible ways of understanding feelings. These include material ones: Robert Boyle's corpuscularianism; Isaac Newton's "Æthereal Medium" introduced in the "Queries" to the *Opticks* (1706, 1730); Hartley's postulation of special particles in the brain; the hydrostatic vocabulary that Hume adopts to discuss the flow of money, and so on. A mysterious quality pervades the contexts of natural science that make use of the idiom, but no single mechanical theory unites them all. The usage exceeds the particular theoretical contexts it serves, and the same goes for its role in less theorized enterprises like fiction, historiography, devotional literature, and other areas of prose. But it seems desperate to give up discussing the idiom's sophisticated and consistent contributions to literary expression simply because it is discursively homeless or because we can find no single source of it, theoretical, technical, or otherwise. While the logic and grammar I have just outlined evoke a sense of the deep power of unfeeling to support feeling, the usages do not together compose a concept such as an eighteenth-century version of the unconscious mind. The idiom is too widely useful and contextually various to do that.

Attempts to recount the prehistory of the unconscious have sometimes turned to the eighteenth century. The tradition of understanding unconscious aspects of mental life is often said to originate with Franz Anton Mesmer's experiments with animal magnetism.[25] Peter Sloterdijk claimed in his *Critique of Cynical Reason* (1983) that "the illusion of a transparent human self-consciousness has been systematically destroyed" as the result of what Mesmerism began.[26] As the 1785 report on Mesmerism to Louis XVI by Benjamin Franklin, Antoine Lavoisier, and others puts it, "The object of this system was a fluid extremely subtle, upon which were bestowed the magnificent titles of soul of the world, spirit of the universe, and universal magnetic fluid; and which was pretended to be diffused through the whole space occupied by the material creation, to animate the system of nature, to penetrate all substances, and to be the vehicle to animated bodies in general, and their several regions in particular, of certain forces of attraction and repulsion, by means of which they explained the phenomena of nature."[27] If the unconscious begins here, with the discovery of a particular occult substance,[28] it constitutes a break with the idioms that depict unfelt change that are the subject of this book, which lack any such "magnificent" fanfare or focus on some special subtle fluid. A system of expression that represents unnoticed passages of time gives way to a comprehensive theory of life and matter.

Mesmer made his appearance in English print right around the time, 1785, that the term *insensibly* began its fall into disuse.[29] And while the term *conscious* appeared, of course, in important literary contexts before this point,[30] it is at least worth noting that *unconsciously* began its conspicuous climb just when *insensibly* declined (see figure 2). Again, concrete examples and context matter more than such vague and often misleading pictures. I will comment in chapter II of this book on a change in Burney's portrayals of her characters' unnoticed affective motions, particularly on alterations to her techniques of antipsychological representation from *Evelina* (1778) to *Cecilia* (1782), a shift occurring slightly before the big drop-off indicated in Google Ngram. The more open idioms in Burney recede, and words more firmly anchored in the minds of individuals (involuntary, unconscious) come forward.

Probably every period has its own ways of recognizing, more or less explicitly, that much more goes into our feelings than what we consciously feel. Like theories of the unconscious would later do, the idioms of unfelt affect in the eighteenth century put "transparent human conscious" into question. But the logic of the idiom distinguishes it from what comes after. English users simply understood the insensible differently from the way we came to understand the unconscious and incorporate it into our views of our minds in later years. Representations of the unfelt aspects of mental life became less adverbial and more about nouns, more about theorized entities and specific kinds of mental processes underneath awareness. As we shall see, the insensible tends to modify not kinds of mental content but rather nonmental processes in the world that affect the mind and feelings.

Affective Genealogies

Scholars in the humanities who employ theories of affect now have also looked back more than a century before Mesmer for the articulation of some of their foundational concepts. Parts 2 and (especially) 3 of the *Ethics* (1677) of Baruch Spinoza have served as a principal source of inspiration in Gilles Deleuze's influential account of affect,[31] and theorists who follow this strand in Deleuze in effect follow Spinoza too. Gregory J. Seigworth and Melissa Gregg's introduction to *The Affect Theory Reader* (2010) relays Spinoza's dictum, "No one has yet determined what the body can do," as an invitation to expand the theoretical

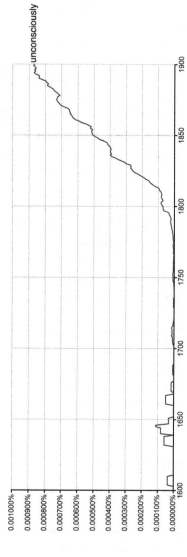

Figure 2. Jean-Baptiste Michel et al. "Quantitative Analysis of Culture Using Millions of Digitized Books." *Science* 331.6014 (2011): 176–82.

field.[32] Spinoza's antidualistic depiction of affect as investing and connecting bodies in fields of physical movement contrasts, as Deleuze and Félix Guattari indicate, with what they call "sentiment," understood as mere "personal feeling."[33] Affect for Deleuze and his heirs extends beyond human emotion and mindedness to encompass all interactions among bodies: "A body affects other bodies, or is affected by other bodies; it is this capacity for affecting and being affected that also defines a body in its individuality."[34]

Deleuze will refine his definition of affect by noting that Spinoza uses two different Latin words for it—*affectio* and *affectus*—with distinct and complementary meanings. *Affectio* refers to a body's physical encounter with another that affects its state, while *affectus* is a body's own ongoing and ceaseless transitioning, from state to succeeding state, resulting from such encounters.[35] As Deleuze puts it in a 1978 lecture at Vincennes on Spinoza, "Affectus in Spinoza is variation . . . continuous variation of the force of existing."[36] And in a lecture in 1981, describing the durations that the affectus comprises in all its variability, he notes that "in a sense, the duration is always behind our backs, it's at our backs that it happens."[37] These definitions of *affectus* will help illuminate the insensibly unfolding processes, the tacit movements from state to state, that this book treats. Unlike an ensemble of subjective emotions, the *affectus* is a "prepersonal intensity" (in Brian Massumi's gloss of the term) attending the body's ceaseless variation.[38] The insensible in British literature of the period exemplifies the nature of *affectus* as passage and variation at its most elusive and minute.

The so-called English Deists of the early eighteenth century—Anthony Collins, Matthew Tindal, and John Toland, among others—step forth as Spinoza's most unambiguous heirs in Britain,[39] and their accounts of the body resonate with this book's theme. In his anticlerical tract *The Natural History of Superstition* (1709), John Trenchard, republican radical and associate of Collins and Toland, offers a remarkable account of mysterious, affective connections among bodies and their passions:

> Nature in many circumstances seems to work by a sort of secret Magick, and by ways unaccountable to us, and yet produces as certain, and regular events as the most obviously Mechanical Operations. Passions of the Mind, as well as Actions of the Body, are not only communicated by all the Senses, but probably by other ways indiscernible to us: . . . The Yawning of one Person infects a whole Company; the Tone, the Motions, the Gestures, and Grimaces of those we converse with steal insensibly upon us, even when we endeavour to avoid them; Not only Nations and Sects, but Professions, and particular Societies of Men for

the most part contract peculiar Airs, and Features, which are easily distinguishable to a nice observer, and one but of moderate skill in Phisiognomy [sic] will discover a Parson, a Quaker, or a Taylor, dress them how you please."[40]

The sense of mystery in Trenchard's examples enlarges, in Spinozan fashion, our appreciation of what bodies can do.[41] They influence each other by affection (*affectio*), and their passages and variations from one state to the next (as *affectus*) "steal insensibly upon us." Social collectivities (sects, nations, professions) cohere according to the same forces that affect the states of individuals. And all this happens, Trenchard adds, "by a sort of natural Mechanism."[42] Here is the insensible as unfelt affect: an array of mechanical motions, notable for their variety, subtlety, and flexibility, that invest and exceed individual bodies and make social bodies possible.

But the novelists, historians, and philosophers discussed in this book who similarly appeal to the insensible are not so firmly in Spinoza's orbit. The very commonness in English of the idiom of the insensible makes any lines of supposed influence from a comparatively little read and often reviled Dutch seventeenth-century philosopher seem beside the point.[43] If the idiom somehow carries an obscure Spinozan residue unknown to those who employ it, the vitality that these usages have in common surpasses such influence. Some scholars moreover have set the English "moderate mainstream Enlightenment" of Locke and Newton, and the later Scottish one of Hume and Smith, against the "radical Enlightenment" promoted by Spinoza,[44] though various affinities, between Hume and Spinoza, for instance, have sometimes been explored.[45] It seems more productive to view the affective resonance of the idiom as arising from a more general set of intellectual practices and attitudes, of which a Spinozan openness to what the body can do is a part. An increasingly detailed attention in the period to a diversity of material anchors of sensate life—to particles and corpuscles, animal spirits, vibrations of nerves, vital and electric fluids—made bridging feeling and unfeeling a compelling task for dualists (as we will see with Hartley) and materialists (as with Hartley's disciple Joseph Priestley) alike.

Apart from such issues of precedence and inheritance, the conceptual vocabulary of affect theory (including Spinoza's *affectus*) helps illuminate the significance and effects of the idiom. What I have called the openness of the insensible to the world, its reference to processes of change often not referred to any particular mind or sensing being, resonates with the ways theorists say that affect works. As Seigworth and Gregg put it, in language heightened by their theoretical interests, affect is now commonly employed in "critical discourses of the emotions (and histories of the emotions) that have progressively left behind the interiorized self or subjectivity ... to unfold regimes of expressivity that are tied much more to resonant worldings and diffusions of feeling/passions—often including atmospheres of sociality, crowd behaviors, contagions of feeling."[46]

The insensible suggests something like a contagion of unfeeling, in part by its grammatical noninherence. The not-feeling it designates is often not referred to any particular nearby mind, so it has a way of opening up to any and all available. Of course, when love insensibly affects someone (as in the passage quoted from Brooke's *Fool of Quality*), we primarily think of the lover himself as not feeling it. But his beloved, as well as onlookers, "friends" of the couple, and others, may be understood as not sensing the onset too. Even the reader herself may be led by the idiom to look for earlier moments when her suspicion of their love began to creep unawares into her reading. As such the insensible can seem a specially novelistic effect. Other descriptions of (for instance) gradual historical change convey this openness even more. Since changes to a person, a group, a town, a region happen insensibly, there is no need to specify who exactly should be said not to sense them.

All such movements remain "positive" by virtue of their attachment to processes that actually produce or describe eventually experienced change. This dynamic interaction between unfelt potential and actual felt feeling finds analogues in the language of Massumi, who speaks of affect as "intensity" that may be "qualified"—arrested—as an identified and thereby felt emotion.[47] Massumi's keyword "virtual" refers to the flow of affect not (yet or ever) actualized in conscious feeling. And in another essay he declares that "virtuality cannot be seen in the form that emerges from it. The virtual gives form, but itself has none (being the unform of transition). The virtual is imperceptible. It is insensible."[48] Massumi's dyad of virtual intensity and qualified emotion is not a simple, static opposition but a pairing, subject to "resonance and feedback."[49] Such accounts help clarify various transactions I will describe in this book. As I show in chapter IV, Bernard Mandeville portrays "the Happiness of the City" as virtual and unfelt, inasmuch as the indexes of the City's prosperity—crowded streets, nasty overflowing gutters—make its inhabitants rather miserable. Yet its thriving condition feeds their own feelings back to them, transformed, to make it possible for them feel a kind of happiness about their success at another level, in another register, after all. Unfelt processes, personal or social, may resonate with our conscious emotions, which may then either heighten or dampen their virtual affective base.

The virtuality of affect has not been much discussed in accounts of sentiment and the passions in eighteenth-century studies. The burgeoning enterprise of the history and theory of emotions, in scholarship about the period and beyond, has instead focused on the shape and historical transformations of more apparent feelings. Important monographs have explored, for instance, the difference between premodern and modern (i.e., eighteenth-century and beyond) conceptions of happiness in illuminating terms,[50] as well as the special affective power of literary love.[51] The literature of sensibility and sympathy will continue to inspire studies that bear on new theoretical approaches to affect,[52] and new essays and collections on the topic in eighteenth-century studies are appearing all the time.[53] These have understandably zeroed in on and discussed discernible passions, and the expressive power of tears, cries, laughter, and the like. A sustained account of unfelt affect, its potential or virtual elements that differ from the palpable and apparent realizations of emotion with which it resonates, has not appeared until this book.[54]

A central motive of this study, however, pulls it away from some of the most often stated aims of affect theory. My emphasis on the insensible as a ready rhetorical maneuver, used by writers to execute otherwise impossible shifts between depictions of incompatible feelings, stands in tension with what Lawrence Grossberg notes is the stress in theories of affect on its "non-representational and . . . non-semantic" dimensions,[55] or—in Seigworth and Gregg's terms—its "pre-/extra-/para-linguistic" standing.[56] A similar impulse to draw a line between affect and language helps define Massumi's project. While insisting that "language, though headstrong, is not simply in opposition to [affective] intensity," he tends to find affect operating on a fundamentally nonlinguistic plane.[57] Much writing about affect exhibits a similar tendency. The strand pursued by Eve Kosofsky Sedgwick, leading not from Deleuze but from psychologist Silvan Tomkins, rejects the dogmas of the so-called linguistic turn of the early "theory" era and instead describes a bodily affect expressly irreducible to the binary oppositions of language deconstructed by poststructuralists.[58] In one of the most often cited critiques of affect theory, Ruth Leys has argued that both Massumi and Sedgwick are invested in a dualism that portrays affects in the body as radically distinct from the mind's "intention and reason," especially as articulated by language. They thus make what Leys calls "the error of separating the affects from cognition or meaning."[59]

The peculiar nature of the eighteenth-century idioms I survey in this book mostly sets them apart from the issues at stake in these debates. Accounts of the body and the structures of psychology do figure in many examples here, and a sense of what the body can do, newly vivid in the period, is one context of appeals to the insensible. But eighteenth-century brain science is not a master key to the idiom across all its uses; nor do I attempt to ground my observations about old literature in current neuroscientific or psychological theories. A humanist such as Massumi turns to the experiments of Benjamin Libet on the will,[60] while others take up the popular theories of neuroscientist Antonio Damasio to site the foundations of nonconsciousness in what he calls the "proto-self."[61] Though nonconscious and therefore not "subjective" (on one definition), the distinct processes that the proto-self orchestrates for Damasio can be listed and located in brain and body.[62] It is tempting to compare Damasio's proto-self, *"an integrated collection of separate neural patterns that map, moment by moment, the most stable aspects of the organism's physical structure,"*[63] to whatever layer of personhood is said by eighteenth-century literature to be affected insensibly.

But the idioms that evoke unfelt affect in the eighteenth century do not point to specific places in the brain or elsewhere in the body in quite the way that Damasio, Gerald Edelman, and other neuroscientists identify the nonconscious bases of feeling now. Even the most concretely sited constituents of the brain discussed in this book, Hartley's particles in the white matter, are defined as fundamentally elusive, "infinitesimal." Writers I treat appeal to the insensible in accounts of mind, brain, and body nearly always to designate their unknowable dimensions, their "secret Magick," their "unaccountable" or "indiscernible" ways (in Trenchard's words)—a place where inquiry halts and, in principle, can go no further. The affiliation of the insensible with a kind of skepticism will be a theme sounded throughout this book. The examples here from eighteenth-century anatomy and psychology, as well as those from other areas of prose, more evoke the mysterious view of affect's virtual nature described by Massumi (e.g., "undecidability fed forward into thought") than his and other theorists' attempts to ground what they call affect in contemporary neuroscience.[64]

So the idiom's status as a rhetorical invocation of what cannot be sensed overrides whatever use it may have to point to specific bodily states or processes. But its adverbial character and function as a mediating term also differentiate it from what scholars usually mean by a "discursive construction" of emotion: taxonomies of the passions, for instance, or specific modes of feeling assigned to gender roles. Again, the insensible commits only to depicting how things happen, not to designating what anything is. Its passing appearances, unlike more assertive and deliberate terms in accounts of emotion, make *construction* seem like the wrong word for what it does. And its grammatically negative function, setting a change apart from what can be felt, known, willed, or intended, opens its reference up even more. What I have called the idiom's openness invites rather than arrests interpretation.

This openness does not neutralize the idiom's cultural uses. I will show throughout this book how it serves particularly charged narratives: the civilization of the passions, the four-stages theory of the Scottish Enlightenment, the disciplining of women's desires, and (perhaps most markedly ideological of all) Smith's story of happy socioeconomic outcomes conjured by the invisible hand. The epilogue of this book will remark on affinities between the insensible in the eighteenth century and how ideology works according to accounts from the nineteenth century and beyond, by moving people in ways they do not notice. The unfelt as well as feeling can be recruited to justify sociopolitical arrangements that serve particular interests. But by leaving a place blank or open in narrations of the emotions, the insensible introduces an element of unpredictability in them. In this too, it resembles what some theoretical writers now hope for from affect: a source of transformative possibility.

How Far the Unfelt Goes

The wide spread of significant usage of the idioms treated in this discussion poses a challenge to any attempt to survey them. This book could never be a conventional history, following a single thread from point A to point C. Nor could it resemble scholarship that traces the migration of concepts from one zone to another—the influence, say, of a medical idea on fiction. The insensible is everywhere at once. But the book's four chapters, on philosophy, fiction, historiography, and political economy, do present their examples in four parallel sequences. Each starts (more or less) around the end of the seventeenth century, moves forward to examples from the heart of the age of sensibility, and then looks ahead—to illustrate the idiom's origins, flourishing, and decline. These developments as I read them are not as neatly unified as a single Ngram line. Though chapter IV refers to seventeenth-century political economists such as William Petty, its first substantial example is Mandeville's *Fable of the Bees*, which began publication in 1714 (1705, if you count *The Grumbling Hive*), and chapter I stops with Eliza Haywood and Adam Smith. (A final philosophical example from William Godwin at the end of the eighteenth century awaits in the epilogue.) What will emerge is a detailed picture of the developing uses to which the idiom was put, with thoughts on why and how it came to be less useful.

The book's second structural principle motivates my choice and sequence of examples, not only to impose order on them but also to reveal what the idiom's range really means. The book progresses from small to big. Chapter I begins by discussing the impulse of the period's philosophy to lay its foundations on the most minute affective components of mental life, exemplified by Locke's attention to the "insensible parts" of matter that cause sensations, and Hartley's infinitesimal particles inside the brain. I then examine Condillac's and Hume's associative accounts of the psychology of the whole person and conclude chapter I with Haywood and Smith, who point the moral sentiments of the individual toward society. Chapter II turns to the novel to understand that form's special zone of interest: the individual character's feelings as manifested in her mind and on her body, and the small social units—families linked by the prospect of her marriage—intensely watchful over these feelings. Chapters III and IV address the power of unfelt affect over still larger social groups. The historiography treated in chapter III uses the idiom to narrate the progress of entire nations or peoples and, at times, suggests how such narratives are subject to question. Chapter IV shows how commerce links the individual to a collectivity not through the passing of time but rather in a cyclical, self-reinforcing system—we now call it "the economy"—driven and steered by "human nature" anchored in human feeling. Schemes of tax policy, for instance, owe their appeal to the systematic, predictable nature of unfelt affect. Yet even here, the insensible also offers to some writers—notably, Smith—a sense of the affective contingency of commerce, as discussed in the last section of the book's final chapter.

This increase of scale allows the book to demonstrate the consistency of the insensible as an idiom across a broad range, from the vanishingly minute to the incomprehensibly vast, such as systems of international commerce whose operations are "impossible not to lose sight of," as Richard Cantillon puts it.[65] The processes called insensible can be both much smaller (for Hartley, infinitely so) and much larger than the individual persons whom they affect. The idiom therefore untethers itself from any particular embodiment. Even examples in the middle of the scale tend to use it to modify processes that affect people from "outside," such as the "four days" with Orville that change how Evelina comes to feel about him. The range of the scale, its reach from sub- to suprapersonal, itself dramatizes the distinctness of unfelt affect from individual subjectivity. My selection of examples, from Locke's *Essay* at the beginning to Smith's *Wealth of Nations* at the end, is motivated in part by a desire to demonstrate this range in an ordered sequence: to survey the space that the insensible takes up, as the four historical progressions in its four parallel chapters express its movement through time.

Also influencing my selection is the conviction that the power and interest of the idiom appear most strikingly in readings of "major" texts and authors (supported by concurrent discussions of less well-known ones). Since I aim to demonstrate the unnoticed but significant help that the insensible lends to the language of feeling in the long eighteenth century, my targets include arguments as well known as Locke's distinction between primary and secondary qualities, Hume's account of associative relations, and Smith's of the invisible hand. The idiom's role in delineating the Richardson–Fielding opposition, so important in accounts of fiction's development in the eighteenth century and after, attracts more attention here than occurrences in less famous novelists. Of course, the category of major authors is always evolving, and now includes Aphra Behn and Eliza Haywood as well as Jane Austen and John Locke, and writers not widely read in their own time can have a different kind of importance (such as Cantillon, only "rediscovered" as an important economist by William Stanley Jevons late in the nineteenth century).

Another motive of my selection of examples is reflected in the status of many as signal texts of what could broadly be designated a British Enlightenment: the early, English one of Locke and Newton (the latter mostly by way of Hartley, in this discussion), and the later, Scottish one of Hume and Smith. Other writers discussed here, including Gibbon, Haywood, and Mandeville, have been productively treated by scholars as Enlightenment figures. (The extent to which the eighteenth-century English novel can be seen as an Enlightenment enterprise remains an open and intriguing question.) The French works examined throughout are included because their use of *insensiblement*—especially as amplified, I show, by the proclivities of translator Thomas Nugent—seems to influence English philosophical and historiographical style. Many of these French works, by Condillac, Montesquieu, and Voltaire, also sit in the Enlightenment's main stream.

This focus on Enlightenment figures across a century and several national contexts runs somewhat against a trend in intellectual history over the last twenty or so years to distinguish ever more local Enlightenments. (So J. G. A. Pocock, for instance, will contrast the Enlightenment of *philosophes* to one of *érudits* in France and describe an "Arminian Enlightenment" that Gibbon encountered in Lausanne.)[66] More apt for this study are broader distinctions, such as the one from Jonathan Israel (invoked above) between a moderate, mainstream Enlightenment in Britain and a radical and international Spinozan one. Insofar as the insensible contributes to a recognizably Enlightenment intellectual style, it expresses such moderation, gesturing toward what cannot be felt and therefore to human limits—a restraint set against dogmatic radicalism. As I will show, however, this restraint performs varying functions. It can serve to magically reconcile incompatible elements (such as selfishness and general happiness), but it can also question any such reassuring resolution. Both impulses, however, match the intellectual moderation broadly seen as characteristic of the Enlightenment in Britain.

The very thing that allows the insensible to roam through all kinds of British writing of the period is what makes a literary study, broadly construed, the appropriate way to approach it. Its status as a portable stylistic device rather than a theme or idea housed in one of the period's protodisciplines, its life on the surface of prose, as it were, indicates that its meaning can best be tracked as part of the period's literary style. The idiom acquires its peculiar resonance, moreover, when writers are focused more intently on other things: important transformations, mechanisms of the mind, plot, history, or money. Attentive reading is needed to draw out such resonances in part because usual practice in intellectual history of reading for the main idea has tended to ignore or not much consider them. Still, this device tends to attach itself to and shape an array of ideas—mental association, stadial history, the specie-flow mechanism, and so on—in comparable ways. So while the chapters of this book do not attempt extended histories of such ideas, their close readings draw in the work of intellectual historians more than a literary study usually would. The book ranges across so many areas of prose usually discussed separately in eighteenth-century studies because the essence of the idiom's meaning resides in its surprisingly general usefulness.

As I proceed through this study, I keep coming back to occurrences of the word *insensibly*. But there are whole sections without this fixation. My pages on Hartley in chapter I explore what he means by "infinitesimal medullary particles," and in chapter IV, I discuss Mandeville's descriptions of a happiness that people do not exactly feel without stressing the word. I examine Smith's phrase "secretly conscious" and treat occurrences of others such as "by imperceptible degrees." Still, the value of a consistent focus on a single semantically rich term has become increasingly clear to me. Such a focus orders my examples and discovers concrete, common ground for comparisons and contrasts in my interpretations of them. It has always been important to me as a literary scholar to approach usage as it actually is, instantiated in actual words, phrases, and sentences, instead of devising general, abstract categories and fitting a range of examples into them. But as will be apparent, my purpose is not to isolate stray moments of usage but rather to show how the term helps create the larger significance of a theory, a fictional story, and so on. My analyses do not stop at the term but use it as a clue to more expansive meanings.

The emphasis here is literary also in the sense that what it examines happens on the page, in a stylistics of affect. The idiom's negative, gestural character could find expression really nowhere else. This raises a question about its status within the larger phenomenon of sensibility, which has been treated in literary and other scholarship not just as a language but also as a "culture."[67] Is there also a culture of what is not felt? It is comparatively easy to view the insensible functioning culturally in its strictly privative, inherent sense, and illuminating studies have (for instance) discussed women's "spells," fainting, and other forms of lost or missing feeling as performed cultural practices.[68] The insensible in its additive, noninherent sense, however, resists being considered a practice such as this because it cannot be sensed while it is happening at all, by anybody subject to or near it. Only retrospectively, at a certain distance, can writers refer to what has occurred insensibly. Yet as we will see, the movements of insensibly unfolding processes for many writers of the period constitute the very condition of society or "culture." People feel their desires, obligations, and needs, but these cohere, by an unfelt movement, into cultural forms larger than the sum of them. So if the insensible in one sense cannot by its very nature materialize as a discernible cultural or material practice, it serves writers in the period as a tool to describe the manner in which culture comes into being.

This introduction began by noting the poetic quality of the idiom that first attracted me to it. But the long discursive poems of eighteenth-century literature pertaining to consciousness, with their own sense of expansive scale—Edward Young's *The Complaint: or Night Thoughts*, and James Thomson's *The Seasons*—do not make much use of such terms.[69] The great poet of the insensible, I think, is William Wordsworth. His fascination with figures who move along the border of feeling and unfeeling—his "solitaries," the Blind Beggar, the Leech-Gatherer, the Discharged Soldier—leads him to depict unfeeling as a peculiarly active state.[70] An inaugural instance occurs in "Old Man Travelling: Animal Tranquillity and Decay," still technically an eighteenth-century poem, included in the first edition of *Lyrical Ballads* (1798):

> He travels on, and in his face, his step,
> His gait, is one expression; every limb,
> His look and bending figure, all bespeak
> A man who does not move with pain, but moves
> With thought—He is insensibly subdued
> To settled quiet: he is one by whom
> All effort seems forgotten, one to whom
> Long patience has such mild composure given,
> That patience now doth seem a thing, of which
> He hath no need.[71]

Here Wordsworth pushes the term's two semantic poles, "in an unfeeling way" and "in an unfelt way," so hard as to nearly collapse their difference. The old man is subdued "insensibly" in an ever-extending, exactingly slow process, so gradually as not to be noticed (not by himself, not by "the little hedgerow birds" in line 1). And he is subdued to a state of near total insensibility. The convergence of the unfelt, ongoing process and the terminally unfeeling state somehow produces his extraordinary, effortless movement through the landscape. A double unfeeling permits what Wordsworth means by moving with thought.

This combination, in its strange Wordsworthian manner, creates the enviable condition of the old man, beyond enlightened patience, a condition that he himself "hardly feels" (line 14). The powerful evocation of such processes in *Lyrical Ballads*, *The Prelude*, and other poems again indicates that graphs of usage fail to capture the capacity of the idiom to generate new profundity after its influence seems to taper off. Wordsworth's figures who move insensibly are heirs to those who move likewise through European history in Gibbon's *Decline and Fall*, and through the marriage plots of eighteenth-century novels as virtuous heroines inculpably succumb to desire. In this way, too, the emergence of feeling from unfeeling in all the eighteenth-century minds and bodies discussed in this book anticipates further profound functions of affect in literature's future.

Chapter 1

Philosophy
Affective Nonconsciousness

Inconspicuous references to the unfelt lace through philosophies of feeling, perception, and sensation, as well as emotions and "sentiment," in Britain throughout the long eighteenth century. Noticing this quiet persistence puts the centrality of feeling in the period's philosophical writing in a new light. A scholarly tradition, inherited and refined by seminal intellectual histories of the late twentieth century, has long seen a specially heightened attention to consciousness, the arena in which the self interacts with its feelings, as definitive of the period's thought. The "self-intimating" impressions of the mind, where sensation and knowing converge,[1] consist of what is sensible, either furnished from "outside" or presented in the mind's reflection on its own operations. This motif in John Locke and his heirs has been seen to place a new emphasis on interiority—the inner space to which objects of sense are conveyed and in which feelings are had—with a corresponding focus on the individuality or separateness of the mind subject to such states, and on the personal identity of the self extending through time as these evolve.[2]

This study's attention to the insensible in some ways resembles the approach of a more recent generation of scholars who look for the defining components of selfhood in the period apart from its specially heightened self-consciousness.[3] Some intellectual historians have shown that British philosophy noticed other factors, including bodily and social ones, in its accounts of the self.[4] Others insist that, whatever the philosophers said, the self was popularly understood as culturally negotiated instead of strictly internal and profoundly personal.[5] And several literary studies have argued that aspects of the self, such as the will or the capacity for moral choice, arise for many writers of the period—novelists as well as philosophers—in our interactions with the world, not in our radically separate conscious states. So legal structures, for instance, portray what a person is in essentially social terms, or theories of agency make willing a matter of external causation instead of a special mental action.[6]

Chapter I, focusing on philosophical writing from Locke through Adam Smith, considers a somewhat different pattern. The insensible tends to come up in this writing's very effort to articulate the unique sensitivities of the mental. It is inside the inside, as it were, inherent in feeling and essential in accounts of the self's interiority. A common theme in affect theory in recent years suggests something similar. It defines affect as "prepersonal intensity" not merely to distinguish it from "personal feeling" but also to show how the latter emerges from and gains its vividness from the former.[7] What a person feels results from what she has not yet felt as a person. The Deleuzean strand of such theories has roots in materialist thought of the seventeenth century, especially Baruch Spinoza's, in which mental images are "corporeal affections (*affectio*)," defined as "traces of an external body on our body."[8] I begin by examining such encounters between affecting and affected at the smallest possible scale: the "insensible parts" of matter identified by Locke as causing sensation, and the infinitesimal particles in the brain hypothesized by Locke's disciple, David Hartley, to bridge spirit and matter. Examples surveyed later in chapter I treat a larger entity, the self, and the unfelt changes undergone by consciousness, a mind, or a person through time. This temporal dimension is evoked by another Spinozan term, *affectus*, which Deleuze defines as "continuous variation of the force of existing."[9] If *affectio* helps us think about miniscule physical traces that affect the mind, *affectus* describes the ongoing, often vanishingly minute transitions that minds undergo: unfelt traces, and the unfelt variations they make. In all these cases, philosophers use the insensible to pass between and underwrite the feelings at the center of their attention.

This passing function indicates why such terms do not come in for much scrutiny from intellectual historians. The insensible plays a supporting role. It facilitates the articulation of prominent ideas—the distinction between primary and secondary qualities, notions of personal identity, the association of ideas, sympathy, and sentimental moral judgment—without being separately conceptualized itself. Beyond that, the period's philosophies of feeling are, after all, mostly about feelings. Calling something insensible effectively removes it from consideration or, more forcefully, from ever being known. As Locke declares at the beginning of book 4 of the *Essay concerning Human Understanding* (1689), "Since *the Mind*, in all its Thoughts and Reasonings, hath no other Immediate Object but its own *Ideas*, which it alone does or can contemplate, it is evident, that our Knowledge is only conversant about them."[10] If immediately sensed ideas supply a paradigm of knowledge in the long eighteenth century, the insensible marks a place where knowledge stops. This affiliates the idiom of the insensible with a kind of skepticism, an epistemological attitude that often attends its usage in examples discussed in this book.

I begin by discussing how the late seventeenth-century British philosophy of sensation, feeling, and selfhood responded to the challenges of mechanism with the idiom of the insensible. I then show how this idiom carries forward from Locke and Robert Boyle to philosophers of the mid-eighteenth century, the age of sensibility, who use it to address a variety of problems—some directly inherited from Locke, others new. The consistent, Lockean element in these usages by Hartley, Étienne Bonnet de Condillac and David Hume, Eliza Haywood and Adam Smith, is that they do not refer to mental contents. We do not hear of "insensible perceptions," the existence of which, as we shall see, G. W. Leibniz asserts to distinguish his views from Locke's. There are no "unconscious thoughts" or "unfelt sensations" in the British tradition surveyed here. Writers in this tradition rather describe insensible *powers* that affect the mind without themselves being mental. They are nonconscious, not unconscious. This is not an articulated idea in the writers I survey here. Rather, it is an implication carried by the idiom into articulations of quite a wide variety of other ideas. All of them indicate the persistent usefulness in philosophies of feeling of a stylistic gesture toward something beyond the reach of both feeling and philosophy.

1. The Insensible Parts of Locke's *Essay*

Minute and Insensible

John Locke is usually seen as a kind of champion of consciousness in the long eighteenth century. It is "impossible for any one to perceive, without perceiving, that he does perceive," he writes in the *Essay concerning Human Understanding*. The tripling of the term makes consciousness seem like a tightly closed loop. Feeling and awareness of feeling are, practically speaking, the same: "When we see, hear, smell, taste, feel, meditate, or will any thing, we know that we do so."[11] When Laurence Sterne in *Tristram Shandy* (1759) calls Locke's *Essay* a "history-book . . . of what passes in a man's own mind,"[12] the word "own" emphasizes the closed character of the scenes and processes that Locke describes. But behind and within all this perception as perception of perception lies an imperceptible class of thing. Locke captures this element in the phrase "insensible Parts," which helps him produce a foundational distinction in modern philosophy. The difference between primary and secondary qualities, introduced in "Other Considerations concerning Simple Ideas," chapter 8 of the *Essay*'s book 2 ("Of Ideas"), hinges on what Locke designates with the phrase.

Many readers misremember this distinction between primary and secondary qualities as one between two kinds of sensations or "Ideas"—a mistake itself indicative of the way unfelt things may drop out of a reading of Locke.

So we may mistakenly recall that roundness is a primary quality, blueness a secondary one. But Locke initially defines the qualities as *powers to produce* sensations, not as the sensations themselves, and it turns out that the powers productive of our sensory ideas lie hidden in an unfelt layer of reality. Locke's argument offers a prominent example of the insensible's peculiar way of coupling with the sensible without being quite at the center of attention—not in the discussion, certainly not in our perceiving minds, and not in our memories of what Locke argues. So while reviewing the sections that elaborate on the qualities, the subject of a vast scholarly literature—that is, sections 7–26 of chapter 8 of Book 2 of the *Essay*—it is worth trying to keep the insensible in view.

Locke begins by defining the word *qualities*: "The Powers to produce those *Ideas* in us . . . I call *Qualities*; and as they are Sensations, or Perceptions, in our Understandings, I call them *Ideas*" (134). Again, it has often been necessary to remind readers that qualities are powers in the world to produce ideas in our minds, not classes of ideas themselves.[13] There is a natural temptation to think of primary qualities, powers to produce ideas of "Solidity, Extension, Figure, Motion, or Rest, and Number" (135), simply as those ideas that represent the world as it really is, and secondary qualities, powers to produce ideas of "Colours, Sounds, Tasts, *etc.*" (135), as those that represent nothing in the world and appear only in our heads. But that is not quite right, at least according to Locke's first definition. (One common way of addressing George Berkeley's critique of Locke's doctrine of qualities is to say that it rests on this misinterpretation.)[14] *Both* types of quality are defined as "external" powers to produce "internal" ideas. So red is not a secondary quality. The power in the world to produce red in my mind is. And though both are aspects of the world, both are also by definition pitched, so to say, only to the mind's capacity to have sensory ideas. (For all we know, there could be many aspects of reality that have no power to produce any ideas in us at all, directly or indirectly.) We learn in the chapter that primary qualities create ideas that match how things are in reality, and secondary qualities do not. But so far as both are qualities, they are nothing but powers to produce ideas.

The appearance of the insensible, however, soon sacrifices this definitional clarity. Locke's thought experiment of dividing a grain of wheat begins a pattern extending throughout the chapter that suggests primary qualities can be said to reside in matter whether they have the power to produce any ideas in us or not: "Take a grain of Wheat, divide it into two parts, each part has still *Solidity, Extension, Figure,* and *Mobility*; divide it again, and it retains still the same qualities; and so divide it on, till the parts become insensible, they must retain still each of them all those qualities" (135). Now, primary qualities seem to subsist even when they are "insensible"—that is, when they lose the power to cause any ideas. Commentators have seen fit, therefore, to divide primary qualities into two sorts. Edwin McCann distinguishes between "primary primary qualities," those qualities subsisting even in bodies' insensible parts, and "secondary primary qualities," those primary qualities presented by larger-than-insensible bodies that produce ideas.

Primary primary qualities, McCann remarks, are "first in the order of being" because they compose elemental reality, while secondary primary qualities are "first in the order of knowledge" because they present the nature of reality to us by causing our ideas of it.[15] Lisa Downing likewise discusses "the issue of microscopic vs. macroscopic primary qualities,"[16] though as we shall see, "microscopic" in Locke's view might turn out to be optimistic. As "properties of the inner constitution of things" (in Downing's words),[17] primary primary qualities may at last permanently lack the power to cause any ideas in us, however hard we try to magnify them. Hence the term *insensible* marks the place where the definition of primary qualities seems to shear in two. The part that emphasizes their power to cause ideas starts to be supplanted by the part tying them to the basic nature of reality, sensed or not. We can only infer that these features of reality still deserve to be called primary qualities because they are the sort of thing that would cause certain types of ideas in us if they were big enough. Insofar as they constitute the insensible "inner constitution" of reality, (primary) primary qualities lose their powers to cause sensation at all. In this they differ from secondary qualities, which can be nothing other than such powers.

The insensible, however, has the odd distinction of pointing out how primary and secondary qualities not only differ but also turn out to be the same. Locke defines secondary qualities as "Powers to produce various Sensations in us by their [bodies'] *primary Qualities, i.e.* by the Bulk, Figure, Texture, and Motion of their insensible parts, as Colours, Sounds, Tasts, *etc.*" (135). He hence *identifies* secondary qualities with a certain kind of primary quality—that is, the insensible kind (what McCann calls primary primary qualities), at least with that swath that produces sensations in us of colors, sounds, tastes, and so on. Both ultimately consist of the same stuff. Or, to put it more paradoxically, sensible primary qualities are primary qualities, while (some) insensible primary qualities are secondary ones. In the latter case we might say that secondary qualities are at once secondary and (insensibly) primary. With the word *insensible*, to put it more broadly, the opposition between world and mind, outside and inside, starts to break down. As Locke concludes, "The *Power* that is in any Body, by Reason of *its* insensible *primary Qualities*" produces what are "usually called sensible Qualities" (140), which he defines as secondary.

Secondary qualities are powers that consist of *nothing but* "insensible *primary Qualities.*" With secondary qualities, the felt derives from the unfelt entirely and in every instance, and the unfelt consists of insensible primary qualities.

Another way of stating this distinction can be pulled from Locke's notorious doctrine of resemblance.[18] As Locke observes, "The *Ideas of primary Qualities* of Bodies, *are Resemblances* of them, and their Patterns do really exist in the Bodies themselves; but the *Ideas, produced* in us *by* these *Secondary Qualities, have no resemblance* of them at all. There is nothing like our *Ideas,* existing in the Bodies themselves. They are in the Bodies, we denominate from them, only a Power to produce those Sensations in us: And what is Sweet, Blue, or Warm in *Idea,* is but the certain Bulk, Figure, and Motion of the insensible Parts in the Bodies themselves, which we call so" (137). While our ideas take their "Patterns" from bodies' primary qualities (in larger-than-insensible form),[19] they do not take any such patterns from secondary ones. So secondary qualities identify more thoroughly with the insensible than primary ones do. Our ideas of colors (and so on) utterly detach from the insensible parts that produce them. We do not see the particles at all. It would be misleading even to say we see them *as* anything—that when the insensible parts vibrate accordingly, we see them *as* red—as if the particles are seen and lead us to construe them a certain way. We cannot think of ourselves having an "unconscious perception" of the particles, or of their causing "unconscious ideas" in us. Sensory ideas of colors, tastes, and so on are instead, in Michael Ayers's phrase, "blank effects" of what causes them at the insensible level.[20] The definition of secondary qualities is pulled, so to speak, in opposite directions on the axis of the sensible. As powers, their ontological reality must be insensible for their phenomenological effects to be sensible.

Primary qualities, on the other hand, directly produce ideas in us that resemble them, at least when they are in larger-than-insensible form. Rocks, for instance, "do really" impart perceptions of their rocky shapes to our minds. But as we have seen, Locke will come to suggest that primary qualities need not have the power to cause any ideas and still be worthy of the name. He will remark, for instance, that primary qualities he lists "*are really in them,* whether any ones [sic] Senses perceive them or no," and hence can be called "*real Qualities*" (137);[21] and (as we have seen) he will finally refer to "insensible *primary Qualities*" (140). Though both primary and secondary qualities are each initially defined as nothing but powers to cause sensation, both find their way finally to the insensible, by different but intersecting routes. One might say that one advantage of (if not motive for) discovering insensible primary qualities is that they identify a causal basis for secondary qualities to which we may say our ideas of them bear no resemblance. Primary qualities consist ultimately of insensible parts of matter. A swath of these insensible parts are secondary qualities.

Variations of the phrase are commonly used to designate the constituents of physical reality in Locke's time.[22] His contemporary and influence Robert Boyle copiously refers in his scientific works to "insensible parts," "insensible particles," "insensible corpuscles," and the like, to designate the constituents of his mechanistic philosophy, corpuscularianism.[23] Locke's invocation of insensible parts leads him to engage, he finally admits, "in Physical Enquiries a little farther than, perhaps, I intended" (140), and he here evinces the influence of Boylean corpuscularianism more directly than anywhere else in the *Essay*,[24] as he entertains a physical theory of perception. At 2.8.12, after one of his typical lists of primary qualities, he remarks that we see them at a distance because "'tis evident some singly imperceptible Bodies must come from them to the Eyes," which cause sensation by interacting with our "Nerves, or animal Spirits" (136). (Darkness and other privations are presumably caused by an absence of such bodies.)[25] Though Locke initially insists that sensed primary qualities cause ideas, he here becomes comfortable with the notion that all ideas may fundamentally be caused by insensible Boylean corpuscles.

I have dwelled so long on the doctrine of primary and secondary qualities because Locke's chapter provides a keen example of the odd way the term *insensible* will behave in subsequent decades in many kinds of writing. In bare semantic terms, *insensible* (as a noninherent adjective) always pulls in two directions.[26] When you say a thing cannot be sensed, you are also saying, in the same breath, that it exists. The word giveth even as it taketh away. Locke offers an additional but unavoidable irony by using the term as the terminal point in his theory of sensation itself, the place where that theory must stop (if it is to stop anywhere). The description of secondary qualities presents the divided effect of the word especially sharply (though as we have seen, primary qualities, as minute elements of the physical world, must also take up the idiom). On the one hand, the parts' effect on us is left "blank" in that what we perceive, our ideas in our heads, bear no resemblance to what produces them. But on the other hand, matter's insensible parts literally do produce sensory ideas. So the powers of secondary qualities are at once fully not felt and yet the only things that can produce feelings of colors, sounds, and tastes. The insensible in Locke expresses this neat unity of nonfeeling and feeling.

The force of Locke's usage for the future of the word in English appears with special clarity in contrast to that of G. W. Leibniz, who takes it in a dramatically different direction. His *New Essays on Human Understanding*, a response to Locke's *Essay* finished in 1704, around the time of Locke's death, but not published until 1765 (some fifty years after Leibniz himself died), has no discernible influence on the writing surveyed in this book. But its decisive turn away from Locke is illuminating for the term's English fate. Leibniz posits the existence of "les perceptions insensibles" (insensible perceptions) to signify unfelt, or unconscious, mental contents in a way he knew Locke could not accept.[27] Leibniz asserts, "In short, insensible perceptions are as important to pneumatology as insensible corpuscles are to natural science, and it is just as unreasonable to reject one as the other on the pretext that they are beyond the reach of our senses."[28]

Insensible perceptions cannot appear in Locke's own "pneumatology" (the science of the soul) because of his steadfast commitment to the notion that all perceptions are conscious ones. Leibniz, conversely, needs the idea to support crucial elements of his psychological edifice, including his view of personal identity and "that marvellous pre-established harmony between the soul and the body."[29] On his use of the phrase and its ramifications in his work rests a claim by scholars of our own day for his origination of the idea of the unconscious mind.[30] But for Locke and his heirs, the insensible will always signify nonconsciousness: forces, actions, or powers that affect the mind without being "in" it like an insensible perception.[31] Throughout this book we will see writers in English using the term to describe affective processes, not mental states or contents such as perceptions or ideas. In Locke, despite the intimate connection between mental ideas and the "insensible corpuscles" that cause them, their relation—between "insensible *primary Qualities*" and the ideas that they cause—remains blank, empty, an unbridged span.

The relation between the qualities in bodies and our sensations rather resembles what Deleuzean affect theorists posit between the virtual and the felt. In the introduction, I cited a comment from Brian Massumi that is especially suggestive here, his notion that "virtuality cannot be seen in the form that emerges from it. The virtual gives form, but itself has none (being the unform of transition). The virtual is imperceptible. It is insensible."[32] Though Massumi does not unfold the implications of this final term, I think he alights on it because it evokes the odd split in its signification that allows its two semantic elements, unavailability to the senses and existence, to complement each other. And however otherwise "the virtual" differs from the qualities, Locke's use of the term *insensible* in chapter 2.8 also lives in this gap, especially between secondary qualities and their emergence as sensations. He asserts both their unavailability to sensation and their power to cause it, the ideas of red, bitter, warm, and so on. (The virtual likewise productively "gives form.")

This tension in Locke's terminology is not a contradiction, but it does exemplify a new way philosophical and natural scientific inquiry can be outrageous to common sense.[33] Locke expects the notion that color, taste, and so on reside not in objects but rather in our minds to come as (at least) a mild shock to readers. Secondary qualities "are commonly thought to be the same in those Bodies, that those *Ideas* are in us, the one the perfect resemblance of the other, as they are in a Mirror; and it would by most Men be judged very extravagant, if one should say otherwise" (137). We see a blue pitcher because, we think, the pitcher is blue, not because the pitcher's insensible parts, themselves not blue at all, produce an idea of blue in us. Locke's first readers would not have found a distinction between appearance and reality unfamiliar, but unlike (say) Plato's doctrine of forms, Locke does not proclaim a hostility between appearance and reality or urge us to see beyond the one to get to the other. Instead of cutting reality off from the senses, the insensible connects them to it, while simultaneously insisting on the unbridgeable gap between them. The explanation of feeling requires an appeal to what is in principle unavailable to feeling. The blank and productive aspects of the insensible are two sides of the same thing. Locke's *Essay*, popular as it was, was one way readers in the eighteenth century got used to the idea that feeling and unfeeling, far from being simply opposed, had a mutual dependence.

A skepticism in Locke about the possibility of our ever witnessing or grasping the ultimate components of matter sharpens the function of the insensible in his thought even further. It also distinguishes his motives from other promoters of a mechanical philosophy of sensation. As Ayers has noted, there is a "tension" between "Locke as sceptic and Locke as corpuscularian."[34] Though Locke seems to embrace corpuscularianism as a plausible guess as to how matter may ultimately be constituted, he also consistently acknowledges that we do not (and perhaps cannot ever) know that it is true. As one famous (somewhat ambiguous) remark in book 2 of the *Essay* has it, "'Tis plain, then, that the *Idea* of corporeal *Substance* in Matter is as remote from our Conceptions, and Apprehensions, as that of Spiritual *Substance*, or *Spirit*" (298)—an observation he repeats near obsessively through chapter 2.23. The nature of "*Substance* in general," he continues, is "secret and abstract" (298). Chapter 23 contends in paragraphs 23–28 that we have no adequate notion of *"the cohesion of solid*, and consequently separable *parts*" (306) and none of the "power of *communication of Motion by impulse*" (311). These considerations lead Locke to conclude that "the simple *Ideas* we receive from Sensation and Reflection, are the Boundaries of our Thoughts; beyond which, the Mind, whatever efforts it would make, is not able to advance one jot" (312).

In Locke's formation of this attitude, the insensible plays an important but double-edged part. On the one hand, Locke recognizes that scientific inquiry can render sensible what is ordinarily insensible:

> Had we Senses acute enough to discern the minute particles of Bodies, and the real Constitution on which their sensible Qualities depend, I doubt not but they would produce quite different *Ideas* in us; and that which is now the yellow Colour of Gold, would then disappear, and instead of it we should see an admirable Texture of parts of a certain Size and Figure. This Microscopes plainly discover to us: for what to our naked Eyes produces a certain Colour, is by thus augmenting the acuteness of our Senses, discovered to be quite a different thing; and the thus altering, as it were, the proportion of the Bulk of the minute parts of a coloured Object to our usual Sight, produces different *Ideas*, from what it did before. (301)

Microscopic inquiry can gain insight into the nature of the corpuscles that may ultimately compose reality. It is difficult to see how or why Locke could think such inquiry would not reveal a lot about the nature of the cohesion or motion of solid objects.

Immediately after this passage, however, he declares that passing beyond the limits of the ordinarily sensible is, practically speaking, not for us: "The infinite wise Contriver of us, and all things about us, hath fitted our Senses, Faculties, and Organs, to the conveniences of Life, and the Business we have to do here" (302). This is Locke's version of what Robert J. Fogelin has called (after Alexander Pope's lines in *An Essay on Man*) "*man's middle-state skepticism*,"[35] which describes human understanding as "narrow" and suited to our place in the universe (above brute, below angel). "Microscopical Eyes" would throw ordinary life into confusion and would not "serve to conduct [a person] to the Market and Exchange" (303). Locke never quite makes the radically skeptical argument that more acute senses would reveal nothing more than more ideas of secondary qualities, while the primary primary qualities that cause them remain forever insensible. Later in book 2, in chapter 29, he will assert unequivocally that "we have but very obscure, and confused *Ideas* of Corpuscles, or minute Bodies, so to be divided [i.e., "*in infinitum*"], when by former Divisions, they are reduced to a smalness, much exceeding the perception of any of our Senses" (370), perhaps suggesting that even microscopically enhanced perception would eventually hit a barrier.

While the insensible may be part of a perceptual theory of how (primary) primary qualities produce secondary ones that produce certain ideas in us, the term also seems to name a limit for Locke. This is not to say that *insensible* in the *Essay* means *unknowable* exactly. The slight distinction between the terms in fact keeps the insensible more active and productive for Locke, more present in our bodily motions and mechanisms. There are instances, however, in his unpublished papers where the term takes on a distinct skeptical coloring. In a 1668 discussion of anatomy (apropos of Lord Ashley's recent liver surgery), he remarks, "it is certaine & beyond controversy that nature performs all her operations in the body by parts soe minute & insensible that I thinke noe body will ever have or pretend even by the assistance of glasses or any other invention to come to a sight of them."[36] Here, at least, the insensibly minute provokes Locke's sense of our epistemic limitations. Our sight must finally reach a point where it can no longer see.

Interrupted Always

The *Essay*'s emphasis on the inescapably conscious nature of all feeling gives its corollary emphasis on the insensible, nonconscious bases of all mental experience a kind of poignancy. The very existence of our feelings, thoughts, and (as we shall see) identities depends on our consciousness of them, as Locke insists from the beginning of book 2. A person "cannot think at any time waking or sleeping, without being sensible of it. Our being sensible of it is not necessary to any thing, but to our thoughts; and to them it is; and to them it will always be necessary, till we can think without being conscious of it" (109).[37] Here Locke pursues a polemic against Cartesians who argue that the soul must be thinking all the time because its essence is thought. Locke claims here that "Consciousness is the perception of what passes in a Man's own mind" (115). He will, later in book 2, insist, "When we see, hear, smell, taste, feel, meditate, or will any thing, we know that we do so" (335). He cannot admit the existence of unconscious thinking or perception (unlike Leibniz). The insensible hence is much more radically removed from the consciousness it causes than anything resembling the Cartesian soul (or, for that matter, the Freudian unconscious). Whatever the mind is insensible of remains entirely cut off from its functioning as conscious.

Yet the insensible also remains causally responsible for this functioning, not only in our immediate perceptions of the qualities but in the ongoing constitution of our identities. The topic of personal identity first arises in the *Essay* in the discussion of consciousness in chapter 2.1 of its first edition: "If we take wholly away all Consciousness of our Actions and Sensations . . . it will be hard to know wherein to place personal Identity" (110). It gets a fuller treatment in the seminal chapter "Of Identity and Diversity" added to the second edition

(1694).[38] In its usage of the adverb *insensibly* to depict how processes move through time and change, this chapter looks ahead to narrative idioms in English in the eighteenth century (which I discuss in chapters II and III of this book). Unlike the account of minute physical encounters between affecting and affected bodies in the discussion of the qualities, "Of Identity and Diversity" applies the idiom to an essentially temporal affective mode.

Locke's argument distinguishes between two sorts of identity subject to time: that of living things, and that of persons in particular (though the less often noticed analogies and interdependencies between the two are crucial). He takes an oak to exemplify the nature of the identity of living beings (as opposed to mere "Masses of Matter," 330), asserting that identity must be seen as an ongoing "Organization of Parts in one coherent Body":

> For this Organization being at any one instant in any one Collection of *Matter*, is in that particular concrete distinguished from all other, and is that individual Life, which existing constantly from that moment both forwards and backwards in the same continuity of insensibly succeeding Parts united to the living Body of the Plant, it has that Identity, which makes the same Plant, and all the parts of it, parts of the same Plant, during all the time that they exist united in that continued Organization, which is fit to convey that Common Life to all the Parts so united. (331)

The organization of matter retains identity, but only through a "Continuity of insensibly succeeding Parts." Here the action of the insensible again performs a kind of mediation, in this case between identity and diversity. On the one hand, the "Parts" differ from and succeed one another. Yet the unperceived nature of the succession also produces the impression of "Continuity," whereby the "Common Life" of the united parts seems like a single thing. If the succession were sensible, our impression of a living thing's identity would never arise. We would see the new and old elements shuffling in and out, and the illusion of sameness would be destroyed. But *illusion* is the wrong word, because it is too positive. Again, our unawareness of succession is nothing like an "unconscious perception" or "unconscious thought." It simply represents a lack or missing part of our awareness.

Locke goes on to differentiate the "Common Life" of organic beings from *personal* identity as based "in the Identity of *consciousness*" (142), something oaks do not have. Individual human beings comprise both sorts of identity. Locke in this regard distinguishes between *man* and *person*. A man, like an oak, remains the same because of the continuity of the succeeding organic parts composing him, while a person consists of "that consciousness, whereby I am my *self* to my *self*" (345). This distinction occasions many often discussed examples through the chapter, as when Locke contends that a prince whose consciousness is transferred to the body of a cobbler remains, in personal terms, a prince, though the cobbler retains the same physical identity as a man by virtue of the organic continuity of the cobbler body, which remains the same (340). Personal identity entails consciousness, while organic identity obviously does not.

Most commentators have emphasized the difference between organic and personal identity, just as Locke does. Consciousness is the key to what makes a person a person, and mere "individual Life" composes an identity fundamentally different in kind. But Locke also conceives strong connections between the two. Both organic and personal identity help Locke make his main point: that identity consists not of substance, material or immaterial, but rather of a system's coherent continuity through time. He finds "Different Substances, by the same consciousness (where they do partake in it) being united into one Person; as well as different Bodies, by the same Life are united into one Animal, whose *Identity* is preserved, in that change of Substances, by the unity of one continued Life" (336). Life provides one sort of coherence, consciousness analogously another. But Locke's "as well as" does more than analogize our organic to our personal identities. He will indicate next that our changeful bodies provide "Evidence" for his account of personal identity by being "vitally united to this same thinking conscious self" (336): a person consciously "sympathizes [with] and is concerned for" (337) his body parts (as long as they are attached). Thus organic identity both models personal identity and provides a basis for it, as conscious concern for our bodies extends from our present to our future.[39]

A kind of nonconsciousness also links the two kinds of identity. The effect of organic identity, again, is achieved by "a continuity of insensibly succeeding Parts united to the living Body." Only by an unnoticing of the succession of parts is the assumption of the oak's identity made. But as always, the idiom raises the question, Insensibly to whom? And the answer in this case is particularly telling. Who is not noticing, and who, by virtue of that unnoticing, is viewing the oak as having an identity? Not the oak, of course. It is neither sensible nor insensible of the continuity or succession of its changing parts, or it is insensible of its changes entirely in the privative sense of the term. It is insensible of its temporal alterations in the same way it is not sensible of anything. That kind of insensibility does not confer identity on the tree. The oak cannot be self-identical through time from its own point of view (because it does not have one).

It must be from the point of view of some conscious observer that the parts succeed each other insensibly so as to create the impression of identity. Only a conscious being can look at an oak as being the same one through time. (Generally speaking, only a conscious being can be insensible in this special sense.) My point is not that some onlooker's unawareness of successive changes in the oak is all there is to its organic identity; that is, I am not asking, If an oak lives in the forest and no one is there to not notice the succession of its parts, does it really have an identity? (Locke thinks that the parts' being "vitally united" [331] is the key.) But insofar as nonawareness of change has any contribution to make to the oak's status as a single living thing, it must be the nonawareness of someone conscious. Such an attribution depends not on the observer's attention to some aspect of the tree, moreover, but on her inattention. This ascription of identity to the tree is a third-person one, from the outside, just as such an ascription to a man is. (While a person presumably could attribute identity to her own body because she does not notice the succession of its parts, that kind of observation still seems, so to say, from outside, with her consciousness regarding her body as an object.) The identity attributed to living things—oaks, men—depends on a kind of nonconsciousness specifically attached to a third-person, conscious perspective.

The unnoticing by which we attribute identity to physically changing systems provides a clue to other insensible components harbored by consciousness. Locke portrays our conscious lives as shot through with interruptions, disconnections, and empty patches. He takes these gaps as evidence that our identities do not consist of "the same Identical substance" because an identical substance would always be there without interruption. Such a belief in the basis of identity in substance, he explains,

> few would think they have reason to doubt of, if these Perceptions, with their consciousness, always remain'd present in the Mind, whereby the same thinking thing would be always consciously present, and, as would be thought, evidently the same to it self. But that which seems to make the difficulty is this, that this consciousness, being interrupted always by forgetfulness, there being no moment of our Lives wherein we have the whole train of all our past Actions before our Eyes in one view: But even the best Memories losing the sight of one part whilst they are viewing another; and we sometimes, and that the greatest part of our Lives, not reflecting on our past selves, being intent on our present Thoughts, and in sound sleep, having no Thoughts at all, or at least none with that consciousness, which remarks our waking Thoughts. I say, in all these cases, our consciousness being interrupted, and we losing the sight of our past *selves*, doubts are raised whether we are the same thinking thing; *i.e.* the same substance or no. (335–36)

A consciousness-based account of personal identity for Locke not only accommodates but also is motivated by lapses in memory, distractions from the "train" of our lives, unthinking sleep, and so on. Without such lapses, this kind of theory of identity would not be necessary. A substance-based theory, conversely, could not tolerate such lapses. (This is one reason why it is misleading to view Locke's account as basing personal identity on memory, as commentators since Joseph Butler have done.)

And *present* consciousness alone maintains personal identity as it moves through time and across the gaps that always interrupt it. Locke continues, "For as far as any intelligent Being can repeat the *Idea* of any past Action with the same consciousness it had of it at first, and with the same consciousness it has of any present Action; so far it is the same *personal self*. For it is by the consciousness it has of its present Thoughts and Actions, that it is *self* to it *self* now, and so will be the same *self* as far as the same consciousness can extend to Actions past or to come" (336). *Repeating* ideas of the past in present consciousness, having them again instead of "remembering" you had them once, extends the self through time. Our identities do not seamlessly extend backward in an expansive memory that holds everything together in the present. Rather, the past returns to us by innumerable acts of repetition across equally innumerable gaps. Though "interrupted always," consciousness for Locke makes personal identity abide. Personal identity is a lossy phenomenon whose coherence entails its inclusion of lacunae in consciousness.

For Locke this is just how consciousness is. Though he locates our identities in it, its lapses do not bother him or endanger his theory. As Galen Strawson has contended, against a long tradition of critique of Locke's theory with roots in Butler and Thomas Reid, "Personal identity through time, understood as human subject-of-experience identity through time, is indeed presupposed" and "taken as a given by Locke."[40] That is, Locke is not seeking to prove that our consciousness provides us evidence of our personal identities. The interruptions and holes in consciousness hence do not present Locke with something that needs to be explained away. He simply presupposes that a consciousness able to repeat bits of its past to itself constitutes the kind of personal identity he is discussing, and that its holes are unfelt features of it. Marya Schechtman thus remarks that Locke "stresses the *affective* side of consciousness" rather than its status as something that provides or stands in need of epistemological evidence.[41] And acts of repetition, and of living with gaps in consciousness in other ways, contribute massively to the way consciousness feels.

Locke's identification of consciousness as the sole ingredient of selfhood gains what could again be called a kind of poignancy from his acknowledgment of its unfelt elements, here its "interrupted always" character. In the *Essay* at large, the unfelt, the unperceived, and the insensible recur as an undercurrent of his most significant accounts of perception and identity. While his focus on consciousness has seemed especially influential on fiction in the century to come, his corollary emphasis on the unfelt evokes another "novelistic" flavor: the representation (or nonrepresentation) of vaguely designated stretches of time. In novels, for instance, we read of vague periods, "a week or more," "a few months," and so on, which pass insensibly yet bring characters to new situations and states of feeling. Less dramatic than the minute portrayal of "inner experience," they nonetheless also depend on a central feature of characters' conscious life: its occasional nonconsciousness. Locke does not directly link the "insensible Parts" of matter that cause secondary qualities to the "insensibly succeeding Parts" composing our organic identities and our perpetual losses of sight of "one part" of our lives "whilst viewing another." But all these unfelt parts perform a similar mediating role: between reality as it is and our perceptions of it, between ceaseless material changes and organic continuity, and between our conscious selves in the moment and their ongoing self-forgetting as they edge into an unknown future.

2. David Hartley's Ghost Matter

The mid-eighteenth-century philosophical language of sentiment and sensibility inherits and intensifies the close attention paid by John Locke and other earlier writers to the material bases of feeling, its temporal flows in consciousness, and (increasingly important) its role in associating ideas. These emphases quietly carry along the insensible into this new language too. Philosopher, theologian, and physician David Hartley, long seen as an important elaborator of the theory of sensibility,[42] begins his *Observations on Man, His Frame, His Duty, and His Expectations* (1749), published by Samuel Richardson, by announcing the foundations of his system: *"the Doctrines of Vibrations and Associations."*[43] He credits Isaac Newton and Locke, respectively, as sources for these. The former influences his account of the materiality of feeling much more than any Lockean doctrine of qualities.[44] But Hartley has his own notion of vanishingly miniscule particles that fundamentally affect the mind. He discreetly borrows the term *infinitesimal* from Newton's differential calculus and uses it to mean something much more elaborate than just extremely small. (Samuel Johnson would define it in his *Dictionary of the English Language*, 1755, as "Infinitely divided.") In his account of the nervous system, Hartley uses the term to reduce the bodily place of feeling to a ghostly medium, unperceivable yet physical. It is the instrument by which Newtonian vibrations cohere into Lockean associations.

Hartley does not acknowledge his debt to the calculus—or the "method of fluxions," as Newton calls it—as explicitly as he does his other influences. His avowed sources in Newton include the "Hints . . . concerning the Performance of Sensation and Motion . . . given at the End of his *Principia*, and in the *Questions* annexed to his *Optics*" (5). By the end of the *Principia*, Hartley must mean the very end, the famous final paragraph of the "General Scholium" that concludes volume 2, which speaks directly to Hartley's interest in anatomy and perception, where Newton describes "vibrations" of "a certain most subtle Spirit" along the nerves that produce sensation.[45] The second source from Newton named by Hartley appears among what are commonly called the *Queries* in book 3 of the *Opticks*, included in 1704 and expanded in subsequent editions, which describe vibrations in the "Æthereal Medium" that produce not only vision ("excited in the bottom of the Eye by the Rays of Light, and propagated through solid, pellucid and uniform Capillamenta of the optick Nerves in the place of Sensation") but also "Hearing" and "so of the other Senses."[46] Hartley's elaboration of these Newtonian hints has seemed to intellectual historians like an early attempt at neuropsychology, a science of the minute physiological bases of feeling.[47]

Less explicitly, Hartley turns to Newton's language of fluxions to emphasize just how radical this minuteness is. Throughout the *Observations* he refers to "infinitesimal medullary particles" in our brains, where our bodies and souls touch. He never claims that Newton's method of fluxions inspires him to see our medullary particles as infinitesimal, but some remarks at the end of volume 1 of the *Observations* imply that it does. For Hartley, nothing but the mysterious, ghostly nature of the infinitely small—as opposed to the merely very small—can provide the subtle, double-sided adhesion of body to soul, soul to body, that his system requires. The most advanced mathematical thinking of his day allows him to conceive of an increment small enough to minimize the difference between feeling and extension, spirit and matter, to nothing. The insensible quality of the infinitesimal, opaque to sense and even comprehension, testifies to the period's increasing appreciation of feeling's *material* subtlety. Unlike the minuteness of particles supposed by natural philosophers after Locke and Robert Boyle to compose all physical reality, the infinitesimal character assigned to medullary particles springs from Hartley's appreciation of how very distant from ordinary dead matter the liveliness of feeling and consciousness must be. To emphasize feeling's special status, only a term entirely resistant to feeling will do. The stuff of subjectivity must differ essentially from anything that could be an object of consciousness yet still be material.

Hartley thus connects the terminology of the *Opticks*, in which the infinitely small plays no part,[48] to that of fluxions. He declares, "*External Objects impressed upon the Senses occasion, first in the Nerves on which they are impressed, and then in the Brain, Vibrations of the small, and, as one may say, infinitesimal, medullary Particles*" (11). He continues, "In like manner we are to suppose the Particles which vibrate, to be of the inferior Orders, and not those biggest Particles, on which the Operations in Chemistry, and the Colours of natural Bodies, depend, according to the Opinion of Sir *Isaac Newton*. Hence, in the *Proposition*, I term the medullary Particles, which vibrate, infinitesimal" (12). So with the phrase "I term," Hartley takes ownership of the idea of infinitesimal particles in the white matter, which he contrasts with Newton's "bigger Particles" of chemistry and colors.

He does not announce that he draws the term *infinitesimal* from the fluxions of Newton who, we will see, invoked the idea of the infinitely small with extreme caution. As some have suggested,[49] Hartley here could seem simply to be groping for some mysterious word to indicate that the medullary particles are smaller than anything we could sense. But some three hundred pages later he reveals what the word means to him by referring again to Newton. There he echoes the earlier invocation of Newton's account of the "bigger Particles" on which colors and chemistry depend, versus the "inferior Orders." Thus he explains, late in volume 1, "It seems to me, that the Rays of Light may be considered as a kind of Fluxions in respect of the biggest component Particles of Matter; I mean those upon which Sir *Is. Newton* supposes the Colours of Natural Bodies, and the Changes effected in Chemical Processes, to depend" (352).[50]

Bringing up fluxions in such close proximity to Newton can leave no doubt that Hartley means to apply a term from the master's calculus to his *Opticks*, which Hartley's "it seems to me," again, indicates is his own idea.[51] He discusses particles of light as "Fluxions" that "bear no finite Ratio to the Quantities of which they are the Increments" (352) and concludes that "Particles of Light, by being infinitely smaller that the biggest component ones of natural Bodies, may become a Kind of *Communis Norma*, whereby to measure their active Powers"—that is, their velocities and powers of attraction and repulsion (353). Hence the "infinitely smaller" must be both imperceptible in itself in principle and useful in measuring the sensible, as in the infinitesimal calculus.[52] And since Hartley's notion of infinitely small particles of light is inspired by Newton's fluxions, it is reasonable to suppose that his notion of infinitesimal medullary particles must be too.

Hartley's embrace of the "infinitely smaller," moreover, is bolder than Newton's had been. A concept more associated with Leibniz, infinitesimals were treated with increasing caution as Newton's work on the calculus developed.[53] In his *Method of Fluxions and Infinite Series*, which appeared in translation in 1736 some ten years after his death but was composed in 1671, the work's editor, John Colson, took care to defend his author against the charge that he thought infinitesimals were real. Colson remarks that Newton "introduces none but infinitely little Quantities that are relatively so."[54] Since infinitely small quantities are, strictly speaking, unthinkable, Newton cannot unequivocally claim they exist. At most he uses them as a tool for measurement. So if it is right to suggest that Hartley's "infinitesimal medullary particles" derive from Newton's fluxions, Hartley goes considerably farther than his master. What are infinitely small are not merely conceptual increments of measurement but infinitesimal *objects*, light particles or brain particles, things in the world—precisely the status Newton would deny to fluxions.

The mysterious character of infinitesimals was widely noted and often ridiculed. The attack that Newton's editor Colson answers came from George Berkeley in *The Analyst; or, A Discourse Addressed to an Infidel Mathematician* (1734). Berkeley targets both the concept of the infinitesimal itself and Newton's hedging characterization of it as merely a heuristic device:

> It must, indeed, be acknowledged, that he used Fluxions, like the Scaffold of a building, as things to be laid aside or got rid of, as soon as finite Lines were found proportional to them. But then these finite Exponents are found by the help of Fluxions. Whatever therefore is got by such Exponents and Proportions is to be ascribed to Fluxions: which must therefore be previously understood. And what are these Fluxions? The Velocities of evanescent Increments? And what are these same evanescent Increments? They are neither finite Quantities, nor Quantities infinitely small, nor yet nothing. May we not call them the Ghosts of departed Quantities?[55]

This mockery of "Fluxions, Momentums, and Infinitesimals" (57) as ghostly underscores the difficulty of finding a home for them anywhere between matter and spirit, or finitude and infinity. Hartley's "relative nothings," again, go farther than the doctrines mockingly attributed to Newton by Berkeley. For Berkeley, fluxions are ghosts because they vanish once they fulfill their heuristic purpose. Hartley's infinitesimals are *particles* that are at the same time "nothings."

This helps us understand the force of Hartley's invocation of the anatomically infinitesimal throughout the *Observations*. He uses it to account for the connection between the material body and "the Soul" in the individual person:

> If we suppose an infinitesimal elementary body to be intermediate between the Soul and gross Body, which appears to be no improbable Supposition, then the Changes in our Sensations, Ideas, and Motions, may correspond to the Changes made in the medullary Substance, only as far as these correspond to the Changes made in the elementary Body. And if these last Changes have some other Source besides the Vibrations in the medullary Substance, some peculiar original Properties, for Instance, of the elementary Body, then Vibrations will not be adequate Exponents of Sensations, Ideas, and Motions. (34)

Hartley requires that "infinitesimal" be endowed with its meaning in the calculus to emphasize the crucial yet ultimately mysterious work that medullary particles do. They are particles of matter so small that they approach the condition of spirit: "relative nothings" that, like spirit, exist in no discernible relationship to what materially is. In principle insusceptible to being mentally represented itself, the infinitesimal makes all mental representation—"Sensations, Ideas, and Motions"—possible.

This third category—ghost matter—somewhat surprisingly allows Hartley to maintain his dualism. "I would not therefore be any-way interpreted so as to oppose the Immateriality of the Soul," he asserts at the end of volume 1 (512).[56] (In this he resembles Locke, who declares in the *Essay concerning Human Understanding* that "sensation . . . cannot be the action of bare insensible matter, nor ever could be without an immaterial thinking Being," 306).[57] In later years, a vitalist such as Joseph Priestley, who re-presented the *Observations* to the British public in *Hartley's Theory of the Human Mind* in 1775, could nonetheless take Hartley as a prophet of his own materialist views.[58] Such an affiliation led Priestley's antagonist Thomas Reid in *Essays on the Intellectual Powers of Man* (1785) to dismiss Hartley's appeal to infinitesimal medullary particles as a mere "castle in the air," along with what he saw as the "tendency of this system of vibrations" of Hartley's to "make all the operations of the mind mere mechanism, dependent on the laws of matter and motion." Attacking Hartley's "votaries," Reid must have Priestley in mind.[59] But Hartley's Newtonian speculations indicate how even dualists attentive to corporeal complexities were driven to enlarge their sense of what the body can do.

And in this Hartley was not alone among physician-philosophers of the early to mid-eighteenth century. A culture of conjecture comprising doctors, theologians, and metaphysicians sought the presence of Newton's "Æthereal Medium" at the subtlest points of the nervous system. George Cheyne, a colleague and associate of Hartley, is known in literary studies as a friend and physician to Richardson, and scholars often cite his medical works (especially

The English Malady, 1733) as crucial in building "the culture of sensibility."[60] But early in his career he published a book of Newtonian mathematics, *Fluxionum methodus inversa* (1703)—to a mixed response—and his other works, particularly part 2 of his *Philosophical Principles of Religion* (1715), explore the notion of infinites and the infinitesimal (which he calls a *"Relative Nothing"*[61]) as a method to describe the continuum between matter and spirit in the universe.[62]

Cheyne carried this interest into his medical and anatomical thinking. Right around the time he met Hartley in Bath in 1742, for instance, he remarks in his *Natural Method of Cureing the Diseases of the Body, and the Disorders of the Mind Depending on the Body*, "I imagin, the *spiritual* Substance uses material Organs, of one kind of Matter or another, in its *Operations*; and it is highly probable, they are the *nervous* Glands, the *Filaments*, the *Nerves*, but especially the membranous Coats of the infinitesimal *Nervuli*, and their wonderful Texture and Mechanism, so little known or understood."[63] As in other contexts that refer to what cannot be felt in the period, Cheyne hunts for terms to describe the point a researcher would most like to see but cannot, the point where perception meets its end at its beginning. With the word *infinitesimal* he can, like Hartley, precisely locate the intersection of spiritual and material substance.

Hartley's infinitesimal particles not only indicate a limit but also actively mediate between the two great terms of his system, *vibrations* and *associations*—located in the body and the soul, respectively. Locke had introduced the principle of association in the fourth (1700) edition of the *Essay* (book 2, chapter 33) mostly to account for odd psychological variations among people. But in the hands of Hartley and other midcentury philosophers, it becomes the central principle of mental activity. In the *Observations*, repetition in the patterns of vibrations cause ideas to be associated: "For the Alterations which Habit, Custom, frequent Impression, &c. make in the small constituent Particles, can scarce be any thing besides Alterations of the Distances, and mutual Actions, of these Particles; and these last Alterations must alter the natural Tendency to vibrate" (61).

And if we could not associate ideas, vibrations (and sensations, a term which for Hartley means physical stimulation as differentiated from ideas of sensation) themselves would fly apart into their infinitely divisible components: "For since all Sensations and Vibrations are infinitely divisible, in respect of Time and Place, they could not leave any Traces or Images of themselves, *i. e.* any Ideas, or miniature Vibrations, unless their infinitesimal Parts did cohere together through joint Impression; *i. e.* Association. Thus, to mention a gross Instance, we could have no proper Idea of a Horse, unless the particular Ideas of the Head, Neck, Body, Legs, and Tail, peculiar to this Animal, stuck to each other in the Fancy, from frequent joint Impression" (70–71). To put it more finely, the medullary particles in the brain, by being infinitesimal themselves, can lay hold of "infinitely divisible" physical vibrations and also integrate them into ideas by means of association. In all of these ways, then, infinitesimal medullary particles reconcile opposites: matter and spirit, vibrations and associations, the infinitely divisible and the "joint." Despite their own inapprehensible character, they thus make ordinary experience and apprehensions possible, much as Locke's "insensible Parts" that cause our ideas do.

Hartley's physical account of the infinitesimals in the brain determines his understanding of what psychological mechanisms and consciousness itself are like. Far more explicitly and directly than in Locke, the insensible physical particles at the basis of feeling for Hartley produce our experience of the evolving self through time from the inside. Hartley saw consciousness itself as a discontinuous affair, as Locke did, and the infinitesimal helps structure these discontinuities. Throughout much of volume 1 of the *Observations* Hartley attends to distinctions between voluntary and automatic actions, making a range of subsidiary distinctions, including "secondarily automatic" motions (105), "semivoluntary" ones (82), and so on. He resorts to the medullary particles' capacity to vibrate especially subtly to explain these gradations of our conscious lives, noting, "Since the same Motion which occasions Sensation, and intellectual Perception, passes thro' the Seats of these into the motory Nerves, in order to excite there the automatic and voluntary Motions, thus pervading the whole medullary Substance, in various Ways, according to the Variety of the Circumstances, but in all with the greatest Precision and Exactness, it follows, that this must be a vibratory one, and that of the most subtle Kind" (87). Beyond the autonomic processes of the body such as the contraction of the iris in bright light and "the Motion of the Heart" (108), Hartley is especially interested in the way "vibratory" motions fill our lives with automatic actions that recede from consciousness and voluntary ones that emerge in it. Much like Locke's consciousness that is "interrupted always," the texture of our conscious lives for Hartley is woven by such receding and emerging.

These alterations can be explained by the association of ideas that is facilitated, naturally, by the brain's infinitesimal particles: "After the Actions, which are most perfectly voluntary, have been rendered so by one Set of Associations, they may, by another, be made to depend upon the most diminutive Sensations, Ideas, and Motions, such as the Mind scarce regards, or is conscious of; and which therefore it can scarce recollect the Moment after the Action is over. Hence it follows, that Association not only converts automatic Actions into voluntary, but voluntary ones into automatic" (104). These conversions themselves are not felt, a nonconsciousness adhering to the action of association itself. Hartley describes a harpsichordist whose learning of a piece consists of an exertion and effort that insensibly fades as it is mastered, noting that "by degrees the Motions cling to one another, and to the Impressions of the Notes, in the Way of Association so often mentioned, the Acts of Volition growing less and less express all the Time, till as last they become evanescent and imperceptible" (109).

For Hartley such transitions model what it is like to be conscious, and the nonconsciousness that accompanies it. In passing from volition to automatic motion, "there is no perceptible Intervention [of the will], none of which we are conscious" (109). Like the infinitesimal particles that hold our ideas together, the motions that "cling to one another" may do so without a conscious exertion. Hartley's account of discontinuity in consciousness is more positive than Locke's vision of consciousness "interrupted always." The unnoticed transitions from automatic to voluntary to secondarily automatic motions and back again constitute mental life. They are less interruptions in consciousness that we perpetually and naturally overcome (upon waking up in the morning and remembering, after a moment or two, who we are) than they are the cement holding mental life together.

Hartley's description of brain anatomy and the psychological mechanisms arising from it, grounded in the nerves' "natural tendency to vibrate," does not, unsurprisingly, anticipate in any precise way the language of electrical signals and synapses of today's neuroscience. But his speculative vocabulary of body, brain, and mind does resemble the language of affect sometimes used by humanists today, and with good reason. Contemporary affect theory draws its keywords at least as much from the history of philosophy, dating back to the early Enlightenment, as from new neuroscientific developments. "Sensation is vibration," declares Gilles Deleuze, who finds versions of this notion at least as far back as G. W. Leibniz.[64] Likewise Brian Massumi describes intensities "filled with motion, vibratory motion, resonation," with a basis in "the unassimilable" of the bodily.[65] Hartley's account, unlike the most common eighteenth-century theory of the nervous system according to which "animal spirits" flow through nerves like hydraulic tubes, finds the source of his vibrations in an incomprehensible place, the infinitesimal, invisible to anatomy. This, too, resembles the language of affect theory today, but at its most mysterious (and least "neuroscientific"), as when Massumi declares that virtual affect resides in "the incorporeality of the body."[66] Such a phrase would work well enough as a euphemism for Hartley's medullary particles. As vividly as Hartley describes the layers of conscious life, he maintains an accompanying sense of the elusive vibrations of the insensible at the root of all feeling.

3. Vivacity and Insensible Association
Condillac and Hume

David Hartley, and John Locke before him, start with the insensibly small in their accounts of sensation and experience. They then construct a larger entity, the self, held together by the insensible through another medium, time, instead of (in Hartley's case, infinitely) small space. This more expansive, temporal significance of the idiom of the insensible will be most relevant to the midcentury philosophy of sentiment surveyed in the remainder of chapter I, and beyond, as subsequent chapters of this book treat novels, histories, and works of political economy that use the unfelt to build ever larger sociotemporal structures. The midcentury philosophers of consciousness to whom I now turn tease out the subtle ways in which unnoticed mental movements structure associative links. Such movements again do not deserve the label "unconscious feelings" or "insensible perceptions." They are instead patterned passages of nonfeeling that do their work in the mind, so to say, *as* nonfeelings, emptiness, missing parts. Pioneers of the theory of association such as Étienne Bonnot de Condillac and David Hume do not propose, like Hartley, an obscure anatomy of the brain, beyond the frontiers of our sensory powers, to support their accounts. They turn away from neurophysiology to provide experiential depictions of the empty spaces holding consciousness together. The Lockean view of consciousness, "interrupted always," and Hartley's account of oscillations between voluntary and automatic activity become in these other hands a psychology of attention and unawareness, of vivacity emerging from the insensible.

The *Essay on the Origin of Human Knowledge* (1746, Eng. trans. 1756), the first major philosophical work by Condillac, explores not only the connections but also the holes that association makes in conscious life. This *Essay* pertains to a discussion of the British tradition because of the closeness it keeps to Locke's (its subtitle advertises it as *Being a supplement to Mr. Locke's Essay on the Human Understanding*),[67] and because it entered English relatively early, in 1756 (unlike Condillac's more substantial *Traité des Sensations*, 1754, which was not translated in the eighteenth century). But it is also interesting because its translator, Thomas Nugent, liked the term *insensibly* and used it more than Condillac's original warrants (though Condillac himself was fond enough of *insensiblement*). We will meet Nugent again later in this book, where this predilection turns up in translations of Montesquieu and Voltaire.

Condillac begins by turning away from the search for the physical bases of the mental, firmly asserting dualism as he concludes that "the body, therefore, as an assemblage and aggregate, cannot be the subject of thought,"[68] and questioning Locke's speculation that matter might be endowed with the capacity to think (16–17). Without being very interested in physiology, then, Condillac elaborates a theory of attention and, more important for this discussion, of inattention in the service of an associationist psychology.[69] But despite his misgivings about Locke's openness to materialism, Condillac—like Hartley— names Locke as a primary influence in respect to consciousness and the power of associative relations. And also like Hartley, he puts special emphasis on the role of language in occasioning and cementing associations. (There is no evidence that either philosopher's work influenced the other's.) Condillac throws in with Locke's view that "the soul has no perceptions of which it does not take notice" and criticizes Cartesian accounts which "have admitted perceptions of which the mind never takes any notice" (28). Like Locke, Condillac comes to what may seem a surprising view: though there are no unnoticed perceptions, our consciousness is filled with unnoticings.

Condillac's account comes alive with narrative examples, and he resolves this puzzle with a story about being at a "public entertainment." He remarks that "among several perceptions of which we have a consciousness at the same time, it frequently happens that we are more conscious of one than the other" (28). Here the insensible performs its mediating function between degrees of awareness:

> Let a person be at a public entertainment, where a variety of objects seem to dispute his attention, his mind will be attacked by a number of

perceptions, of which it certainly takes notice; but insensibly some of these will be more agreeable and engaging to him than others, and of course he will more willingly give way to them. As soon as that happens, he will begin to be less affected by the others, his consciousness of them will even insensibly diminish, insomuch that upon his coming to himself he shall not remember to have taken any notice of them. (29)

Condillac relies on the word *insensiblement* throughout his *Essay*, though the first of the two instances here is "peu à peu,"[70] changed to "insensibly" by his translator Nugent. Neither term in this passage gestures to anything like the subliminal or unconscious. It is crucial for Condillac to insist, like Locke before him, that the person here, insofar as he is affected by anything, is consciously affected. There is no Leibnizian unperceived perception, no lower-level mental registering of what the conscious mind does not notice. Locke's view of consciousness as "interrupted always" had focused on our tendency to attend to the present moment and lose sight of the past. Condillac presents a more dynamic and uneven picture of present consciousness, which always prioritizes among the things affecting it and as it does, ceaselessly forgets as it notices and notices as it forgets.

Our present is woven together with this hectic forgetting and micro-neglect. In illuminating remarks on Condillac's *Essay*, Suzanne Gearhart argues that his treatment of inattention undermines his Lockean rejection of unperceived perception. She cites a passage immediately following the one quoted above, about the experience of a spectator in a theater, who finds himself more absorbed in the performance because he takes cues from the absorption of those around him. Gearhart concludes, "Our attention for the stage may even be a result of our emulation of the other, attentive spectators . . . in an 'attentive' audience, all the spectators in fact must be at once attentive to and forgetful of the other spectators. Condillac has rejected the notion of an unperceived perception only to create the notion of an inattentive attention."[71] While Gearhart is right to argue that such gaps must complicate any commitment to the unity of consciousness, I think the phrase "at once" misrepresents attention's successive, temporal nature. According to Condillac's model, we attend to the other spectators but then forget them so fast that our minds produce the "deception" (the French original has *l'illusion*) that the stage holds our undivided attention (29). Condillac indeed insists that our minds perpetually "give way" to one object after another.

He acknowledges that "there are some moments in which our consciousness does not seem [*ne paroît pas*] to be divided between the action represented, and the rest of the entertainment; by which I mean, the theatre, the audience, the actors, &c" (29). But by asserting that consciousness does not *seem* to be divided, Condillac is, of course, continuing to insist that it is. Our insensibly shifting attention allows this illusion to occur. The example of the theatrical spectator hence cannot be Condillac's attempt to preserve "the unity of the perceiving subject."[72] He will subsequently note that "there are perceptions in our mind, which we do not remember, not even the very moment after their impression" (31). The point is not that they abide unperceived but that they are perceived and then instantly gone. The gaps in our consciousness are essentially temporal, holes in the flow of awareness created by the often extremely minute span of time it takes to forget what does not matter to us. There can be no "inattentive attention," only attention and inattention forever replacing each other. And the term *insensibly* makes all the difference because it signifies an unfelt movement instead of the simultaneous copresence of a conscious and an unconscious perception.

The term refers, moreover, not to what is itself forgotten, the stimuli out there in the world that slip away from us, but to our lack of awareness *that* we notice and forget this quickly and fluidly. Nugent's rendering of the first instance, "insensibly some of these will be more agreeable and engaging," refers to the noticing, while the second, "his consciousness of them will insensibly even diminish," the forgetting. Hence the term *insensibly* gestures to a kind of lubricant in consciousness that allows us to single one thing out as we allow others to recede. Condillac enhances this effect of the mind sliding along without awareness of its attention and inattention by the passivity prominent in passage. The mind is "attacked" by perceptions, and the person will "give way" to them. Though the person's consciousness takes everything in, its retention and loss of perceptions are not at his command. He not only notices and forgets insensibly. His awareness itself insensibly resists his control. Thus Condillac identifies another way in which consciousness is a lossy phenomenon whose texture and shape are created by the gaps that fill it up, like air bubbles in bread.

As Condillac's *Essay* continues, it becomes apparent that the insensible as deployed in his theory of inattention lies at the heart of the association of ideas itself. He remarks on the power of physiognomic reflections over our thoughts: "In general the impressions we feel under different circumstances, induce us to connect ideas, which we have it no longer in our power to separate. We cannot, for instance, frequent company, without insensibly connecting the ideas of a certain turn of mind and character with a particular figure and make" (82). Here again the milieu is social interaction and "company," in which a variety of stimuli shapes both our awareness and our unawareness of our mind's actions. The self's passivity earlier remarked in his account of inattention here reappears as inherent in associations. We are induced to make them and have no power to separate them once they are made. That we do so insensibly is a crucial aspect of their power.

The constitutive role played by the insensible only becomes more pronounced in more sophisticated activity of the associating mind. For Condillac, the acquisition of associations in language and the greater awareness of our world also emerge from unnoticed processes.[73] Cries of passion gradually form into a system of signs in our minds: "The same circumstances could not be frequently repeated, but [the first learners of language] must have accustomed themselves at length to connect with the cries of the passions and with the different motions of the body, those perceptions which were expressed in so sensible a manner" (173). The vivid, "sensible" character of natural bodily expression strikes us and only afterward becomes customary: language learners "began to acquire some sort of habit, they were able to command their imagination as they pleased, and insensibly they learned to do by reflexion what they had hitherto done merely by instinct" (173).

Oddly, "reflexion" seems to operate more insensibly than instinct does. We gain through signs a fuller awareness of meaning, but a loss of intimacy with the process of sophistication that accompanies this acquisition: "The use of those signs insensibly enlarged and improved the operations of the mind, and on the other hand these having acquired such improvement, perfected the signs, and rendered the use of them more familiar" (173–74). It begins to seem that Condillac's use of the idiom of the insensible is itself a kind of reflex, used to describe any gradual process, even the heightening of our capacities to consciously reflect. The persistence of the device is not meaningless, however. It testifies to Condillac's abiding sense of the mind's "operations," in which noticing and forgetting, consciously improving and habitually associating, go hand in hand. Finally, the insensible has become a feature not only of our neglect of what is going on outside and inside of our minds but of our coming to the highest levels of consciousness.

David Hume's own theory of the association of ideas also depends on the quiet collaboration of vivid feeling with the insensible. This affective complexity forms the foundation of his project, his account of our belief in associative relations in book 1 of *A Treatise of Human Nature* (1738–40). This is well before his taxonomy of the passions in book 2 or his account of sympathy in book 3, to which contemporary discussions of affect in Hume more frequently turn.[74] Hume considered his theory of association to be his prime achievement in the *Treatise*. As he puts it in *An Abstract of a Book Lately Published; Entituled, A Treatise of Human Nature* (1740), "If any thing can intitle the author to so glorious a name as that of an *inventor*, 'tis the use he makes of the principle of the association of ideas, which enters into most of his philosophy."[75] And association could not occur without affect. An association, according to James A. Harris, represents for Hume "a change in how the idea *feels* to the mind."[76] And as we might expect, Gilles Deleuze's book about Hume, *Empiricism and Subjectivity* (1953, his first, based on his dissertation), finds "affectivity" at the heart of Hume's doctrine of association.[77] On the one hand, belief in particular associations—say, of causes to effects—is a vivacity of feeling, as again the *Abstract* has it: "the belief, which attends experience, is explained to be nothing but a peculiar sentiment, or lively conception produced by habit."[78]

Yet the experience of a liveliness of sentiment that drives association also requires an unnoticed movement: not a hidden impression or idea, nor any "unconscious" content, but an unregistered mental passage. As Hume notes in book 1 of the *Treatise*, the *communication* of *"force and vivacity"* that associates one idea to another is itself unfelt:

> When the mind fixes constantly on the same object, or passes easily and insensibly along related objects, the disposition [of the mind when it performs its operations] has a much longer duration. Hence it happens, that when the mind is once inliven'd by a present impression, it proceeds to form a more lively idea of the related objects, by a natural transition of the disposition from the one to the other. The change of the objects is so easy, that the mind is scarce sensible of it, but applies itself to the conception of the related idea with all the force and vivacity it acquir'd from the present impression.[79]

This "change of objects" is the central action of association. Its essence is movement. The very vivacity that associates objects in the mind has an underside of unfeeling on which the association also depends.[80] If the force were not vivid, it could not associate, but if its action were itself felt, objects in the mind would remain merely distinct. Some eight years later, in the *Philosophical Essays concerning Human Understanding* (1748), Hume's emphasis on association had somewhat receded.[81] But the insensible likewise figures in his summary definition of it: "Nature has establish'd Connexions among particular Ideas," he remarks, and "no sooner one occurs to our Thoughts than it introduces its correlative, and carries our Attention towards it, by a gentle and insensible Movement."[82] Though Hume more openly insists on the "intense and steady" character of "the Sentiment of Belief" (84), its insensible component, the movement, is what makes this intensity possible.

The sentiment of belief in general depends on both vivacity and a version of the unfelt affect described throughout this book. Hume founds this dual sentiment on "Custom" (what the *Philosophical Essays* call "the great Guide of human Life," 75), which itself may suggest unthinking, automatic patterns of mental action. Yet it is not easy to pinpoint exactly what is insensible in customary associations, which themselves are not unnoticed at all. Our minds vividly associate a portrait with its subject, a room with another adjacent to it, or a wound with pain (*Philosophical Essays*, 32–33). Nor does the insensible lie in any tendency to consider our beliefs to be rational when they in fact arise from sentiment. We certainly often make such a mistake unawares, but Hume does not refer to that when he mentions the "gentle and insensible Movement" of association.

Rather, the insensible characterizes the very facility with which associative movements occur. Like Condillac, who designated as insensible not the impressions that we instantaneously forget as we move through a room but rather our not noticing that we accumulate impressions by forgetting other ones, Hume does not describe insensible mental ideas. Instead the insensible is again a kind of lubricant of mentation, referring neither to thought's objects nor to the mental mechanism itself. In her treatment of association in the *Treatise*, Annette Baier has asked, "Could the associative relations between thoughts be . . . covert, unconscious relations between unrecognized relata?" She concludes, "So the association of ideas that explains our complex ideas of lasting 'substances' may well have to be taken to be often unconscious."[83] This insight can be refined by insisting that "unconscious relations" do not equal something that is itself an (unconscious) idea, with some kind of tacit content. That is, my association between a wound and pain does not consist of some unconscious proposition, hidden in my mind, like "wounds of that kind hurt." As Baier points out, very often the content of associations is explicit, as when someone exclaims "Ouch!" upon seeing another's injury, or "That boy really looks like his father!" Baier's word "often" above indicates that such content is sometimes recognized and sometimes not.

The kind of nonconsciousness that Hume gets at with the "gentle and insensible Movement" instead functions consistently as insensible, or something we are "scarce sensible" of. It is not some idea or proposition that we do not *think*, but rather the movement itself, which we do not *feel*. This is always insensible, or nearly so, while the question of whether or not we assign some propositional content to an association—this cloak makes me proud because it resembles beautiful cloaks I have seen and because I own it—simply depends on whether or not we spell out such thoughts to ourselves. The "unconscious" component of the association of ideas for Hume is not, then, some unthought proposition—X typically relates to Y—but the unfelt slide itself. As he puts it in the *Treatise*, "The passage betwixt related ideas is, therefore, so smooth and easy, that it produces little alteration on the mind, and seems like the continuation of the same action; and as the continuation of the same action is an effect of the continu'd view of the same object, 'tis for this reason we attribute sameness to every succession of related objects. The thought slides along the succession with equal facility, as if it consider'd only one object; and therefore confounds the succession with the identity" (356). Succession confounded with identity: Hume brings us back to the perspective of Locke on the seeming self-identity of the oak tree and its "insensibly succeeding Parts." Vividness itself for Hume depends on this gentle, sliding, nonvivid movement. The fire so vividly evokes heat, the son so strikingly recalls the father he takes after because the mind moves insensibly to link them. In this way, then, the insensible makes our sentiments of belief what they are.

Hume characteristically recognizes the rhythm and progress of his own sophisticated philosophical pursuits in these basic movements of consciousness. His working of the insensible into the sentiments of belief on important occasions comes to characterize the formation of his belief in his own philosophical insights. In the *Treatise*, he dramatizes his recognition of the true basis of the association of causes to effects as something of a surprise: "THUS in advancing we have insensibly discover'd a new relation betwixt cause and effect, when we least expected it, and were entirely employ'd upon another subject. This relation is their CONSTANT CONJUNCTION. Contiguity and succession are not sufficient to make us pronounce any two objects to be cause and effect, unless we perceive, that these two relations are preserv'd in several instances" (156–57). This surprising effect arises in part from Hume's uncertain shifts between the authorial *we* and the *we* that includes all human beings who learn from experience. In the preceding paragraph, remembering and learning to expect previous conjunctions lead us to an understanding of cause and effect. Here Hume the philosopher recognizes the relation's theoretical relevance. This dramatization of the sophisticated intelligence recognizing its own subjection to insensible processes will find an echo in a passage that will be discussed in chapter III, by one of Hume's heirs, in *The History of the Decline and Fall of the Roman Empire*, where Edward Gibbon finds his critical powers as a historian insensibly emerging from his reflection on his sources. In Hume the "advancing" of both philosopher and ordinary person by means of experience produces parallel discoveries: for the person a sense of cause and effect, and for the philosopher a theory of it. The crucial work performed by *insensibly* in both cases derives from its arising from the movement of experience. In both, the accumulation of associations, not "reason," creates the sense of relation. The insensible resides within this movement or consolidation of what finally produce vivid expectations and perceptions.

Finally, the insensible helps indicate something of the complexity, if not tension, in Hume's grand reconciliation of theoretical exploration and common life, a durable theme in Humean exegesis.[84] Taking on the persona of "The Sceptic" in the essay of that title, he concludes, "Here then is the chief triumph of art and philosophy: It insensibly refines the temper, and it points out to us those dispositions which we should endeavour to attain, by a constant *bent* of mind, and by repeated *habit*. Beyond this I cannot acknowledge it to have great influence; and I must entertain doubts concerning all those exhortations and consolations, which are in such vogue among speculative reasoners."[85] The insensible in such cases again plays its crucial mediating role. Art and philosophy both inculcate salubrious habits and "point out" dispositions of mind to be deliberately chosen. Presumably we choose to take up art and philosophy for our own good, yet their benefit accrues insensibly, not because of whatever "exhortations and consolations" they issue. Only *after* we have already gained the benefit are we enabled to perform the crucial Humean move of choosing our habits and embracing our "bent." The insensible, then, forms not only our unthinking good habits but also our capacity to *endeavor* to live well without relying on windy platitudes of moral philosophers. It can function this way only by *not* being a content or moral proposition (e.g., "thou shalt live according to refined habits"). It must instead be a process. The insensible hence helps Hume reconcile habit and philosophy.

4. Sentiment and Secret Consciousness
Haywood and Smith

As the prestige and power of sentiment expand in midcentury philosophy, writers appeal to the insensible to enable feeling to perform an enlarged array of new tasks. Beyond accounts of particles in the brain or the "core consciousness" of individual persons, the idiom helps articulate moral philosophies that turn the individual toward society. Eliza Haywood's use of it in her monthly periodical *The Female Spectator* (which ran from April 1744 to May 1746 and appeared as a four-volume book in 1745–46) testifies to this increase in the scale of its application. In these essays, Haywood offers numerous reflections, moral exhortations, and anecdotes that exemplify the kind of popular philosophy offered by periodicals since the first *Spectator* earlier in the century.[86] She already had experience with the idiom as a novelist (as chapter II of this book will show), particularly to characterize the subtle onset of desire in the tradition of romance and scandalous fiction. She hence comes to her thoughts about insensible aspects of sentiment not by self-consciously trailing in a set of philosophical influences but by exploring the suggestions inherent in a prevalent stylistic device. Consistently *The Female Spectator* testifies to the odd double action of feeling, its overt power to fill consciousness and its quieter manner of controlling and directing it.

Haywood recalls in the periodical's introductory essay that her own philosophical sensitivity is a product of unfelt processes. Describing how she "commenc'd Author," she remarks that her worldly experience has "enabled me, when the too great Vivacity of my Nature became temper'd with Reflection, to see into the secret Springs which gave rise to the Actions I had either heard, or been Witness of—to judge the various Passions of the human Mind, and distinguish those imperceptible Degrees by which they become Masters of the Heart, and attain the Dominion over Reason."[87] The processes of passion's advancement and dominance that are "secret" and "imperceptible" to others are revealed to and recognized by Haywood, and this masterful insight enables her to edify her readers as author of her own *Spectator* papers. She here apparently aligns herself with "Reason" in her criticism of the prevalence of passions.

But she is quick to celebrate how her feelings have shaped her own perspective. Again stressing the social context of her acquisition of insight, she continues, "A thousand odd Adventures, which at the Time they happen'd made slight Impression on me, and seem'd to dwell no longer on my Mind than the Wonder they occasion'd, now rise fresh to my Remembrance, with this Advantage, that the Mystery I then, for want of Attention, imagin'd they contain'd, is entirely vanish'd, and I find it easy to account for the Cause by the Consequence" (1:3). Like those thoughtless people she observes, Haywood herself is initially led only by her feelings, her "too great Vivacity" and propensity to "Wonder." Also as with them, her passions do not, initially at least, bring her any great insight. Like the philosophers already discussed, she portrays her own conscious life as shot through with inattention and forgetting, a leavening that imparts a shape to a life of social feeling.

But her vivacity and wonder also help redeem such distraction and inattention, fixing the incidents in her memory so as to be available for reflection later. While passion dominates thoughtless people, it brings her to her own philosophical reflections on causes and effects. In this process, the insensible plays its familiar mediating role, here bridging the gap between thoughtless feeling and deliberate reflection on it. The content of ideas—her remembrance of past "odd Adventures"—figures more largely in the insensible processes of mentation here than it did in writers such as Hume and Locke. But like them, Haywood notes an opacity in such mental processes, that fix ideas and allow them to return when wisdom is ready for them. Like Hume's "Sceptic," Haywood attains a philosophical attitude through experience that accrues insensibly. In her case, however, this experience is driven not by "constant bent" and steady habit but by the "too great Vivacity" of her coquettish nature. Haywood by these means perhaps discovers her unique vocation as a woman philosopher, a "female Spectator." She finds in what are initially the unconstrained passions of the thoughtless coquette the way to reason and wisdom.[88]

More comments scattered throughout *The Female Spectator* likewise remark on the way unnoticed processes both create a context for vivid affections and endow them with meaning that may be subsequently recognized. For instance, in a long account of the natural-philosophical observations made by a party of fashionable women in the countryside, Haywood comments, "The Mind is insensibly attracted by the Senses to Contemplation of that which is most pleasing to them" (3:301). Here the word, passing as it is, again plays its mediating role, establishing a relation of conscious feeling to conscious mental attraction, adding an opacity that affect must cross to get from one to the other.[89] The striking proximity of "insensibly" to "the Senses" exposes the secret character of the process. As before, Haywood extols the power and influence of sensation by suggesting that its sway over the mind cannot be felt. The senses assert their power not simply by filling up the conscious mind but by maintaining, in a process antithetical both to sensory vivacity and mental consciousness, their distance from it.

Another essay, on taste, makes a more dramatic point. An insensible temporal process is what establishes sensitivity. Haywood writes, "But they who can once resolve to employ themselves in such a manner as becomes a Person of *fine Taste*, however repugnant they may be at first, will, by Degrees, be brought insensibly to have it in reality" (3:138). As always, a pertinent question is, Insensibly to whom? Perhaps it is to onlookers scrutinizing the repugnant person, unable to tell just when he becomes truly tasteful, but certainly it is also to the person himself. He deliberately "resolve[s] to employ" himself tastefully and consciously attains taste, but his taste, though it is discriminating sensitivity itself, seems blind to its own emergence as a real attainment. Even he does not notice when his taste becomes real, and even his newly real taste cannot help him tell. Haywood's assertions of the power of feeling throughout *The Female Spectator* hence tend to include references to feeling's opacity, not only to "Reflection" and "Reason" but to feeling itself. In all these cases, one is insensible not of some idea or proposition, but of the process of coming to awareness and acuity.

Adam Smith's more systematic display of the powers of feeling in *The Theory of Moral Sentiments* (1759) less frequently relies on the insensible to bind the elements of his account together. Also building individual psychology on social interaction, the *Theory* insists that our observations of others affect us sensitively and that this sensitivity constitutes our capacity for moral behavior: "If virtue," Smith remarks, "be desirable for its own sake, and if vice be, in the same manner, the object of aversion, it cannot be reason which originally distinguishes those different qualities, but immediate sense and feeling."[90] He moreover describes a lack of sensitivity as the chief obstacle to moral civilization. For instance, his discussion of "savages and barbarians" (205) in the section "Of the Influence of Custom" refers to their "insensibility," in contrast to "the virtues which are founded upon humanity" that hold sway "among civilized nations" (204). "The savages in North America, we are told" (205), are able to bear injuries and insults "with the appearance of the greatest insensibility" (206), and a crowd of "savages" can look upon scenes of torture with "the same insensibility" (206). Throughout the treatise, the noun designates the blockage of those sentiments that are the essence of our moral responses.

At a crucial point, however, Smith recruits the insensible to serve moral sentiment rather than to identify what obstructs it. Bare sentiment, Smith knew, could not alone support what we think of as a consistent moral life. Basing morality on sentiments opened him to the charge that his theory was merely a "Refinement of the selfish System" of Bernard Mandeville (as Thomas Reid would later put it).[91] Ethics could seem reduced to what pleases us in social interaction. As a letter he wrote to Gilbert Elliot makes especially clear,[92] Smith thinks that the impartiality of the impartial spectator, the imaginatively constructed "man within," is able to elevate moral sentiments above mere selfishness. In one important passage in *The Theory of Moral Sentiments*, this impartiality rests on the fact that we are "scarce sensible" (135) of the spectator's authority over us. This kind of insensibility allows our moral feelings to be felt more fully and yet selflessly.

Smith introduces this idea in part 3, "Of the Foundation of our Judgments concerning our own Sentiments and Conduct," by drawing an analogy from vision.[93] I realize that the mountain I see out my window, if I think about it, takes up no more space in my visual field than objects in the room where I sit:

> I can form a just comparison between those great objects and the little objects around me, in no other way, than by transporting myself, at least in fancy, to a different station, from whence I can survey both at nearly equal distances, and thereby form some judgment of their real proportions. Habit and experience have taught me to do this so easily and so readily, that I am scarce sensible that I do it; and a man must be, in some measure, acquainted with the philosophy of vision, before he can be thoroughly convinced, how little those distant objects would appear to the eye, if the imagination, from a knowledge of their real magnitudes, did not swell and dilate them. (135)

The correction comes habitually, not deliberately, and habit in this case prevents distortion. Having this habit does not exactly mean that I subscribe to some tacit proposition or belief: "that mountain really is much bigger than this vase." It is instead simply something done: "habit and experience have taught me to do this."

Likewise, unthinking habit ensures that we sympathize with others and place their interests on a scale with our own. This is the authority of the impartial spectator at its most automatic and perhaps most compelling. Instead of cleaving to "the selfish and original passions of human nature" (135) in assessing the hardships of another person, we find ourselves irresistibly adopting a more detached attitude:

> Before we can make any proper comparison of those opposite interests, we must change our position. We must view them, neither from our own place nor yet from his, neither with our own eyes nor yet with his, but from the place and with the eyes of a third person, who has no particular connexion with either, and who judges with impartiality between us. Here too, habit and experience have taught us to do this so easily and so readily, that we are scarce sensible that we do it; and it requires, in this case too, some degree of reflection, and even of philosophy, to convince us, how little interest we should take in the greatest concerns of our neighbour. (135–36)

In direct parallel to Smith's account of vision, the moral authority of the impartial spectator—a fictional "third person"—furnishes us a selfless perspective in a manner of which we are "scarce sensible."

Yet Smith wavers somewhat here. He claims that the spectator guides us in moral life so compellingly that it requires an exertion of "philosophy" for us to act selfishly. But he also seems to make the spectator's authority a matter of our conscious rational will, not merely automatic impartiality. We must consciously appeal to "reason, principle, conscience, the inhabitant of the breast, the man within, the great judge and arbiter of our conduct" (137) when facing moral dilemmas. Here he departs from Hume, who denigrates the idea that rational principles substantially motivate us. Such declarations in the *Theory* lead Eric Schliesser to contend that "Smithian conscience is a synthesis of feeling and reason."[94] How this synthesis of antitheses may come about and function is the question. The impartial spectator is a firm, principled arbiter, and yet there are ways in which we are "scarce sensible" of his sway. The insensible hence again acts as a mediator, here between consciously consulted conscience and habitually compelling moral sentiment. Smith needs both for his theory to be both sentimental and moral.

The middle position occupied by the insensible comes into view more clearly a little later in part 3, when the moral agent's impartiality comes under most stress. Smith confronts just how difficult it is to impartially assess our own actions, noting, "There are two different occasions upon which we examine our own conduct, and endeavour to view it in the light in which the impartial spectator would view it: first, when we are about to act; and secondly, after we have acted. Our views are apt to be very partial in both cases; but they are apt to be most partial when it is of most importance that they should be otherwise" (157). This most important moment is the moment of action itself. Afterward, when the deed is done, the impartial spectator has a decent enough (though still attenuated) chance of stepping in to cause guilt and encourage self-reproach. Here the impartial spectator does not exert anything like an unquestionable sway over our moral judgments. The analogy of morality to our automatic way of correcting our estimations of objects' sizes at relative distances breaks down. Here it takes "philosophy" (or at least effort) to achieve adequate moral feeling during the heat of the moment, not to divest ourselves of it.

At this potential crisis of confidence in sentiment as a basis of moral life, Smith finds a special way to introduce the notion of general moral rules. Any appeal to rules at all could seem to run against the grain of his theory, which all along insists that morality is a matter of sentiment, not obedience to authority. But his account casts rules' origin and power in sentimental terms: "Nature, however, has not left this weakness, which is of so much importance, altogether without a remedy; nor has she abandoned us entirely to the delusions of self-love. Our continual observations upon the conduct of others, insensibly lead us to form to ourselves certain general rules concerning what is fit and proper either to be done or to be avoided" (159). Far from being passively heeded as distant, static, "juridical" authorities,[95] these rules arise as it were organically through our "continual observations" of social life. The adverbial form of *insensibly* is crucial here. It indicates a *how*, a process whereby the rules become personally meaningful for each of us. We "form" them "to ourselves."

Smith does not quite claim here that we maintain unconscious beliefs in moral rules. (As it happens, everybody more or less consciously knows what the moral rules are anyway.) Rather, he insists that our manner of forming them (to ourselves) is what is insensible. The unfelt nature of this process of coming under the sway of "certain general rules" is precisely what makes them effective in ways that any mere belief in them, conscious or unconscious, could not be. If moral rules here can be described as "formulated by induction,"[96] it is formulation and induction of peculiar kinds, not a thoughtful process of generalization from philosophically considered individual cases but an insensible accumulation of affecting examples that form a personal structure of response.

Later, in part 7 of the *Theory*, Smith will use the word *induction* to describe this process, but again he insists on its sentimental nature: "The general maxims of morality are formed, like all other general maxims, from experience and induction. We observe in a great variety of particular cases what pleases or displeases our moral faculties, what these approve or disapprove of, and, by induction from this experience, we establish those general rules. But induction is always regarded as one of the operations of reason. From reason, therefore, we are very properly said to derive all those general maxims and ideas" (319). What "pleases or displeases" comes first, followed by the rational establishment of the rules. This account also retains verbal links to his earlier portrayal of the way our observations "insensibly lead us to form to ourselves certain general rules." If anything, the description in the passage about how rules "are formed" more fully emphasizes the passivity of reason in the process to insist that the gathering of experience proceeds without advance direction. Through his discussion of general rules in part 7, Smith uses the passive to describe how rules take shape and gain their power. Such expressions emphasize the experiential, affective side of induction. Again, the rules themselves are consciously enough recognized. The insensible pertains not to what the rules are but how they are affectively formed.

The rules' insensible formation and their "rational" recognized content together help make Smith's moral system what it is. Rules do correct sentiment's excesses and serve, as commentators have noticed, as a defining element, even the "apex," of Smith's moral system.[97] As he claims in a later passage from part 7, "It is by these [rules], however, that we regulate the greater part of our moral judgments, which would be extremely uncertain and precarious if they depended altogether upon what is liable to so many variations as immediate sentiment and feeling, which the different states of health and humour are capable of altering so essentially" (319). But Smith's theory requires delicate language to bridge sentiment and the rationality and propositional character of rules, which otherwise could seem incompatible. After all, chapter 2 of part 7, "*Of those Systems which make Reason the Principle of Approbation*," rejects arguments that identify reason as the foundation of morality and supports sentiment instead: "It is altogether absurd and unintelligible to suppose that the first perceptions of right and wrong can be derived from reason, even in those particular cases upon the experience of which the general rules are formed" (320). Such formulations could make reason's rules seem too remote from our actual experience in particular circumstances to serve us when we most need them. The language of passives, habit, and the insensible works to balance the two functions. If moral feeling were too consciously and completely to give way in Smith's theory to adherence to rationally abstracted rules, morality would lose its fundamentally sentimental basis. But if feeling did not include our capacity to form rules "to ourselves," our feelings would make morality a potentially haphazard affair.

Hence even following a moral rule (as opposed to forming one) requires an element of unfelt affect. In the heat of the moment, the rules guide us as a kind of pressure coming from past experience rather than a body of moral maxims to be consulted. Back in part 3, considering a bad case—a person who does ultimately end up acting violently—Smith writes, "At the very time of acting, at the moment in which passion mounts the highest, he hesitates and trembles at the thought of what he is about to do: he is secretly conscious to himself that he is breaking through those measures of conduct which, in all his cool hours, he had resolved never to infringe, which he had never seen infringed by others without the highest disapprobation, and of which the infringement, his own mind forebodes, must soon render him the object of the same disagreeable sentiments" (161). The drama here lies between contending feelings, mounting rage versus hesitation and trembling, not exactly between feelings and rules, which are not quite there in the moment. They hold sway in the pluperfect indicative, as he thinks back to his "cool hours" when "he had resolved" not to infringe them (as "measures of conduct"), and when all the experience that had formed them had seemed to coalesce.

Crucial here is the phrase "secretly conscious to himself." Some barrier exists between his present, passionate state and the rules that would prevent the impending wrong. The word "secretly" perhaps just means that the transgressor does not tell his victim or anybody else around that he is having scruples. But whether they know or not is beside the point, since Smith is most interested now in what is going on in the mind of the transgressor himself. The secret consciousness instead seems (at least to a degree) a secret "to himself" (that is, from himself), a consciousness secreted from consciousness, a not fully self-aware counterpressure working against his conscious fury, resembling the way rules are said to be formed "insensibly . . . to ourselves" earlier. Being "secretly conscious" at the moment of action is subtly different from holding an "unconscious belief" (such as "it is wrong to kill"). The former phrase depicts an adverbial pressure in the present built from past feelings instead of a static, abiding structure of unrecognized convictions. Similarly the foreboding of his own mind is more like a feeling, a presentiment somehow recessed from his foremost awareness. Smith uses the insensible as a device to enforce the dependence of moral consciousness on the secrets to itself it keeps.

This not to say, again, that Smith thinks we cannot consciously deliberate about moral rules. We all know what they are, so there is little point in claiming we believe in them unconsciously too. They are "fixed in our mind by habitual reflection" (160), he asserts, suggesting our responsibility for mentally maintaining them. But the rather passive way they "are fixed," and their habitual character, work against our reading them as a fully deliberated practice of moral discipline.[98] The examples get worked reflectively into our minds as "formed" residues, as it were, of past sensitive experiences: he will talk about "the rule which past experience has impressed upon him" (161) instead of the rule that the agent's moral intelligence has abstracted from experience. We do form them, out of our own experience. Yet in many cases, we are led to do this and are insensible, unaware, that we are thus led. The insensible element of rule following, again, synthesizes feeling with the rational dictates of the impartial spectator. Maria Alejandra Carrasco compares such a synthesis in Smith's moral theory to an Aristotelian conception of practical reason or *phronesis*, which blends attention to particular moral situations with a generally rational outlook. Such a synthesis, she explains, works "habitually . . . and we are usually not conscious of it except in situations of conflict."[99] Conflict may force us to formulate and reflect on rules, but insensible habit preserves their vital link to what we feel.

In his appeal to the insensible to reconcile difficult relations among elements of his system, Smith participates in a long tradition of philosophical usage. The idiom's inclusion in the diversity of philosophical writing about feeling in the long eighteenth century in Britain indicates a kind of intellectual presence different from that of the period's big ideas. The term performs as a character actor who always seems to be on hand, a little off to one side in movie after movie, passing the scalpel or handkerchief to the stars when they have their dramatic scenes. It is hard to see any very direct link connecting Locke's distinction between primary and secondary qualities to Smith's impartial spectator, or to what Hume viewed as his signal accomplishment, the theory of the association of ideas. Yet the functions performed by the idiom in philosophy, from the late seventeenth century to the age of sentiment, remain remarkably precise and consistent. It bridges or mediates between contrasting states of consciousness, or between our feelings and the unfeeling material from which they arise. It places power in unfelt performances rather than in stated or even "unconscious" beliefs or propositions. In a sense, the idiom itself does this, not the philosophers. It serves them because it signifies the function of the unfelt in fabricating feelings and hence can be endowed with whatever subtlety of movement that philosophers require to make their theories of feeling work.

Chapter II

Fiction

Unfelt Engagement

Unfelt affects are among the most subtly potent ones in eighteenth-century fiction, and they often decisively delineate character, advance plot, and confer a distinctive texture on narrative. At a significant moment, Henry Fielding's narrator in *Tom Jones* remarks of Sophia's feelings for Tom, "The reader will be pleased to recollect that a secret affection for Mr Jones had insensibly stolen into the bosom of this young lady."[1] The capacity of characters not to feel and not to notice feelings vitally supports the expressions of high emotion and intense desire long seen as among the novel's reasons for existence. In their privative sense, words like *insensible* and *imperceptible* sometimes serve as a plot device. Heroines' unawareness of the schemes of seducers leads them into danger. But as with Sophia, the insensible also fortifies feelings and desires. In the sentimental novel, women's vivid, demonstrated emotions, tears and distress, passions and revulsions are, of course, far from unnoticed or unsensed by those undergoing them, by other characters, or by readers. Yet novelists also gesture to the insensible to evoke deeply meaningful affect, not merely as an alternative to the high-flown feelings evident in such fiction but also as a way of quietly enhancing their profundity.

These gestures also help novelists navigate the perilous tensions and congruities between virtue and desire that are definitive of heroines' predicament in the marriage plot. "There is something monstrous frightful, my dear Harriet, in marrying a man that one likes," says Jane Austen's Miss Grandison, by way of raillery, in Austen's rediscovered dramatic version of Samuel Richardson's last novel.[2] By discreetly employing the insensible as a stylistic device, novelists can solve this problem. An affection growing unawares can move a heroine toward a love match without implicating her in a frightful desire like an avid affection would. And the feeling of Sophia and other virtuous characters for a long while crucially remains a secret *to* themselves, as well as to others. As with that of Adam Smith's wrathful man, secret consciousness serves moral ends in eighteenth-century novels of desire. But instead of intimating an affective restraint, insensible affection impels heroines forward. While a virtuous woman's moral responsibility for her desire is softened by its way of tacitly overcoming her, the idiom signals not an evasion or "repression" of desire but its unfelt mode of growth. The insensible plays a Janus-faced role in novels about sentiment, subduing its moral jeopardy but strengthening its affective hold. The term allows the culture of sensibility, at the height of its power, to incorporate kinds of affect and motivation that seem antithetical to it.

The unfelt affections of characters in fiction obey the logic of the insensible I have treated earlier. As a negation, the idiom removes affective motives from the characters' awareness yet also refrains from siting them very apparently in some yet-to-be-hypothesized "unconscious mind." In this, the following account resembles those of other critics who have viewed literary characterization in the period as less exclusively pitched toward the representation of "inner" states than it has seemed. From its beginnings, sentiment in literature was recognized by readers as socially performed as well as privately felt.[3] And from the 1980s on, criticism has stressed the ideological dimensions of such performance.[4] Later critics have shown that the eighteenth-century novel in general is not so exclusively devoted to representing will, moral choice, and the like as "inner," private processes after all, by applying materialist philosophies of action, legal accounts of liability,[5] and so on—often taking Richardson's proto-sentimental novel *Clarissa*, 1748, as a prime case. Ian Watt's description of the novel's fundamental motive to depict the inner life of its characters has supplied a remarkably durable point of view to dissent from.[6] As diverse as this body of criticism is, a common impulse has been to argue that an external dimension in eighteenth-century fiction supplements, dialectically motivates, or even replaces representations of "inner meaning."[7]

The insensible in fiction sits somewhat askew to these currents. On the one hand, the account here resembles those that shift attention away from the inside of characters. Inasmuch as the insensible can be understood as a force or movement of affect at all, it refers to something unavailable to introspection of characters even as it depicts, in negative terms, changes to them. It unfolds in time, not in any apprehensible or locatable inner space. But neither does it appear on the outside very obviously either. Its potency in fact depends on its antitheatricality. Unlike cries and tears—dramatic, visible events that elicit general concern—insensibly encroaching changes gain their special character by happening too slowly and subtly to be perceived, by their subject or by spectators. The mode of the insensible I am describing also differs from the sudden losses of consciousness—fainting, swoons, blackouts—that some commentators have seen as themselves theatrically performed conventions,[8] as well as from the insensibility that defines classes of cold, dull, or indifferent characters.

The insensible is less a spectacle even than the state of absorption, which, as Michael Fried pointed out some time ago, can be read as performed, in paintings or in fiction of the eighteenth century.[9] The unfelt by definition cannot be turned into any such performance because it refers to an absence of attention to change by beholders and the person undergoing the change herself. Its temporal nature—its occurrence by imperceptible degrees—removes it from the inherently perceptible dynamics of event and plot. The term designates a kind of blank time essential to narrative yet not substantially narrated. (In this, it resembles affect's distinctive function in nineteenth-century realist fiction as described by Fredric Jameson: "affect denarrativizes and dechronologizes the action ostensibly being narrated.")[10] The unfelt in fiction of the period does not, then, provide a simple contrast to the inner. It instead evokes a sense in which the dichotomy between inner and outer, between consciousness and externally defined action, intention and emplotment, breaks down.

Attending to the idiom illuminates in a new way the special zone of sociality that the novel, particularly the domestic novel, seems designed to represent: the individual's body and mind as witnessed, discussed, hypothesized about in the family and among families drawn together by the prospect of a marriage. Things happening insensibly to the feelings of a heroine are unnoticeable to her and onlookers, yet they have a curiously active life. As we shall see, in the case of Clarissa Harlowe, the insensible functions most potently as a hypothesis precisely because she has no way to deny, even though she doubts, its effects. The intimate social world of domestic fiction presents a revealing segment of the scale of the idiom's applications surveyed in this book. Neither like minute particles (discussed in chapter I), nor like the vast changes of a nation or an economy (discussed in chapters III and IV, respectively), insensible movements of desire go out of sight in the most socially intimate of circumstances, when everyone is watching and would most like to see them. While novelists use the idiom to resolve moral difficulties inherent in the sentimental novel of courtship, it also adds uncertainty by evoking processes that live somewhere beyond minds, and beyond the power of onlookers to observe them on bodies.

The insensible does not quite work in fiction like any of the adjectival nouns with negating prefixes that critics have long used to identify peculiar aspects of its representations of persons, the nature of their mental states, or of their actions: the (free) indirect, the unintentional, the involuntary and, at the top of the list, the unconscious. The insensible does not allude to unplumbed personal depths or a hidden site of mindedness, to any latent content, or even to a structure or system of experience, behind or beneath what characters are shown to consciously feel. All that has been described as unconscious (in Freudian or Lacanian terms) in eighteenth-century fiction,[11] or indeed as involuntary, or unintended, or otherwise "external" to consciousness, cannot be equally well described by the term *insensible*, which performs a less clearly demarcated, vaguer, and less easily isolated role. For those reasons, however, the idea suggests a kind of deep background of the feelings and actions of characters in time and a context for more easily nameable features of their experiences.

1. Unfeeling before Sensibility

References to the insensible but overwhelming power of love could seem especially at home in the breathless, heightened style of seventeenth- and early eighteenth-century fiction, perhaps more so than in scrupulous and alert courtship novels of the age of sentiment. Such gestures fit within what literary historians have called a florid, even "flatulent" fictional language of high-flown passion prevalent before Samuel Richardson and Henry Fielding.[12] But the rhetoric of love in romance is usually understood as deploying a system of visible signs, displayed on the body and in conventional, often list-like literary representations of such displays. These can be revealing or deceptive and read well by characters or poorly. The insensible, never manifest in quite this way, cannot be used to set up any such challenges.

Instead it occupies an incongruous zone in romance, palpably an element of the genre's descriptive style and, as we will see, of the philosophical disquisitions on love often taken up in it, yet not exactly part of its "externalizing" language of sighs and darting eyes. The idiom's own way of testifying to the power of love lies in its refusal to find a location for it, either inside a heart or mind or outside in rhetorical, bodily, or social cues. The following discussion treats a few passages from three examples taken from this vast body of writing—a mid-seventeenth-century French romance, an epistolary roman à clef by Aphra Behn, and an amatory novel by Eliza Haywood—to identify the place of these gestures among the elements of romance style. If this place seems odd, it does so because it pulls against conventions of affective legibility often associated with romance. And as we will see, the idiom's tendency to dislocate and render elusive the formidable powers of love is just what allows it to carry forward into the more restrained affective domain of later novels, while giving important transactions in them something of a romance flavor.

The vast idealistic French romances of the 1640s into the 1660s, so influential on English literature that they near seamlessly conjoin with it, quietly but consistently employ *insensiblement* and like terms to testify to the irresistible power of love. One instance of such influence is Georges de Scudéry's *Almahide; or, The Captive Queen* (1661),[13] translated and supplemented in 1677 by John Milton's nephew John Phillips,[14] and (before that) a source for John Dryden's play *The Conquest of Granada* (1670). At one point in part 2 of *Almahide*, a group of characters discusses the advantage that male "submissive Lovers" have over violent, domineering ones. A character concludes, "that submission which seems so feeble, is more strong, than all the Machines which Love employs against a Heart; It insinuates insensibly, it renders it self Mistress, without perceiving it, and a long time after it is vanquish'd, it believes yet to be Victorious."[15] Here as elsewhere, the unfelt nature of an affect correlates with its intensity. In keeping with romance idealizations, in which love among the virtuous is powerful without being morally corrupting, the passage throws the very intention of the lover to vanquish in doubt, contrasting the effect of his submissiveness with "Machines" expressly designed for conquest. (Though one character will call submissive lovers "spies," another will insist they succeed "neither by stealth, nor by force.")[16]

The looseness of pronoun reference in the English passage enhances this effect of unknowing and unfelt power. "It" (submission) becomes "Mistress" (presumably of the beloved's affections) unawares, but "it" is also what is "vanquish'd." By being so vaguely characterized, as both ruler and ruled, the insinuation is essentially unsited, associated with neither party in the affair. Even the question of whether the adverb characterizes something done *by*, or something done *to*, remains unresolved. The vagueness here results in part from bad translation, though it is perhaps encouraged by a tendency of *insensibly* to drift toward modifying various nearby words. In the original French passage,[17] gendered pronouns assign the active and passive roles clearly. The "soûmission" (designated with *elle*) insinuates itself so as to be mistress without the "cœur" (*il*) perceiving the process. But even here, the act's occurrence insensibly ("insensiblement") suggests that the lover who loves with "soûmission" feels it no more than the heart he vanquishes. The passage's irony moreover relies, of course, on the fact that "soûmission" is passivity itself. The unfelt aligns with the unwilled character of the transaction. While *Almahide* in other places uses "insensibly" to describe the success of deliberate seduction,[18] here and elsewhere it helps characterize love's power as more or less unfelt and unchosen by both parties.

Later in *Almahide* this emphasis on love's impersonality directs a more abstract, philosophical discussion, yet one that links the insensible more directly to affecting and affected matter. The dialogists are asked which "of the two they judge to be the most powerful, Love or Time."[19] Mahomad answers love, and notes love's dominion "over all Nations, over all Ages, Sexes, Temperaments, and Conditions, over Brutes, as well as Men: Nay, even over the very Inanimates [*choses insensibles*] themselves, which are not exempted from feeling his power" (lodestones, flowers bending to the sun, etc.). He concludes that love "Insinuates unperceivably [*imperceptiblement*] into the Heart, insensibly [*insensiblement*] gets possession of the Soul, reigns, tyrannizeth, inspires with Fear, with Hope," and so on.[20] Here "feeling," an overwhelming emotional "power," turns out again to depend on unfeeling. The turn to the "Heart," the "Soul," and the passions at the end does more to rank them along with "Brutes" and "Inanimates" than to distinguish them in some separate inner or immaterial space. If "Fear," "Hope," and the like evoke what we might call "psychology," it is one as subject to a physicalized attraction as a lodestone.

This sense of equivalency among attractions extending throughout the world, from organic to inorganic matter, resonates with the seventeenth-century philosophical speculations that have served as inspiration for writing about affect today. The fanciful, passionate exchange in *Almahide* of course is not equivalent to a theoretical declaration that inorganic matter can be seen as "sensitive."[21] But an urge to spread feeling around is part of the work's intellectual milieu. "Distrust of Cartesian mechanism was prevalent in the de Scudéry circle," notes Erica Harth, in part because René Descartes denied feelings to animals.[22] Harth offers a reading of Madeleine de Scudéry's *Histoire de deux chaméléons* (1688) that debates with Claude Parrault concerning the anatomy of the creatures (two of which she owned herself), in which Scudéry "writes empathically of her animals' feelings," including the male's lovelorn grief at the female's death.[23] This natural-scientific dispute, in which other members of the salon participated, resonates with the passage quoted above about the sensibility of "Brutes."

And without denying the difference between spirit and matter—a denial unlikely to issue from the Scudéry group[24]—the passage does bring "Inanimates" into the ambit of love. The word *insensibly* permits this equivalency between feeling and unfeeling beings (even more than *unperceivably*, which suggests something not perceived but which possibly could be). Pertaining on the one hand to living bodies (which feel or do not, depending on the circumstances), and on the other to everything in the world commonly thought incapable of feeling, the word's equivocation joins feeling and matter on a continuum. The connection is even more apparent in the language of the original, in which love's insensible possession of the "Soul" is prefigured by the *choses insensibles* also under love's power. The unfeeling of inanimate matter seems akin to the soul's unfeeling as it comes under love's sway. By differentiating between the "Soul," "Brutes," and "Inanimates," the text seems to accept real divisions between them even as the insensible force of "Love" affects them all. The overriding of the line between inner and outer, spiritual and physical, minded and mindless is made possible by the unfeeling that drives love. The conversation thus suggests a modality of love's power opaque in principle to feeling, materially deep and not at all "psychological."

In *Love-Letters Between a Nobleman and His Sister* (1684), Aphra Behn explores a more nakedly erotic world of seduction and scandal, less lofty than that of the romances of either Georges or Madeleine de Scudéry.[25] The work's epistolary form also makes the crucial turn to the first person, which allows the insensible to intrude in an especially dramatic manner on a mind intent on its own movements. Silvia, the protagonist, depicts herself as helplessly succumbing to seduction unawares. In her letter to Philander toward the beginning of volume 1, as she is sliding into her affair with him (intricately elaborated through this volume which, with subsequent ones, also reflects on the Monmouth Rebellion), she strains to account for the power of love in an expanded conception of its "Rhetorick":

> The Rhetorick of Love is half-breath'd, interrupted words, languishing Eyes, flattering Speeches, broken Sighs, pressing the hand, and falling Tears: Ah how do they not perswade; how do they not charm and conquer; 'twas thus with these soft easie Arts, that *Silvia* first was won! for sure no Arts of speaking cou'd have talk'd my heart away, though you can speak like any God! oh whether [sic] am I driven, what do I say; 'twas not my purpose nor my business here, to give a character of *Philander*, no not to speak of Love! but oh like *Cowley*'s Lute, my Soul will sound to nothing but to Love! talk what you will, begin what discourse you please, I end it all in Love! because my Soul is ever fixt on *Philander*; and insensibly its byas leads to that Subject.[26]

Silvia insists initially that the brokenness of Philander's "Rhetorick of Love" attests to his sincerity, in contrast to any more calculated "Arts of speaking" he might have employed. His displays of overwhelming feeling, "half-breath'd, interrupted words, languishing Eyes," and the like cannot be feigned. (So runs a convention of wishful thinking in romance.) Michael McKeon remarks that

Silvia's submission in this passage to a near-violent power evokes a "Petrarchan masochism."[27] Silvia here, however, needs to believe that both she and Philander equally have relinquished power, agency, and artful intent—that there is no "tyranny" of one lover over the other in their case. "Love" seems to have overtaken not only her but also him, and its broken rhetoric undoes his intent as well as hers.

But the passage's first person allows Silvia to undergo an affect even more forceful than the one she attributes to her lover. Though bodily instead of verbal, his love remains "Rhetorick," a set of signs to be read. For this reason, she can at least consider the question of whether his visible passion is artless or performed. (Behn here may be thinking of the Longinian question, which had recently been raised in Nicolas Boileau's 1674 translation of *On the Sublime*, of whether there can be an art of passionately disordered expression; Longinus thinks there can.)[28] Silvia's own wayward passions are known differently, from her experience, and she finally comes (with unfortunate results) to judge Philander's sincerity by his effect on *her*: "for sure no Arts of speaking cou'd have talk'd my heart away, though you can speak like any God!"

And this effect is insensible in some powerful way. The past tense and subjunctive suggest she can only wonder about how she lost her heart. Her answers indicate that she is searching for a narrative of her own emotions to fill in the gaps that love has left in it. And even if Philander's mostly bodily rhetoric guarantees his sincerity, even if it really is unintentional and involuntary, as Silvia wants to believe, she can at least witness his behavior and locate it in time. (It will turn out, of course, that she will be betrayed by him.) Her love, on the other hand, has overtaken her unawares. It reveals its affective power not by an act of profound introspection but rather by the opposite: the suggestion that she cannot fully tell how or when her feelings have consumed her.

Silvia's loss of control in the first person demonstrates an affective force most powerfully when she struggles to reflect on her own epistolary writing,[29] only superficially similar to Philander's rhetoric of love: "wh[i]ther am I driven, what do I say"? Like the dialogists in *Almahide*, she turns to the language of material causes and effects to find this place for love beyond rhetoric and beyond her own introspective powers. The image of her heart like *"Cowley's lute,"* which can only sound on the theme of love, suggests a physical attunement like sympathetic vibration.[30] When she concludes that "my Soul is ever fixt on *Philander*; and insensibly its byas leads to that Subject," she describes the unfelt as an almost gravitational pull. That connotation of "byas" indicates a continuity if not an identification of lofty emotion and material force. And "insensibly" helps makes this connection between the unfelt physical and the felt emotional possible. Again it is not a question of any dogmatic assertion of materialism or mechanism. Rather, Behn portrays the "Soul" of Silvia as sounding compulsively, pulling or being pulled insensibly, physically resonating. Behind all such overwhelming emotion, the capacity of the soul to be affected insensibly ensures that the intense feeling of love is finally felt.

This passage also anticipates a future of the insensible's usefulness in sentimental fiction, as it allows a reconciliation of desire with virtue that writers such as Frances Burney will need for their own heroines' advances toward marriage. The "byas" allows Silvia to invoke her conscious virtue while excusing her deviation from it: "No, I did not when I began to Write, think of speaking one word of my own weakness; but to have told you with what resolv'd Courage, Honour and Vertue, I expect your coming."[31] The verb tenses again play out the drama of ever-elusive intention that the insensible demands. While Silvia's experience of writing the letter unfolds in the present tense, she comes to realize that her "byas" has led her unawares to express something that, she now recalls, she had no intention of writing, much like Alexander Pope's later dramatization of the uncontrolled compositional process of Eloisa.[32] This play with a present-tense desire whose unintentional unfolding can only be retrospectively rejected insists on a conscious purity while desire is forcibly introduced to an (as yet, in Silvia's case) honorable heroine and an honorable text. That is, "Courage, Honour, and Vertue" are not rendered merely ironic values or aspirations when they are only insensibly overcome.

This passage in *Love-Letters* could be read according to a tradition within feminist criticism that views women's sexual passivity in amatory fiction as a kind of ruse to enable them to express their desires. They resist, but must do what they must. In a classic essay, Patricia Meyer Spacks notes that women authors of the period—she refers specifically to Haywood—sometimes portray feminine erotic agency as "unknowing," and she argues that women must "enact a vision of irresponsibility, expressing female sexuality without being subject to judgment."[33] This helps clarify the gender-ideological role of the insensible in Behn and Haywood, as well as in the more morally watchful sentimental tradition. But it could be misleading if it suggests that unfelt desire in the period is a mere pretense or a "repression and denial" (in Spacks's Freudian vocabulary) of feelings actually felt.[34] The passage in Behn and ones in Haywood too (as we will soon see) invoke the insensible not to repress but to support the expression of vehement passion. Desire runs on two converging tracks. Far from a charade of weakness, the insensible in these fictions amplifies love's affective power.

The usage of *insensibly* to indicate the unsuspected but overwhelming power of desire carries forward from seventeenth-century romance and seduction narratives into the so-called amatory fiction of the early eighteenth century.[35]

Perhaps even more popular is the similar portrayal of love as obtaining its power over heroines "by degrees."[36] Such expressions have the effect of attenuating the complicity of the heroine's will and desire by slowing them down. They seem as much functions of her external environment and the expectations of a social world around her as an inner impulse. Since desire does not erupt directly, fully formed, from the heart in a moment, it can seem less a matter of interior volition or feeling than a project of context and circumstance. Jonathan Kramnick has persuasively argued that in amatory fiction, especially the novels of Haywood, putatively interior states or acts such as desire or consent tend to be externalized. He takes up a scene in one of her most discussed novels, *Love in Excess* (1719), in which Amena, in love with the rake-hero D'Elmont, finds herself with him in the Tuileries, at night and the edge of ruin, saved when her maid interrupts. Kramnick, noting how Haywood's language externalizes agency in the passage and wobbles its point of view so as to dissociate it from any particular mind available in the scene, remarks, "Bodies and parks do all the necessary work until the intrusion of social expectation in the person of the maid puts the measures to an end."[37]

The language of imperceptible degrees and the insensible in one way abets such an exteriorization of the mental states, motives, and acts of characters. As we have seen, however, such locutions tend to facilitate crossings from mental to physical, from outer to inner and back, rather than permit us to distinguish very clearly between what is mental and what is outside.[38] They do not very stably or consistently point to "external" and visible contexts such as parks or social expectation. The oddly positive negativity of whatever is called insensible—its way of pertaining to the senses by not stimulating them—tends to make it particularly difficult to find. And by transposing the evolution of "inner" things like desire from the medium of space to that of time, both slow degrees and the insensible can be said to happen pretty much anywhere and everywhere.

Haywood's *The Mercenary Lover: or, The Unfortunate Heiresses* (1726), now considered minor but which ran to three editions in its time,[39] depicts the seduction of one of the two heiresses, Althea, in both such ways. First, Clitander's opportunities for intimacy with her afforded by his marriage to her sister (recalling the scenario in Behn's *Love-Letters*) "made him not fear but that a little Time and Assiduity, might by Degrees steal into her Soul those Inclinations which wou'd give him the absolute Possession of his Wishes."[40] This stealing into her soul is accomplished by both impersonal and Clitander's own means, by "Time" itself and by (his) "Assiduity." This combination, not merely his own strategic methods, comprises the ingredients of seduction. More important, he furnishes her with writing that he expects to work on her by itself:

> The first Step he made towards the Accomplishment of this barbarous Enterprize, was to redouble the Civilities and Tendernesses with which he had been accustom'd to treat *Althea*, and knowing she was naturally a great Lover of Reading, took Care to bring her home every Day something new for her Amusement; I say Amusement, for I believe the Reader will easily imagine, the Books he desir'd she should peruse, were neither Religion, Philosophy, nor Morality; there are certain gay Treatises which insensibly melt down the Soul, and make it fit for amorous Impressions, such as the Works of *Ovid*, the late celebrated *Rochester*, and many other of more modern Date.[41]

Again, the blurring of the agency of and responsibility for desire ensues from terms such as *insensibly*. The books prepare Althea for seduction, but she is already susceptible to such susceptibility, which stems from her being already "naturally a great Lover of Reading."

As a more or less blameless disposition darkens insensibly into a more culpable one, Althea retains her innocence, at least far as her own agency goes. She does not so much fall in love by acting involuntarily as become ready, without feeling it, to feel. The insensible hence prevents heroines from facing their principal challenge, in *The Mercenary Lover* and other amatory fiction by Haywood, which is, according to Michael Prince, "the challenge of reading social circumstances and other people as if they were texts," and results in "the consequences of failing to do so accurately."[42] Like the "Rhetorick of Love" in Behn's *Love-Letters*, the external, legible codes of amorous literature given to Althea depend for their effect on what cannot be sensed or "read." Though Althea is initiated in amorous feeling and intent by reading itself, such initiation undoes her ability to master the text-like cues that lead her toward disaster. The rhetoric of passion and love, not only in this but in the earlier examples, functions in a nonrhetorical way by means of its unfelt force. Not recognized or able to be codified, this underside of the language of love does love's most difficult work.

2. External and Invisible

In parallel to its role in romance and amatory fiction, the idiom of the insensible quietly pulls against long-standing critical expectations about the representation of desire in the midcentury novel. The importance of Henry Fielding and Samuel Richardson as a pair—"the most eminent writers of our country," declares Clara Reeve in *The Progress of Romance* (1785)[43]—has long been seen to turn on their contrasting ways of depicting feeling.[44] Fielding, so the critical commonplaces have run, takes an "external" view of character (he is, as Samuel Johnson said, "a man who could tell the hour by looking on the dial-plate"), and Richardson an "internal" one (he is "a man who knew how a watch was made").[45] Richardson sacrifices an interest in "story" for a full expression of sentiment,[46] to find (in Reeve's words) "a short way to the heart."[47] This distinction helps create another commonly observed contrast, of their authorial functions. Fielding's magisterial third person in *Tom Jones* (1749) watches the social appearances and contexts of feeling, while Richardson builds *Clarissa* (1748) as a web of passionately engaged, private first-person accounts. But their joint inheritance of the insensible from romance and amatory style unites them in their sense of the unique dangers of feeling's unfelt onset. The idiom also puts comparable strains on Richardson's multidirectional intimacies and Fielding's supposedly all-knowing detachment.

The most significant depiction of feminine desire in *Tom Jones* exhibits emotion as especially potent while avoiding or bypassing the mental realm altogether. Fielding uses the term *insensibly* only once to describe the beginnings of Sophia's desire for Tom, but its full meaning unfolds over some fifty pages. The narrator points us in the right direction by reminding us, "The reader will be pleased to recollect that a secret affection for Mr Jones had insensibly stolen into the bosom of this young lady."[48] Of course the bosom, especially for readers accustomed to Fielding's erotic frankness, is an equivocal place, signifying an inside and also a surface of Sophia's body, as well as the enfolding of an outside into a kind of bodily depth. Wherever the affection is, Sophia is not aware of it. As commentators have noticed, Fielding sometimes marks strong feelings, especially Sophia's, by omission. He either invokes an authorial "modesty topos," refusing to tell us what would embarrass him or his heroine, or declares that some feelings (of love, for instance, between Sophia and Tom) are felt too profoundly to be adequately conveyed in writing.[49] But the insensible process of Sophia's desire that he narrates is something like the opposite of these.

For one thing, Fielding delights in pointing out its manifestations to us. And if he uses the idiom to hint at the feeling's profundity, the feeling itself is expressly the reverse of something Sophia experiences in a way we cannot. As in other affective transactions in the period, this "secret" is one kept from the person keeping it. But Fielding does not keep it from the reader, and what the narrator asks us to "recollect" here is the process of Sophia's explicitly nonconscious embodiment of desire: "Sophia, with the highest degree of innocence and modesty, had a remarkable sprightliness in her temper" that "greatly increased whenever she was in company with Tom" (144). As visible as Fielding makes this to his readers, the narrator points out its distinctly invisible nature within *Tom Jones*'s diegesis: "But indeed it can occasion little wonder that this matter escaped the observation of others, since poor Sophia herself never remarked it, and her heart was irretrievably lost before she suspected it was in danger" (144). Her unnoticing of her own desire matches its general hiddenness from the rest of her social world (though it is important to Fielding, as will be shown, that it is, in some fundamental sense, noticeable in principle).

The transaction presents a peculiar obverse of what Jill Campbell, a critic who has profoundly enriched our understanding of Fielding, describes in her essay "Fielding's Style." She remarks that Fielding characteristically "focuses far less on the nuanced evocation of a particular character's psychology and much more on the fluid and often fleeting suggestion of a variety of points of view."[50] Here Sophia's "psychology" or conscious mental life is indeed not very fully represented. She is woven into her social world, however, not by having a point a view among many others but through a shared unnoticing. If we think, as Campbell does, that Fielding's style is often experienced "on the level of feeling rather than cognition,"[51] it becomes striking here how careful he is to explore the gray areas between feeling and unfeeling in Sophia, between mental and physical, inside and outside. Expecting erroneously that Tom "intended to make love to her" (145), Sophia falls victim to a kind of nonconsciousness of the idea: "yet, whether Nature whispered something into her ear, or from what cause it arose, I will not determine; certain it is, some idea of that kind must have intruded itself, for her colour forsook her cheeks, her limbs trembled, and her tongue would have faltered had Tom stopped for an answer" (145). Fielding seems deliberately to avoid saying that the idea entered into Sophia's "mind." It merely "intruded itself"—but where? He lists its bodily manifestations.

And yet "intruded" suggests entry, if not penetration: a movement to an inside somewhere. At this crucial point, while Sophia's desire and her innocence of it coexist, her mindedness seems not so much denied as spread all over her body. Even the fascinating final detail, her tongue that "would have faltered" if Tom had given her the chance to try to speak, does not quite point to a state of mind. The tongue's inarticulate weight, its stuckness, is virtual, already there in her mouth, ready to fail. This is an emblem of Brian Massumi's virtual as an *"incipience*, incipient action and expression,"[52] all the more apt because her tongue now embodies an incipient *failure* to express. The insensible again does not really negate the "inside" of characters, or turn away from "a particular character's psychology" (in Campbell's words), but rather places inside and outside on a single continuum. The tongue is inside Sophia's mouth, not her mind. Critics have persuasively disputed the view that Fielding has no interest in mental states,[53] but these crucial moments prior to Sophia's recognition of her own desire offer something different. She certainly feels the idea, but she seems not to feel it *as* an idea—that is, to know her feeling as such. Fielding seems keen to demonstrate that Sophia "has" the feeling, the idea, *before* she knows it, contradicting John Locke's dictum, "When we see, hear, smell, taste, feel, meditate, or will any thing, we know that we do so."[54]

All this description of Sophia's mind-body of desire functions as prolegomena to her feeling's finally coming to consciousness. What separates her feeling and her knowledge of it, then, is less a veil than a lag. When Tom kisses her hand in gratitude, "the blood, which before had forsaken her cheeks, now made her sufficient amends by rushing all over her face and neck with such violence that they became all of a scarlet colour. She now first felt a sensation to which she had been before a stranger, and which, when she had leisure to reflect on it, began to acquaint her with some secrets, which the reader, if he doth not already guess them, will know in due time" (145–46). The narrator comically endows the blood with the will and knowledge (making her sufficient amends) that Sophia, at the time of its rushing, explicitly lacks. Then the feeling, which she has somehow already been having, is "first felt" by her. Fielding seems to imply that for a feeling really to be "felt" it has to become aligned not only with knowledge but also with a bodily change that cannot be ignored as an event. The mental obviousness of these feelings correlates with their physical obviousness. They find a place on her body, and they also find a place in a moment in time.

It could be tempting to turn to contemporary neuroscience to explain how Sophia could first feel a feeling after her body had been having it for some time. The popular books of Antonio Damasio have proposed the idea of the "proto-self" to understand unfelt feeling. The proto-self is active within "the ensemble of brain devices which continuously and *nonconsciously* maintain the body state within the narrow range and relative stability required for survival."[55] In later work, Damasio has stressed that the primary products of the protoself are *"primordial feelings* . . . [that] provide a direct experience of one's own living body" as it maintains itself and responds to new stimuli.[56] Though these feelings rise near to consciousness, they are "wordless, unadorned, and connected to nothing but sheer existence . . . [and] originate at the level of the brain stem rather than the cerebral cortex."[57] This might help us conceptualize what is happening to Sophia's body, which has a feeling in advance of *her* first feeling it. But it goes without saying that Fielding lacks anything like the understanding of brain anatomy we have now, let alone of the interacting bodily and mental layers of selfhood that are the basis of Damasio's theory. Every historical period finds its own way of describing the emergence of feelings from the nonconsciousness of the material body, and Fielding takes up a metaphor from the corporeal language available in his own time.

This tool is the medical symptom and its accompanying distinction between latent and manifest. After Fielding glances back over the preceding pages and remarks in the pluperfect that "a secret affection for Mr Jones had insensibly stolen into the bosom of this young lady," he notes that this affection "had there grown to a pretty great height before she herself had discovered it. When she first began to perceive its symptoms, the sensations were so sweet and pleasing that she had not resolution sufficient to check or repel them; and thus she went on cherishing a passion of which she never once considered the consequences" (171). Fielding digs deeper into this medical vein, referring to the "nauseous physic" of Molly Seagrim's visit that for a while "expelled [Sophia's] distemper," and so on: "The diseases of the mind do in almost every particular imitate those of the body," Fielding declares, and begs leave of "that learned faculty," physicians, "to lay [violent hands] on several words and phrases, which of right belong to them, and without which our descriptions must have been often unintelligible" (171). Often we think of Richardson, inspired by his friend, physician and anatomist George Cheyne, as viewing sentiment in medical terms.[58] But here Fielding compares Sophia's secret affection to a symptom and encourages us to think of it as nonconsciously corporeal, or at least recognize an "exact analogy" between "distempers of the mind . . . [and] those which are called bodily" (171). As a symptom moves from latent to manifest, so may a feeling.

Fielding will alter his vocabulary significantly to describe effects of this symptom after it has announced itself to Sophia. While he maintains the medical analogy, he also deepens Sophia's consciousness: "Notwithstanding the nicest guard which Sophia endeavoured to set on her behaviour, she could not avoid letting some appearances now and then slip forth: for love may again be likened to a disease in this, that when it is denied a vent in one part, it will certainly break out in another. What her lips, therefore, concealed, her eyes, her blushes, and many little involuntary actions, betrayed" (187–88). It could seem that her "little involuntary actions" resemble the "secret affection" that grows like a symptom until it reveals itself to her. But as in other cases, the involuntary and the insensible sharply differ here. The former becomes meaningful in the context of her consciousness: her intention not to do what she involuntarily does. She is on her "nicest guard." And unlike the affection that "had insensibly stolen," the "little involuntary actions" occur at distinct moments. Conversely, the insensible, an unnoticeable gradualness that happens in advance of her feeling's coming to consciousness, prevents her from acting meaningfully at all, either voluntarily or not. Again, the insensible unfolds unsited in place or time, and its secrecy depends not on an agent's success or failure at not doing something but on the flows and feedbacks that undo the distinction between mind and body, feeling and unfeeling.

The insensible in this transaction reveals a crucial element of Fielding's distinctive third person, what D. A. Miller, or Jill Campbell in response to him, might call his "style."[59] Within the fictional frame of *Tom Jones*, neither onlookers nor Sophia herself notice the signs of her desire. Yet the increase of her "sprightliness" (144) happens when Tom is around—inspired, by definition, by social circumstances, because he is there. The signs of it, too, are there in our world. Fielding thereby indicates that her desire is sensible to onlookers even though it happens not to be sensed by them. He hence offers a subtle alternative to the epistemological barrier that "insensibly" usually erects when it suggests something is absolutely unavailable to the senses. The narrator in these circumstances is neither the absolute outsider who sees things others cannot, as Miller portrays the impersonal third person of Jane Austen, nor the orchestrator of a multitude of social perspectives, as Campbell has it (though, as she demonstrates, he often is that).

Instead, Fielding positions himself by means of the insensible within the world of sensible social phenomena. He refrains, at these points, from peering from above like a god into the private thoughts of characters to represent them, yet assumes the role of one who sees and feels what others will not. In Fielding's hands the insensible becomes a kind of paradox, an unseen spectacle, that only he, and the reader trained by him, sense. It is essential to Fielding's purposes that the "secret affection" of Sophia be embodied because it permits the intimacy that the narrator feels with the world he represents.[60] If this affection were hidden behind a mask of indifference, or deep in Sophia's unconscious mind, he would have to remove himself, like God, from the world to see it. Instead he sees sights, and feels feelings, that are right there in front of everybody, but which his characters, even the subjects of the feelings themselves, do not.

Fielding at times announces something like this as a principle of his fiction in this novel and elsewhere. In book 5, when Tom is powerfully affected in saving Sophia's muff from the fire, the narrator makes a famous pronouncement: "The world may indeed be considered as a vast machine, in which the great wheels are originally set in motion by those which are very minute, and almost imperceptible to any but the strongest eyes" (195). And there is, of course, the famous reminder to the reader in book 18 of the "many strange accidents" that kept Partridge and Mrs. Waters apart at Upton in book 9, on which the plot hinges, suggesting how "the greatest events are produced by a nice train of little circumstances" requiring the reader's "accurate eye" (810–11). John Bender echoes a common view of such famous passages when he claims they evoke "Fielding's godlike machinations."[61] But for my purposes it is important to insist that "the strongest eyes" are not godlike or transcendent but worldly, not outside but part of the human context. The "almost imperceptible" must be not wholly so for people in the world, though it happens to be that way for nearly everybody. The figure of the narrator is an exceptional person within a world of unnoticed but noticeable things.[62]

Another telling instance of Fielding's narrator's special situatedness occurs toward the end of *Amelia* (1751), when he, after revealing some crucial plot points, remarks, "These were several Matters, of which we thought necessary our Reader should be informed; for, besides that it conduces greatly to a perfect Understanding of all History, there is no Exercise of the Mind of a sensible Reader more pleasant than the tracing the several small and almost imperceptible Links in every Chain of Events by which all the great Actions of the World are produced."[63] Fielding's fictional purpose described here aims to bring the "sensible Reader" and the "almost Imperceptible" together, and their fruitful interaction confirms the power of the former (tutored by the author) to make the latter perceptible. Again, Fielding strongly means the "almost": almost but not quite imperceptible are the circumstantial links that produce great actions. While *almost* in other authors can work (almost) as an intensifier of the imperceptible or insensible—insisting on how very far a transaction is from being fully perceptible—in Fielding the word signifies the availability of the links to sensible, well-guided minds. Here and throughout his fiction, Fielding tends to emphasize the nearly inapprehensible gradualness and subtlety of processes, of desire and of narrative itself, only to confirm their legibility in the author-world he superintends. The insensible functions in his style to emphasize an oddly significant area of novelistic space, between the unfeeling but moved body and the mostly unnoticing observer of it.

The insensible in Samuel Richardson's *Clarissa* is used by characters to refer more to a potential desire, somewhere, than to an actually forming one, as with Sophia. The idiom's appearances in *Clarissa* are nearly as sparse as they are in *Tom Jones*, though it has been cited as a component of the novel's "vocabulary of sensibility."[64] But because insensible processes place affect somewhere else besides the sensing mind, Richardson's usage offers an opportunity to expand our conception of his special interest in representing consciousness. Generations of critics have contested or at least supplemented Ian Watt's observations that Richardson's distinctive way with characters lies in the fact that "we get inside their minds" (as well as their private homes), and that his principal achievement is "giving fiction this subjective and inward direction."[65] Tom Keymer, for instance, has stressed that the novel's letters, far from simply opening windows onto the characters' mental states, are rhetorical performances intended for particular interpersonal effects.[66] But the insensible processes alluded to in *Clarissa*, as elsewhere, evade the terms of this distinction. They cannot be publicly performed or even detected, but neither do they reside in some private world of feeling, conscious or unconscious. For that reason, the novel presents them as a special danger.

From the beginning Clarissa recognizes but seems to dismiss the threat of a desire whose onset cannot be felt. Lovelace, she remarks in the early pages, has "so good an opinion of himself, as not to doubt, that his person and accomplishments would insensibly engage me."[67] She thinks he knows her well enough to know that a frontal assault, a passionately performed attempt at seduction, cannot work. Even she seems to acknowledge that her insensible engagement to him would have to precede any formal one, with Lovelace down on one knee, if such were at all possible. Her mother uses similar turns of phrase to acknowledge the yet more profound impossibility of Solmes winning her over, hoping his "good treatment" will "engage her Gratitude, and by degrees her Love" (1:260). Other characters in the novel, and critics as well, typically read Clarissa as committed to the idea of her own self-possession, a believer in her sensible mastery of her own consent.[68] These appeals to "insensibly" arising desire "by degrees" indirectly acknowledge that mastery by desperately imagining some way around it.

And though Clarissa herself implies that insensible affection for Solmes or Lovelace is no more possible for her than the sensible kind, it remains a threat to her because it cannot be disputed, from inside or out. Early in volume 1, Anna Howe's often discussed letter 10 that diagnoses Clarissa's unacknowledged desire for Lovelace includes an idea of its insensible nature, set alongside other ideas of it. Critics have often used the word *unconscious* to account for what Anna perceives in her friend in this letter, as when John Dussinger remarks that "Anna Howe has the important function of interpreting for us this unconscious motive in Clarissa's correspondence with Lovelace."[69] Anna speculates about many things, among them that Lovelace "has seen more than *I* have seen; more than you think *could* be seen;—more than I believe you *yourself* know, or else you would have let *me* know it" (1:61). She next observes, "You are drawn in by a perverse fate against inclination: But custom, with such laudable purposes, will reconcile the inconveniency and *make* an inclination" (1:62). And the letter concludes with the remark that will become her most famous, "To be sure Lovelace is a charming fellow. And were he only—But I will not make you *glow*, as you read—Upon *my word* I will not.—Yet, my dear, don't you find at your heart somewhat unusual make it go throb, throb, throb, as you read just here?" (1:62). None of these quite suggests an invisibility of Clarissa's feelings locked away in an unconscious mind. All are in one way or another predicated on feeling's at least partially "external" character. But only the second comment suggests something both external and not visible.

The first concerns what Lovelace has seen. Unlike Anna, Lovelace has been with Clarissa to see how she reacts to him. Anna in effect tells her, "Lovelace seems to be encouraged, so he must have seen an expression of your desire; you apparently do not know you have shown it, and perhaps you do not even feel it yourself; if you did, you would have told me about it." But every step in this tensile inference depends on the visible character of Clarissa's desire. And we know that Lovelace himself, the man on-site, is never very confident of having witnessed it. The third remark, that Clarissa must "*glow*" and her heart "throb throb throb" when reading Anna's letter, also pertains to visible expressions of feeling and is even more easily rejected, by Clarissa herself. She says she "cannot own any of the *glow*, any of the *throbs* you mention.—*Upon my word* I will repeat, I cannot." Here *own* means "to claim as being one's own" or even "to acknowledge . . . as affecting oneself."[70] She easily enough disowns the throbs and glows because they are bodily events that produce awareness, as when Sophia "first felt" her insensibly growing feelings for Tom after her blush. Here the dual privacies of Richardson's fictional world observed by Watt—mental and domestic—peel apart.[71] The first-person perspectives that compose *Clarissa* (arguably, at least) reveal mental states well enough, but crucially the characters still read and write letters unwatched, for the most part. No ideally perceptive, Fielding-like third-person narrator, who sees what the characters could see if only they were observant enough, may confirm or disconfirm Clarissa's glow. Anna can only speculate at a distance (wrongly, in this case) about how demonstrative Clarissa has been around Lovelace and what she looks like when reading Anna's teasing accusations.

But Clarissa cannot so easily dismiss Anna's second remark—"You are drawn in by a perverse fate against inclination: But custom, with such laudable purposes, will reconcile the inconveniency, and *make* an inclination"—and says nothing of it. (Quite a bit later, in fact, she affirmatively echoes this language of Anna's.)[72] The remark characterizes feeling as both invisible and "external," or as some compound in which the distinction between inner and outer is not especially relevant. Clarissa has a positive *disinclination* to pursue the affair with Lovelace, but two external forces, "fate" and "custom," will produce the requisite affection.[73] Anna is vague as to whether the feeling will actually be felt by or only imputed (by custom) to Clarissa because the location of its existence does not matter. (*Custom* could mean what the social world widely expects and credits, or her habituation to him.) Here inclination need not be felt to be operative.

Most crucially, unlike a throb, a glow, or an expression of feeling witnessed by Lovelace, such an inclination spreads through time. It is not an event, mental or physical, but an unnoted unfolding. As such, even though its essence is temporal, it cannot really be narrated. It presents something like the opposite, in fact, of the aim to offer (as Richardson announces in the preface of *The History of Sir Charles Grandison*) "familiar Letters, written, as it were, to the Moment,"[74] which has been seen by some as the essence of his technique: "to catch living voices in a dramatic present."[75] Insensibly unfolding processes cannot be written to the moment, since they weave together strands of blank time, and can only be characterized by those subject to them in retrospect, as vague temporal stretches incompatible with minute narration. Such processes are so bereft of dramatic feeling that they can be imputed to Clarissa without her knowing anything about them. And if the insensible need not be felt to exist, it cannot be disowned by its subject. Clarissa acknowledges something of this jeopardy when she admits that her own phrases "lay me open" to such constructions, and owns her inability to "tell what turn my mind had taken to dictate so oddly to my pen" (1:63). Whatever desire she has exists outside, in words open to interpretation, and here they result from a "turn" of mind, a disposition rather that an isolatable intention or even an involuntary impulse.

The idea that Clarissa's desire could affect her insensibly and exist in some profound way outside her conscious mind is consonant to some degree with the main line of argument of Sandra Macpherson's discussion of eighteenth-century fiction in *Harm's Way* (2012). Invoking the legal category of strict liability, which holds people responsible for results of their actions whether they intend them or not, Macpherson contends that Clarissa (like other characters of the period's fiction) knows that her moral responsibility extends beyond merely what she wills, chooses, or desires. Macpherson comes to claim that, morally speaking, "there is nothing we can unequivocally claim is *not* our doing," and that "this is an insight *Clarissa* insists on and that the novel's characters—all but Clarissa herself—refuse."[76] Responsibility on this "tragic" model lies in consequences of actions out in the world, not in the will or motive of the agent, which is irrelevant. My claim that desire conceived to function insensibly poses a special threat to Clarissa runs parallel to Macpherson's general argument. (And she at times takes the term *insensibly* as evidence for her case that a logic of strict liability divorces moral responsibility from conscious intent in the English novel, though not in *Clarissa*).[77]

Insensible desire and the kind of inclination Anna says that custom and fate sponsor tend, however, not to be manifest exclusively anywhere, neither strictly outside nor inside Clarissa. They are not necessarily confirmed by outcomes and the strict liability of people for them. The insensible in its negativity and temporal diffusion extends itself beyond other kinds of unintended experience, notably the involuntary. Macpherson takes Clarissa's acknowledgment of responsibility for her involuntary acts as prime evidence that she understands the tragic logic of strict liability better than other characters. And the principal involuntary act Clarissa owns, of course, is what she calls her "involuntary step" (7:107), when she leaves the Harlowe household under duress with Lovelace. But here, as in many other places, Clarissa notes the act's involuntary character to extenuate her guilt, not to insist on it: her full sentence to Uncle Antony reads, "Yet I think I may defy calumny itself, and (excepting the fatal, tho' involuntary step of *April* 10.), wrap myself in my own innocence, and be easy" (7:107). Her "tho'" in this context indicates that the act's involuntary character lessens her responsibility for it and for its grave consequences. And unlike an insensible process, the involuntary act is a single "step" taken at a particular time, containable and identifiable enough to have a line drawn around it. Clarissa's acknowledgment of the act expresses the higher significance she accords to her will and intentions. (Macpherson finally concludes that all *Clarissa*'s characters, even Clarissa herself, "universally fail to recognize how the novel thinks about blame—refusing for themselves and others the strictures of strict liability.")[78] The insensible, the processes that "*make* an inclination" from time, custom, and social expectation, conversely cannot be so clearly identified or delimited.

This is not to allow that everyone is right to suggest that Clarissa harbors insensible desires. As many have noted, such accusations from critics align them with Lovelace and replicate a pattern of aggression against her.[79] It is only to recognize how other characters use the idiom to suggest that Clarissa is to blame without her having actually desired any of it to have happened. The novel has long been seen as enacting (in William Warner's phrase) "struggles of interpretation,"[80] and the insensible in such struggles is a potent weapon due to its undisprovable negativity. After Clarissa's unfelt but supposedly real desire for Lovelace, another self-defining desire imputed to her in the novel is the one to die. Lovelace remarks after the rape, "So this Lady, as I suppose, intended only at first to vex and plague me; and, finding she could do it to purpose, her desire of revenge insensibly became stronger in her than the desire of life" (7:404). Lovelace subtly transforms a direct intent ("to vex and plague me"), fallaciously ascribed though it is, into a vaguer "desire of revenge," which yet more vaguely strengthens "insensibly" enough to kill her. Again, the point is not to assign credibility to Lovelace's (always overheated) fantasies but to suggest how the insensible permits him to ascribe motives to her unchecked by any evidence of the senses. Such ascriptions actually require that these motives evade her own awareness of them to be effective.

As such, the insensible process in Richardson operates at its characteristically peculiar level of plot and narrative. It refers to something that might actually have happened, somewhere between points A and B, a middle time different from narrated episodes and longer spans merely designated as blocks (e.g., "these past months"). Yet it demands to be invisible, even unplottable, often because of the implausibility of what people like Lovelace seek to accomplish with it. When Richardson's correspondent Lady Bradshaigh (under the name of Belfour) wrote, just before an advance copy of the novel's fifth volume reached her in November 1748, to urge him to furnish his novel with a happy ending and a reformed Lovelace, she appealed desperately to the idiom in her plotting of such an outcome: "I would, by choice, have him drawn by easy steps, and as it were insensibly, to reflection; though there are many and great instances of sudden and sincere transformation, of such as have been struck with remorse by various ways. And has not Loveless sense?"[81] Though Lovelace's "sense" leads her to imagine a dramatic event, sudden and sincere, she still prefers that this sense be worked on insensibly, doubtless because of the story's demonstration to this point that Lovelace does nothing much with his sense but misuse it. Lady Bradshaigh not only violates Richardson's moral purpose in the novel with this suggestion.[82] She also suggests something narratively at odds with the technique of writing to the moment. She continues, "And may he not, by the sufferings of Clarissa, occasioned by himself, be brought to reflection with the help of his friend Belford, who seems to be paving the way towards so good an end?"[83] As with Lovelace's imputation of insensible desires to Clarissa, the idiom here functions as a kind of affective wishful thinking, a way to imagine a plot resolution at the level of feeling without requiring a credible representation of it.

Richardson's next performance, *The History of Sir Charles Grandison* (1753), permits a final reflection here on the tightly constrained placement of unfelt feminine desire in his work. The epistolary first person and a candid, innocent heroine—both requirements of Richardsonian fiction—could seem to make the heroine's acknowledgment of insensible desires or motives impossible. Yet Harriet Byron manages one. It is perhaps a sign of the growing prestige of the idiom as "polite" after 1750, with the continuing development of the discourse of the civilization of the passions, that Richardson could allow Harriet herself to adopt it.[84] But the circumstances of its appearance still indicate its peculiar narrative and moral functions. At a crucial moment at the beginning of volume 2, when Harriet first allows herself fully to express her desire for Sir Charles, the insensible comes into play. She narrates her feelings upon his entry into the room after what everybody fears is a dangerous encounter with Sir Hargrave Pollexfen: "I thought him [Sir Charles], the moment he enter'd, the handsomest man I ever saw in my life. What a transporting thing must it be, my Lucy, to an affectionate wife, without restraint, without check, and performing nothing but her duty, to run with open arms to receive a worthy husband, returning to her after a long absence, or from an escaped danger!"[85] Here Harriet imagines intimacy through distancing gestures, thinking not of herself as his wife but of what some wife of some "worthy husband" must feel.

More personally and dramatically, she comes next to describe herself, starting in the third person as Sir Charles appears:

> And I'll tell you how the Fool, the maiden Fool, looked, and acted. Her feet insensibly moved to meet him, while he was receiving the freer compliments of my Cousins. I courtesied bashfully; it was hardly notice-

able; and, *because* unnoticed, I paid my compliments in a deeper courtesy. And then, finding my hand in his, when I knew not whether I had an hand or not—I am grieved, Sir, said I, to be the occasion, to be the cause—And I sighed for one reason (perhaps you can guess what that was) and blushed for two; because I knew not what to say, nor how to look; and because I was under obligations which I could not return. (2:31)

The first-person adoption of the third person both preserves Harriet's "maiden" modesty and notes its unfelt movement toward the object of desire. This self-critical account, at least in retrospect, somehow notices and comments on her approach, which in the moment neither she nor perhaps anybody else nearby notices. She continues in this vein, as the "hardly noticeable" curtsy evokes the narrative world of Fielding, where almost unperceived expressions of feeling reveal themselves to no one only because those on the scene are not attentive enough.

The third person that Harriet adopts makes her own noticing of it possible, even though she narrates a series of obliterations of her consciousness. She finds her hand in Sir Charles's even though she says she did not know if she had one or not. These oscillations between heightened feeling and unfeeling become possible only because of her ability to use the third person to reflect on her first. In this the idiom of the insensible activates an obscure analogue of free indirect discourse. Critics and theorists have described the interpenetration of third and first person characteristic of that mode of writing as a productively ambiguous mix of perspectives, that can focalize a third-person narration with the "private" thoughts and feelings of a character or represent, ideologically or otherwise, a community's purchase on an individual's seemingly private, interior world.[86] Harriet's case here does something of both. Her third-person mockery of herself—"the Fool, the maiden Fool"—conveys the embarrassment she feels reflecting on the episode by taking an external perspective on it. But she also steps outside herself to judge her insensible behavior by "community standards" given that her letters are narrations of events at Colnebrook intended for a family of different readers, from naive to satirically minded, at Selby-House.[87] Yet the insensible both motivates Harriet's shift to the third person and frustrates its capacity to represent details of her emotion, as free indirect discourse normally would do. Since the insensible cannot be narrated from the inside, Harriet takes an outside view of herself. But this outside perspective can only remark on the blankness of its subject's affect, since there is nothing sensible there to be narrated.

An innocence that cannot feel its own embodiment of desire needs the help of a critical intelligence that can at least recognize that desire's meaning, especially in a novel centered on an impassive male hero. "I advise nothing, Madam," Sir Charles will soon say, when Harriet asks him whether or not she should see Sir Hargrave: "Pursue your inclinations" (2:32). This withholding of authoritative direction has been seen as crucial to Sir Charles's bizarrely total—even "totalitarian"—power in the novel. So the blank in her consciousness that Harriet narrates here itself serves as an effect of her abjection before him as an aloof absolute.[88] We have no Lovelace here to ascribe insensible desires to the heroine as a pretext for his aggressive actions. She must do it herself, in effect becoming her own Anna Howe. (Lucy, her naive correspondent, cannot detect evasion in Harriet's accounts.) So the insensible provides Harriet with an idiom to narrate feminine desire both innocently and critically, as it moves her through physical space toward its masterful object.

Both Fielding and Richardson use the insensible to navigate an otherwise perplexing terrain that their fiction surveys—between a virtuous, marriageable heroine and a suspicious community. They preserve the term's emphasis on love's unlocated, temporally diffuse power stressed in earlier romance and amatory fiction. But they add a more intense focus on what this lack of placement does to the judgment of the heroine—by herself and by the community—as well as on the fictional representation of it. As we will see in section 3 of chapter II, the insensible in Frances Burney's fiction will work as a mode of exoneration, a way for her character Evelina to come to feel desire slowly enough to remain inculpably innocent. But both Fielding and Richardson infuse the unfelt onset of love with a danger appropriate to the social worlds they depict. In the case of Clarissa, its potential lack of existence only heightens its effectiveness as a weapon against her, while for Sophia, love's insensible intrusion, however ultimately salutary, can only seem a threat from some unknown place. At the level of technique, the idiom helps precisely identify what Fielding's narrator and the reader he coaches can just barely sense, and what slips between the social scrutiny assembled in Richardson's letters.

3. Insensible against Involuntary in Burney

The deployment of the insensible is Frances Burney's subtlest response to the basic problem of feminine desire confronted in her first novel, *Evelina* (1778). How can a young woman innocently feel it? John Richetti, among others, finds the question fundamental in a range of fiction in the period. He notes that Burney faces in *Evelina* "the classic dilemma of the eighteenth-century moralizing woman novelist: how to preserve her heroine's innocence and moral integrity without lapsing into static didacticism and, more difficult, how to express her heroine's complex desire for all the pleasures that worldly experience can bring to a young beauty (in this case one deprived of her proper social status) without turning her into the sexually active and materially omnivorous woman whose shadow haunts the eighteenth-century imagination."[89] He adds that Burney herself recognizes the lifelessness and disengagement of her "abstemious paragons," Lord Orville and Evelina, and balances them with more forthright, "voraciously self-seeking personalities who reveal the truth . . . of desire and appetite that prevail in market society."[90] But Burney's narrative use of the insensible deepens her depiction of Evelina and Orville by bridging their desires to their commitment to virtue and propriety. The insensible in the novel of feeling again performs its mediating role, now between personal gratification and codes of social restraint.

Critics have long noticed that *Evelina* seems to announce itself as a kind of conduct book,[91] when its heroine exclaims early on, "really, I think there ought to be a book, of the laws and customs *à-la-mode*, presented to all young people, upon their first introduction into public company."[92] Thus the novel depicts, as Michael McKeon contends, Evelina's "privatizing internalization, of those public laws and customs" that support both her virtue and her social confidence.[93] And the idiom of the insensible may be used to characterize the salutary effects of the novel itself on the conduct of young people. Perhaps picking up a term from Burney's depiction of the most critical affective transaction in *Evelina*, the *Critical Review* praises the novel in 1778 by remarking that it "will imperceptibly lead them [sons of families] as well as their sisters, to improvement and to virtue."[94]

But diverse as it is, the body of conduct literature often explored as a relevant context for the novel tends to be wary of the insensible,[95] which is the very opposite of moral vigilance and publicly acted propriety. For instance, Wetenhall Wilkes's *Letter of Genteel and Moral Advice to a Young Lady* (1740) warns young women away from "Novels, Plays, Romances, and Poems" because they may "inculcate such Light, over-gay Notions as might by unperceiv'd Degrees soften and mislead the Understanding."[96] James Fordyce's *Sermons to Young Women* (1766), which Burney mentions in an early journal,[97] thus describes how young women may become habituated to lax moral standards: "By little and little their natural fearfulness begins to abate . . . custom soon begets familiarity; and familiarity produces indifference. The emotions of delicacy are less frequent, less strong. And now they seldom blush, although perhaps they often affect it. At the image of sin they tremble no longer: their minds are already debauched. All the internal fences of modesty are broken down."[98] The role of time is decisive, though Fordyce appeals to the techniques of what I have been calling blank narrative. He depersonalizes the process described, as abstractions like "custom" and "familiarity" are granted agency, and the passive voice predominates. The passage erases the moment of decisive change and projects it into a past, as women hardened to sin "are already" receptive to its corrupting power.

A little later in volume 1 of the *Sermons*, Fordyce genders the power of the unremarked process: "Men, I presume, are in general better judges than women, of the deportment of women. Whatever affects them from your quarter they feel more immediately. You slide insensibly into a certain cast of manners; you perceive not the gradations."[99] The difference between male judges and female objects of judgment unfolds as a difference of affective temporality. Men "immediately" feel what women perform in front of them, as the course of feminine behavior presents itself as series of moral excellences or lapses, divided up into "gradations" by which men are affected. Women conversely experience or at least undergo their judged lives, good and (here mostly) bad, as an unfelt flow or "slide," and when they finally feel, they do so after an often fatal "cast of manners" has already been established. Women's feelings lag behind the establishment of character that gives their feelings meaning.

Similarly, in her *Letters on the Improvement of the Mind, Addressed to a Young Lady* (1773), Hester Chapone depicts the moral hazards facing women in blank narrative terms, noting that "even those vices which you would most blush to own, and which most effectually defile and vilify the female heart, may by degrees be introduced into yours."[100] As much as Chapone—an acquaintance of Burney's whose *"seriousity"* she smiles at[101]—associates the dangers of such unnoticed degradation with the feminine, she will later indicate that this susceptibility is not inherent in women's nature: "I know not, whether that strange caprice, that inequality of taste and behaviour, so commonly attributed to our sex, may be properly called a fault of temper—as it seems not to be connected with, or arising from our animal frame, but to be rather the fruit of our own self-indulgence, degenerating by degrees into such a wantonness of will as knows not how to please itself."[102] Moral dissolution arises not directly out of the feminine body ("animal frame") but rather from taught self-indulgence. But as with Fordyce, the constitution of women's affective identity moves in time, "by degrees," and is time's object and product. Though some devotional works, including some important Methodist texts,[103] occasionally portray spiritual and moral improvement as also coming to its subjects insensibly, conduct literature often views lapses of "sense" as leading directly to moral ones.

The commonness of such anxiety makes Burney's appeal to the insensible to resolve and fulfill Evelina's desire all the more striking. Burney prepares the reader for her character's passion for Orville by distinguishing her in many scenes with her performances of sensibility. She often reacts to situations and people with great, even overwhelming, emotion. Her behavior at such moments conflicts to some extent with strict social propriety, from her unusually immediate (and somewhat awkward) appreciation of opera (volume 2, letter 21) and other theatrical performances to her highly emotional response to the attempted suicide of the Scottish poet (as it will turn out, her half-brother) Macartney (volume 2, letter 12) and his sad tale—a figure of sensibility if there ever was one.[104]

But toward the novel's end Burney puts (at least) two obstacles in the way of Evelina's direct expression of passion for Orville, both indicating propriety's superior claims. First is the letter to Evelina supposedly sent by Orville (though actually a forgery by Sir Clement Willoughby), in which Orville seems to reveal himself to be as voracious and self-seeking as most everybody else in the novel. No amount of Evelina's feeling for him could override the barrier put up by this shocking breach of decorum. Second, the novel introduces Orville's sister Louisa Larpent, a parody of the woman of excessive sensibility, who languishes and complains to get attention: "it's quite horrid to have such weak nerves!—the least thing in the world discomposes me" (361). Unrestrained feminine sentiment looks particularly bad at this point in the novel, and Burney seems intentionally to rule out any appeal to pure feeling to resolve her love plot.

So she turns to unfeeling to do the job. In letter 4 of volume 3, addressed to Mr. Villars, Evelina recurs to the term *insensibly* in a way that reads as obsessive-compulsive on her part and deliberate on Burney's. All the warnings against unfelt affect raised in the conduct literature supposedly informing the novel go unsounded. A slowly advancing intimacy with Orville at Clifton overcomes both Evelina's distrust of his intentions and her awe of his personal perfections and lofty social status: "Almost insensibly, I find the constraint, the reserve, I have been wont to feel in his presence, wear away; the politeness, the sweetness, with which he speaks to me, restore all my natural chearfulness, and make me almost as easy as he is himself; and the more so, as, if I may judge by his looks, I am rather raised, than sunk, of late in his opinion" (295). Politeness provides an incitement to intimacy instead of resistance to it. It both puts her at Orville's mercy and exonerates her of wrongly being too acquiescent to his charms, knowing what she thinks she knows of him. The "almost" could hint that Evelina has just enough awareness of the process to witness without being able to resist it. In this way Burney resolves the problem of unfeeling in the epistolary first person, as if the "almost" wins, from a nonconsciousness (all but) insensible of what is happening, just enough ground for third-person self-scrutiny. This self-consciousness of nonconsciousness is also what allows her to speak the voice of judgment even as she finds herself mirroring his easiness.

The next installment of the same letter fills in the gap between it and the last with more "almost" unfeeling: "Almost insensibly have three days glided on since I wrote last, and so serenely, that, but for your absence, I could not have formed a wish. My residence here is much happier than I had dared expect. The attention with which Lord Orville honours me is as uniform as it is flattering, and seems to result from a benevolence of heart that proves him as much a stranger to caprice as to pride" (295–96). Again politeness, especially when uniformly enacted, proves a medium in which intimacy can grow, but the term *insensibly* again enhances Evelina's effusions with an unrecognized dimension, with something more than social gratitude. That is, her (near) inability to sense the process unfolding invites the reader to assign her feelings a meaning that she (almost) cannot. Here the old warmth of the idiom in romance begins again to be felt. *Insensibly* permits the otherwise impossible copresence of innocence and desire.

A couple of sentences later, Evelina declares that "a thousand occasional meetings could not have brought us to that degree of social freedom, which four days spent under the same roof have, insensibly, been productive of" (296). Now instead of her impressions of politeness, time—"four days"—is the agent in the sentence. Only by depersonalizing the effects of Orville's attentions yet further can Evelina finally acknowledge her desire for the possibility of his desire for her, though her desire must still be couched in evasion and circumlocution: "Indeed, my dear Sir, I have reason to hope, that the deprecating opinion he formerly entertained of me is succeeded by one more infinitely more partial" (296). "Infinitely" cannot quite be a euphemism for sexual desire because the forged letter Evelina thought Orville wrote was soaked in sexual innuendo that she found repellant. It expressed his "deprecating opinion" more powerfully than his judgment of her as a "poor weak girl" (37) in the novel's early pages. Here infinite partiality suggests an unspecific romantic love, beyond the politeness that was its vehicle.

Throughout these crucial passages, the insensible erases the offense of Orville's letter without quite accounting for or excusing it as an expression of his character (let alone exonerating him by identifying its true author, Willoughby, which happens later).[105] So as far as Evelina knows, his desire for her is preserved as a fact, but it is made innocent by the slow workings of his polite behavior. To accomplish this, the insensible's power moves from being subtractive, negative—Evelina's own constraint "wear[s] away" in Orville's presence—to being both productive and depersonalized. The days, not the lovers, are what "glide . . . on" and are "productive of" new feelings, for which Evelina is grateful. The insensible does not so much gesture at what we might call hidden, "unconscious" depths *within* the agents as indicate the transformations that time makes possible when its effects and its affects are unfelt by them.

The blankness of these days of intimacy reveals a distinct narrative character of unfelt affect in the period's fiction. In some ways such a transaction resembles those affective ones described by Fredric Jameson in *The Antinomies of Realism* (2013) that are determinative, for him, of the nineteenth-century realist novel. The prime antinomy he has in mind comprises plot on the one hand and, on the other, affect, "a pure present in which little by little transition itself replaces the more substantive states (or musical 'named emotions') that precede and follow it."[106] In this Burney's "insensibly" could also be said to represent or gesture to "a temporality specific to affect," the "sliding scale of the incremental, in which each infinitesimal moment differentiates itself from the last by a modification of tone and an increase or diminution of intensity."[107]

But Jameson's language also furnishes means to differentiate *Evelina* from the realist novel. We readers do not witness the increase or diminution of intensity that must have occurred over the "four days." Burney leaves them blank, not offering the nonnarrative, "realist" details (such as those in Émile Zola's descriptive passages that exceed narrative meaning or easy allegorization) that Jameson claims convey affect at the expense of plotted and named emotions.[108] The four days are not filled with bits of "realism" outside the plot's forward momentum—sunlight dappling the tea things, a smell of newly mown hay through a window—that could build up Evelina's and Orville's affective change by depicting the unplotted, felt reality of the world. And, left empty, the insensibly passing time in *Evelina* becomes free to instrumentally serve plot after all. Here "transition itself" is both affectively rich and empty and allows a timorous heroine to overcome fears and scruples to love the man whom she already loves.

Orville's path is somewhat different. Some pages later (volume 3, letter 14), in Evelina's transcription of a tense conversation between him and Willoughby (reported to her by Mrs. Selwyn), he likewise both excuses and acknowledges his desire by means of the insensible. Willoughby challenges Orville's motives for sponsoring Evelina, and the exchange turns up the pressure that the novel puts on words like *interest* and *disinterestedness*. Orville proclaims his "unaffected interest in Miss Anville's welfare" (345); Willoughby a little later will counter, "your praises make me doubt your disinterestedness" (346). Orville's "unaffected" has at least two meanings: his interest is not pretended (an affectation), merely strategic, nor is it moved or motivated by his private feelings, by affect. But at the conversation's culmination, Orville offers a more frank and complex acknowledgment of how his "unaffected" concern might be understood. Evelina, he observes, "is not, indeed, like most modern young ladies, to be known in half an hour; her modest worth, and fearful excellence, require both time and encouragement to shew themselves. She does not, beautiful as she is, seize the soul by surprise, but, with more dangerous fascination, she steals it almost imperceptibly" (347). Orville avoids directly owning that he is the one who is fascinated. He also leaves his "dangerous" unattributed and unspecified: dangerous to whom? But it seems clear that he is thinking of himself as in danger and his interest in her as being at least partially erotic (though the danger might also include his becoming ensnared by his own desire to marry Evelina). Nonetheless he speaks in euphemism and abstraction. In contrast, other men, including Lord Merton and Willoughby himself, have found no impediment in being erotically and directly captivated by Evelina's beauty.

Like Evelina's repetition of "insensibly," Orville's "almost imperceptibly" here both cleanses his desire of agency and choice and acknowledges its irresistible power. As a man talking to another, he can be forthright in recognizing it is "dangerous"—that is, erotically involving. Also, as a man, he can project responsibility for his desire onto its object. It is Evelina who "steals" his soul "almost imperceptibly," not he whose desire grows within him and draws him closer to her. His account, unlike hers, assigns agency not to time but to her. While time takes a leading role in Orville's account of his desire (her attractions "require time" to show themselves), he readily adopts the masculinist convention that Evelina has stolen his soul. The "almost imperceptibly" nonetheless absolves her of any predatory motives, since the phrase's evocation of gradualness ensures that the process must be imperceptible to her too. Orville acknowledges the dangerousness of desire, its erotic content, even while culpability for it is cleansed from all involved.

Burney represents nonconscious action in other ways, in *Evelina* and through the rest of her literary career. Unlike *insensibly* and affiliated terms, these representations more concretely tie unintentional feelings and expressions to individual minds and particular moments. She brings to notice automatic movements and reactions that perform their own narratively complex functions. After Evelina's abduction by Willoughby at Vauxhall, she feels a kind of shame at being seen by him in the company of the Branghtons and Madame Duval. Addressing Villars, she says, "I must own to you, my dear Sir, that an involuntary repugnance seized me, at presenting such a set to Sir Clement" (200). Burney shines a satirical light on the psychological power of social standing. Far from being disgusted at introducing her would-be rapist to her relatives, she is mortified at letting him see her relationship to them, and the involuntary character of this emotion points to how deep such social or "class" shame goes.

A later example can be moralized differently. After Orville proposes to her and her titled father finally acknowledges her as his daughter, Evelina finds herself Louisa Larpent's object of regard: "there seemed something so little-minded in this sudden change of conduct, that, from an involuntary emotion of contempt, I thanked her, with a coldness like her own, and declined her offer" (380). The involuntary character of the harsh emotion acquits Evelina of deliberate aggression even while her natural good sense forces her to see Louisa's behavior for what it is. As with the unawareness conveyed by terms like *insensibly*, these expressions of involuntary feeling—repugnance and contempt—help Burney differentiate Evelina from the appetitive and aggressive social world through which she must move.

But the differences between the insensible and the involuntary are equally crucial, and not just because the latter is privative (it negates the will) and the former additive. The insensible designates extended processes of narrative development and signifies a manner in which Evelina changes and matures as a character. Its essential slowness endows it with a particularly intimate meaning. Her emotions themselves deepen and change. By contrast, the involuntary consists of spasms that occur momentarily and mechanically. These aid Burney's characterization of Evelina precisely by *not* sticking to her for too long. Though feeling contempt, she is not thus shown to be a contemptuous person. The involuntary responses display a function of her mind, her individual "psychology," and so represent a truth about how unwilled, automatic reactions are among the repertory of possible mental behaviors. Again some distance appears here between my view of the workings of the involuntary in fictional accounts of moral responsibility and Sandra Macpherson's (who does not discuss Burney at any length). Instead of expanding Evelina's responsibility (or "liability") for morally questionable acts, the involuntary allows her to express herself automatically in such a way as not to affect her fundamental moral character. The insensible process of her growing feelings for Orville, on the other hand, seems more profound for being less tied to the mechanics of human psychological action and reaction. It is a depiction not of how the mind works but of how change in time works, not localized in or directed by "the mind" at all.

A survey of quantitative data suggests the two words' fates in usage may be entwined. Google Ngram graphs show that while the usage of *insensibly* declines sharply after around 1786 (see figure 1 in this volume's introduction), *involuntarily* begins a steady ascent around 1750 that does not stop until around 1855 (see figure 3).

The words, of course, mean different things: the former suggests only a lack of sensate awareness of something happening or being done, while the latter indicates a person's clearly doing something without intending to do it. It is striking, however, how much easier it is to substitute forms of *involuntary* for those of *insensible* in many of the sentences discussed in this section than the other way around. That is, we can (though with a distinct change of meaning) easily understand "almost *involuntarily*, I find the constraint, the reserve, I have been wont to feel in his presence, wear away." But it is considerably harder to understand a phrase like *"insensible* repugnance" or *"insensible* emotion of contempt." The latter phrases name emotions too clearly felt and

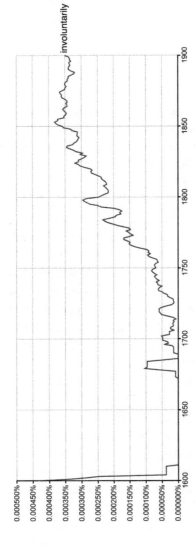

Figure 3. Jean-Baptiste Michel et al. "Quantitative Analysis of Culture Using Millions of Digitized Books." *Science* 331.6014 (2011): 176–82.

distinctly situated at a moment in time to be insensible, though not too much so to be involuntary. It is possible to speculate—and difficult to get beyond this degree of caution—that English-language users after 1750 began to prefer the more precise, temporally delimited, and morally clearer implications of the involuntary to the vaguer, more alarming processes described as insensible. The involuntary pertains to one will and one mind, often at one moment. The insensible plays in a considerably wider field.

A neat, emblematic contrast between the involuntary and the insensible appears in Burney's famous encounter with Miss White in June 1780, recorded in her journal and relayed to her sister Susanna. Burney describes the onset of the unnerving part of the interview this way: "Our Conversation, for some Time, was upon the common Bath topics,—but when Mrs. Lambert left us,—called to receive more Company, we went, insensibly, into graver matters."[109] It is not an especially alarming narrative signal, and far less dramatic than Burney's response to Miss White's remark that "the reason the men are happier than us, is because they are more sensual." That comment provokes Burney's extreme disturbance: "'I would not *think such thoughts*,' cried I, clasping my Hands with an involuntary vehemence, 'for Worlds!'"[110]

Burney herself participates, that is, in the insensible drift into the dangerous part of the conversation with Miss White—"*we* went"—while the involuntary reaction to the outrageous thoughts is Burney's alone. The danger of the initial insensible movement lies in its involvement of Burney without her awareness in a way that implicates her. We may believe her when she says she "would not *think such thoughts*," as if the thoughts come to her without her wanting to think them, or thinking them at all. They instead affect her, in this semiprivate social moment, without being consciously thought. Conversely, the "involuntary vehemence" with which she clasps her hands presents an entirely different kind of unwilling. The hand clasp is visible, dramatic, and done by her, tied to a personal psychological shock, a reaction to and open rejection of *"such thoughts."* While the insensible leads her into exposure to such thoughts, the involuntary gets her out. Again, the power of the insensible lies in its being undramatic and impersonal, unfolding by slow degrees thoughts and feelings to which Burney may then react (involuntarily or not).

In her next novel *Cecilia, or the Memoirs of an Heiress* (1782), the term *involuntary* takes over much of the delicate work performed by the insensible in *Evelina*. But the differences are again apparent and reflect distinct moralizations of desire and its hold on the mind and body. In an account cognate to Evelina's insensibly developing intimacy with Orville, Cecilia finds herself, in a chapter titled "A Sympathy," captivated by young Delvile without fully realizing it. As the novel's third-person narrator relates,

> She had been struck from her first meeting young Delvile with an involuntary admiration of his manners and conversation; she had found upon every succeeding interview something further to approve, and felt for him a rising partiality which made her always see him with pleasure, and never part from him without a wish to see him again. Yet, as she was not of that inflammable nature which is always ready to take fire, as her passions were under the control of her reason, and she suffered not her affections to triumph over her principles, she started at the danger the moment she perceived it, and instantly determined to give no weak encouragement to a prepossession which neither time nor intimacy had justified.[111]

Many elements contribute to distinguish the character of this passage from those that describe Evelina's insensible pull toward Orville. The somewhat chilly demeanor of the novel's third-person narrator here mimics Cecilia's cool self-supervision, itself built on a social and financial position more secure than that of Burney's first heroine. The term *involuntary* paradoxically contributes to this sense of self-control. While *insensibly* suggests a dangerous lack of containment of feeling's growth and encroachment on the will, Cecilia's "involuntary admiration" is ripe for her scrutiny precisely because it throws her will into prominence by so clearly arising against it. Unlike the insensible, it is the work neither of "time nor intimacy." It is temporally delimited, apparent at the first meeting, not oozing over vaguer stretches of time. None of the fuzzy outlines of the insensible that implicate Evelina's secreted feelings in the social intimacy with Orville, that make the process so hard to contain or even notice, trouble Cecilia's admiration. The involuntary has the virtue of being easily spotted and so monitored.

As the passage continues to describe the effects of Cecilia's extended visit to the Delviles' London home, however, she finds herself confronting something like the insensible's vaguer, more formidable powers:

> Qualities such as these, when recommended by high birth, a striking figure, and polished manners, formed but a dangerous companion for a young woman, who, without the guard of any former prepossessions, was so fervent an admirer of excellence as Cecilia. Her heart made no resistance, for the attack was too gentle and too gradual to alarm her vigilance, and therefore, though always sensible of the pleasure she received from his society, it was not till she returned to Portman-Square, after having lived under the same roof with him for a fortnight, that she was conscious her happiness was no longer in her power. (252)

Here that time scale of a certain middle region of narrative, "a fortnight," comes into play. The danger of the gradual lies in its hiding its true meaning and tendency until it is too late, and the belated recognition only confirms her loss of control. But from the security of Portman-Square and the unseductive society of the Harrels, Cecilia is able to control her feeling again by using the more circumscribed and contained word: "Yet this loss of mental freedom gave her not much uneasiness, since the choice of her heart, though involuntary, was approved by her principles, and confirmed by her judgment" (252).

Again the narrator's cool perspective approximates Cecilia's own, as the too gentle and too gradual attack in retrospect can be demarcated as a temporary "loss of mental freedom." While the involuntary nature of her choice confirms its depth and sincerity and perhaps is never fully dissipated, its danger is stifled by principled approval and the confirmation of judgment. The involuntary is hence enlisted as an element of a comprehensive mental attitude of deliberation and self-control, and recognizing it is part of a regime of moral hygiene. Unlike Evelina, who falls more deeply for Orville insensibly even though she still suspects him of impropriety, Cecilia is able to redeem the involuntary by configuring it in a pattern with deliberate choice. The involuntary tidies up the insensible.

Cecilia's involuntary affections do bear some responsibility for her unhappiness as the novel advances toward its only partially satisfying conclusion. Some hundreds of pages after her fondness for Mortimer Delvile originates, the narrator recounts, in free indirect discourse, that "she had met with an object whose character answered all her wishes for him with whom she should entrust her fortune, and whose turn of mind, so similar to her own, promised her the highest domestic felicity: to this object her affections had involuntarily bent, they were seconded by esteem, and unchecked by any suspicion of impropriety in her choice" (520). Here, too, though the entanglement begins involuntarily, it soon comes to harmonize with propriety. It is true that her agreement to marry Delvile without his parents' consent, extracted from her in a state of emotional confusion, nearly leads Cecilia to a sad end. But the psychological violence she undergoes, at least as her own thoughts are narrated, stems from her taking not an unconscious step but an intentional one. The involuntary nature of her weakness in the affair allows it to be discounted as she exerts her moral intelligence: "Where frailty has never been voluntary, nor error stubborn, where the pride of integrity is unsubdued . . . how fearfully delicate, how 'tremblingly alive,' is the conscience of man!" (576). What she cannot reconcile her herself to, instead, is "her consent," her "wilful fault" (576) in agreeing to marry Delvile without a parental blessing. However interesting it may be to apply to fiction a model of moral agency in which consent does not matter, in Cecilia's moral universe the involuntary has the virtue of being forgivable, like Clarissa Harlowe's involuntary step. Though the novel at large depicts dangers initiated by involuntary emotions, Cecilia's rectitude again depends on her will's capacity to affirm or deny, esteem or reject, emotions that involuntarily besiege her. Despite its dangers, the involuntary is an agent of moral clarity.

As the complexities of the fictional tradition of sensibility in which Burney participates resist easy summation, so do those of the insensible. (In Burney's next novel, *Camilla*, the additive sense of *insensibly* all but drops away, while there appear some fifty instances of *involuntary* and *involuntarily*.)[112] The claim that historians have sought to substantiate in recent decades, that individual character in Britain gradually ceases to be defined by fluid social and intersubjective factors and becomes more tied to a firmer form of personal identity as the eighteenth century draws to a close,[113] may draw an odd sort of support from this observation, local as it is. If the insensible characterizes a fluid time and an unfolding of affect that is not strictly embodied in individuals, the involuntary is grounded in particular moments, bodies, and (strange to say) conscious wills. A figure like Cecilia, vigilant as to what she wishes and does not wish to do, can comfortably sort her voluntary from her involuntary actions and feelings. At least within Burney's career, the representation of affective character moves away from the impersonal vagueness that the insensible imparts and toward the firmer if still dangerous world of involuntary actions.[114]

4. Austen as Coda

This chapter on fiction has shown how the insensible oddly both fulfills and exceeds the stylistic expectations commonly associated with particular fictional projects through the long eighteenth century. In romance, the idiom amplifies the powers of love by suggesting how these may move so as scarcely to be felt. Inherited by the moralized sentimental novel, in parallel fashion, it allows a desiring heroine to be both guiltless and (in a special way) out of control. A final, brief reflection on a novel of courtship that appears after the eighteenth century's end and critically engages the tradition I have been discussing will bring this sequence of examples to a close. The idiom appears only once in Jane Austen's first published novel, where it helps reconcile what seems like the opposition announced in its title. *Sense and Sensibility* (1811) has often been viewed by critics as a retrospective commentary on sentimental attitudes of the so-called high sentimental period of 1745–90, though an ambiguous one.[115] It has been common, of course, to read the book as a rather schematic working out of the superiority of sense to sensibility, with the figure representing the latter, Marianne Dashwood, subdued by the former when she marries Colonel Brandon.[116] Maybe even more common have been attempts to break the title's apparent opposition down (it refers, after all, to sense *and*, not sense *or* sensibility) and suggest that Austen here and throughout her career cares a good deal about feeling, even sentimental feeling.[117] The novel's restricted but crucial use of the term *insensible* exposes this mixed attitude toward sensibility while reflecting on the subtradition of the unfelt in the fiction of sensibility I have been describing. When Austen's career as publishing novelist began in the second decade of the nineteenth century, the special additive sense of the insensible and similar terms had waned, and she will not use them much. The word *insensible* appears in a purely privative sense seven times in *Sense and Sensibility*. But the one additive instance, passing as it is, helps the novel partially redeem the language of sensibility, again by means of that negating prefix, after it had apparently been discredited.

This ambiguous redemption arrives in chapter 44, when a privative usage of the word, denoting a cynical absence of sentiment, leads to a subsequent, additive one that brings genuine feeling back. Willoughby arrives unannounced during Marianne's illness at the novel's end to explain his behavior and feelings to Elinor. He manages to make her believe he really felt for Marianne, despite his abandonment of her. This rescues, after a fashion, sensibility for the novel. It allows a kind of truth in evident feeling. Willoughby's affection for Marianne had not been dissimulated or cynically or casually performed, but was as significant and real as it seemed to her as well as to Elinor, the figure of sense (or at least acute observation), and to other onlookers. If he cannot convince Elinor of this, not only the affair but also the entire "sensibility" part of the novel, its language and its ethos, could seem a sham, a mere effect of "the charms of enthusiasm and ignorance of the world" or a willful projection of Marianne's abstract "systems" of thought upon an indifferent reality.[118]

At the start, Willoughby's speech conforms to the latter reading: "Your sister's lovely person and interesting manners could not but please me; and her behaviour to me almost from the first, was of a kind—It is astonishing, when I reflect on what it was, and what *she* was, that my heart should have been so insensible" (298). Here the term flatly signifies a lack, however "astonishing," of affective engagement. Pleased, Willoughby nonetheless does not feel in his heart. The sentiment that seemed to overload their intimacy seems only an amalgam of insignificant pleasures and "amusement" (298), supplemented with conventionalized sentimental performance, as well as his vanity and self-indulgence. Elinor is ready to end the conversation there.

But Willoughby's lack of true feeling, he says, was transformed by an unfeeling of quite another sort. His sentimental attachment to Marianne, at first a kind of disguise used to manipulate her, gradually becomes real, like Eliza Haywood's man in *The Female Spectator* who pretends to have taste until he really does. Intending to trifle with Marianne because he thinks he cannot afford to marry her, Willoughby finds himself in love: "To have resisted such attractions, to have withstood such tenderness!—Is there a man on earth who could have done it!—Yes, I found myself, by insensible degrees, sincerely fond of her; and the happiest hours of my life were what I spent with her, when I felt my intentions were strictly honourable, and my feelings blameless" (299–300). Given his confession of levity as he initiated his flirtation with Marianne, the "insensible degrees" help guarantee the veracity of his fondness and sincerity, not only to Elinor now, but to himself, as he "found" himself feeling. The insensible in its additive sense proves a vital, and in this case really the only, support to feelings. Again, the idiom is introduced in a retrospective first person that is able only to identify a special kind of blank that cannot be filled in with "realistic" details. Distinct moments of increasing intimacy—"degrees"—existed, but their insensible character makes writing to the moment impossible. Between the narration of his initial "libertine" intentions and his disgracefully mercenary departure, the unnarratable process of the insensible serves to legitimate feeling's irresistible truth and honor. Only the insensible can wear away the cynicism and callousness that obstruct and discredit sensibility and partially restore it as a language and a "system," as it makes one man receptive to affection. The insensible allows feeling to be itself.

And in the clarified world of Austen, the gender of the person subject to the insensible matters. Of course, insensible degrees of feeling affect men in the sentimental tradition; as we have seen, Orville's heart in Burney's *Evelina* is stolen almost imperceptibly. But Austen's Willoughby is a seducer and casual libertine (like Burney's Willoughby, as it happens), bent on his own pleasure and amusement. His conversion to the world of deep feeling, which he at first only pretended with Marianne, means something. So the redemption of an earlier, worse libertine, Lovelace in Richardson's *Clarissa*, had to be imagined by Lady Bradshaigh as coming about insensibly, but of course Richardson could not gratify her with such an outcome. In the decades of fiction preceding Austen, it is mostly women, and the desires that compromise them, who are subject to the sway of unfeelingly developed feelings.

Austen's discovery of the power to seduce a seducer by insensible degrees thus represents a gender equalization of such powers and a partial redemption of the discourse of sensibility itself. Willoughby ends miserably, and Marianne marries outside the ambit of sensibility, but the affections between them were real, and their reality is what allows Marianne to finally get past him. She says after her recovery, "if I could be allowed to think that he was not *always* acting a part, not *always* deceiving me;—" and Elinor responds, "If you could be assured of that, you think you should be easy" (321). She happily obliges her sister with such assurance, relaying the gist of Willoughby's account of his irresistible, insensibly grown attachment. So a culmination—

not *the* culmination, but one—of the tradition of insensibly seduced heroines in sentimental fiction comes at this moment in Austen when the unfelt advent of a man's true feeling accredits not only him but the judgment of the sentimental heroine, who may now depart the dangerous world of sensibility for something more sensible.

The tradition of narrative functions of the blank motion and temporal scale of the insensible hence achieves a kind of end. It reforms a rake, if not plotwise by turning him into the "best husband," at least at the level of his moral sentiments. In the foregoing survey of diverse fictional examples over a very long period, the insensible has played a remarkably consistent role. It supports the passions that impel British fictional plots by offering an affective alternative to both—the passions and the plotting. Doing so requires that it offer writers narrative strategies that function differently from those commonly singled out in the critical tradition. The idiom supplements and qualifies the externally performed "rhetoric of love" of romance, as well as Fielding's godlike master narration and Richardson's writing to the moment, and the techniques, such as epistolary self-scrutiny and free indirect discourse, that explore gaps between narratorial assessment and first-person motive and feeling. And recent critical emphases on the external status of agency and moral will in some fictional contexts may be enhanced by attention to the insensible. While the former reconfigure subjective states and actions spatially, moving from inside to outside, the latter explores temporal processes in which such spatial distinctions drop away altogether. The days insensibly pass, submission insinuates itself without being perceived, and after these affective blanks, a new state of feeling has arrived. Some critical perspectives might view the use of the idiom as relinquishing the opportunity to provide a psychologically detailed account of unfolding feeling. But the withholding practiced by the insensible offers something positive: an opening up of feeling to the world.

Chapter III

Historiography
Insensible Revolutions

Radically new content and concepts enter British historiography around the middle of the eighteenth century and require new language and narrative techniques to represent them. Among these, the insensible is doubly useful. It not only helps historians narrate the large-scale changes to society, nations, populations, and commerce that were increasingly treated alongside the usual topics—kings' reigns, statecraft, and wars. It also, in its paradoxical way, serves their descriptions of the fundamentally affective bases of historical change. As we have seen, the negating prefixes of terms like *insensibly* tend oddly to draw unfelt forces into proximity to more apparent human feelings. Such terms, popular as they were becoming through the long eighteenth century, had found their way into histories of an earlier date. Landmark works like *The History of the Rebellion* (1702–1704) by Edward Hyde, First Earl of Clarendon and Gilbert Burnet's *History of His Own Time* (2 volumes, 1724 and 1734), both published posthumously, employed it on occasion. So Burnet describes Charles II's fear during the Exclusion Crisis that giving Parliament the power to forbid the accession of the Duke of York "insensibly would change the nature of the *English* monarchy: So that from being hereditary it would become elective."[1] And the great partisan histories of England of the first half the eighteenth century, from the popular, judiciously Whiggish one by French protestant Paul Rapin de Thoyras to that of the Jacobite Thomas Carte, naturally find the term useful.[2] Any account of slow tendencies and insidious effects is bound to take up the idiom when it is available.

But new roles for gradualness appear at midcentury. Accounts of insensible processes find an especially significant place in the historiography of the age of sentiment. The term figures in what Dugald Stewart would call in 1793 "*Theoretical* or *Conjectural History*": lacking "direct evidence, we are under a necessity of supplying the place of fact by conjecture; and when we are unable to ascertain how men have actually conducted themselves upon particular occasions, of considering in what manner they are likely to have proceeded, from the principles of their nature, and the circumstances of their external situation."[3] Developed by Montesquieu (whose *Spirit of Laws*, 1748, first appeared in English in 1750) and historians of the Scottish school including David Hume, William Robertson, and Adam Ferguson, this style of history writing commonly viewed such principles of historical agents' "nature" largely as matters of feeling, that must be seen to reflect and link to "external" circumstances in new ways. A mediating term between feeling and the impersonal forces shaping history is required.

The new categories of *moeurs* and *manners*, which came to be central concepts in the period's historiography, help delineate this area where individuals and these forces interact. English translators conventionally used the latter English term, defined by Johnson as "general way of life; morals; habits," to translate the former French one.[4] (The French word *manières* is often rendered "customs.") "*Moeurs* constitute a philosophical and an Enlightened concept," J. G. A. Pocock remarks,[5] a centerpiece of theoretical or conjectural history, and tend to pertain to sentiment and the social shape of human passions. While these often take vivid and noticeable forms, the tendencies that cultivate them and give them their bent—whether from *"moral"* or *"physical"* causes, as Hume divides them in his essay "Of National Characters" (1748)—unfold unnoticed. Seen to embody a nation's peculiar dispositions, form its institutions, and often (though not for Hume) express its climate, geography, and other physical factors, manners prepare and shape particular eruptions of passions and acts of emotion while themselves operating collectively, mutely, and gradually. A nation's manners change in unrecognized ways, but more fundamentally, the *relation* of manners to events, expressions of feeling and purpose, deeds, and acts of will, which tend to capture the attention of historians, is itself insensible to historical agents. The insensible mediates between affective events and abiding structures of feeling. The condition of possibility (to use a Kantian notion) of historical actions is their unfelt relation to manners.

This insensibly forged link between agent and circumstance, private feeling and *moeurs*, event and slow process, situates the idiom discussed in this book at a grander, more expansive place on the scale of its uses in the period's writing. I began chapter I with minute particles that precede all sensory experience, and chapter II treated that social zone of the courtship novel where insensible processes play out between a heroine and the watchful men and families converging on her. In every context the idiom characterizes something happening prepersonally, in advance of any feeling being owned by the people affected by it. This prepersonal implication operates equally at every part of this scale. A sociohistorical "atmosphere" is just as prepersonal as a particle.

And in the former, in history, the insensible performs its effects at their most vast. So Edward Gibbon characteristically remarks, early in *The History of the Decline and Fall of the Roman Empire*, that at the empire's height, the Italians "insensibly coalesced into one great nation."[6] Without anyone feeling it, the local and separate become "great." Such coalescence is deindividuation itself, yet it comes to forge a new national identity, and a person may eventually say, "I am an Italian."

In history writing, the insensible can seem especially prone to depict movements much bigger than whatever might consciously be happening in any particular brain or body. In this, the idiom resonates with writing in the humanities attuned to nonconscious affective and cognitive performances that exceed individual psychology.[7] Unnoticed affect is dispersed through crowds, even among unspecified individuals remote from one another in space and time. Gibbon will remark later in *The Decline and Fall* that "the nations of the empire insensibly melted away in the Roman name and people,"[8] and the adverb does not single out any particular individual or group as not noticing, either the ones joining the empire or those being joined by the melting. Such dispersion is its essence as a species of massive historical change. The term's reference to affective processes that nobody feels or is even identified as not feeling allows it to float free of any particular human embodiment. When characterizing historical movements, the insensible has a way of enfolding the world, its human subjects included, in an impersonal but affecting passage of time.

And like historical agents, readers of history may find themselves insensibly involved in it. As in accounts of many other areas of sentimental engagement after midcentury, writers portray our immersion in historical narrative as coming upon us in unnoticed ways. Early in the century, describing the appeal of a rather traditional form of historiography, Joseph Addison remarks in the *Spectator* (1712),

> It is the most agreeable Talent of an Historian, to be able to draw up his Armies and fight his Battels in proper Expressions, to set before our Eyes the Divisions, Cabals, and Jealousies of Great Men, and to lead us Step by Step into the several Actions and Events of his History. We love to see the Subject unfolding it self by just Degrees, and breaking upon us insensibly, that so we may be kept in a pleasing Suspence, and have Time given us to raise our Expectations, and to side with one of the Parties concerned in the Relation. I confess this shews more the Art than the Veracity of the Historian, but I am only to speak of him as he is qualified to please the Imagination.[9]

Here Addison's picture of historiographical affect seems to mimic the gradual unfolding of "Actions and Events" themselves, as "the Subject" opens to the reader at the suspenseful pace at which history itself develops.

After midcentury, the insensibly affective power of written history can turn less on narrative suspense than on its overriding the difference between then and now. In his account of sentimental historiography of the period, Mark Salber Phillips stresses how historians recognized that novelistic techniques bring the reader vividly close, without her realizing it, to past events and scenes. Quoting Joseph Berington, author of *The History of the Reign of Henry the Second* (1790), Phillips remarks that "allowing their characters to speak for themselves 'insensibly transports the reader into the company of their heroes and sages, obliterating, by a momentary magic, the distance of years, and the consciousness of present existence.'"[10] Though Phillips does not make much of the point, his quotation of Berington reveals the striking proximity and mutual dependence of sentiment and the insensible. For the content to be affectively vivid, its form or manner of engagement must be unfelt. By "obliterating" distance by "magic," by "insensibly" transporting readers, historians generate the very opposite of insensibility: a connection to people of the past, their concerns and emotions.

But the capacity of the insensible to connect historians to their readers and the present to the past serves purposes beyond facilitating sympathetic identification with historical personages. Historians' depiction of our insensible way of engaging with written history mimics aspects of time's own advancement: its gradual evolution into new shapes and configurations. By using such devices, historical texts represent how time passes and carry us along with its momentum. As we shall see, the histories of Hume and the Scottish Enlightenment have a reflexive quality. They narrate the "insensible revolution" that drives European progress and cast their own narratives, refined and polite as they are, as outcomes of it. But a sense of the insensible motions of time can serve more skeptical, less triumphalist apprehensions of its advance. The idiom brings Gibbon not to boast his mastery of historical truths but to confront his own subjection to processes that challenge the judgment. Versions of this doubleness appear elsewhere in this book: the insensible seems both to invite and to discourage an enlightened account of what is out there that cannot be sensed. In historiography, the unfelt inspires both an urge to see deep into the movements of time and a recognition, equally expressive of the British Enlightenment, of the historian's limitations. The insensible allows historians to join or connect with history, either to understand it or to accept its mute power over their own understanding.

1. The Force of the Thing
Unfelt Moeurs in French Historiography

In the works of the French historical thinkers most influential in Britain, Montesquieu and Voltaire, the idiom of the insensible quietly provides an occult ingredient that Enlightenment history requires to present itself as enlightened. This kind of language characterizes in particular the operation of manners. Mutely and unnoticed, they affect historical agents and activate sentiments. In contrast to, say, rational improvements in the legal code or social institutions, moeurs exert their power without being deliberated on or planned. They shape a nation's history in advance of any such deliberations. They could hence seem simply forces of antienlightenment, obstructing the rational, polite, masterful achievement of enlightened eras (such as the reign of Louis XIV, as Voltaire portrays it). Yet in both writers, moeurs operate in a kind of productive tension with social advances. They may impede positive change but may also, following their own inherent tendency, polish and civilize a people and create the precondition of enlightenment. This understanding of the way tacit moeurs underwrite social change in French historical writing, different as it is in Montesquieu's and Voltaire's projects, finds a response in the British, and especially Scottish, historical thought that developed alongside it.

While not exactly a work of history, Montesquieu's account of the consolidation of peoples and nations in *L'Esprit des lois* (1748) helps stimulate, sometimes through opposition, the British Enlightenment understanding of change and continuity.[11] David Hume corresponded with Montesquieu and perhaps helped see a pamphlet-size publication of two chapters from *The Spirit of Laws* into print in Edinburgh in 1750, before the English translation of the full work by Thomas Nugent appeared later in the year.[12] Hume's argument in his essay "Of National Characters," which appeared the same year *L'Esprit des lois* did in French, seems to anticipate and contest Montesquieu's identification in book 19 of climate as among the "various causes" that create *l'esprit général* (along with, as Montesquieu lists them, "the religion, the laws, the maxims of government" and "precedents, morals and customs").[13]

Later, Edward Gibbon's attitude toward the philosophical and historical ambitions of *L'Esprit des lois* will evolve in complex ways.[14] His early work, the *Essai sur l'étude de la littérature* (Essay on the study of literature, 1761), praises Montesquieu for penetrating into causes that escape the "vulgaire,"[15] though Gibbon critically comments on him at various places in *The Decline and Fall*.[16] Finally, in his posthumously published memoirs (1796), Gibbon seems to renounce his early infatuation altogether: "Alas! how fatal has been the imitation of Montesquieu!"[17] Whether endorsed unreservedly or not, Montesquieu's works among many British writers came to stand for an ingenuity in discerning hidden causes and regularities beneath the variegated surface of historical phenomena—an inspiring if dangerous example for historians seeking an enlightened view of otherwise mysterious historical forces.

The insensible and cognate terms play an intriguing part in both Montesquieu's own general pronouncements about the nature of history and his narration of particular historical transactions. In his early unpublished (and untranslated) fragment *De la Politique* (1725), he remarks that "most effects come about in such singular ways, or depend on such imperceptible and remote causes, that they can hardly be foreseen." (La plupart des effets arrivent par des voies si singulières, ou dépendent de causes si imperceptibles et si éloignées qu'on ne peut guère les prévoir.)[18] David Carrithers has taken the reference to "imperceptible and remote causes" to suggest a "view of history stressing necessity rather than chance" (as opposed to the first part of the sentence concerning "voies si singulières"), and therefore a history open to enlightened philosophical explanation.[19] On the other hand, Isaiah Berlin quotes the sentence as evidence that Montesquieu thought "human history is not susceptible to the simple laws which had so deeply hypnotised many noble thinkers."[20]

This double view in part results from the characteristically peculiar power of terms like *imperceptible*. They point, on the one hand, to something unavailable not only to the agents subject to them but also to the historian's enlightened retrospect. On the other hand, they do seem to posit *something*—especially when modifying "causes"—that shimmers like a lure, motivating especially profound historical speculations (though this something is decidedly not "simple"). Of course, much depends, as will be apparent in subsequent examples, on whether the causes are imperceptible only to those affected by them or must remain so to historians as well. Two different types of historiographical authority may potentially issue from the notion of the unfelt. The idea either indicates the historian's enlightened mastery over causes that his subjects could not perceive or casts a kind of magisterial doubt on the possibility of anyone, the historian included, finally making sense of the historical processes in which all of us are immersed.

Montesquieu's published historical writings freely use "insensiblement" and "insensible" to express the nature of gradual historical change, and his English translators reflect his idioms, occasionally even substituting the terms for his other expressions (e.g., "peu à peu").[21] In this we witness concrete instances of a heightening of the English infatuation with such gestures. In *The Spirit of Laws* itself, insensible effects ramify from the full range of causal factors Montesquieu considers, from the three governmental types (monarchy, republic, despotism) to climate to legal codes. Most consistently, though, the insensible characterizes the force of moeurs and *manières*, discussed in book 19, which stands "literally at the centre" of *The Spirit of Laws*, "at the crossroads between the material and ideal factors,"[22] as Brian Singer observes. This crossing of the physical and the mental, human and nonhuman, is typical of the idiom's function in history writing. Material factors alien to feeling attach seamlessly to the structures of sentiment of any nation. The insensible characterizes the foundation of sensible thought, action, and behavior.

Such factors prove to be linked especially closely to the slow force of time; in Singer's words, "The moeurs and manners may have their origins in relations of rule, but over time they can take on a thickness and inertia that renders them relatively immune or, at least, resistant to political events such as foreign conquest."[23] This "thickness" and slowness of moral effects show up in other books as well, as when Montesquieu remarks in book 15 ("In What Manner the Laws of Civil Slavery are relative to the Nature of the Climate") that a slaveholder "contracts all manner of bad habits with his slaves, he accustoms himself insensibly [*insensiblement*] to the want of all moral virtues, he grows fierce, hasty, severe, choleric, voluptuous, and cruel" (1:336). The power of custom results in a change in sensibility that emerges between exploited and exploiter as a product of the perverse relations of rule that debase both. While the feelings activated by this situation are volatile, the time that constitutes them cannot be felt.

CHAPTER III. HISTORIOGRAPHY

In the central book 19, Montesquieu describes again in different terms how rule and moeurs work together in contrasting ways to shape feelings. He here makes his well-known distinction between laws and moeurs:

Manners and customs [*les moeurs & la manières*] are those habits [*usages*] which are not established by the laws, either because they were not able, or were not willing to establish them.

There is this difference between laws and manners [*moeurs*], that the laws are most adapted to regulate the actions of the subject, and manners [*moeurs*] to regulate the actions of the man. There is this difference between manners [*moeurs*] and customs [*manières*], that the first principally relate to the interior conduct, the others to the exterior. (1:428)[24]

Moeurs pertain particularly to the "interior conduct" of the "man" or person, shaping how he feels and thinks. Montesquieu will continue to note, in the cases of China and ancient Sparta, that laws, *moeurs*, and *manières* have become "confounded" (1:428). But in China's case, on which he lingers for a few chapters, he seems mostly impressed by how well the mixture works. In book 19 he remarks that "this empire is formed on the plan of the government of a family" (1:433): any weakening of the *manières* of civility, and the governmental order "would insensibly be lost. Retrench but one of these habits, and you overturn the state" (1:433). In other cases, too, Montesquieu seems more struck by the interconnection between laws, *moeurs*, and *manières* than by their natural distinction. In the concluding chapter 27 of book 19, "How the Laws May Contribute to Form the Manners, Customs, and Character of a Nation" (which takes England as its prime example), the three elements, far from being separable, again blend seamlessly into one another.

And if not always characterizing the way in which laws, *moeurs*, and *manières* become confounded, the insensible in Montesquieu typically describes how they function in concert. The term depicts a medium in which this variety of causal factors interact in history. For instance, in book 28—one of the three essentially "historical" books of the *Spirit of Laws* (the others are 30 and 31)—Montesquieu describes a shift, decisive for French society, that occurs without anyone being especially attentive to it: the decline of Salic law and the revival of Roman law in medieval France. The regular, consistent administration of the laws gained ground slowly, impelled by an unarticulated mass of indifference, neglect, and habitual attitudes. He repeats that "no law" was positively responsible for the more regularized institution of justice: "Thus there was no law to inhibit the lords from holding their courts themselves; no law to abolish the functions of the peers; no law to ordain the creation of bailiffs; no law to give them the power of judging. All this was effected insensibly, and by the very necessity of the thing. [*Tout cela se fit peu à peu, et par la force de la chose.*] The knowledge of the Roman law, the arrests of the courts, the new digests of customs, required a study of which the nobility and illiterate people were incapable" (2:321). So a former state of affairs over which the nobility presided, in which judicial combat and other haphazard and customary forms of justice were common, transforms into the more consistent and learned procedures and jurisprudence of the Roman law. Moeurs and manners (such as the nobility's indifference to technical procedures of pleading) dictate French society's way of adapting to a more professionalized and orderly system, not any deliberate structural innovation. Order itself, in other words, relies on unfelt processes to take hold; ironically, the move to a more conscientiously consistent system itself partly depends on the nonconscious force of evolving custom. The "spirit" of French social customs, moeurs, and manners constitutes the force, translated as the "very necessity," of the thing. While "the thing" is the character of social transformation itself, its "force," in a phrase more powerful and much more uncommon in Montesquieu's prose than his usual "la nature de la chose," designates the insensible as a dynamic movement.

Montesquieu hence presents not the nation's simple transition from a customary to a formal legal system but rather a more complex view of how the former evolves alongside, to support, the latter. Two chapters later, in "Of the Customs of France," he notes the "prodigious diversity" of the old legal system and its origins both in the country's intense localism and in the practice of legal duels, "it being natural that a series of fortuitous cases must have been productive of new usages" (1:323). But again, the displacement of this system itself by procedure and regularity obeys the previous customary principle of unnoticed change; Montesquieu notes that "these customs were preserved in the memory of old men; but insensibly laws or written customs were formed" (1:323). His equating of laws and "written customs" makes the point in a nutshell. The phrase preserves a sense of the deep continuities accorded by insensible transformation even as a new, less "customary" order comes into being. Something like enlightenment comes to a social order through the force of custom that drives progress toward rationalization. And if order and consistency ultimately transform not only the customs but also the "spirit" of the French, these rely on something they cannot be sensible of.

Even in interpretations of French history opposed to Montesquieu's, the insensible sway of moeurs evokes a similarly complex attitude toward change and progress. In contrast to his rival,[25] Voltaire advocates the so-called royal theory (*thèse royale*), ascribing the advances of the French nation to the power of an enlightened monarchy. Montesquieu promotes a version of the *thèse nobilaire* (nobiliary theory), arguing for the ancient constitutional right of the nobility to guard French liberty by limiting the sovereign's power—a historical view, on the face of it, more invested in slow tradition and unarticulated sources of authority than celebrations of the masterful legislative and executive powers of the monarch. But Voltaire's major historical works, *La siècle de Louis XIV* (The age of Louis XIV, 1751) and the *Essai sur les mœurs et l'esprit des nations* (1756), like Montesquieu's *L'esprit des lois*, refer to insensibly affecting and changing moeurs to develop his own model of historiography *à la philosophe*. His English translators, among them Thomas Nugent, reflect and again sometimes enhance the rendering of the processes of history as insensible. Nugent is identified as the translator on the title page of the first English version of the later book, *An Essay on Universal History, the Manners, and Spirit of Nations, from the Reign of Charlemaign to the Age of Lewis XIV* (1759), and while the identity of the translator of the earlier one, *The Age of Lewis XIV* (1752), is not certain, it has also been attributed to Nugent.[26] Again, the free way in which the translators add *insensibly* to Voltaire's historiography suggests how readily British readers thought of time's passage rendered by the new philosophical history as unfelt.

The significance of the idiom in *The Age of Lewis XIV*, as the 1752 version printed by Robert Dodsley and subsequent ones are titled, lies in its discreet supplementation of the brilliancy and height of achievement embodied by its subject. Voltaire begins by placing Louis's reign among the "four happy ages" of humanity,[27] a rare historical moment grouped with the ancient Greece of Philip and Alexander, the Rome of Augustus, and the Florence of the Medici. These shining ages of vitality and success stand out from the common order of history. But what surrounds them is not always mere barbarism for Voltaire. At the end of volume 1, after the tumult and occasional failures of Louis's rule, he discusses the age that follows, and the quieter administration of Cardinal Fleury during the regency:

> Political affairs insensibly [*insensiblement*] returned into their natural chanel.[28] Happily for Europe, Sir Robert Walpole, the prime minister of England, was of a disposition equally pacific. These two men maintained almost all Europe in that tranquillity which lasted from the peace of Utrecht to the year 1733; and which was but once interrupted by the short war in 1718. This was an happy time for all nations, who, cultivating commerce and arts with emula[t]ion, forgot their past calamities. (1:421)

This is an account of what Pocock has called the "Utrecht Enlightenment,"[29] a picture of a "republic" of European nations mutually improved by commerce that is an alternative to Louis XIV's age of light and bellicosity. The "natural channel" (Voltaire's phrase is slightly stronger, "ordre naturel") is the usual course of history embodied by the mild dispositions of Walpole and Fleury, tacitly reestablished and maintained, and contrasts with the previous reign, which is portrayed, in Karen O'Brien's words, as "a spectacle discontinuous with the natural order."[30]

Later, Voltaire's English translator would add "insensibly" to point out Louis's own way of acting against this natural order as he rules. In volume 2, Voltaire describes in the chapter "Of Calvinism" the fatal decisions to persecute the Huguenots as running against the stability that the king's own administration had conferred unawares on French society. Unlike the more dangerous Calvinist elements that challenged the monarchy in the late sixteenth century during the French Wars of Religion, the Huguenots of Louis XIV's time posed no serious threat. In pressing against the Calvinists, Louis and his advisers had "not considered, that the Hugonets [sic] were no longer the same as at Jarnac, Montcontour, and Coutras; that the rage of civil war was extinguished; that the malady which had so long afflicted the nation was almost spent; that time was insensibly restoring things to their first state; that if the fathers had been rebels under Lewis XIII, their sons were become good subjects under Lewis XIV" (2:211). The French original of the phrase rendered here as "that time was insensibly restoring things to its first state" simply reads "que tout n'a qu'un tems [sic] chez les hommes."[31] A Glasgow translation the following year, which complains of "some hundreds of mistakes in the London editions," translates the phrase as "that every thing among men has its period."[32] The rhetorical heightening in Dodsley's London version—not only the gratuitous addition of "insensibly" but the placement of time as the clause's subject and agent—indicates how the translator is working overtime to present temporal passage as an active and unseen force. And time here is an affective medium, subduing "rage" and other destructive passions. Louis reduces himself by failing to notice this action of time—by failing, in short, to apprehend the shifts of feeling in history itself.

The power of time in such accounts has its own distinctive tendency toward enlightenment. The passage continues: "Lewis XIV, who upon seizing Strasburg in 1681, engaged to protect Lutheranism, might have acted in the same manner with respect to Calvinism, and left it to time to abolish it insensibly" (2:212). Again "insensibly" is added gratuitously (and the 1753 Glasgow translation inserts it here just as the 1752 London one does): Voltaire's original reads "pouvait tolérer dans ses états le calvinisme que le tems [sic] aurait aboli."[33]

As above, the English translator seems to take the mere reference to time as license to insert the idea that its power is unfelt, or would have been had Louis left well enough alone. Time in these passages in effect acts as the alternative site of power, a force contrasting to the gaudier theatrical power of the king. Wanting both to defy Innocent XI and to crush Calvinism, Louis "considered these two enterprizes as productive of that lustre of glory, of which he was in all things fond even to idolatry" (2:213). As exceptional as Louis XIV is, he fails to recognize his own agenda and submit it to an alternative form of enlightened agency, that of mere passing time.

In the English translation of *Essai sur les mœurs et l'esprit des nations*, titled *An Essay on Universal History, the Manners, and Spirit of Nations* (1759), the term *insensibly* continues to infiltrate Voltaire's vocabulary, now traceable to Nugent's predilection for it, though often with a license from his original. In a chapter on medieval France and England, the translation of the *Essay* reads, "After such a long series of calamities, after the elements and human passions had conspired to desolate the earth, it is surprising that Europe should be still in so flourishing a condition. The only resource of the human species was in a few towns, which were despised by the great sovereigns. Commerce and industry has insensibly [*sourdement*] repaired the mischief done by those princes [Edward III of England and Philip VI of France]."[34] Here is the Enlightenment story of commerce as the agent and cement of civilization. Voltaire's word *sourdement*, with its connotations of deafness, muffledness, and secrecy, characterizes the improving action of commerce and industry working at the edge, as it were, of human sensation and awareness, in contrast to the volatility of human passions, unnoticed not only by the "great sovereigns" but perhaps also by the people in the "few towns." Again, the saving agency of time is portrayed as unsensed and unknown yet elaborated in the context of sensation, and constitutes a salutary alternative to a different kind of Enlightenment history, the one created by sovereigns and their battles.

But Voltaire does not allude to unfelt time merely to depict diminutions of violent feelings. In a summary chapter titled "A Recapitulation of the Whole of the Foregoing History, with the Point of Light in Which It Ought to be Considered," added to a completed version of the *Essay on Universal History* that incorporates *La siècle de Louis XIV*, he concludes dourly that "all history then, in short, is little else than a long succession of useless cruelties."[35] While some commentators have argued that Voltaire appeals to the concept of moeurs only to prepare the way for a more conventional neoclassical history of Louis XIV's glorious achievements,[36] here Voltaire again invokes moeurs as operating at a deeper, more civilizing level that is more salutary even than Louis's great deeds: "In the midst of the ravages and desolations which we have observed during the space of nine hundred years, we perceive a love for order which secretly animates [anime en secret] human kind, and has prevented its total ruin. This is one of the springs of nature which always recovers its tone; it is this which has formed the code of all nations, and this inspires a veneration for the laws and the ministers of the laws at Tonquin, and in the island of Formosa, the same as at Rome."[37] Here the principle directing history is a love beyond feeling, quiet but persistent. The secret in this context is one kept from conventional history itself, as well as from the ordinary people who do not consciously "love civilization" but whose love of order nonetheless preserves it. Karen O'Brien has astutely written about this and other passages from the *Essai sur les mœurs* (citing the one including *sourdement* quoted above). She notes that Voltaire at times uses the "highly unusual" reflexive verb *se civiliser* "to signify that the civilising process is voluntary and not mechanical."[38] Yet such voluntary improvements also operate secretly, silently, and collectively. Not the result of deliberate action by individuals or even specific groups, this improvement for Voltaire is enacted by "human kind," "the springs of nature," or (as in the earlier passage) "commerce and industry." While not exactly a mechanical enactment of general historical principles, the secret character of the process, a secret even from those who enact it, also makes it something less than fully voluntary or deliberate. To civilize itself, humankind reflexively, collectively, and slowly acts to realize its general nature.

For both Montesquieu and Voltaire, the insensible refers to something more specific than a disparate array of obscure historical causes. It points to a sensitive membrane upon which impersonal time imprints patterns of human feeling. These patterns, manners, quietly mediate between temporal passage and vividly conscious human motives and sentiments in history. In both writers, "nature"—whether that of a particular people or human nature in general—expresses an affect especially intimate, even identified with this passage. Moeurs mediate for Montesquieu between custom and law, linking them and aligning the French spirit with an emerging and regular legal code. In Voltaire, moeurs provide a mode of European self-civilization that is both secret and affectively deep, a corrective and also an accompaniment to the violent brilliancy of enlightened rule. Though the insensible in each historian is antithetical to rationalization and self-awareness, they consistently use it to gesture to something that historical enlightenment requires to realize itself.

2. The Insensible Revolution and Scottish Historiography

The classic texts of Scottish Enlightenment history reflect and at times contest the thinking about temporal processes found in the great midcentury French efforts to discern history's deep causes from a magisterial perspective. The mode of Montesquieu helped bring notions especially associated with Scottish attempts to master history into being. He was, for instance, an inspiration (with Lord Kames) for John Dalrymple's *Essay towards a General History of Feudal Property in Great Britain* (1757), "the first publication in the English language to make use of the four stages theory" (as James Moore puts it)[39]: the contention that human history normally unfolds according to the succession of four dominant modes of subsistence and production—hunter-gatherer, pastoral, agricultural, and commercial—with different political, social, and cultural systems appropriated to each. The turn from neoclassical emphases on great leaders and statecraft to the consideration of more diffuse, structural conditions and change helped give Scottish historiography its "philosophical" flavor.[40] The stages, like moeurs, determine not only the form of social and political life, but also how people whom they affect are able to feel.

Voltaire's formidable historical works were also always seen as a relevant context in which to assess Scottish historiography, and particularly David Hume's *History of England* (1754–62). As Hume acknowledges in a letter to Abbé Jean Bernard le Blanc, "In this Countrey, they call me his Pupil, and think that my History is an Imitation of his Siecle de Louis XIV," though he adds that he had composed the first volumes of his *History* before Voltaire's work had appeared (1751).[41] And while Voltaire's *Essai sur les mœurs et l'esprit des nations* was published as Hume's full *History of England* was nearing completion, Hume requested a copy of it from Gilbert Elliot in 1760, remarking that Voltaire's "general Views are sometimes sound, & always entertaining" (but adding that he is untrustworthy with regard to facts).[42] Hume saw Voltaire's eminence as the historian of "general Views" as something to be acknowledged and perhaps emulated.

The description in Hume's *History* of historical processes as insensible, while nowhere near as frequent as Gibbon's use of the term twenty years later in *The Decline and Fall*, helps him depict the large-scale changes in British attitudes toward liberty, politics, and law that give his work its political bite. In Hume's account, the unfelt plays its quiet but significant role in determining how the "minds of men" collectively undergo gradual changes (and mostly, for him, improvement) of sensibility. Mark Salber Phillips has noted that Hume lacks anything quite like the nineteenth-century notion of "public opinion," to attribute historical agency to masses of people without identifying a precise, directive source or power.[43] The Humean appeal to processes beyond notice suggests something comparable yet distinct. Human consciousness enters history for him not by being materially located in a "public" but instead more secretly and inexpressively as an obscure, collective sentiment.

And without reference to the intentional character of public opinion by which a public "wants" or "decides," the idiom of the insensible supports the political program of the *History*, which delights in pointing out how good outcomes arise despite the intentions of politicians. An unfelt affect better secures political advances than scheming or patriotic ardor. British liberties do not have their basis, according to Hume, in a long-cherished and passionately defended ancient constitution (a view promoted in anticourt polemics like those published in Viscount Bolingbroke's *Craftsman*) but rather arise from slowly evolving social, legal, and commercial conditions starting around the reign of Henry VII—conditions that make a formalization of British liberty in 1688 possible. Participants in this evolution mostly do not intend such an outcome, and Hume often savors the historical ironies that arise from disparities between immediate purposes and long-term results.[44]

The historical meaning of the insensible in Hume is more focused, however, than the general idea of unintended consequences much discussed in scholarship treating British and particularly Scottish thought in the period.[45] The idiom in the histories of Hume and other Scots tends to portray specifically the emergence of new feeling and capacities to feel. The sensibility of the social collective refines, develops, and effervesces until British society and the individuals it comprises have sensibly changed. Such a depiction of history's affective development solves a particular problem for Hume. It allows him to maintain his view of passion as humanity's prime motivator while preserving his sense that British constitutional freedoms evolved without much influence, as he remarks, "from any fixed passion towards civil liberty."[46]

Chapter IV of this book describes a different pattern, which distinguishes the idiom's function in political economy from that in the writing of Enlightenment history. Both occupy the most vast end of the scale of insensible affects that I have surveyed. But in writing about commerce, the idiom expresses a repeating cycle. Rather disreputable passions—greed, envy, vanity, and others associated with "private vices"—remain consistent and unchanging but are also the very things that eventually produce what Adam Smith and Bernard Mandeville before him call "public happiness." As we shall see, that public feeling is unfelt in some profound sense by those whose private feelings produce and maintain it. The unintended consequences celebrated in political economy result from constant passions, grounded in "human nature," while the insensible in Scottish historiography points to transformations in human feeling itself. The former is cyclical, the latter linear.

Early in the history of publication of Hume's work, in the first of the Stuart volumes (volume 1 of what he then called *The History of Great Britain*, 1754), he narrates one such crucial alteration in human sentiments. This is also a large statement that introduces his conception of what we might now call the force of enlightenment in history. Beyond merely effecting a recovery or renaissance of ancient learning by men of letters, this force triumphs by exceeding the confines of a few inspired, distinguished minds. At the turn of the seventeenth century, a generalized, unfelt, but orderly alteration of sensibility brings forth the new epoch:

> About this period, the minds of men, throughout Europe, especially in England, seem to have undergone a general, but insensible revolution. Though letters had been revived in the preceding age, they were chiefly cultivated by those sedentary professions; nor had they, till now, begun to spread themselves, in any degree, among men of the world. Arts, both mechanical and liberal, were every day receiving great improvements. Navigation had extended itself over the whole globe. Travelling was secure and agreeable. And the general system of politics, in Europe, was become more enlarged and comprehensive.[47]

Viewing change as insensible again tends to increase its power by obviating the intentions of those it affects. The passage's style, its odd tenses and distribution of agency, attenuates the power of "minds of men" to direct or even recognize the revolution they promote. The minds do not simply undergo the change during a particular period but "seem to have undergone" it already by the time it may be noticed by historical narrative. Passives fill the passage, and the series of abstract entities (letters, arts, navigation, traveling, the general system of politics) either perform or receive the effects of the revolution without much indication of conscious direction or even awareness of the change by individuals. Though minds change, they do so "in general," not as the result of being "cultivated" deliberately by a few.

It is not difficult, moreover, to hear a note of sympathetic identification in Hume's account. His own career represents an extension of the revolution begun in the early seventeenth century. He has played his own part in such a process by abandoning the abstruse, dense argumentation of the *Treatise of Human Nature* for the more elegant, polished style of his successive volumes of essays and the *History* itself—a miniature reenactment of learning's expansion from the "sedentary professions" to "men of the world" in the seventeenth century.[48] Of course, Hume made such choices deliberately, and he also consciously strives in the *History of England* to rise above the forces of history by transcending the partisanship of previous historians. Yet he also both theoretically and practically embraces the idea that individual literary talent, including his own, emerges from antecedent, collective circumstances—as when he declares in "Of the Rise and Progress of the Arts and Sciences" that individuals' "spirit and genius must be antecedently diffused throughout the people among whom they arise, in order to produce, form, and cultivate, from their earliest infancy, the taste and judgment of those eminent writers";[49] and when he celebrates the flourishing of Scottish genius, not just his own, in his time. The picture of multifarious forces insensibly creating conditions under which literary talent may arise is one in which he assuredly placed and recognized himself.

These conditions, moreover, are ones of heightened and refined sentiment: in short, "spirit." Hume continues,

> In consequence of this universal fermentation, the ideas of men enlarged themselves on all sides; and the several constituent parts of the gothic governments, which seem to have lain long unactive, began, every where, to operate and encroach on each other. On the continent, where the necessity of discipline had begotten standing armies, the princes commonly established an unlimited authority, and overpowered, by force or intrigue, the liberties of the people. In England, the love of freedom, which, unless checked, flourishes extremely in all liberal natures, acquired

new force, and was regulated by more enlarged views, suitably to that cultivated understanding, which became, every day, more common, among men of birth and education. (5:18)

The "universal fermentation" carries a specific metaphorical weight in Hume: it is a process affecting organic matter, at once a physical, metabolic action and an excitement of the passions. (Hume had used the figure of fermentation to describe cultural liveliness in an essay published two years before, "Of Luxury,"[50] in which he noted that achievement in the mechanical arts correlates to that in the liberal arts.) This conjunction of physical and passionate agitation governs the rhetoric of the passage, in which ideas are "enlarged," the constituents of governments "operate and encroach," and the love of freedom "acquire[s] new force" like a spherical body rolling down a slope.

As in the philosophical discussions treated in chapter I, then, Hume here passes from a quasi-physical force to a mental or psychological one by means of the insensible. The transaction partakes of both unfeeling and feeling as a way to transform one into the other. And the sensitivity that grows out of the insensible is something like liveliness itself. Hume notes that one advantage that men of the world have, after all, over those in sedentary professions is their superior capacity to feel and disseminate feeling: "A familiar acquaintance with the precious remains of antiquity excited in every generous breast a passion for a limited constitution, and begat an emulation of those manly virtues, which the Greek and Roman authors, by such animating examples, as well as pathetic expressions, recommend to us" (5:18–19). Hume's characteristic appreciation of the power of strong feeling (with its attendant dangers, as we will find in the volume's subsequent accounts of James I's and Charles I's fortunes) takes over the passage, which had first dwelled on passives and obscure forces. (The metaphors turn organic at a higher level than fermentation, too, as the acquaintance with ancient sources "begat" emulation.) Now the enthusiastic reading of "animating examples" from the past projects socially transforming sentiments into the present.

A similar account of epochal but unplanned and nonlocalized change comes at the beginning of the Tudor volumes, in his summing up of the reign of Henry VII: "Thus a general revolution was made in human affairs throughout this part of the world; and men attained that situation with regard to commerce, arts, sciences, government, police, and cultivation, in which they have ever since persevered."[51] Again, change comes as a matter of refined sensibility, not deliberate policy, and attains social substantiality not so much by positive law as by manners, for Hume as for his French counterparts. That term plays, of course, a prominent role throughout *The History of England*, both in the main text and in the appendixes of each volume that treat, as he puts it in the James I volume, "government, manners, finances, arms, trade, learning."[52] In the third appendix of the second Tudor volume, he will remark, "the manners of the age were a general cause, which operated during this whole period" (4:519). In this case, manners help reduce the barons' and enhance the crown's power. Hume also uses manners to sound a historical note in his philosophical essays, as in "Of the Standard of Taste," when he acknowledges how "the particular manners and opinions of our age and country" must affect even our most evenhanded judgments.[53]

A glimpse into the background of Hume's thinking about manners is offered in his correspondence of the 1730s, at the very start of his literary career, to his friend Michael Ramsay. Hume was already thinking about history; in an undated letter to Ramsay from that period, he had requested a loan of "the Carrier Pelisson's History, & the last volume of Rapin."[54] A 1734 letter, posted from Rheims where he spent his French sojourn and undertook a course of study leading to his composition of the *Treatise of Human Nature*,[55] offers the young Hume's insight not just into French manners but also into how manners in general work:

> After all it must be confest, that the little Niceties of the French Behaviour, tho' troublesome & impertinent, yet serve to polish the ordinary Kind of People & prevent Rudeness & Brutality. For in the same manner, as Soldiers are found to become more couragious in learning to hold their Musquets within half an Inch of a place appointed; & your Devotees feel their Devotion encrease by the Observance of trivial Superstitions, as Sprinkling, Kneeling, Crossing &c, so men insensibly soften towards each other in the Practice of these Ceremonies. The Mind pleases itself by the Progress it makes in such Trifles, & while it is so supported makes an easy Transition to something more material: And I verily believe, that tis for this reason you scarce ever meet with a Clown, or an ill bred man in France.[56]

The entirely physical nature of the behavioral "Trifles" provides the best way to initiate mental and sentimental improvement in individuals. The placement of the musket "within half an Inch" of an appointed spot, the "Sprinkling, Kneeling, Crossing" that constitute religious observance begin as trivial fixations as "the Mind pleases itself" in mastering them, but they come to produce an "easy transition" to more significant feelings of courage or devotion. When it comes to politeness, such practices "insensibly soften" the social collective—in part, it seems, because of their origination in unmeaning bodily behavior. Hume thus notes early on the vital role played by the insensible in both constituting a nation's moeurs and improving individuals' sentiments. And again, it is not hard to recognize Hume's amused implication of himself in such acculturation, as he finds himself polished insensibly through his experience of French society.

The decisive role of the dyad of feeling and unfeeling in Hume's historical enterprise emerges by way of contrast to one of his work's main competitors, Catharine Macaulay's republican, eight-volume *History of England from the Ascension of James I to that of the Brunswick Line* (later changed to *from the Ascension of James I to the Revolution*), some twenty years in the making (1763–83). Like other British historians after midcentury, Macaulay turns her attention to the role of moeurs in history, and especially their support of the English embrace of liberty and virtue in the seventeenth century, as when she remarks in volume 1 that "the revival of letters co-operated" with the shining example of the Dutch "to effect an alteration in the modes of thinking of the English nation."[57] She is also alert to the rise of seventeenth-century parliamentary power as an unintended consequence of a long history of royal scheming, including "the crafty policy of the First Henry of the Tudor line."[58] These features mark Macaulay's *History* as an Enlightenment project, in these respects reflecting the historiographical spirit of her time.

But her work differs from Hume's in its tendency to de-emphasize affect as a primary engine of history. As Karen O'Brien has stressed, Macaulay promotes an "ideal of individual rationality, responsibility and patriotism."[59] As such an emphasis leaves little place for recognizing the historical efficacy of mass feeling, it does likewise for mass unfeeling. The idea of an "insensible revolution" could not appeal to Macaulay's sense of active republican virtue. Whatever sparse appearances of such idioms there are in her work tend to mark a falling away from liberty rather than a secret support of it.[60] In contrast to "almost insensible" historical factors underscored by other historians to depict political and social advancement, she employs an entirely different rhetoric of temporality—noting, for instance, that "the Commons almost suddenly roused to a spirit of free enquiry and high independence, and opposed, with unremitting ardor, that civil and ecclesiastical power to which they had hitherto paid an almost-implicit obedience."[61] As reason instead of affect determines historical progress for Macaulay, the slowness of the almost insensible gives way to an "almost suddenly roused" neo-Roman republican virtue.

A body of work more aligned with Hume's sentimental history is that of William Robertson, including *The History of Scotland* (1759), *The History of the Reign of Emperor Charles V* (1769), and *The History of America* (1777). These express his largest ambitions in historical explanation by identifying processes not noticed by historical agents, yet intimately linked to sentiment. His *View* of the Progress of Society in Europe, from the Subversion of the Roman Empire, to the Beginning of the Sixteenth Century*, the first volume of *The History of the Reign of Emperor Charles V*, even more amply than Hume attests to a devotion to the idea of sentimental progress, ultimately reliant on the unfelt, while acknowledging both Hume's influence and Montesquieu's. Robertson praises the latter in typical terms as one who sees deep into hidden causes, singling out his "industry in tracing all the circumstances of ancient and obscure institutions, and sagacity in penetrating into the causes and principles which contributed to establish them."[62] A similar aliveness to the interaction between deep causes and the otherwise obscure or insignificant events and circumstances that express them animates Robertson's work as a historian.

Something like that interaction appears in an anecdote in his first major work, *The History of Scotland*, a text not usually seen as a work of true conjectural history (unlike his *View of the Progress of Society in Europe*). An attention to Scottish manners helps Robertson explain what would otherwise seem an event touched off by the vagaries of passion. The glue attaching accident to the historically meaningful is, again, manners. During the so-called War of the Rough Wooing, he remarks that the Scots, "naturally an irascible and high-spirited people . . . seconded the French in their military operations with the utmost coldness, and this secret disgust grew insensibly to a degree of indignation that could hardly be restrained; and on occasion of a very slight accident, broke out with fatal violence"—a quarrel between a French solider and "a citizen of Edinburgh."[63] In this story it is not exactly Scottish manners—their irascibility and high spirits—that are unnoticed. Nor, of course, are the events in it hidden from view, the "very slight accident" and the subsequently "fatal violence." What is insensible is the way in which Scottish moeurs work beneath the surface, finally translating into a historical incident, which to superficial observers might seem merely accidental or random. Episodes like this demonstrate how terms like *insensible* allow historians to weave nonserial into serial modes of explanation: a description of what Scots are like allows a narration of events. Here the "secret disgust," with its basis in the nation's steady irascibility and spirit, operates slowly and collectively, throughout the social body, and creates a convergence of a historical situation with Scottishness, embodied and acted on at a decisive moment.

In his *View of the Progress of Society in Europe* Robertson presents a bigger, more cosmopolitan picture,[64] in which the insensible is yet more powerfully connected to the feelings required for enlightenment to emerge. In that volume he consistently turns to the idiom to depict the crucial processes that make the progress indicated by the title possible. Robertson writes of the rise of cities as a stimulation to the people's dormant sensibilities, "The acquisition of liberty made such a happy change in the condition of all the members of communities, as roused them from that stupidity and inaction into which they had been sunk by the wretchedness of their former state" (35–36).[65] Near the paragraph's conclusion, he remarks that "all became sensible" of the benefits of a well-regulated society, but at the climax, all this spirit and sensibility becomes diffuse: "laws and subordination, as well as polished manners, took their rise in cities, and diffused themselves insensibly through the rest of society" (36). For sentiment to create civilizational progress, it must be insensibly collectivized.

On this passage Daniele Francesconi has remarked that "the 'silent or insensible revolution' in the manners, a phrase used also by Hume, was a keyword in the eighteenth-century language of the unintended consequences."[66] But again it is worth stressing the special relation between the refinement of manners—the components of heightened social feeling—and the insensible. Unlike a range of other unintended consequences, sentiment is especially susceptible to, or stands especially in need of, affective forces beyond feeling. Certainly it can work the other way too: feelings may also coarsen or be corrupted insensibly. But the insensible recurs as a conduit through which sensibility may enhance its historical role, a way to generalize the effect of enhanced feeling, making it more than the experience of a few enlightened minds.

Later passages in the *View of the Progress of Society in Europe* extend this use of *insensible* to characterize a yet more diffused sociability among European nations. The term proves vital to Robertson's version of the Voltairean (or Humean) *thèse royale*, the idea that enhanced royal power and centralization of authority promote progressive political developments, yet it involves several monarchs across the continent, not just one. The benefits of a balance of power in Europe could for a long time be foreseen by its kings—they were not stupid—but they lacked the authority over "civil government" (90) that they needed to exert themselves on its behalf. A range of factors increased crown authority in general (France's recovery of its territory from England, the subsequent creation of standing armies, etc.) by putting conditions favorable to it in place: "But during the course of the fifteenth century, various events happened, which, by giving Princes more entire command of the force in their respective dominions, rendered their operations more vigorous and extensive. In consequence of this, the affairs of different kingdoms becoming more frequently as well as more intimately connected, they were gradually accustomed to act in concert and confederacy, and were insensibly prepared for forming a system of policy, in order to establish or to preserve such a balance of power as was most consistent with the general security" (90).

The passive language ("various events happened") indicates that greater monarchical power, long desired by "Princes," ultimately depends on factors beyond their control. Further, the deliberate policy of the balance of power itself follows princes' gradually increasing tendency to accustom themselves to it. Power and policy lag behind circumstance and custom in the construction of a European balance crucial to modern civilization. A few pages later, Robertson will remark on how various royal marriages, wars in Italy, military innovations, and so on, none deliberately aimed at a balance of power, nonetheless produce it: "These engaged them in such a series of enterprizes and negociations, that the affairs of all the considerable nations in Europe came to be insensibly interwoven with each other; and a great political system was gradually formed, which grew to be an object of universal attention" (104). Though Robertson will at times remark that the notion of balance among European nations indeed deliberately guided participants in the midst of this process,[67] he is attracted to the idea that the system arose insensibly and was attended to *as* a system and a policy only after it was established.

The civilizational function of the unfelt extends, in Robertson's *History of America*, to a context and a set of factors and forces unprecedented in Eurocentric historiography. The right kind of unfeeling discreetly distinguishes European tribes, no matter how "barbaric" or "rude" they are, from the peoples of North America, who are insensible in the wrong way. In the early pages Robertson describes the formation, over centuries, of conditions leading to Europeans' desire to explore the world: with "the rude tribes which settled there [in the western provinces of the Roman Empire], acquiring insensibly some idea of regular government, and some relish for the functions and comforts of civil life, Europe began to awake from its torpid and unactive state."[68] Again the causal power of the unfelt tends to heighten a refined capacity to "relish."

In contrast, the North American tribes (as in Smith's *Theory of Moral Sentiments*, discussed in chapter 1) remain trapped in a bad, immobilizing insensibility—a cold insusceptibility—that makes them both brave and uncivilized. The Iroquois "appear to be not only insensible of pain, but to court it," Robertson writes, but this "magnanimity . . . instead of exciting admiration, or calling forth sympathy, exasperates the fierce spirits of their torturers to fresh acts of cruelty."[69] The contrast demonstrates the difference between an insensible process that civilizes and enlightens and the insensibility that simply blocks civilization. The idiom's gestural blankness again allows it to play a role in solving historiographical problems: one kind of unfeeling advances, another retards the accession to civil life.

The insensible is not always applied, however, as a finishing element of triumphalist pictures of European cultural advancement. As a blank, it can be used to present deviations from the usual historical script. While historiography of the period generally strikes an optimistic note, especially when treating the transition from feudalism to the modern age, the unfelt at times provides an opening to less predictable or complacent narrative currents. For instance, in *An Essay on the History of Civil Society* (1767), Adam Ferguson, in keeping with his work's less sanguine views of progress, remarks, "MANKIND, when they degenerate, and tend to their ruin, as well as when they improve, and gain real advantages, frequently proceed by slow, and almost insensible, steps. If, during ages of activity and vigour, they fill up the measure of national greatness to a height which no human wisdom could at a distance foresee; they actually incur, in ages of relaxation and weakness, many evils which their fears did not suggest, and which, perhaps, they had thought far removed by the tide of success and prosperity."[70]

Here, too, the insensible addresses the transformations in feeling wrought by unfeeling—either those feelings fostered by "activity and vigour" or those by "relaxation and weakness." In each case, the insensible and the unforeseeable are identified, though the vigor seems the unforeseen product of progress, and relaxation the unnoticed cause of degeneration. And in both, the character of the feeling carries with it a kind of obliviousness to its own historical tendency. While historians use the unfelt to narrate a mysterious process whereby civilization advances affectively in ways the exceed the immediate feelings of individual agents, its blankness allows them also to narrate collective failures of enlightenment.

3. Gibbon in History

The device of the insensible has uniquely dramatic consequences for Edward Gibbon's style of history writing, and his thinking about history as well. He uses it more than any other writer I discuss in this book and is the only one whose predilection for it has been widely noted. Frank E. Manuel remarks, "the idea that events happen 'insensibly' . . . became a tick [sic] in the later volumes of *The Decline and Fall*."[71] But the term crops up not just in the later volumes of that work; it appears from Gibbon's early piece in French, the *Essai sur l'étude de la littérature* (1761), as "insensiblement,"[72] through every volume of *The Decline and Fall*, to his posthumously published memoirs (1796). Accompanying the common understanding of Gibbon's usage as a tic, an automatic stylistic mannerism, is the frequent attribution of a particular historiographical meaning to the word—a meaning, even, of what it means to be a historian. Leo Braudy remarks, "Throughout the *Decline and Fall* Gibbon's favorite adverb for the growth of causes is 'insensibly.' Both accident and causes unrecognized by the actors are a great part of the movement of events."[73] Similarly, David P. Jordan notes, "Gibbon frequently speaks of 'insensible' developments. What he means by this is that the development was 'insensible' to contemporaries"[74]—a definition David Womersley endorses when he claims the term signifies that a historical process (such as decline) "is visible only from the standpoint of the present."[75] This interpretation emphasizes the present and masterful perspective of Gibbon himself, the philosophical or conjectural historian, who has attained insight into the slow, meaningful processes that the "actors" or "contemporaries" he writes about cannot have.

Thinking of Gibbon's usage as both an assertion of mastery and a stylistic tic—the very opposite of self-control, recurrent within one of the most fully achieved styles in English—suggests something paradoxical about its status in his writing and thought. He means it, even as it often seems mechanical and unreflective. He is subject to it as he uses it. Earlier versions of this double movement have already appeared in this book. In chapter I, I described how Eliza Haywood's insights into the "imperceptible Degrees" by which others' hearts are mastered arise from her own insensibly acquired knowledge. And it was easy enough in the present chapter to see how Hume extends the "insensible revolution" in "the minds of men" that began in the seventeenth century to himself, which enables him to narrate that very historical phenomenon. In such cases, however, this immersion in the processes of refinement produces a kind of crowning insight into both the processes and the self. Gibbon's addiction to the idea of the unfelt at times results, however, in something more intimate and extensive. He sometimes subjects not only himself but also his judgment, even as it is exercised, to the insensible movements of which history consists. This pushes the Enlightenment use of the idiom to its limit.

Instead of applying the term only to historical actors immersed in incomprehensible processes, Gibbon also uses it autobiographically. In his memoirs it depicts important changes in his personal life. Often it signifies the recession of intense feeling into something less, as when he describes his father's grief at the death of his mother, when Gibbon himself was nine years old: "The storm of passion insensibly subsided into calmer melancholy."[76] (This again raises the question, Insensibly to whom? Gibbon senior, or junior, or both?) The term also characterizes his recovery from own disappointment at his break, at his father's insistence, with Suzanne Curchod: "I sighed as a lover, I obeyed as a son; my wound was insensibly healed by time, absence, and the habits of a new life."[77] But the notion works by addition as well as by diminution—for instance, in his crucial account of his conversion to Roman Catholicism as a young man. That conversion, he explains, was precipitated by reading the *Free Inquiry into the Miraculous Powers* (1749) by Conyers Middleton—though it has been argued this was unlikely and represents his memoirs' retrospective revision of events.[78] In any case, Gibbon means the anecdote in the memoirs to depict a crucial encounter of his young self with historical thinking.

The process of thought said to be set in motion by Middleton leads Gibbon to recognize, or forge, a link between his belief as a young man in the miracles performed in the fourth and fifth centuries and his acceptance of innovations in Christian doctrine and ritual in that time: "The marvellous tales which are so boldly attested by the Basils and Chrysostoms, the Austins and Jeroms, compelled me to embrace the superior merits of celibacy, the institution of the monastic life, the use of the sign of the cross, of holy oil, and even of images, the invocation of saints, the worship of relics, the rudiments of purgatory in prayers for the dead, and the tremendous mystery of the sacrifice of the body and blood of Christ, which insensibly swelled into the prodigy of transubstantiation."[79] That is, the compelling character of the miracles leads him to embrace the church's new teachings at the time in which they happened. As we shall see, this passage echoes (and if trusted as memory, anticipates) a crucial one in volume 1 of *The Decline and Fall*, which also invokes Middleton and the progress of the belief in miracles. And there as well as here, the term *insensibly* ambiguously connects the mind of the (here, young) historian and the historical process itself. Plainly the primary sense of the passage is that young Gibbon's own embrace of the "tremendous mystery of the sacrifice" swells insensibly into his personal belief in transubstantiation. But the omission of personal pronouns suggests how his own progress of belief mimics what is, after all, a historical process, whereby the early church's respect for Christ's sacrifice swells into belief in a ritual miracle. Here Gibbon indicates that the insensible movement of his own mind recapitulates that of history of itself.

A slightly different dynamic animates a more direct description in the memoirs of his initiation into history. Here he dramatizes as insensible not his succumbing to processes that are usually the conjectural historian's object of analysis, but rather his own budding erudition and fascination with ancient sources. (Arnaldo Momigliano remarks in a classic essay that the essence of Gibbon's achievement lay in his "blending in himself the philosopher and the antiquarian."[80]) It is apparently important to Gibbon to depict his embarkation on his great work as not fully conscious:

> As soon as I was released from the fruitless task of the Swiss revolutions, (1768,) I began gradually to advance from the wish to the hope, from the hope to the design, from the design to the execution, of my historical work, of whose limits and extent I had yet a very inadequate notion. The Classics, as low as Tacitus, the younger Pliny, and Juvenal, were my old and familiar companions. I insensibly plunged into the ocean of the Augustan history; and in the descending series I investigated, with my pen almost always in my hand, the original records, both Greek and Latin, from Dion Cassius to Ammianus Marcellinus, from the reign of Trajan to the last age of the Western Cæsars.[81]

Here "the Augustan history" is writing in the archive. The insensible plunge into "original records" seems to mimic the gradualness of his formation of the ambition to write *The Decline and Fall*, though they are not the same process. Gibbon describes the divided affect of his researches, unnoticed or perhaps even benumbing on the one hand, yet on the other a vividly conscious, painstaking investigation (his pen is almost always in his hand) inspired, we next read, by the "inimitable accuracy" of the pious Jansenist *érudit* Louis-Sébastien Le Nain de Tillemont.[82] The insensible character of the plunge into the oceanic archive expresses a kind of connection with the material itself, the slow descent into an ever deeper engagement with it. Gibbon's point is not that the material is mysterious or opaque; his line-by-line reading of the written records is vivid, detailed, and accurate. Rather, his engagement with the task is what develops insensibly. The part of Gibbon that is insensible blends with the objective condition of the records, which his accurate erudition brings into the light of consciousness.

Gibbon invokes the term throughout *The Decline and Fall*, often in just the manner commentators have noticed. It allows him to differentiate his enlightened sense of the past's meaning from those immersed in it. But it works in more subtly revealing ways too. In a passage from chapter 15 on the belief in miracles that finds an echo in the one from his memoirs quoted above, Gibbon again ties his acquisition of historical insight to the insensible:

> From the first of the fathers to the last of the popes, a succession of bishops, of saints, of martyrs, and of miracles, is continued without interruption, and the progress of superstition was so gradual and almost imperceptible, that we know not in what particular link we should break the chain of tradition. Every age bears testimony to the wonderful events by which it was distinguished, and its testimony appears no less weighty and respectable than that of the preceding generation, till we are insensibly led on to accuse our own inconsistency, if in the eighth or in the twelfth century we deny to the venerable Bede, or to the holy Bernard, the same degree of confidence which, in the second century, we had so liberally granted to Justin or to Irenæus.[83]

Gibbon's "almost imperceptible" and "insensibly" could at one level seem to set up an anti-Christian irony. Since we cannot put our finger on the moment miracles can be shown to have ceased, and "the progress of superstition" has tainted the tradition of miraculous relations, are we not enjoined to disbelieve even the earliest "miracles of the primitive church," as Middleton urges in his *Free Inquiry* (referred to in Gibbon's footnotes)?

But while we may simply wish to read such moments in *The Decline and Fall* as implicitly but confidently scoffing at miracles,[84] the passage contains a deeper comment on the relation of the historian's mind to history. It links a slow historical process, "the progress of superstition" that is "almost imperceptible," with the historian's "insensibly" gained power to "accuse [his] own inconsistency" in respect to believing in miracles of different eras. Note that he does not assert that "we are insensibly led into inconsistency"—from which we must be rescued by acute, enlightened scrutiny. Rather, he observes that "we are insensibly led to *accuse* our own inconsistency." Critical insight arrives insensibly. This reverses what most commentators say about Gibbon's use of the word. Here it is not a way to contrast the blindness to causes of historical agents with the vital insight of the present historian. It rather aligns his own gradual arrival at an understanding of history with the "imperceptible" processes of history itself.

This transaction, by the way, does not quite discredit miracles. It merely comes to recognize the inconsistencies that plague a mind interested both in beliefs and in their historical evolution—an interest that Gibbon here has in common with his earlier self, struggling with his conversion to Catholicism. The evolution of insight now reaches a point at which it seems to the historian that he must believe in all miracles or none. As a product of an insensible process, such an insight does not commit him to take the next step in either direction. The term *insensibly* therefore helps Gibbon preserve the kind of skepticism or suspension of belief that J. G. A. Pocock's monumental work on him has insisted on, committing Gibbon neither to a dogmatic rejection of religion nor to an affirmation of it. This suspension lies deep within Gibbon's understanding of historical process, which is portrayed in these instances as a nonconscious evolution of attitudes. Here, as in the passage in his memoirs about the archival ocean, Gibbon seems concerned more to align himself with this nonconsciousness of "slow degrees" than to dissipate historical obscurity with the enlightenment of modern criticism.

To some extent, this account of Gibbon and the insensible resembles what Ruth Mack concludes in her book *Literary Historicity* (2009), which also reflects on the words *insensibly* and *sensibly* as clues to the deep meaning of Gibbon's writing of history. She argues that in *The Decline and Fall*, Gibbon endows the empire, or "the past," or "history" itself, with both sensibility and insensibility to "insist . . . on historical change and causation as matters of sensation."[85] Mack sees the insensible in Gibbon's prose as especially gesturing to our only dim ability to intimate the empire as a set of past experiences. This, for Mack, evokes what the philosopher of history F. R. Ankersmit calls "sublime historical experience"[86]: the past or history comprises (in Ankersmit's words) "fleeting sets of sensations, moods, and feelings . . . sets of experience without there being a *subject* of experience."[87] This aspect of the past is sublime because it exceeds the limitations of our present historical perspective even while stimulating it. Mack concludes, "in Gibbon what we find is a suspicion that we cannot simply assimilate the past, especially when written about in the modern way that history demands: its experience will forever appear both like ours and apart from it."[88]

As an account of Gibbon's references to the insensible, however, this seems to me both too dramatic and too conventional in its taking such terms to refer to some past, lost object, however obscure or desubjectified. It further presumes that he applies this language to past experience to distinguish it from a temporal experience "like ours." But the examples from his memoirs and *The Decline and Fall* show that the insensible unites Gibbon with the movements of history rather than separates him from them. The idiom evokes not a sublime encounter with otherness but the common, intensely gradual evolution of the affective state, as *affectus*, of everyone. It happens all the time. As an adverb, *insensibly* does not allude to some thing, some elusive force or set of experiences, that exists or existed but cannot now be sensed. Rather, it signifies bare process, an unnoticed temporal passage. It does not, for Gibbon, gesture to a "body or landmass of feeling" or a barely intimated pastness "without a transcendental subject" (as Mack, following Ankersmit, asserts).[89] The adverb does not point to an object at all: not "experience," nor "the past," nor "history itself" (whatever that may mean). Again, it designates a *how*, not a *what*. And as such, it is no more "other" than it is a creature of any subject. In recognizing his own immersion in insensible processes, even when he is "insensibly led on to accuse [his] own inconsistency"—that is, even at the dawning of critical insight—Gibbon at once owns the insensible and finds himself mimicking the deindividuating processes moving through history.

Finally, then, it makes sense to see *insensibly*, especially as used to characterize his own engagement with the process of writing history, as of a piece with Gibbon's skepticism, since it does not posit some obscure experiential substrate, but rather only gestures to the unknowing or unfeeling effect of time's gradualness. Here, too, a distinction between the insensible in Gibbon and the ideas of affect theorists today emerges. As much as writers such as Brian Massumi insist that affect involves process, they still consistently refer to its physical reality, however nonconscious, in the autonomic body, the nerves, the flesh, and so on. But Gibbon refrains from espousing a doctrine of materialism or monism, from centering insensible experience on some thoroughgoing commitment to the physical body, or from dogmatically denying the existence of spiritual substance.

The difference appears in Gibbon's attitudes toward a figure influential in his own time, Baruch Spinoza, whose monism and panpsychism Gilles Deleuze and his followers have taken as a model. Jonathan Israel has claimed that the English had "a pervasive, even at times obsessive, preoccupation with Spinoza,"[90] at least into the early part of the eighteenth century. For Gibbon, however, the influence seems slight and largely negative, though his imputed atheism led some to accuse him of Spinozism.[91] A direct reference comes once in Gibbon's own works,[92] in his anonymously published tussle with Warburton, *Critical Observations on the Sixth Book of the Aeneid* (1770). He discusses lines in book 6 of Virgil's poem that edge near pantheism: "Principio cælum, ac terras, camposque liquentes, / Lucentemque globum Lunæ, Titaniaque astra / Spiritus intus alit, totemque infusa per artus / Mens agitat molem, & magno se corpore miscet" (First, a spirit within them nourishes the sky and earth, the watery plains, the shining orb of the moon, and Titan's star, and Mind, flowing through matter, vivifies the whole mass, and mingles with its vast frame).[93] Gibbon comments, "the mind which is INFUSED [here he includes a footnote citing a passage in Cicero's *De Natura Deorum*] into the several parts of Matter, and which MINGLES ITSELF with the mighty mass, scarce retains any Property of a Spiritual Substance; and bears too near an affinity to the Principles, which the impious Spinoza revived rather than invented."[94]

The Spinozan panpsychism that still resonates with today's writers about affect, as they discover modes of sentience or cognition distributed throughout the material world, may seem to some readers used to distrusting any indignation from Gibbon as to the "impious" to be only ironically rejected here. He continues, however, commenting on the Virgilian lines: "I am not insensible, that we should be slow to suspect, and still slower to condemn. The poverty of human language, and the obscurity of human ideas, makes [sic] it difficult to speak worthily of THE GREAT FIRST CAUSE."[95] This comment sounds a doubt of *any* attempt to comment definitively on the nature of the deity and the universe: "the Materialist's System" for Gibbon is no less dubious than any positive piety.[96] As Pocock contends in his effort to taxonomize "the Enlightenments of Edward Gibbon," Gibbon's skepticism consistently distances him from the dogmatism of Spinozistic assertions of "a pantheism in which creator and creation, mind and matter, were one because the mind was part of what it perceived and could be considered the universe grown conscious of itself."[97] Pocock recognizes that Gibbon, and Hume before him, "were sceptics; and in them the Enlightenment which tried to set limits to the human mind confronted the Enlightenment which made the mind the object of its own self-worship."[98] This skepticism finally distinguishes Gibbon's attachment to the insensible from the aims pursued by Spinoza's heirs in affect theory.

The use of *insensibly* for Gibbon, as for other writers in the period, often assumes such an antidogmatic task. It refers to time's opacity rather than to any positive attempt to characterize the nature of reality or turn toward the otherness conjured by the thought of unmediated historical experience. Its lack of theoretical elaboration in Gibbon, as in other writers, suggests that it is not some entity to be postulated, but rather an unfeeling built into the way time unfolds. In showing that history affects those subject to it in ways they cannot feel, Gibbon joins other historians discussed in this chapter who gesture to the pervasiveness of the unfelt to suggest the elusiveness of causes and effects. Such gestures at times confirm, in Gibbon and others, the historian's powers of penetration.

But the idiom also provides Gibbon occasion to suggest how even his own understanding evolves with an insensible passage of time. At some moments he goes beyond even the skeptical historian Hume, himself always happy enough to view his own polite and learned perspective as a product of custom and historical circumstance. Gibbon, in finding himself "insensibly led on to accuse our own inconsistency" while assessing testimony from the past, more resembles Hume the epistemologist, as discussed in chapter I of this book, who relates how he "insensibly discover'd a new relation betwixt cause and effect" as he reflected on other matters. Gibbon's approach to "the progress of superstition" likewise comes insensibly to a new idea, but in him the idea is self-critical, as the enlightened scholar puts his own enlightenment in question without providing or even strongly intimating a solution to his problem. Critical acuity here reaches its height when it advances unawares to the limit of its powers.

4. The Embrace of Unfeeling

If Gibbon's submission of his judgment to insensible processes leads him to a terminal point in the idiom's use in Enlightenment historiography, the same vocabulary allows a figure at the century's close to take one small step beyond it. Edmund Burke in his late writings on the French Revolution more positively than most writers discussed in this book accepts the near paradoxical linkage between feeling and unfeeling. He rises to a pitch of sentiment in portraying the unsensed way in which cherished social forms have come into being. Viewing Burke as a sentimental writer, especially about the past and its traditions, has been a feature of the critical response to his writing from the beginning. Catharine Macaulay in her pamphlet attack (1790) on Burke's *Reflections on the Revolution in France* refers to the *"methodized sentimental barbarism"* of chivalry that has led Burke astray.[99] But among other functions, the insensible helps Burke differentiate his own fervor from the "eager and passionate enthusiasm" animating the English radicals.[100] His espousal of the idiom suggests a new sense in which he may be seen as an anti-Enlightenment figure, beyond the commonly recognized, more pronounced one, as a critic of revolutionaries' assertions of rational and abstract ideals of rights and liberty. Instead of quietly gesturing to the unfelt to underwrite an enlightened theory of history, of the progress of politeness or the four stages, he more fully embraces it and succumbs to its embrace.

Though he published no work of history, strictly speaking, in his lifetime, a particular understanding of English constitutional development permeates Burke's political writings. Lord Acton declared Burke "the most historically minded of English statesmen."[101] Burke's unfinished but substantial fragment *An Essay Towards an Abridgment of the English History* (1757, running to some ninety thousand words) expresses historiographical views that will shape his subsequent writing and thought. He refers in the *Abridgment*, for instance, to Montesquieu as "the greatest genius, which has enlightened this age."[102] Burke's career-long emphasis on manners derives in part from Montesquieu,[103] and in the *Abridgment* itself, manners take a central place.[104] Burke brings his *Abridgment* only to 1215, Magna Carta and the reign of King John. But in it he articulates a defining regard for gradual historical change and a particular interest in how such change forms a nation's characteristic sentiments.

The *Abridgment* shows Burke's thought to be consonant with the depictions in David Hume and other Scottish thinkers of the gradual historical refinement of both sensibility and liberty.[105] For instance, in his discussion of Roman Britain under Agricola, Burke remarks, "He moulded that fierce nation by degrees to soft and social customs, leading them imperceptibly into a fondness for baths, for gardens, for grand houses, and all the commodious elegancies of a cultivated life."[106] Such slow processes are not confined to England. Like Hume's account of the "insensible revolution" and William Robertson's *View of the Progress of Society in Europe*, Burke's *Abridgment* presents this expansion of liberty as an international phenomenon. In discussing contests between papal and imperial factions in France and Germany in the time of Charlemagne he remarks, "Whilst these parties disagreed in the choice of a master, by contending for a choice in their subjection they grew imperceptibly into freedom, and passed through the medium of faction and anarchy into regular commonwealths."[107] Like the Scottish Enlightenment historiographers, Burke narrates the gradual expansion of sentimental and political powers of European populations, but with a slight difference in emphasis.

This difference may ultimately derive from subtly contrasting political sympathies. The *Abridgment* articulates a Humean view that the constitution developed slowly and haphazardly and that aspects of Saxon governance such as the Witenagemot (the Saxon assembly that advised the king) are too uncertain to serve as a basis for the English constitution: Burke writes, "All these things are, I think, sufficient to shew of what a visionary nature those systems are, which would settle the ancient Constitution in the most remote times exactly in the same form, in which we enjoy it at this day; not considering that such mighty changes in manners, during so many ages, always must produce a considerable change in laws, and in the forms as well as the powers of all governments."[108] All the same, despite this circumspection, the *Abridgment*'s "view of English history had a distinct Whig flavour," T. O. McLoughlin remarks,[109] with its stress on Magna Carta as a watershed and its view of the Witenagemot and other elements of the Saxon inheritance that made liberty a consistent, if often only felt, theme in English political development. Hume, who insists that English constitutional liberties really had their birth at 1688, would not go this far. (Recognizing the importance of Magna Carta, he sees it as a composite expressing Norman and Saxon impulses, as well as universal natural law.)[110] Burke furthermore identifies religion as largely responsible for the insensible revolution in English manners in a way that Hume, who foregrounds religion's volatility, could not countenance.[111]

In these similarities and differences, the lineaments of Burke's distinctive attitude toward insensible historical change appear. Like Hume and Robertson, he stresses the unintended development of manners that come to shape laws. But a kind of inarticulate feeling accompanies and also somehow directs this process. Discussing a crucial juncture in the conflict between the barons and King John, Burke remarks, "The English barons had privileges, which they knew to have been violated: they had always kept up the memory of the ancient Saxon liberty."[112] Thus liberty as an (at least baronial) English birthright subsists as knowledge and memory and so exerts a historical force of which the nation is conscious. But a sentence later, he offers this qualification: the barons "rather felt their wrongs, than understood the cause of them."[113] English liberty abides more as a feeling than as a concept of governance. By thus distinguishing the feeling for liberty from the understanding of it, Burke may the better maintain the link between such feeling and the unfelt historical processes out of which it arises. He may narrate, that his, how the English "grew imperceptibly into freedom" while still putting liberty forward as something they consistently felt if not knew, abiding and developing through "mighty changes in manners."

This doubleness distinguishes Burke both politically and, in a subtle way, also historiographically from Hume. In his review of Hume's complete *History of England* in *The Annual Register, or A View of the History, Politicks, and Literature, of the Year 1761*, the journal he ran for Robert Dodsley, Burke accepts Hume's contention that England's politics developed gradually, like a plant: "The idea of the growth, as I may call it, of our present constitution seems to be the principle of the whole work compleated by the part now published" (i.e., the medieval volumes). He also shares Hume's view of the accidental, unplanned nature of this growth, praising his portrayal of the "strange chaos of liberty and tyranny, of anarchy and order, [from which] the constitution, we are now blessed with, has at length arisen."[114] But a small, suggestive difference between the two writers appears when the review complains that Hume leaves crucial historical transactions out of the main narrative, consigning them instead to appendixes: "Yet, with deference to so learned and sensible a writer, we think some matters, as the history of the Wittangemot [sic], might in his hands have appeared to advantage in the text, and have relieved the reader i[n] a period, where the recital of uninteresting facts seems to demand some argumentative or discussive matter to engage the attention, and so perhaps might the origin of the feudal law."[115] Burke knows that Hume's placement in an appendix of his account of the Witenagemot could be a way of announcing its lack of "discussive" importance in understanding England's political evolution.[116] For Hume, the Witenagemot did not represent the people and so could not be seen as an ancestor of the House of Commons.

Yet despite all its uncertainties and haphazard manifestations, a Saxon spirit of liberty, which found expression in such hazily distant institutions, for Burke somehow brought forth signal moments like Magna Carta, though it was liberty "rather felt . . . than understood." Likewise, the historian surveying such developments must find a way to narrate them, now seen as "argumentative or discussive matter," within England's main political storyline. If this story progresses by insensible steps, it is also tied together by feeling, however inarticulate—a feeling that the historian must recognize, include, and perhaps share. (Thus, much later, his remarks on English historiography in *Reflections on the Revolution in France*, while discounting the accuracy of previous pedigrees of the ancient constitution, will nonetheless insist that "the powerful prepossession towards antiquity" of English legal historians alone decisively maintains the constitution.)[117]

Another much more discussed early work of Burke's, *A Philosophical Enquiry into the Origin of Our Ideas of the Sublime and Beautiful* (1757), offers an account of insensible affective change that is brief but more psychologically precise than the political and historical pictures presented in the *Abridgment*. Still, like the *Abridgment*, the *Enquiry* at large demonstrates (in F. P. Lock's words) that for the young Burke, "feeling is more reliable than reason."[118] A wealth of scholarly literature in recent decades has explored the "aesthetic ideology" of Burke's *Enquiry* and connected it to his later revolutionary writings and historical views in general. Many, including Tom Furniss, have emphasized the special pertinence of the sublime to Burke's account of politics. The mental exercise demanded by the sublime has been read as a kind of allegory of actual physical labor in the economy; for Furniss it is associated with "the political and economic project of the rising middle class," which valued the exercise of talent.[119] The beautiful, though significant enough in the *Enquiry*, has been placed by Furniss and others on the side of an enervating, "feminine" luxury, associated with the aristocracy, which Burke is said to despise.[120]

Commentators in this vein sometimes go so far as to identify the beautiful with a kind of stupefying privative insensibility, an "evil" slackness for which the laborious sublime acts as "remedy."[121] But Burke does not portray beauty as quite so slack as all that. In two chapters, "Gradual Variation" (part 3, chapter 15) and "Variation, Why Beautiful" (part 4, chapter 23), he associates beauty with an insensible of the more positive, additive kind. While affirming that "the genuine constituents of beauty, have each of them separately taken a natural tendency to relax the fibres," Burke maintains that a kind of quiet change or dynamism maintains the beautiful object as such:

> Another principal property of beautiful objects is, that the line of their parts is continually varying its direction; but it varies it by a very insensible deviation, it never varies it so quickly as to surprise, or by the sharpness of its angle to cause any twitching or convulsion of the optic nerve. Nothing long continued in the same manner, nothing very suddenly varied can be beautiful; because both are opposite to that agreeable relaxation, which is the characteristic effect of beauty. . . . Rest certainly tends to relax; yet there is a species of motion that relaxes more than rest; a gentle oscillatory motion, a rising and falling.[122]

Here beauty's "very insensible deviation" causes not a senseless stupefaction at all but rather an "agreeable relaxation." (The sublime certainly rescues us from disagreeable relaxation, but it is hard to read Burke as viewing the mind as in need of rescue from beauty as here described.) William Hogarth's discussion in *The Analysis of Beauty*, which appeared four years earlier (1753),[123] contains a similar point, of which Burke approved.[124] Change is essential, Burke notes, because "nothing long continued in the same manner" can be beautiful, but it must be change of an insensible sort. Sentiment thrives not on the privative sort of insensibility but on the insensible character of the right kind of variation.

The account in the *Enquiry* of the "positive pleasure" taken in insensibly varying objects sheds light on the historical thinking that infuses Burke's later political writing. It does so not as some crude allegory of politics—as if the English constitution, or the traditions and customs that stabilize a society, were beautiful objects like the neck of a dove or the breasts of a woman (Burke's examples). More precisely psychological, the *Enquiry*'s account of beautiful variation illustrates how a positive, powerful sentiment in the human mind may originate from objects whose active and effective powers are not sensed.

As in other examples discussed in this book, the point here is *how* the unfelt may affect feeling, not *what* specifically in any given context may be affecting (a neck, the constitution) or what truths such things may stand for.[125] So beautiful affect does not allegorically represent some social class or other, or any particular political aspiration, but rather activates a feature of human psychology, the more widely shared by persons in groups and reinforced for being included among the "passions which belong to society."[126]

A few examples from Burke's late political writing only begin to suggest how the idea of unfelt affect helps him to articulate his sentimental grasp of historical processes. As any usage of the term *insensibly* must, they all designate significant change, not the comforts of consistency, of static custom, habit, and tradition, sometimes seen as the core of Burke's political ideals. And such change ultimately touches and brings into being significant sentiment. Like the beauty in the *Enquiry* that results from insensible variation, such sentiments are remarkable, not merely the product of inert customary norms; as the *Enquiry* puts it, "if we suppose proportion in natural things to be relative to custom and use, the nature of use and custom will shew, that beauty, which is a powerful and positive quality, cannot result from it."[127] The Burkean politician is *affected* by contemplation of insensible changes in manners from which he feels his own affections grow. (Those merely immersed in "use and custom," on the other hand, do not feelingly recognize the arc of insensible change that brings them to their immediate, practical concerns.)

So in a famous passage in *Reflections on the Revolution in France*, Burke insists on both the basis of such processes in the unnoticeable and the intensity of attention they arouse. In the Burkean political effort "at once to preserve and to reform," the legislator's "vigorous mind, steady, persevering attention, various powers of comparison and combination, and the resources of an understanding fruitful in expedients" are assisted by time: "It is one of the excellences of a method in which time is amongst the assistants, that its operation is slow and in some cases almost imperceptible."[128] Again, the point is not that it is right to call what the legislator does "beautiful." But his activity is nonetheless remarkable, not merely an indifferent falling in with custom. He does not resemble a snuff-taker who passively and insensibly falls into his habit. What the legislator does, "to preserve and to reform," is a species of motion, productive of change, fruitful, vigorous, persevering (and if not quite a "gentle oscillatory motion, a rising and falling" like the beautiful stimulus, at least one that moves between gently opposite impulses). Yet it is often so "slow" as to be "almost imperceptible"—to the legislator, to the society he benefits, and to the observer-historian.

And with Burke, as with others discussed in this book, such imperceptibility, far from negating sensibility, is what constitutes it. He continues, "If circumspection and caution are a part of wisdom, when we work only upon inanimate matter, surely they become a part of duty too, when the subject of our demolition and construction is not brick and timber, but sentient beings."[129] Burke's architectural metaphor reverently presents a continuum between the renovation of ancient buildings and that of human beings. Both become affecting by the unnoticed way they are affected. Finally, he declares, "the true lawgiver ought to have an heart full of sensibility"[130]—notably fuller, it seems, than the "sentient beings" he helps construct. The reverence of the legislator is not only directed at maintaining a social and governmental fabric that has insensibly evolved through time. His own sentiment is the product of such evolution. In such passages, then, the insensible provides the ground on which the wisdom of the legislator and the meaningfulness of social history may meet. In this gentle embrace of the insensible, Burke distinguishes himself from those historians and their societies who find themselves merely subject to it.

Burke's political writings of subsequent years will return to this near paradoxical imperative to attend with special feeling to the insensible. The slowness of political change produces the sentiment of its subject, who in turn feelingly maintains this change. The irrelevance of the divide between passive and active, spectator and spectacle, is part of Burke's point. In *A Letter from Mr. Burke, to a Member of the National Assembly* (1791) he remarks that politically, the British "have always cautiously felt our way": "The parts of our constitution have gradually, and almost insensibly, in a long course of time, accommodated themselves to each other, and to their common, as well as to their separate purposes."[131] Again, the peculiar combination of feeling our way (cautiously, deliberately) as the object we feel changes (insensibly) distinguishes Burke's specially direct approach to the unfelt. Our own agency and that of the "parts of the constitution," far from being opposed, amount to the same thing. Our way with the almost insensible accommodation can be "felt" only because it almost cannot be. And yet Burke's impassioned prose must make a kind of rhetoric of such feeling.

The next year Burke elaborated on the role that a people must play in allowing change to occur in ways they cannot feel. In his *Letter from the Right Hon. Edmund Burke, M. P. in the Kingdom of Great Britain, to Sir Hercules Langrishe, Bart. M.P. on the subject of Roman Catholics of Ireland* . . . (1792) he declares, "We must all obey the great law of change, it is the most powerful law of nature, and the means perhaps of its conservation. All we can do, and that human wisdom can do, is to provide that the change shall proceed by insensible degrees. This has all the benefits which may be in change, without any of the inconveniences of mutation."[132] Here physical law, "the most powerful law of nature," proves itself continuous with moral and political law. The comparison of historical change to change in nature represents a culmination of the naturalization of sentiment and its unfeeling bases in accounts of history in the period. It again may seem a paradox that Burke asks human wisdom to "provide that change shall proceed by insensible degrees," as if wisdom were asked to look after something whose defining element is its unavailability to inspection. But inasmuch as our feeling and attention, our passions and interests, are themselves always and continuously products of unfeeling, the gulf separating them from almost imperceptibly gradual processes of political, social, and historical change seems less unbridgeable. The "almost" in many of Burke's formulations (though it is not in this last) testifies to their vanishingly subtle point of contact. When the "almost" is omitted, one might say their identification only becomes more complete.

Hence, for Burke, the insensible is a moral imperative that we must "provide" for if not experience, and its function is historical. Part of this view derives from his inheritance of the previous half-century's reflections on the evolution and historical function of moeurs. At the end of his life, in the first of his *Letters on a Regicide Peace* (1796–97), a passage (often quoted) decisively elevates manners above laws and epitomizes his understanding of the political significance of historical change: "Manners are of more importance than laws. Upon them, in a great measure the laws depend. The law touches us but here and there, and now and then. Manners are what vex or sooth, corrupt or purify, exalt or debase, barbarize or refine us, by a constant, steady, uniform, insensible operation, like that of the air we breathe in."[133] Burke will observe that the "French Legislators" have learned this heightening of the lessons of Montesquieu too well, settling a new and debased system of manners on the French people. His string of verbs soon moves from immediately and presumably individually experienced moods ("vex or soothe") to slow, collective processes of corruption, purification, and so on. Yet all signify subtle changes to sentiment and manners, not the indifferent extension of custom and habit, not the insensibility of privation but the insensible of addition. We keep breathing moment after moment, but the air operates on us constantly without being noticed. *Air* itself is a synonym for manner, both taken breath by breath and inhabited through time. We breathe it in but also breathe in it.

Burke was interested in air. He corresponded with Joseph Priestley about his experiments in the 1770s and helped Priestley in his efforts to dedicate an abridged edition (1790) of *Experiments and Observations on Different Kinds of Air* to the Prince of Wales. But by the time of Burke's writings about the Revolution, he began to see the violence of chemical and governmental experiments as linked, comparing the action of air to that of liberty: "The wild *gas*, the fixed air is plainly broke loose," he would exclaim in the *Reflections*.[134] The air of the new manners concocted by the revolutionaries is plainly toxic. Only air left to its insensible nature, not experimented on and forced to be an object of theoretical scrutiny, may support our social life.

Burke's derivation of political sentiment from insensibly operating natural laws and his comparison of their action to air reenact the common tendency I have noted in chapter III of this book to illustrate, and even link, unfelt social change with material or physical processes. But these linkages preserve an antidogmatic view of such materialism. Like Montesquieu's "force de la chose," Hume's liberty that "acquire[s] new force" of its own inertial motion, and Gibbon's unfeeling immersion in the ocean of history, the insensible in Burke portrays our feelings as having a basis in the laws and unfeeling matter of the physical world. But far from proposing a materialist theory, these turns of writing identify the energy, the natural force of matter, as the profoundest source of feeling—a profundity consisting of the fact that feeling cannot feel it. Most historians I have discussed have stylistically employed the insensible as the extra ingredient needed for an enlightened account of historical movement to complete itself. Burke's more deeply felt acceptance of the insensible takes him in a subtly different direction. The elusive nature of what the idiom designates ensures that this acceptance cannot be theoretical or even conscious, exactly, and it is certainly not comparable to any revolutionary rationalism. He alludes to the insensible movements in history as a kind of affect to provide for the working of affect on us.

Chapter IV

Political Economy

Moving with Money

Money moves people, as depicted in eighteenth-century writing about commerce, in two ways. Obviously, it incites and gratifies powerful passions: greed, envy, and "self-liking," in Bernard Mandeville's terms early in the century—or, as Adam Smith later has it, feelings appropriate to different social stations, such as merchants' slow-burning passion for gain or the consuming vanities of the rich and great. Strong feelings serve as the prime movers of commerce. But money also affects people in ways they feel just barely or not at all. Their personally, passionately motivated acts lead them unawares to participate in the movement of money as a social force. A typical example: in 1767 James Steuart remarks that "money insensibly began to circulate" in Europe as a result of the seventeenth-century imperialist adventures of Spain and other nations.[1] People are collectively moved without sensing it to make economic life what it is, even as they are moved individually by keenly felt passions for money. The feeling and unfeeling generated by commerce intertwine as themes in the period's writing, and together they expand the affective range of commercial life beyond what scholars have usually thought of as "economic sentiments."[2]

Like the impersonal historical processes said to unfold insensibly in eighteenth-century historiography, the unfelt movements of commerce operate at the most vast end of the scale of applications of the idiom discussed in this book, which began with infinitesimal particles affecting the individual mind. But the structure and significance of the affective assemblages of people in commercial relations differ from those of nations' movements through history discussed in chapter III. Historians like Edward Gibbon and David Hume typically appeal to deindividuating processes to account for the emergence of new modes of feeling. An insensible revolution occurs "in the minds of men" that confers on them new affective capacities. A sense of being Italian, or part of the Roman Empire, emerges insensibly from more local kinds of identity.

The collectivization of affect in commerce that I will describe in this chapter is not a linear emergence of feeling from a lack of it, but rather works as a repeating cycle. Before and after Mandeville, commercial writers presume that the crude, rather disreputable passions that drive commerce (greed, vanity, etc.) remain constant, an aspect of "human nature." But something else has to steer it. Unfelt, collectivizing movements coalesce to confer a predictable order on trade and finally, if all goes well, result in a final affective state—what Smith calls "the publick happiness." This resultant affect does not replace the individual avarice and self-love which, as political economists insist, must continue on as before for the whole ensemble to operate. A narrative of linear emergence has been dominant throughout this book, in accounts not just of polite feeling emerging from barbarism but also of lively sensation from material particles and of a heroine's desire for a husband from her indifference or aversion. Commercial harmony—affectively denominated happiness—also emerges from base, individual commercial passions, but it can never replace them. Rather, the interaction between felt and unfelt affects maintains a dependable loop.

This dependability makes unfelt affect particularly useful as an element in writing designed to justify commercial policy. All along I have not only stressed that the idiom of the insensible expresses, inconspicuously, a common way many eighteenth-century genres gesture to feeling's emergence from unfeeling. It also discreetly solves problems particular to each discourse. A term is needed to mediate between the soul and the material body, or allow a moral heroine to actually come to feel desire. In commercial writing, more clearly perhaps than elsewhere, the insensible solves a problem. It articulates the manner in which jarring, selfish economic passions may result in a general happiness. People ought to feel or at least acknowledge this happiness, commercial writers argue, even if they often do not—even if they remain fixated on their own feelings regardless of how well (or poorly) "the economy" as a whole does.

Writers of the period depict the relation between felt and unfelt affect in this transaction often as not much of an interaction at all. The insensible movements of money, prices, tendencies of taxation, and the like seem to float free of any particular human feeling, motive, or agency, to happen naturally, on their own, according to regular "laws." (And so the science of economics will become possible.)[3] But it is always people, after all, who move money. They *perform* transactions and exchanges even though the large patterns and meanings created by these take shape without being felt or noticed. To rearrange the emphases in a famous sentence of Karl Marx from his remarks on commodity fetishism, "we are not *aware* of this, nevertheless *we* do it."[4] So when writers say things like "money insensibly began to circulate," they make it easy to forget that people are the ones who circulate it. By assigning the verbal action to money, writers such as Steuart portray people, individuals collected in a society, as objects of money's agency, even though the actual movement is simply the sum of what people themselves do.

But such assertions perform more than a mere syntactical sleight of hand. They erect a double structure of commercial agency. Individuals act on their passions and desires and then, collectivized, find themselves objects of vaster movements that they do not notice. Such accounts portray commercial individuals as both feeling agents and patients who are moved unawares—in one more than notable account, "by an invisible hand"—to behave in large, socially meaningful ways, even as they themselves move the money that moves them: a peculiar affective form, an unfelt commercial autoaffection. Some of the most discussed elements of eighteenth-century thought appear in a new light when seen as involved in this affective structure. The familiar notions, especially active in the Scottish Enlightenment, of unintended consequences, spontaneous order, and self-organization continue to be treated freshly in scholarship,[5] and the always growing mound of commentary on Adam Smith's little phrase in book 4, chapter 2 of *The Wealth of Nations* continues to be astonishing. Scholars pondering the invisible hand often understand its unnoticed force as "a mechanism outside human influence"[6]: a secularized providence,[7] or some abstract principle like automaticity or self-organization. But viewing it as unfelt affect portrays it as nothing if not under human influence, even as such a view expands a notion of what human influence is.

In conceptualizing this expanded idea, it helps to remember the Spinozan suggestion that affects consist of more than just emotions. One thing can be affected by another in any number of possible physical encounters (among which emotion, itself a physical process, is a single case). Gilles Deleuze glosses Spinoza's main idea this way: "a body is defined by relations of motion and rest, of slowness and speed between particles" and by its "capacity for affecting and being affected" by them.[8] The continuities between "moving" in physical and emotional senses find an analog in the way the idioms of eighteenth-century commerce describe money, which people move around ardently while it moves them to build the commercial order without being aware they do so—an order that itself provokes new feelings. In the language of affect theory, money's unfelt motions are a kind of virtual "intensity" that is "qualified" by the emotional engagement of people in it. The two resonate with and feed back into each other.[9] Instead of pitting human motive and feeling against some outside force that orchestrates them at a distance, we can find, in Smith and other writers, the immanence of the unfelt in the feelings of human beings. We would still not ask, What does it *feel* like to be moved by an invisible hand? By definition, it does not feel like anything. But we can ask, In what sense might the pressure of the invisible hand be understood as an unfelt affect? What is it like for our bodies to be moved unawares (as if) by an invisible hand, whose impulses consist, after all, of nothing more than our own?

These movements often produce predictable and good outcomes, a fact that indeed provides writers on money with a motive for identifying them. The insensible helps commercial writing to build a vision of corporate happiness out of passionately competing individuals. But affects can sometimes produce surprising results. Though the logic of self-organization is inherently optimistic, we know unintended consequences can be good or bad, and affect has a way of introducing the suboptimal along with the happy or fortunate. So in Smith's account of European economic development, discussed in section 4 below, "the insensible operation of foreign commerce" transforms the feudal order somewhat awkwardly, in not exactly the best possible way. The predictability of passion falls out of harmony with the happiness of the economic whole.

1. Mandeville and the Other Happiness

Many writers in the pre-Smithian period of British economic thought identify the pressing motives of the body as the origin of commercial energy. "The main spur to Trade, or rather to Industry and Ingenuity," writes Dudley North in 1691, "is the exorbitant Appetites of Men, which they will take pains to gratifie, and so be disposed to work, when nothing else will incline them to it; for did Men content themselves with bare Necessaries, we should have a poor World."[10] In a similar vein, Bernard Mandeville some twenty years later in the first *Fable of the Bees* (1714) pronounces "Man" to be "a compound of various passions." The point of his poem *The Grumbling Hive* (1705), he notes, is that these passions "are the great Support of a flourishing Society."[11]

But passion and affect in Mandeville operate on different levels. People feel their own passions, of course, but these create social results that are not experienced in the same way, though they remain affective in some sense. In this he provides a model to subsequent writers who separate personal economic motives from the collective feelings that characterize the commercial order. Though Mandeville does not very frequently use terms like *insensibly* to configure the relation between them, his works offer other devices, including metaphorical "hypochondria," to account for it. If we follow scholarly commentators in seeing Mandeville as one of the discoverers of the notion of "society,"[12] his layering of felt and unfelt affect proves a surprising precondition for socially cohesive functioning and provides a template for later writers who take up the topic.

Mandeville begins his intellectual enterprise by extolling a happiness other than one people actually feel. At the end of the preface of the *Fable*'s first (1714) edition,[13] he presents a vivid account of life in a successful modern city:

> There are, I believe, few People in *London*, of those that are at any time forc'd to go a-foot, but what could wish the Streets of it much cleaner than generally they are; while they regard nothing but their own Clothes and private Conveniency: but when once they come to consider, that what offends them is the result of the Plenty, great Traffick and Opulency of that mighty City, if they have any Concern in its Welfare, they will hardly ever wish to see the Streets of it less dirty. (1:10–11)

Mandeville continues to evoke what walking in the streets is like, with crowds "continually harassing and trampling through every part of them" (1:11). Yet he insists that "dirty Streets are a necessary Evil inseparable from the Felicity of *London*" (1:12). Harassed and annoyed inhabitants sacrifice their immediate "Conveniency" to the happiness of the city, and this secondary happiness may feed back to become the happiness of the city's stakeholders when they consider this fact. Their wishes and desires themselves will change, and they will enjoy, after a fashion, the undelightful signs of prosperity at street level.

It can only be ironically that the preface's final paragraph entertains the thought of what alternative social arrangement might produce actually felt happiness "without any regard to the Interest or Happiness of the City" (1:12). Mandeville muses, "I would esteem a fragrant Garden, or a shady Grove in the Country" (1:12) as places where "Men might enjoy true Happiness" (1:13), living off the land's produce without foreign wars or foreign luxuries. But the better happiness, the other happiness "of the City," must have the advantage for Mandeville over such bucolic ease. When describing London's happiness, of course, he means its prosperity—an "objective" condition that could characterize it no matter how people actually feel about living there from moment to moment. Scholars and historians of emotion have stressed the difference between happiness as "an objective state of affairs" and happiness as "affective," an emotion. Sometimes they characterize the former sense as a "classical" usage, the latter as a "modern" one.[14] As the *Oxford English Dictionary* shows, however, *happiness* in English has, of course, meant both pleasurable contentment of mind and prosperity or good fortune since well before the modern period and, as Adam Potkay points out, this double meaning still affects usage today.[15] Yet Mandeville here and elsewhere illustrates not just a difference between two senses of the word but a complex socioaffective interaction between them. Individual passions—for gain, for self-approval—create the happiness of the city, and that happiness will, or at least should, return transformed to individuals to make them feel happy too.

This complex noncoinciding relation between individual and collective affect differs, moreover, from comparable relations proposed by writers of antiquity. The concept of eudaemonia, the virtue that establishes an individual's happy life, does extend in Hellenistic philosophy to include a communal dimension. As Aristotle remarks in book 9, chapter 9 of the *Nicomachean Ethics*, "It is perhaps strange also to make the blessed person solitary: no one would choose to have all good things by himself, since a human being is political and is disposed by nature to live with others."[16] The good person seeks a society of good people. The happiness of commercial London, conversely, is composed of the thoughtless, appetitive, selfish, consumerist activities of individuals—the very impulses that commentators contrast with those defining the good and happy life of the classical tradition. Mandeville's idea of flourishing also differs from the concept of *Felicitas Publica* in late Republican and Imperial Roman thought and religion, a public flourishing in which individual citizens partake, uniting personal happiness with a condition of communal blessedness. This is decidedly not what Mandeville means by "the Felicity of *London*."[17] Again, the crucial fact stressed at the end of Mandeville's preface is the individual annoyance caused by general prosperity.

But despite this divergence, the objective condition of commercial happiness in Mandeville, again, has a subjective payoff. It means the individuals of this society *are* themselves happy and should recognize and feel it. We have seen throughout this book that strands of affect theory encourage a recognition of how affect can be "objective" and supraindividual and characterize systems and groups, even as it remains connected, however immanently, to feelings of individual people. As Mandeville deepens his account of our motive passions throughout his work, he will elaborate ways in which passion can be both immanent (or "virtual") in the body and spread over the social, corporate life of human beings. His juxtaposition at the beginning of *The Fable of the Bees* of some hypothetical "true Happiness" of human beings—rural, simple, fragrant, easeful—with the complex happiness of the city itself has two effects. First, it opens a gap between the feelings of individuals and their collective, social condition. But second, it hints that this gap may be bridged, though rather oddly. Urbanites may reflect on the idea that their immediate exasperations are indexes of social felicity—and so may actually feel, though in some way necessarily more remote than a splash of nastiness from a gutter, happy about them.

In affective terms, then, we may transform *Private Vices, Public Benefits*, the subtitle of Mandeville's *Fable*, to "private irritation, public happiness." The latter equation runs deeper than the former, expressing something like an irony of the human social condition, beyond our efforts to define what morality is or fix the bounds of vice and virtue. The affective divide of people in society goes beyond ethics. The inconvenience of crowded prosperity is not a vice, so called or not, like covetousness or intemperance. It rather accompanies the condition of human flourishing. Our capacity to attain a bigger social happiness from thriving commerce and sociability even while we feel somewhat socially miserable inspires many of Mandeville's deeper insights into our social being.

This doubleness of happiness and feeling in general appears as a motif throughout the *Fable*. For instance, in his extensive body of "Remarks" on particular passages in *The Grumbling Hive* in volume 1, Remark C on "the Desire to be thought well of" (1:63) states, "It is incredible how necessary an Ingredient Shame is to make us sociable; it is a Frailty in our Nature; all the World, whenever it affects them, submit to it with Regret, and would prevent it if they could; yet the Happiness of Conversation depends of it, and no Society could be polish'd, if the Generality of Mankind were not subject to it" (1:68). Again, this convergence of vivid, palpable pain and the externalized "Happiness" created by it reveals how the felt and the unfelt depend on each other.

Mandeville does not suggest that we would be better off if we could jettison the shame, or somehow not "Regret" it, and unreservedly embrace the happiness of conversation. In fact, he goes on to assert that we rightly "endeavour to Increase instead of lessening or destroying this Sense of Shame" (1:68) as we educate children. So the shame itself, or at least the fear of it (shame at potentially being ashamed), must be cultivated for a social happiness to flourish. And again, Mandeville indicates that the happiness of conversation comes back to *us* to make us all happy, ashamed though we are. This happiness of social life, again, is not merely abstract, "objective," or definitional, not entirely cut off from the socially miserable people who compose it. Mandeville seems to refer to something more, that is, than the mere "prosperity" of conversation, whatever that might be. Conversational happiness must include its power to confer enjoyment on its participants, despite its basis in their unpleasant feelings of shame.

Nearly a decade after volume 1 of *The Fable* was published, but before volume 2 appeared, Mandeville again takes up the question of a corporate happiness that is more than the sum of its component feelings in his tract *Free Thoughts on Religion, the Church, and National Happiness* (1720). The book is mostly devoted to espousing toleration and anticlerical views, but the final chapter, "Of National Happiness," revisits the problem of unhappy individuals living on "a happy Island."[18] Through the opening pages of the chapter, Mandeville toggles between the objective meaning of happiness, whereby "*Great Britain*" is a uniquely happy nation, and the subjective or actually felt kind of happiness, which the nation's citizens notably and perversely lack.[19] "Our Climate is still more Happy" than our wealth, he remarks. Nowhere else do the working multitudes "get and spend more Money chearfully than they do in this City."[20] Politically, too, a happiness distinguishes the situation of Britons: "The most substantial Blessing, and the peculiar Happiness we enjoy above all other Countries, are the Laws and Liberties of *England*."[21] Yet the people do not, somehow, feel their own happiness. Mandeville asks, "Since so many Blessings then conspire, what hinders us from being happy; for it is certain we are not so?"[22] Mandeville's language through these passages makes any simple distinction between objective happiness—prosperity—and subjective happiness difficult to sustain. Plainly we *feel* the climate, and the people "chearfully" make and spend money and "enjoy" happy laws and liberty. Yet these feelings are more objectively, factually oriented than the unhappy feelings that we feel in spite of them. The unhappy feelings make the happy ones, in some strange way, less felt.

Mandeville's name for this peculiarly divided affective condition is hypochondria. Such a diagnosis sees happiness as a deep state of the body that can be brought back to sensibility and properly felt, by "reason." As he continues in "Of National Happiness," "Should any State Physician behold our goodly Countenance, and having felt our low dispirited Pulse, examine into the real Cause of all our Grievances, he must infallibly pronounce the Nation hypp'd. No Woman in the height of Vapours is more whimsical in her Complaints than some of us, and melancholly Madmen have not more dismal Apprehensions of Things in the blackest Fits of the Spleen, than our State Hypochondriacks are daily buzzing in our Ears. In Distempers, where the Imagination is chiefly affected, Men, without any other Remedies, may often reason themselves into Health."[23] Again, even as the passage distinguishes the corporeal from the affective, it blurs them together. As a happy constitution shines in the countenance, subjective unhappiness appears in autonomic activity, in the "low dispirited Pulse." Mandeville, of course a physician himself, here portrays the malady as a zone where corporeal and emotional conditions mix irritably and unnaturally, and health as their natural harmony, in which the organism's feeling matches its actual state.

His earlier medical work, *A Treatise of the Hypochondriack and Hysterick Passions, Vulgarly Call'd the Hypo in Men and Vapours in Women* (1711), also occasionally notices this odd divergence and convergence of happy feelings and happy conditions. He remarks there, for instance, that "People of lower Fortunes" are content with securing life's necessities, "which if they accomplish to satisfaction, they are commonly pleas'd and happy, because they think themselves so"—again, an intriguing separation *and* connection between happiness as an emotional state and happiness as a situation.[24] To "think" yourself objectively happy—well favored, fortunate—of course causes you to feel happy. Here and in Mandeville's later works, the line between felt and unfelt feeling remains, but always as a site of intercourse (as well as a separation) between them, and actively open to revision.

After volume 1 of *The Fable*, and after the *Free Thoughts*, the weightier among the army of Mandeville's critics, such as Joseph Butler and Francis Hutcheson, attack the very existence of this distinction. They see that denying the possibility of unfelt happiness—the idea that irritated, ashamed, or otherwise unhappy people may compose a happy society—strikes Mandeville's system in *The Fable* at its root. These respondents will claim that "private" happiness and the happiness of the whole must be essentially compatible, if not identical. Thus Butler, answering Mandeville (though not by name) in the first of his *Fifteen Sermons* (1726), describes the relation "between the Nature of Man as respecting Self, and tending to private Good, his own preservation and Happiness; and the Nature of Man as having respect to Society, and tending to promote publick Good, the Happiness of that Society." He concludes, "These Ends do indeed perfectly coincide; and to aim at publick and private Good are so far from being inconsistent; that they mutually promote each other."[25] (Here "Good" covers both moral goodness and well-being, contentedness, happiness.) Later he will claim that "Men are so much one Body, that in a peculiar Manner they feel for each other, Shame, sudden Danger, Resentment, Honour, Prosperity, Distress . . . each of these being distinct Cements of Society."[26] To block Mandeville, Butler must do more than assert the notion common among British moralists that benevolence comes as naturally to human beings as self-love does. He must reject a prior, more radical Mandevillean claim, that public "feeling" can be built out of individual feelings that differ from it: the idea, that is, that some unhappiness of individuals is essential to society's happiness.

Around the same time, Hutcheson denies, in a manner similar to Butler, that such an equation can add up. First published in the *Dublin Journal* in 1725, and later posthumously in *Reflections upon Laughter, and Remarks upon The Fable of the Bees* (1750), Hutcheson's critique of Mandeville seems to reject the notion that there could be any distinction between the happy feelings of particular people and those of society, in which the former are simply summed. "What then remains," Hutcheson remarks, "in order to public happiness after the necessary supply of all appetites, must be to study, as much as possible, to regulate our desires of every kind, by forming just opinions of the real value of their several objects, so as to have the strength of our desires proportioned to the real value of them, and their real moment to our happiness." He will a few pages later remark that "the greatest public good of the whole" is "the surest way for each individual to be happy."[27]

As a theory of the origins of ethics, Hutcheson's position proved more satisfying to many readers, or at least closer to what they wished to believe, than Mandeville's. By denying that vice really produces social benefits and insisting that Britain would be just as prosperous if temperance were broadly practiced, Hutcheson answers Mandeville's challenge at an ethical level. But at the deeper, affective one, Hutcheson's equation of personal and social happiness disregards all the nonethical ways in which the two may diverge. Irritation, shame, and other forms of misery not vicious in themselves, Mandeville insists, conduce to the happy functioning of society and (again, in feeding back to us) may make us happy later in a different way. We feel unhappy feelings personally, and these are necessary for a collective, less immediate happiness.

This affective split in Mandeville that I have been discussing differs from, even reverses, the relation between avowed and "repressed" or "unconscious" motives in social life that many scholars have found in his work.[28] In that relation, an unfelt cause such as self-love antecedes and produces the polite and moral behavior that we consciously embrace and extol. My foregoing examples move in the opposite direction, from felt—irritation, shame—to unfelt: the "happiness" of a flourishing society. As Mandeville puts it early in volume 1 of the *Fable*, "nothing can render the unsearchable depth of the Divine Wisdom more conspicuous, than that *Man*, whom Providence had designed for Society, should not only by his own Frailties and Imperfections be led into the Road to Temporal Happiness, but likewise receive, from a seeming Necessity of Natural Causes, a Tincture of that Knowledge, in which he was afterwards to be made perfect by the True Religion, to his Eternal Welfare" (1:57). The transaction between "Frailties and Imperfections" and their meaning and purpose, "Temporal Happiness," may be obscure itself and take time. But here we unquestionably notice and act on our frailties—they are not hidden—and these produce a feeling temporally distinct from them, and one that resides not in the individual but (eventually) in a collective body.

Still, Mandeville's account of repressed or hidden personal feelings remains closely connected to his picture of unfelt social ones. Personal and social feelings dynamically give way to one another, and in the process, their degree of being sensed may flip. The six dialogues that compose volume 2 of the *Fable* (1729), written in part to answer critics like Butler, deepen the complexity of passion's comprehensive influence on what Mandeville had called "the invisible Part of Man" in volume 1 (1:145). As he later boasts in Remark N, the *Fable* is outstanding in the history of social philosophy because "it describes the Nature and Symptoms of human Passions, detects their Force and Disguises; and traces Self-love in its darkest Recesses; I might safely add, beyond any other System of Ethics" (1:405). Though interested in the hidden, passionate origins of social life, he also exposes the passions' surprising "Force," their way of materializing in social practices beyond the immediate notice of the individual.

The opacity of passionate motivation itself, moreover, shifts with time. An initially obvious motive becomes a hidden one. In the Second Dialogue, Mandeville's mouthpiece Cleomenes remarks, "When a Man has behaved himself with so much Prudence as I have describ'd, lived up to the strictest Rules of good Breeding for many Years, and has gain'd the Esteem of all that know him, when his noble and polite Manner is become habitual to him, it is possible, he may in time forget the Principle he set out with, and become ignorant, or at least insensible of the hidden Spring, that gives Life and Motion to all his Actions" (2:79).[29] What starts as palpable self-love *becomes* "a hidden Spring" that the man forgets or no longer feels. In terms I have explored earlier, self-love, like shame, is the felt component that makes society "happy" in Mandeville's special sense. But as this social happiness becomes paramount—here realized in the "Esteem" of others for "his noble and polite Manner"—it displaces his awareness of the rather unsavory, antisocial passion that led to it, which is forgotten.

As in other accounts discussed in this book, the slowness of time in Mandeville proves to be unfelt affect's principal mode of force. The man becomes insensible "in time." In these cases, Mandeville presents not so much a history of cultural progress (as would be offered by David Hume or William Robertson) but a sense of how human nature and society in general jointly have a temporal dimension. The texture of civilized social life, Cleomenes will later say, is "the Product, the joynt Labour of several Ages" (2:322). As E. J. Hundert remarks in his study of the *Fable*, for Mandeville "Providence manifests itself in the workings of our passions over long periods of time, while society emerges independent of any human design in a slow evolutionary process."[30] Though Mandeville will note in places in volume 1 that cunning politicians manipulate our passions to produce the social effects that they want, even there he acknowledges, "I would have no body that reflects on the mean Original of Honour complain of being gull'd and made a Property by cunning Politicians, but desire every body to be satisfied, that the Governors of Societies and those in high Stations are greater Bubbles to Pride than any of the rest"

(1:220).³¹ An all-motivating pride "bubbles," as it comes to be opaque to, everyone. It must precede all efforts (which are innumerable) of manipulative people to turn it to account, and these cunning manipulators succumb unawares to the same gradual processes as everyone else.

The motive power of passion in Mandeville's account, then, depends on its way of not being noticed sometimes, whether at the individual or social level. It can, in fact, be difficult to distinguish these levels. We may feel our social passions much more fully than our selfish ones. Cleomenes uses a striking series of analogies in the Third Dialogue of volume 2 to illustrate the principle that people always obey "The Passions within, that, unknown to themselves, govern their Will and direct their behaviour" (2:139). He explains that good manners are like a person leaping, who disposes his body in the proper position to leap farthest without knowing what he is doing (2:140–41). Cleomenes remarks that neither the motive for these postures nor the optimal character of its outcome enters his awareness. The latter applies especially to good manners: "What I have said of this Stratagem made use of in Leaping, I desire you would apply to the Doctrine of good Manners, which is taught and practiced by Millions, who never thought on the Origin of Politeness, or so much as knew the real Benefit it is of to Society" (2:141). A kind of passion suffuses the entire practice of good manners—we feel we want to behave well—but by most this passion remains unfelt both at its origin in self-love and in its result in social happiness.

Next Cleomenes applies the analogy of shipbuilding and other feats of collective technical achievement that advance slowly through centuries of accumulated knowledge (2:141–45). As before, he insists that shipbuilders and sailors, like those who gradually refine the practice of good manners, are ignorant both of the "true Cause, the real Foundation those Arts are built upon in Nature" and of the social *"Rationale"* they support (2:144). Our vivid experience of good manners as we practice them, like the feeling of leaping well or steering a well-built ship, relies and feeds on the nonfeeling that attends their slow construction through time. It is important, again, that Mandeville here does not attempt a full, linear history that traces the progress of European refinement (of the sort discussed in chapter III of this book) but rather declares natural principles that make gradualness a transhistorical, recurrent component of what it means to be human (e.g., "in the Pursuit of Self-preservation, Men discover a restless Endeavour to make themselves easy, which insensibly teaches them to avoid Mischief on all Emergencies," 2:139).³²

This ensemble of analogies makes "the Passions within" that direct and give social meaning to our actions seem like something other than unconscious thoughts, let alone repressed ones. When we make a leap, our minds are not tacitly performing calculations about velocity, weight, and efficient force; people rather feel, in their bodies, the optimal speed and positioning when "they take a Run before they throw themselves off the Ground" (2:140). If the motive force of good manners is like that, it resembles a deep, nonconscious physical impulse more than a repressed thought. The other analogies, that compare politeness to sailing, shipbuilding, or other arts improved by time, also locate its force beyond any knowledge possessed by the person, conscious or not: "We often ascribe to the Excellency of Man's Genius, and the Depth of his Penetration, what is in Reality owing to length of Time, and the Experience of many Generations, all of them very little differing from one another in natural Parts and Sagacity" (2:142). The efficient functioning of manners says little about the beliefs, knowledge, and motives of individuals, and much more about the collective wisdom and purposes of our social lives. An individual embodies such knowledge in practice, not in any unconscious system of knowledge he possesses, which is dispersed across and externalized in a collectivity of people and a vast span of time. Taken together, then, these illustrations of "the Passions within" portray them as a kind of embodied affect that bears a collective stamp. Inasmuch as the individual does not perceive the "knowledge" that motivates her politeness, she also is not aware of its social origins and aims. While we vividly experience the impulse to be polite to one another, as we have an embodied experience of a good leap or steering a ship on a true course, the affect that has optimized these actions, for us and those on board with us, remains unnoted.

Mandeville's appeal in the *Fable* to the notion of unfelt affect supports two of his most significant intellectual contributions. In one direction—the one most discussed by commentators—it advances his radical critique of ethics, which leads to Nietzsche and beyond. Our fine moral feelings and behavior ultimately have their roots in hidden or forgotten and not especially admirable passions like pride and its source, self-liking. But in the other direction, the unfelt casts the role of passion in his economic and social thought in an unexpected light. Feelings exist on a social plane in ways individuals do not directly experience, in the happy, prosperous society to which we privately, sometimes unhappily, contribute. Our skilled social practice, politeness, embodies an accumulation of knowledge across generations that we ourselves do not really "know" or master consciously. So a corporate kind of affective success draws on individual contributions yet remains more than the mere sum of them. In this, Mandeville points a way to conceptualize the affective nature of political economy.

2. Feeling Untaxed

Writing on taxation in the long eighteenth century finds a kind of perfection in the idiom of the insensible. Though casually deployed as usual, the term captures an ideal way to bring the feelings of individuals into line with collective, national imperatives. If money solicits and expresses the former—passion for gain, vanity, and so on—in a social form, taxes are money that compels citizens to share in the latter whether they personally care about them or not. British writing about taxation in the eighteenth century consistently reflects on what this only partly intentional sharing means and, more practically, how much or how little the people ought to feel the extraction of taxes from them. A consistent answer given is that taxes should be collected as insensibly as possible, and writers develop techniques of representation to depict degrees of feeling that kinds of taxation may elicit. Individuals' way of being insensibly affected turns out to be a manipulable feature of human nature. Alongside servicing the growing national debt, British tax revenues mostly supported the "fiscal-military state" as it developed to fund what historians have called Britain's Second Hundred Years' War with France, from the Restoration through the Napoleonic era.[33] The peculiar nature of this conflict, with its apparently distinct wars (the War of the Spanish Succession, the Seven Years' War, etc.) interrupted by periods of peace that enabled preparation for more wars, helped dictate that level of feeling deemed suitable for the appropriation of funds from the citizenry. Surges of patriotism gave way in peacetime to other concerns, and tax collection through the long eighteenth century to some degree tracked these rhythms.

The period witnessed the growth of indirect taxes, which were designed to be unfelt. These—the excise, customs duties, the stamp tax—contrast with the direct taxes on wealth and property such the land tax, the window tax, and so on.[34] Though direct taxes on wealth rose, for instance, late in the century to support the nation's war efforts against revolutionary France, Patrick K. O'Brien, a historian of the topic, remarks that "throughout the period"—that is, from the reign of William III to 1815—"taxes fell mainly and increasingly upon expenditures on goods and services. They were indirect, that is to say, collected from businessmen and passed on (more or less in their entirety) to consumers in the form of higher prices."[35] This passing on is what makes indirect taxes hard to notice. The insensible performs a crucial function in the fiscal production of the modern state, and British writers on taxes knew it.

The terms in which indirect taxation was promoted remain remarkably consistent through the long eighteenth century. Early on, William Petty in his *Treatise of Taxes and Contributions* (1662) advocates for an excise tax, "the very perfect Idea of making a Leavy upon Consumptions."[36] Taxation for Petty depends on the people's willingness to pay, but he also recognizes the desirability of their not feeling the exaction very keenly: "But supposing, that the several causes of Publick Charge are lessened as much as may be, and that the people be well satisfied, and contented to pay their just shares of what is needfull for their Government and Protection, as also for the Honour of their Prince and Countrey: It follows now to propose the several wayes, and expedients, how the same may be most easily, speedily, and insensibly collected."[37] As with other instrumental affections in the period, felt and unfelt are here configured in a complementary relation by optimal taxation according to Petty. On the one hand, people should feel as "well satisfied and contented" about paying as possible—this because of their sense of national "Honour" and of what is "needfull" for defense and government. Despite this goodwill, the best taxes are nonetheless insensible ones. A split opens between the sense of public need and the desirability of unfeeling at the point and moment of collection. A general patriotic sentiment is all well and good, but paying for it should evade notice as much as possible. (At the beginning of his subsequent tract on taxes, *Verbum Sapienti*, 1691, Petty lists taxes that people "pay more insensibly and directly, as Customs, Excise, Chimny-Money, &c." than the land tax.)[38] So taxation works best when it bridges individual feelings and social needs, while maintaining a kind of gap, an affective blank, between them.

Similar remarks on the efficacy of this kind of taxation are scattered throughout the economic literature in the eighteenth century. The writer on commerce and founder (with Nicholas Barbon) of the land bank, John Asgill,[39] describes in 1715 the unfelt excise in colorful terms: "And tho the Excises on Food and Rayment may be at bottom as extensive and universal as this Window-Tax; yet they being not so visible, are paid more insensibly, and with a less Eye-sore to the People: *(for what the Eye don't see, the Heart don't rue.)* I can walk all day long with a hole in my Stocking (very well contented) if I my self don't know it, nor any one else tells me of it. *Non videmus id manticæ quod a tergo est* [*sic*]." [We do not see the knapsack on our back.][40] Asgill denounces the window tax (essentially a property tax, calculated by the number of windows in a house above ten) in conventional terms as "a Tax *upon the Lights of Heaven.*"[41] The excise on commodities exacts no less, but has the advantage, again, of being unsensed. Asgill develops the social psychology, or nonpsychology, of taxes suggested by Petty.

Attaching a tax to "Food and Rayment" that essentially becomes part of the prices of such commodities renders it insensible in a way that attaching a standing obligation to windows (or land) cannot be. This has as much to do with the nature of the item itself as the way the taxes are collected. Somehow we "see" a house's windows as subject to taxation in a way we do not see a mug of beer or a piece of clothing as such. The fluidity of such commodities, like that of money itself, masks the tax better than the static reminder of obligation to the government announced by a fixed number of windows in a house (and especially irritatingly perceptible when it encourages a practice, common in the eighteenth century, of bricking over some windows to reduce the tax bill). For Asgill, tax collection is made more bearable, less felt, by being attached to fugitive commodities instead of stable property—a position with the obvious potential to spark ideological conflict between landowners and the rest of society and raise questions about regressive taxation.[42]

It is ironic but unsurprising that a form of taxation said to be nearly unnoticeable should provoke some of the most furious, visible public disputes about tax legislation in the long eighteenth century. Though fearful of the unseen nature of such taxes, many controversialists followed Andrew Marvell's lurid visualization in 1667 of "Excise" as "a Monster, worse than e'er before / Frighted the midwife and the mother tore."[43] The tendency of such taxes to enhance Court power provoked much of the opposition. Early on in its English history the excise, according to Henry Roseveare, "doubled the elasticity of royal revenue and was the best bargain Charles [II] ever made."[44] Charles Davenant, who began his career as a playwright (like his father William, the laureate) but served as an excise commissioner under James II, sounds a dominant note in the political disputes over such taxes in his *Essay upon Ways and Means of Supplying the War* (1695). Certain patriots, Davenant observes—"real

Lovers of their Country, and Jealous of its Liberties"—fear the way in which excises are "so easie and little felt": "Excises being an easie way of Contributing, insensibly paid, and falling chiefly upon the common sort, they apprehend our Representatives may, some time or other, by the Arts and Power of the Court, be prevailed upon to let them pass into a lasting Supply to the Crown."[45] Though himself a promoter of excises, Davenant knew that their unfelt nature was exactly what alarmed many about them and corresponded to what anticourt factions feared was the creeping advance of tyranny.

The later furor over Robert Walpole's Excise Bill of 1733 arose in part because of a fear of the unfelt increase of governmental power that it would supposedly guarantee. The bill sought to change the form of tax on wine and tobacco (both, of course, imported commodities), from customs duties assessed on importers to an excise on domestic trade, in an effort to stanch revenue loss due to smuggling and relieve landowners of a high land tax.[46] But this relatively modest initiative gave rise to a fear of a "general excise" that would creep in to be levied on commodity after commodity. The prodigious pamphlet war waged that year against the excise found a focus in Viscount Bolingbroke's *Craftsman*. The numbers devoted to the dispute were collected in *An Argument Against Excises* (1733) by Caleb D'Anvers, the pseudonym under which Nicholas Amhurst edited the periodical. The collection uses Marvell's passage describing excise as a monster for an epigraph and declaims against the tax's potential violence and oppression. (Numerous pamphlets of that year also portray excise as a monster in particularly ghastly terms.)[47] In this, the *Craftsman*, like other contributors to the controversy, stresses the oppression of merchants by excise commissioners, their abridgment of the freedom of commerce, their unconstitutional, arbitrary powers, and so on, in contrast to the less predatory assessments of customs officials.

As anticipated by Davenant, the invisible nature of the tax will finally conduce, according to the *Craftsman*, to an unfelt encroachment of the power of court and crown. Though they now propose that only tobacco and wine come under the tax, "they carry it on gradually, and bring only *some Commodities* under this severe Yoke at a time."[48] The slowly coming general excise will result in the destruction of Britain's international commerce and thereby of the nation itself: "The Consequence must be, that our *Riches* and *Power* will sink away with our *Trade*; a general Scene of *Poverty* will spread it self by Degrees amongst all Ranks of People; and I am afraid it will appear that *our Liberties* will decline in Proportion."[49] The excise, openly reviled as it is, will operate according to the larger imperceptible principles of commerce, whereby its destructive power lies in its slow, corrosive spread. An economic tendency replaces political principle by the collectivizing action of money, displacing the conscious liberties of the constitution.

Nearly twenty years later, David Hume in his *Political Discourses* (1752) approaches the insensible character of indirect taxes more dispassionately. The *Discourses* (which contain Hume's most important essays on trade, commerce, and money) tend to occupy a "philosophical" terrain above practical political and controversial wrangling about policy.[50] In the essay "Of Taxes," he praises the excise in by now conventional terms, but his picture is notable for its psychological complexity:

> The best taxes are such as are levied upon consumptions, especially those of luxury; because such taxes are least felt by the people. They seem, in some measure, voluntary; since a man may chuse how far he will use the commodity which is taxed: They are paid gradually and insensibly: They naturally produce sobriety and frugality, if judiciously imposed: And being confounded with the natural price of the commodity, they are scarcely perceived by the consumers. Their only disadvantage is, that they are expensive in the levying.[51]

As commonsensical as these remarks are, they expose the strange power of indirect taxes both to involve the taxed subject in a social order and to screen that involvement. Many commentators about the period note the "voluntary" character of such taxes: you choose how much beer you want to drink and so "in some measure" choose how much tax to pay—as opposed to having a set amount assessed by an external agent on property you already own.

Yet even as he remarks on the quasi-voluntary character of indirect taxes, Hume notes how "they are paid gradually and insensibly," because they evade the notice of the will. They are chosen without a very full awareness of choice. Such taxes also impose a kind of unnoticed moral rigor. Unlike the exercise of them as virtues, the "sobriety and frugality" caused by tax policy arise without an exertion of moral will or even a desire to be good. Hume's "naturally" is a euphemism for the recession of this moral progress from moral awareness. The raised price blocks excessive consumption in a way the will cannot. The cost (as it were) of this progress is a kind of confusion, when the tax is "confounded" with the "natural price." Hume hence presents the tax as a mechanism to socialize the feelings in ways that cannot be felt. Liberty and moral imperatives are not destroyed but are rather transfigured by indirect taxation, and a new kind of free, modern subject is born.

The insensible for Hume hence mingles not only willed and unwilled but also artificial and natural, personal and political. Such combinations ultimately produce more of a gap than a link between the two elements. In the case of taxes, they provide "an instance of what frequently happens in political institutions, that the consequences of things are diametrically opposite to what we should expect on the first appearance."[52] To illustrate this principle, Hume ends the essay by noting that the power to impose new taxes surprisingly unites "European princes" and their subjects in a common interest, by being general in affecting the entire economy, unlike the arbitrary impositions of local "bashaws and governors" that work their way up to the *"Grand Signior"* in the Ottoman Empire.[53]

Finally, then, the small gap between the payment and the noticing of tax opens into a larger vision of a society bound together by unfelt affect. Writers after Hume attend to the psychology of taxation along similar lines. James Steuart, in his *Inquiry into the Principles of Political Oeconomy* (1767), for instance, describes the advantage of "proportional" taxes such as excises over "cumulative" taxes on property. Both mislead the taxpayer: the payer of property taxes imagines the imposition to correlate with what the government thinks he can pay. But as Steuart continues, "In the proportional, the deceit is of another nature. When a person buys a consumable commodity, which has paid an excise, he does not perceive that the price he pays for it comprehends a tax upon his past gains, in favour of the public; but he concludes the whole to be necessary, in order to procure what he has an inclination to consume."[54] Here the "deceit" of taxation is more radical than that of the "cumulative," where the exaction is felt but its nature is mistaken. The "proportional" taxes instead fundamentally reconfigure the relation of subject to society. Now the subject thinks he solely pursues personal "inclination"—choosing and paying for a consumer item—when he really pays "in favour of the public." The social impulse is thoroughly cloaked in private desire. Acutely felt when arbitrary, unnoticed when tending to the general good, taxes for Hume, Steuart, and others, including Adam Smith himself,[55] may take advantage of the double affective character of "human nature" to build a new kind of good citizen and newly secure social order.

3. The Money Flow

The power of indirect taxes to hide in prices points to a bigger truth about the role played by the insensible in British commercial discourse of the eighteenth century. The fluidity of commodities—priced goods and services—and of money itself tends to mask our engagements in commerce as a system, passionate though they are. Landmarks of pre-Smithian economic writing frequently recur to the insensible to describe money's affective status in a complex, temporally extensive system of transactions, both within and across national boundaries. The latter movements figure in one of the period's principal obsessions, achieving a favorable balance of trade and amassing gold and silver to secure national wealth—a body of doctrine that Adam Smith and later generations will call "mercantilist." Increasingly, commercial writers portray the flow of money as a natural phenomenon, obeying fixed laws. And as in Hume's "Of Taxes," the naturalness of economic movements correlates to their unnoticed and unwilled character, their resistance to deliberate human manipulation. Still, writers also realize that money does not move by itself. It is always people who move it, and often passionately motivated people. Out of a tension between money's metaphorically natural, nonconscious flows and the busy hands of merchants seeking very consciously to draw it to themselves emerges this body of writing's central affective dynamic.

A classic work of pre-Smithian economics, now considered among the most accomplished, describes how money and markets are always moving into and out of our range of feeling. The *Essai sur la nature du commerce en général* by Richard Cantillon, the Irish-French banker and speculator with numerous British and French financial interests,[56] exerted an international influence among specialists in the growing field as it circulated in manuscript in the early to middle decades of the century (it was published in French in 1755 but had been written around 1730). The *Essai* frequently employs the term *insensiblement* to describe movements of money and economic change in general, a fact somewhat obscured in the standard English translation of 1931 by Henry Higgs, who variously renders the word (as "gradually," "imperceptibly," "by imperceptible degrees," etc.).[57] Cantillon is often praised for dissociating his analysis of commerce from questions of morality and politics,[58] though policy recommendations are scattered throughout the *Essai*. He views commerce as operating according to abstract laws that move money and people regardless of individual wills and desires, which policy makers must understand if they wish to favorably affect a nation's economy. These movements Cantillon consistently depicts as occupying a dynamic, affective zone, in which they are in some sense noticeable, in another unavailable to our senses.

For Cantillon, himself a successful currency trader, the complexity of money's movements renders them invisible, even though we see and move it ourselves all the time. A passage in his admired chapter on monetary theory, "Of the Increase and Decrease in the Quantity of Hard Money in a State,"[59] remarks on the manner in which the nature of exchange itself must evade scrutiny:

> I have also observed that the increase or decrease of prices in a distant Market, home or Foreign, influences the actual Market prices. On the other hand money flows in detail through so many channels that it seems impossible not to lose sight of it seeing that having been amassed to make large sums it is distributed in little rills of exchange, and then gradually accumulated again to make large payments. For these operations it is constantly necessary to change coins of gold, silver and copper according to the activity of exchange. It is also usually the case that the increase or decrease of actual money in a State is not perceived because it flows abroad, or is brought into the State, by such imperceptible means and proportions [*par des voies & des proportions si insensibles*] that it is impossible to know exactly the quantity which enters or leaves the State.[60]

Rather than simply asserting that exchange is too complex to be directly perceived, Cantillon describes a ceaseless process wherein money gathers in visible proportions ("amassed to make large sums"), dissipates in "little rills of exchange" we cannot keep track of, and then reconstitutes itself in "large payments." His water metaphor suggests something both "natural" (a favorite word of Cantillon's) and gravitationally forceful about the process, as does the way money "flows abroad" and back again by its insensible means and proportions. The meaning of the insensible here is again not merely privative but literally additive. We lose and gain sight of amounts in exchange repeatedly, and the gaining testifies to the insensible movement in little rills that we could not otherwise recognize.

The unsensed quality of money's flow in Cantillon's account cannot be separated from its status as an object of the senses. We see it all happen, and we do it all, yet in its scale and complexity, we somehow lose sight of it at the same time. He next remarks, "However all these operations pass under our eyes and everybody takes part in them. I may therefore venture to offer a few observations on the subject, even though I may not be able to give an account which is exact and precise."[61] Now you see the "operations," now you don't. The interplay between obvious and obscure, then, helps establish the particular character of Cantillon's analytical approach: not "exact and precise" but nonetheless susceptible to his theoretical "observations on the subject." Hence Cantillon uses the idiom of the insensible to point not to a failure or limitation of his theorizing but to a precondition and motivation for it. The device allows him to depart from what is available to immediate observation to achieve a larger, more abstract view of how money works.

The understanding of economic activity as both saturating and evading sensible awareness is general in Cantillon's account and closely correlates with what he considers its "natural" movements. Another of his characteristic contentions, that the increase in a nation's wealth must tend to an eventual decline, also portrays the collectivity of transactions "under our eyes" as insensible. Considering a hypothetical increase in the domestic money supply stemming from a development of mines at home and a favorable balance of foreign trade, he concludes, "When a State has arrived at the highest point of wealth . . . it will inevitably fall into poverty by the ordinary course of things. The too great abundance of money, which so long as it lasts forms the power of States, throws them back imperceptibly but naturally [*insensiblement, mais naturellement*] into poverty."[62] The crucial linkage of the insensible to the natural enables Cantillon's achievement of analytical distance throughout the *Essai*. The unfelt, unmanaged, and undirected just *means* the natural in the period's political economy, and Cantillon's insight into it helps historians see him as a protoeconomist instead of a mere policy maker. And as in other appeals to the unfelt in eighteenth-century writing, time is Cantillon's theoretical medium. Terence Hutchison remarks that economic developments for Cantillon can extend over "a fairly long-term phase,"[63] not just the business cycle. (As Hutchison notes, Cantillon mentions the decline of Spain due to the influx of New World precious metals, which happened over two hundred years.) The insensible movements of economic history operate by a kind of natural force that evades direct human scrutiny in part because of their extreme gradualness.

At other instances Cantillon contrasts the natural, insensible movements of commerce with what policy might do to divert them. Like many writers of the period (though unlike Hume), Cantillon takes a negative view of the macroeconomic effects of luxury over time, but also portrays them as entirely natural. Luxury creates a particularly sharply divided interdependence of felt and unfelt, a tension we will see again in Smith. Those who can afford luxury items passionately pursue them, even as the larger tendency of such consumption wholly eludes notice. Cantillon describes the long-term process this way:

> It is true that the continued increase of money will at length by its abundance cause a dearness of Land and Labour in the State. The goods and manufactures will in the long run cost so much that the Foreigner will gradually cease to buy them, and will accustom himself to get them cheaper elsewhere, and this will by imperceptible degrees ruin the work and manufactures of the State [*ce qui ruinera insensiblement les ouvrages & les Manufactures de l'Etat*]. The same cause which will raise the rents of Landlords (which is the abundance of money) will draw them into the habit of importing many articles from foreign countries where they can be had cheap. Such are the natural consequences. The Wealth acquired by a State through Trade, Labour and Oeconomy will plunge it gradually [*insensiblement*] into luxury. States who rise by trade do not fail to sink afterwards. There are steps which might be, but are not, taken to arrest this decline. But it is always true that when the State is in actual possession of a Balance of Trade and abundant money it seems powerful, and it is so in reality so long as this abundance continues.[64]

The slow process of decline and the allure and power of wealth gradually pull apart. A kind of fatalistic "mercantilism" grips the narrative here. Money and a favorable trade balance really are power, but they naturally, inherently tend toward decline. Policy, "steps which might be, but are not taken," seems somewhat frail in the face of such natural gravity, inasmuch as "are not" resigns the possibility of action. Earlier Cantillon offers some ideas for resisting luxury's downward pull. The "Prince or the Legislator" ought "to withdraw money from circulation, keep it for emergencies, and try to retard its circulation by every means except compulsion and bad faith, so as to forestall the too great dearness of its articles and prevent the drawbacks of luxury."[65] Yet the force of the real, sensible power of wealth, there "under our eyes," tends to make such resistance difficult. Cantillon's natural consequences of commerce hence tend to override wise policy by means of their insensible operations.

Other important works in the literature of commerce and political economy of the 1750s and 1760s also portray the sensory status of money in these dual terms. For instance, the English commercial writer and advocate of the slave trade and of the Royal African Company, Malachy Postlethwayt,[66] drew freely in his major works (without acknowledgment) from Cantillon's *Essai*,[67] from which he perhaps contracted the habit of referring to the insensible motions of trade and money. He strikes Cantillon-like notes in his account of the decline of industry through processes of international competition in *Britain's Commercial Interest Explained and Improved* (1757): "In proportion as the price of a commodity rises to a certain degree, the profit tempts other nations, or enables them to compete in what they before did not dare to hazard. Their rivalship lessens the price insensibly; that diminution of price is sometimes on a sudden such, that the people, with whom the price of labour is dearest, are unable to bear it, and therefore renounces that branch of trade, of which it's [sic] rivals possess themselves for ever."[68] This motion in and out of sensible awareness again defines the action of commerce. The price that insensibly lessens and suddenly undergoes a surprising and quite noticeable diminution, causing managers to vacate a trade, expresses the peculiar doubleness in the affect of economic processes. For Postlethwayt these are different aspects of the very same pricing process, as he indicates with "that diminution." The economic development of international "rivalship" does its unnoticed work to lower the price—operating, as it were, on another scene, even as those put out of business by low prices that make labor costs untenable notice it all too clearly. The impression Postlethwayt conveys is of economic processes working at both an insensible (natural, forceful) and an evident (human) level. A kind of alienation of the senses lurks within our very sensible engagements with commerce.

A more explicit rendering of the close relation between the felt and the unfelt in economic movements appears in another essay from Hume's *Political Discourses* (1752), "Of the Balance of Trade," much broader and more international in scope than "Of Taxes." In it, Hume presents his celebrated account of the specie-flow mechanism, a central element of his theory of money.[69] A sharp contrast between the two affective modes of the movement of money comes toward the essay's end: "For above a thousand years, the money of EUROPE has been flowing to ROME, by an open and sensible current; but it has been emptied by many secret and insensible canals; And the want of industry and commerce renders at present the papal dominions the poorest territory in all ITALY."[70] The passage illustrates the essay's broader polemic against what later writers would call mercantilism. Worry about trade imbalances and national losses of gold and silver, Hume thinks, is misplaced. A government, he continues, "may safely trust" its money supply "to the course of human affairs."[71] Hume here presents credentials to be considered a father of the "classical" economic model.

But money's dual affective power in the passage to move both sensibly and insensibly makes it relevant to my discussion now. Tribute flows to Rome and the Catholic Church out of religious fervor or compulsion. People perceive what they are doing. They do not notice the multiple movements of money away from Rome again, though they are responsible for them too, exchanging and investing out of Italy, all according to "the course of human affairs." As Cantillon asserted, all the motions of money happen right "under our eyes." People, real individuals, are always the ones actually moving it. Yet in the scale and complexity of the movement of money, they do not recognize its backflow. To paraphrase the Marxian dictum, they do not *know* it, but *they* do it. The metaphor says, however, that money moves in both felt and unfelt ways. (Reversing what we might expect, the observed flow here is figured as a natural phenomenon, a "sensible current," while the "insensible canals" evoke human engineering.)

The water metaphor in the passage develops from patterns in Hume's essay at large. Near the beginning Hume remarks, "I should as soon dread, that all our springs and rivers should be exhausted, as that money should abandon a kingdom where there are people and industry."[72] A few pages later he elaborates in hydrostatic terms, noting that "all water, wherever it communicates, remains always at a level. Ask naturalists the reason; they tell you, that, were it to be raised in any one place, the superior gravity of that part not being balanced, must depress it, till it meet a counterpoise; and that the same cause, which redresses the inequality when it happens, must for ever prevent it, without some violent external operation."[73] The dumb, irresistible flow of water illustrates the flow of specie and commodities, regularizing their distribution across borders and exposing the counterproductivity of mercantilist, Colbertian measures to bottle them up. "It is impossible to heap up money," Hume insists, "more than any fluid, beyond its proper level."[74] Human will cannot successfully transcend the relations of what Gilles Deleuze, characterizing Spinozan affect, calls "the relations of motion and rest, of slowness and speed" that constitute the basis of our affective lives.[75] Without insisting that Hume (here or anywhere else) is any kind of Spinozist,[76] we can see his account linking monetary affect to physical motion.

Comparing money to water finding its level could hardly be more common in eighteenth-century discussion of the topic. Hume himself used the analogy a couple of years earlier in his letter to Montesquieu of 1749, which addresses the balance of trade, among other things.[77] The image recalls Cantillon's picture of money flowing in and out of sight in "little rills of exchange." It is possible Hume got to know Cantillon's work through his early acquaintance with Andrew Michael Ramsay in France,[78] but the analogy appears everywhere in commercial writing of the long eighteenth century. It is perhaps more difficult to find a writer who does not use it than one who does. William Petty, in his chapter "Of Customs and Free Ports" from *A Treatise of Taxes and Contributions* (1662) concedes, after making a few mercantilist recommendations, "I conceive even this were better then to perswade Water to rise out of it self above its natural Spring."[79] Later, the Italian economist Ferdinando Galiani, with whom Hume argued in Paris about monetary policy, offers similar images.[80] Such depictions could seem to subject the motions of money to dumb physical laws and leave human feeling entirely out of it. Money moves on its own, obeying forces like gravity that operate on *their* own, not diverted by economic sentiments.

But Hume does not set out to prove that human feeling is irrelevant to economic processes, which are "really" determined by brute physical force. Rather, he places them on a single continuum, with human feeling, will, and intention at one end and affective physical motion at the other. While we perceive some economic motives, others affect us like physical impulses, move us to move, to transact according to relations of slowness and speed that we feel only dimly or not at all. Hume describes just that, as he explicitly brings his analogy of gravity and fluidity back to the human, "moral" realm: "We need not have recourse to a physical attraction, in order to explain the necessity of this operation. There is a moral attraction, arising from the interests and passions of men, which is full as potent and infallible."[81] This "moral attraction" *arises from* human feelings, from "the interests and passions of men,"[82] without quite being identified with them. It is something extra, embedded in and driven by interests and passions without being felt itself.

The connection between water and commerce in Hume's essay moreover turns out, unsurprisingly, to be more than just an analogy. A little farther on, he comments, "Men naturally flock to capital cities, sea-ports, and navigable rivers. There we find more men, more industry, more commodities, and consequently more money."[83] Money flows not only *like* water but also *to* it, and people flow to and with it also. Entirely characteristically, Hume stresses continuities between the natural and moral realms, and money has a way of affecting people like a physical force whether they feel it or not.[84] Water, money, people: the continuum preserves and intensifies the physical, natural character of commerce even as it remains linked to motive and feeling, as men of business "naturally flock" to the water like birds. Thus Hume's final distinction between the "open and sensible current" of commerce and its "secret and insensible canals" does not contrast feeling with dead physical force but felt with unfelt affect. The latter is contiguous with the former, all part of the same interconnected affective waterway, all moved by and motivating the passions and interests of men.

4. Invisible versus Insensible

The affective range of economic life portrayed in the examples discussed in the foregoing three sections of this chapter sets the most famous piece of figurative language in the period's commercial writing in a new light. Adam Smith's account of the invisible hand is one of numerous references in *The Wealth of Nations* (1776) to unsensed forces that steer the economy while fully felt passions, such as greed and vanity, power it. Commentators have proposed various candidates for the hand's true identity from the early twentieth century on. (The phrase drew little attention before then.) The list includes the market, the price system, self-interest, self-regulating self-interest, competition, private property, a secularized providence, "the obvious and simple system of natural liberty" (Smith's phrase),[85] and so on, and the goal to which the hand directs the economy has been identified as "order," "automaticity," "coordination," "general equilibrium," or "general harmony and benevolence."[86]

But something different emerges when considering the invisible hand proper alongside other unsensed economic processes in *The Wealth of Nations* and in light of this chapter's sequence of examples of unfelt economic affect. In Cantillon, in Hume, people moved money and money moved people in interrelated ways; and of these, some were sensed and some not. This makes it difficult to see commerce as ordered from above by "a mechanism outside human influence" since human affective influence is all there is to the mechanism.[87] The immersion of commerce in affect does not make it any less susceptible to quasi-scientific explanations, as examples from Mandeville onward have shown, though feeling must always give more scope to contingency than physical laws of nature. Private vices will result in public benefits, and public happiness may well produce some private discomfort, though people may learn to feel happy about that too. The hydrostatic terms elaborated by Hume and others bring commercial life under principles akin to the law of gravity. Human motives and feelings remain relatively predictable, and the cycles they initiate are consistent exactly insofar as "the interests and passions of men" are too. Smith likewise brings in an understanding of human nature to his explanation of trade and commerce, which is why *The Wealth of Nations* stands as the edifice of classical economics that it is.

But scholars have found that Smith's invisible hand does more than execute a single function. Warren J. Samuels emphasizes the idea of "an invisible-hand process or mechanism" over "any candidate for the identity of the invisible hand" and suggests that "the economy is comprised of numerous invisible hands."[88] An affective reading of the hand as one example among many in Smith of unsensed processes also recognizes the multiple roles they may play without viewing them as expressing a single executive principle directing all from above. The figurative dimension of Smith's famous phrase reinforces such multiplicity. A hand—the body part most associated with touch and with intention—can do many different things: point, push, touch, feel. The phrase has been viewed as a "literary" effect,[89] a "rhetorical" flourish,[90] a sally of humor not especially important to his thought,[91] even an expression of gothic menace.[92] Often commentators call such figures in Smith literary to suggest that they are less than fully serious.[93] But their literariness also enhances their flexibility of meaning, as well as their resistance to simple moralization.

Such flexibility means their function can extend beyond optimization, a production of the best possible economic and more general social outcomes. Smith uses these devices in that optimizing way, of course, but the insensible in *The Wealth of Nations* has an ambiguous range. A renewed scholarly interest in the notion of unintended consequences in the Scottish Enlightenment has taken the invisible hand as a prime example,[94] and mostly it has been seen to work for the best—a reassuring, harmonious "self-organization." But unintended consequences can, of course, be good or bad or, in affective terms, gratifying or appalling—and mix good and bad feelings in various degrees. Smith's attention to the insensible as an affect exceeds the limitations of any simply happy narrative of self-organization that some economic historians found in his thought.

It is telling that this affective complexity emerges most palpably in the most historically minded part of *The Wealth of Nations*, book 3, "Of the Different Progress of Opulence in Different Nations," before the invisible hand makes its appearance by name in book 4. (The use of the term "opulence" itself has suggested to some that book 3 was drafted early, before Smith had settled on the word "wealth.")[95] Here Smith describes an insensible economic development that fails to conform to expectations. This account does not follow the cyclical logic of commercial writing that I have described in the first three sections of chapter IV, where money tends to flow visibly, then invisibly, and then comes back into view again, all according to the predictable passions of human beings. While Smith never loses his keen sense of natural human passions in treating the historical "progress" pursued in book 3, his appreciation of their complexity unfolding in linear time ensures that the story does not merely conform to a predictive, theoretical principle. His historical perspective here leads him to attend to what actually happened instead of what ought to have happened.

Though the title of the first chapter of book 3 promises an account "Of the Natural Progress of Opulence," the book as a whole delivers something like the opposite. In brief, the story goes like this: The natural way for any society to develop is by bringing agriculture to an improved state before centering itself on the pursuit of commercial trade. Smith here evokes a version of stadial theory, whereby society advances through defined stages—hunter-gatherer, nomadic herding, agricultural, and finally commercial—through history, of which Smith's most sustained discussion appears in the *Lectures on Jurisprudence* (delivered 1762–63).[96] The case of England and Europe in general, according to book 3, did not work that way. As chapter 1 concludes,

> But though this natural order of things must have taken place in some degree in every such society, it has, in all the modern states of Europe, been, in many respects, entirely inverted. The foreign commerce of some of their cities has introduced all their finer manufactures, or such as were fit for distant sale; and manufactures and foreign commerce together, have given birth to the principal improvements of agriculture. The manners and customs which the nature of their original government introduced, and which remained after that government was greatly altered, necessarily forced them into this unnatural and retrograde order. (380)

European society advances out of feudalism not naturally, by developing agriculture first and then commercial trade, but in this "entirely inverted" manner. The resulting "unnatural and retrograde order" cannot, of course, look like an entirely happy kind of progress or an optimal form of self-organization.[97]

Yet as we will see, there are still good things to say about it. The outcome represents real progress, unnatural though it is: the progress Europe actually got instead of the progress a four-stages theoretician might have predicted and wished for.

Driving this story affectively is "the vanity of the great proprietors" (407). Instead of improving their lands, the great indulge a taste for foreign luxuries, which comes to stimulate home manufactures. The great *then* improve their lands so that they can afford yet more luxuries. Smith argues in chapter 2 of book 3 that the hard facts of the feudal law, particularly concerning primogeniture and entails, discouraged agricultural improvement. But the engine of feelings—vanity and greed—powers the processes that deform European economic development. Smith is highly critical of the legal causes,[98] but he is positively disgusted at and contemptuous of the affective ones. Later in book 3, for instance, he will denounce the "trinkets and baubles, fitter to be the playthings of children than the serious pursuits of men" (421) that stimulate the vanity of feudal proprietors, in terms very close to his expressions of contempt in book 2 for the tastes of the rich and the great of his own time (see, e.g., 346). Book 3 presents a double layer of affective intensity, then: the pride and vanity of the great proprietors driving Europe's unnatural development, and Smith's own opprobrium for these motive passions, which seems to aggravate his sense of its unnaturalness.

Alongside these feelings, however, Smith reserves a place for the unfelt. Appalling as the vanity of the barons is, it nonetheless brings forth a historical development of which Smith approves. The narrative concludes,

> What all the violence of the feudal institutions could never have effected, the silent and insensible operation of foreign commerce and manufactures gradually brought about. These gradually furnished the great proprietors with something for which they could exchange the whole surplus produce of their lands, and which they could consume themselves without sharing it either with tenants or retainers. All for ourselves, and nothing for other people, seems, in every age of the world, to have been the vile maxim of the masters of mankind. As soon, therefore, as they could find a method of consuming the whole value of their rents themselves, they had no disposition to share them with any other persons. For a pair of diamond buckles perhaps, or for something as frivolous and useless, they exchanged the maintenance, or what is the same thing, the price of the maintenance of a thousand men for a year, and with it the whole weight and authority which it could give them. The buckles, however, were to be all their own, and no other human

creature was to have any share of them; whereas in the more antient method of expence they must have shared with at least a thousand people. With the judges that were to determine the preference, this difference was perfectly decisive; and thus, for the gratification of the most childish, the meanest and the most sordid of all vanities, they gradually bartered their whole power and authority. (418–19)[99]

So quite animating feelings—"the most childish, the meanest and the most sordid of all vanities"—propel an entirely unfelt process, "the insensible operation of foreign commerce and manufactures." The two hand in hand, felt and unfelt, eventually destroy the power of the great proprietors as a "class" and inaugurate a new commercial order.

The conclusion of this process, even the just deserts reaped by the barons whose vanities cause their destruction, does not dissipate Smith's disapproval. Far from taking a Mandevillean delight in the private vices of his fellow citizens and the happy outcomes they produce, he moralizes about the "vile maxim"—"all for ourselves, and nothing for other people"—that distinguishes the rich and the great as a social sector throughout history. Smith's dislike of the rich and their motive principles remains remarkably consistent, whatever the economic, social, and historical circumstances. He does not like them when they aggrandize themselves by squandering capital on wasteful feudal feasts and exorbitant entertainments instead of improving their lands. And he does not like them here when they spend money on stupid luxuries, which look mean compared to medieval generosity.[100] He just does not like them. This animosity arises from and helps intensify, I think, his sense that the progress initiated by their vanities is "unnatural and retrograde," progress though it may be. The very mismatch of their attempts to aggrandize themselves with "frivolous and useless" things and their insensibly approaching self-destruction add a further sense of disorder and illogic to the undoing of feudalism.

But the unnatural character of this unfelt movement is not bad enough for Smith to renounce it. He finally moralizes book 3's history this way:

A revolution of the greatest importance to the publick happiness, was in this manner brought about by two different orders of people, who had not the least intention to serve the publick. To gratify the most childish vanity was the sole motive of the great proprietors. The merchants and artificers, much less ridiculous, acted merely from a view to their own interest, and in pursuit of their own pedlar principle of turning a penny wherever a penny was to be got. Neither of them had either knowledge or foresight of that great revolution which the folly of one, and the industry of the other, was gradually bringing about. (422)

Commentators interested in the invisible hand cite this passage as another example of economic self-organization in Smith's thought[101]—and to some extent it is. But Smith will not let go of the perverse aspects of the development. He concludes by restating reasons to feel bad about it: "This order, however, being contrary to the natural course of things, is necessarily both slow and uncertain" (422). The insensible processes arising from the interest of merchants and especially the childish passions of the great cannot be moralized as an unambiguous triumph of optimization or "general harmony and benevolence," even though they resemble such tales. The sordid feelings and insensible operations they set in motion produce something awkwardly placed in history.

A final affective state emerges at the end of this sequence. First childish vanity, then "the insensible operations of foreign commerce and manufactures," and at last "a revolution of the greatest importance to the publick happiness." Smith equivocates slightly here. He does not directly state that the "publick" went from being unhappy to being happy; he merely acknowledges that the "publick happiness" underwent a revolution. The passage implies that things changed very much for the better, but this slight hitch in his account again indicates his unwillingness to celebrate all aspects of the change without reserve, and especially the affective aspects. Still, as in many other passages discussed throughout the present volume, from beginning to end, the insensible mediates in this account between two sorts of fully felt feelings—in this passage, between the contemptible feelings driving the avidity for foreign luxuries and the final generalized happiness they help procure. It allows Smith's account to get from one to the other.

He does not elaborate on the idea of public happiness to the degree that Mandeville does earlier in the century, but the phrase here (which appears nowhere else in *The Wealth of Nations*) raises questions like those Mandeville's *Fable of the Bees* considered. It is worth wondering how Smith thinks the final state, "the publick happiness," is really felt, and by whom. The rich and the great in commercial societies, the present socioeconomic configuration of the nations of Europe, remain contemptibly trivial. As we know from book 2, the rich as they are in Smith's day tend to exhibit "not only a trifling, but a base and selfish disposition" (349). Despite their "passion for present enjoyment" (341), their existence is not exactly happy, in Smith's eyes.

And the word also seems too simple to describe the affective state of relentlessly accumulating merchants and artificers, laudable though their activity is. As he remarks earlier, on "the desire of bettering our condition" that predominates among men of business, between birth and death "there is scarce perhaps a single instant in which any man is so perfectly satisfied with his condition, as to be without any wish of alteration or improvement, of any kind"

(341). Somehow such feelings of these contrasting social stations, very different from each other and from any simply enjoyed happiness, come together to make the "publick happiness" what it is. The public affect as a whole is called happiness, as the word shades again into an objective, even materialist meaning: prosperity or good fortune. If not entirely unfelt itself, "the publick happiness" in Smith transcends while thriving off of the affective constituents—vanity, passion for gain—that motivate and produce it. In it Smith offers another way we can think of affect as residing somewhere other than in what people actually feel.

Considering the insensible process that Smith discusses in book 3 aids an understanding of the more famous invisible one introduced in book 4. There Smith speaks about a general tendency of individuals to maximize their advantages, without anything comparable to the historical context offered in book 3. He remarks:

> As every individual, therefore, endeavours as much as he can both to employ his capital in the support of domestick industry, and so to direct that industry that its produce may be of the greatest value; every individual necessarily labours to render the annual revenue of the society as great as he can. He generally, indeed, neither intends to promote the publick interest, nor knows how much he is promoting it. By preferring the support of domestick to that of foreign industry, he intends only his own security; and by directing that industry in such a manner as its produce may be of the greatest value, he intends only his own gain, and he is in this, as in many other cases, led by an invisible hand to promote an end which was no part of his intention. (456)

There it is, the only reference to the invisible hand in *The Wealth of Nations*. As is frequently pointed out, the phrase appeared in two earlier texts of Smith's, the "History of Astronomy" as "the invisible hand of Jupiter,"[102] referring to supernatural explanations for earthly phenomena; and an economic instance in *The Theory of Moral Sentiments*, about the distribution of goods by the expenditures of the rich, who likewise promote widespread social well-being "without intending it, without knowing it."[103] In *The Wealth of Nations* Smith's formulation links a general principle—capitalists will, ceteris paribus, prefer domestic markets to foreign ones, for safety's sake—to a general tendency: often, our pursuit of private interest promotes the public one.

The "insensible" process discussed in book 3 operates rather differently. In one way, its scope is wider, involving both domestic and foreign economic movements. Smith describes "the silent and insensible operation of *foreign commerce and manufactures*" and shows how these have affected domestic production. But in another sense, book 3's account is more narrow: it focuses on historical particularities, what actually happened in Europe as a result of the feudal law and the affective subjects it created. The unfelt affect noticed in book 3 has its own unintended benefits, but its historical actualities mix in a sense of how the insensible may drive suboptimal processes to which bad affects cling. It does not contradict or invalidate the more optimistic, abstract, invisible tendency articulated later. Yet together they demonstrate how the unfelt imparts an openness to unpredictable impulses in Smith's work that scholars have in recent years insisted on. For Smith, in Jack Russell Weinstein's words, "human tendencies are not inviolable in the same way that the laws of physics are." Smith's examples ensure that the former have a "normative" character, in which actual and optimal mutually inform each other.[104]

The exchange in Smith between invisible and insensible demonstrates how lawlike principles in *The Wealth of Nations* remain, as Christopher J. Berry remarks characterizing Scottish Enlightenment attitudes toward historical inquiry in general, "ineliminably open to contingency."[105] The unfelt works as a kind of double medium in Smith's account. On the one hand (the invisible one), it provides a way for particularized, private actions and motives to be assimilated in a socially larger structure and so brought under a kind of economic law. But on the other, the insensible helps characterize a historical distortion, a kind of accident that expressly deviates from the natural course. Both the lawlike and the contingent may hence emerge out of this blank affective matrix.

The examples surveyed in this chapter in all their variety point to the intimate ways in which felt feelings inform the unfelt ones that help constitute larger social structures. Far from establishing an implacable, generalizing field of force that derives its power and authority from its remoteness from actual human feelings, the insensible ceaselessly draws on and incorporates such feelings, taking direction from as well as directing them. In an obvious sense, the insensible would be nothing, neither in its motive origin nor in its outcomes, without feelings. So the proximate unhappiness of Mandeville's citizens constitutes happiness of the city. And the large movements of money through commercial transactions within and across borders, in one sense invisible to us, are in another sense always happening "under our eyes." But unfelt affect also transforms feelings, making the most antisocial of them social, even when this affect differs from the feelings that create it, as public happiness differs from urban exasperation, greed, and vanity. And in Smith, especially, the two kinds of affect, felt and unfelt, have a way of seeping into each other. So his contempt for the vanity of those who propel prosperity can make progress itself somewhat contemptible, while his own philosophical confidence in commerce can make its unnatural retrograde history in Europe feel like something to be happy about.

Epilogue

Insensible Emergence of Ideology

A radical text written for an epoch to follow the one treated in this book identifies unfelt and active forces holding humanity back from social happiness. At the outset of his *Enquiry concerning Political Justice* (1796), William Godwin disputes with those who see the operations of "government or social institutions" to be "as rather of a negative than positive nature,"[1] mere restraints on us instead of productive powers. The *Enquiry* starts with the contrary contention that government "insinuates itself into our personal dispositions, and insensibly communicates its own spirit to our private transactions."[2] The insensible performs politically insidious work on behalf of the status quo. It disposes our sympathies and beliefs before political reason can be exerted and so forestalls meaningful progress toward justice. Oddly (but now familiarly after all the examples in this book), this kind of unfeeling has a "positive nature." Its inertial force is not static but that of a body in motion, slowly, positively affecting our beliefs and their effects in our actions.

Later Godwin's picture of how such affects work takes on more detail. The chapter "Of the Mechanism of the Human Mind" follows in the tradition of the psychological philosophy I surveyed in chapter I of this book, referring to Hartley's "medullary substance" and his "vibrations,"[3] as well as, indirectly, to David Hume and John Locke. The ongoing input to our senses, according to Godwin, always overfills us with more than we can ever actually experience. "The sense of feeling is diffused over every part of my body," he remarks, "but all these impressions are absolutely simultaneous, and I can have only one perception at once."[4] This is Godwin's version of the divide between virtual and felt feelings that interests affect theorists now and that has been the subject of the present volume. "Every perception," Godwin continues, "is complicated by a variety of impressions" that we do not exactly feel; in fact, "every idea that now offers itself to the mind, is modified by all the ideas that ever existed in it."[5] This virtuality of feeling for Godwin is a potential menace. The very mechanism of the human mind perpetuates a tacit politics of nonconsciousness, a politics embedded in tacitness, and "it is this circumstance that constitutes the insensible empire of prejudice."[6] In the interaction between felt and unfelt, perceptible and imperceptible, lie the deepest roots of oppression.

The many kinds of writing I have surveyed in this book that use the idiom of the insensible in some ways anticipate what must look to us now like Godwin's theory of ideology. What the writers I have discussed—from the late seventeenth century onward—have treated as natural changes wrought by the slowness of time can be seen through Godwin's eyes as entailing a political dimension: an oppressively slow mode of acquired and reinforced beliefs that humanity is desperate to overcome. Beyond that, the four areas of eighteenth-century prose treated in this book's four chapters each employs the idiom to describe what could look, if described broadly and roughly enough, like the basic components of an ideology of modern Western liberalism.

The treatment in chapter I of Locke's account of our apprehensions of reality and our self-constituting identities, of David Hartley's brain science, and of the affective nature of experience in Étienne Bonnot de Condillac and Hume, Eliza Haywood and Adam Smith notes a mysteriousness common to all these, an unfeeling that enables our perceptions, mental processes, and feelings to function. The ideological construction of "the modern subject," then, its self-transparency and conscious freedoms, relies on a productive, affective blank. In chapter II, the fiction of the long eighteenth century (especially of Henry Fielding and Frances Burney) was shown to reconcile the freedom of women's desire with its disciplining by means of its insensible motions, to ready them for marriage. The historiography of the period, as described in chapter III, understands enlightened progress, refinement, and the civilization of the passions as natural in an account of their unfelt and undirected growth. And chapter IV showed that writing about trade and commercial life reconciles (in Dudley North's words) "the exorbitant Appetites of Men" with a happy, harmonious social collective by means of an affect that individuals cannot feel.[7] As much as this recapitulation leaves out, it suggests how the idiom of the unfelt enables writers to construct four basic formations—the free subject, disciplined feminine desire, progress, the self-optimizing economy—that the ideology of modernity has commonly been seen to comprise.

It is important to stress that the insensible does not, in the first instance, characterize how *belief* in these things is inculcated. That is, my examples have not primarily illustrated how historical individuals insensibly assume beliefs in their own free subjectivity, in progress, and so on—assumptions that dispose them to behave as passionately committed participants in a particular social and political order. Rather, the *things themselves* are said to emerge through insensible processes in time. Such processes may often, if not usually, entail the affective embodiment of them by the writer who describes and therefore believes in them. So the "insensible revolution" in the early modern period described by Hume implicitly extends, in recursive fashion, to his own subsequent personal enlightenment, and in Edward Gibbon's more ambiguous example, the historian finds himself enwrapped in the insensible movements of history that he researches. The writer who notices an insensibly changing process may be a part of the very process she describes, as in Haywood's account of the unfelt development of her own insight (treated in chapter I). Such performances run deeper than the writer's mere belief in what she says. She *undergoes* and is subject to the process as a consequence of her writing and self-understanding. It happens to her.

At the beginning of chapter IV, I alluded to a classic definition of ideology from Karl Marx as a doing, instead of a mere knowing or believing. Preceding the remark I quoted, in the same chapter of *Capital* ("The Fetishism of the Commodity, and the Secret Thereof"), is a longer, also familiar passage that resonates with my discussion's themes in more specific ways. The alienation of social relations in objects, Marx explains,

> is the reason why the products of labour become commodities, social things whose qualities are at the same time perceptible and imperceptible by the senses. In the same way the light from an object is perceived by us not as the subjective excitation of our optic nerve, but as the objective form of something outside the eye itself. But, in the act of seeing, there is at all events, an actual passage of light from one thing to another, from the external object to the eye. There is a physical relation between physical things. But it is different with commodities. There, the existence of the things quâ commodities, and the value relation between the products of labour which stamps them as commodities, have absolutely no connection with their physical properties and with the material relations arising therefrom. There it is a definite social relation between men, that assumes, in their eyes, the fantastic form of a relation between things.[8]

The remarks on commodity fetishism have commonly been seen as a suggestive account of ideology, though Marx does not here use that word.[9] In this passage, he asserts the copresence of felt and unfelt in our affective lives to illustrate ideology's characteristic powers and operation. Our social existence has qualities that "are at the same time perceptible and imperceptible by the senses." Ideological experience arises out of this affective split. And in this passage, ideology, beyond something we do, is something that happens to us. We have no choice in the matter as to whether or not to believe in it, just as we have no choice as to whether or not our optic nerves are excited by light reflected from objects.

But the passage also distinguishes between such physical processes and fetishism's hold on our minds. The former are "objective" and "actual," while the objective existence of the latter is nowhere to be found. And this distinction further illuminates the potential ideological significance of the examples of unfelt affect treated in this book, themselves often described, literally or figuratively, as physical processes. The optical metaphor in *Capital* of course recalls Locke's account of primary and secondary qualities in the *Essay concerning Human Understanding* at its most "corpuscular," its description of the "insensible parts" of matter that actually cause (in Marx's words) the "subjective excitation" of our eyes. My discussion cites many other gestures to the physicality of the unfelt, from Hume's references to fermentation and gravitational forces, to the attractions among "Inanimates" raised in Georges de Scudéry's account of love in *Almahide*, to the hydrostatic metaphors that run through the period's commercial writing. Marx will go on to insist that commodity fetishism, unlike ocular stimulation, occurs only in a certain kind of social world. It cannot happen on Robinson Crusoe's island, nor does it arise among the clear hierarchical dependencies of feudalism. The insensible, conversely, happens all the time. Writers in the eighteenth century portray it as a feature of our temporal existence in the world. It affects reality positively even as it refers to an affect that cannot ever be felt or known. This double valence, additive and blank, structures the idiom's meaning and usages.

Recalling this basic structure clarifies what may be said of its ideological tendencies. Nothing could be more useful in narrating otherwise impossible affective improvements and resolutions than an idiom designed to hint at a productively blank feeling. But as a blank, of course, this feeling must wait for such meanings to be assigned to it, usually at the story's end. So Burney can use the notion of the insensible to describe, in a novel in which women's desire is itself a trap, how her heroine can discover in herself the right desire for the right marriage without compromising her morality. Burney can also use the insensible, however, to find her way to otherwise unthinkable thoughts—libertine, sensual—in her conversation with Miss White. The insensible similarly helps Smith describe the emergence of a kind of "publick happiness" from "unnatural and retrograde," "slow and uncertain" developments in British and European economic history.

Even Godwin, who seems to align the insensible with the power of government and institutions to oppress, can find it opening paths on which political justice may advance. In the final book of the *Enquiry*, "Of Property," he asserts the equal right of everyone to all goods and proposes a resolution of any potential conflict among people with competing claims to the same thing. The doctrine of equality of property may "be expected to make hourly progress in the convictions of mankind . . . to sink deep in the human understanding, insensibly to mix itself with all our reasonings, and ultimately to produce, without shadow of violence, the most complete revolution in the maxims of civil society."[10] Competing claims to property will hence disappear. If the insensible characterizes the weight of injustice for Godwin, it also may bring forth the nonviolent revolution. These examples in their totality indicate that the insensible cultivates a kind of openness to narrative possibility in British discourse of the long eighteenth century. Writers doubtless use it to realize whatever affective ends they would choose, but the range of choice is too broad to serve just one set of ideological purposes.

If it is right to understand the insensible as a kind of affect, its political meaning remains undetermined and a function of this indeterminacy. To an extent, this assertion resembles what affect theorists have commonly claimed. Differentiating affect from emotion, Lawrence Grossberg refers to this political dimension: "I am not sure that emotions can simply be described as affect, even as configurations of affect. I have always held that emotion is the articulation of affect and ideology. Emotion is the ideological attempt to make sense of some affective productions."[11] So affect, as preemotional, is pre-ideological. Perhaps the insensible as I have described it is not so very open as bodily affect, as now theorized, to an indeterminate range of political outcomes. The account in this book has stressed the status of the insensible as an idiom, a useful way of writing, and not a reference to a deep reservoir of unarticulated feeling. As such it assimilates itself to various writers' purposes (some of which we may call ideological) perhaps more readily than the full, rich, multivalent potency of affect now appreciated by its theorists. But even as a mere stylistic feature, the idiom holds its politics in reserve, until an "ideological attempt to make sense" of it comes along. The variety of literature surveyed in this book alone, I think, testifies to the idiom's open-endedness.

An important preoccupation of writers about affect today has been its supposed "emancipatory potential."[12] Theorists may present what Clive Barnett calls "the *affirmative vision of the politics of affect*" or "the *critical vision*" of it—the latter alert to ways affect "opens up new surfaces for the exercise of manipulation."[13] But in respect to the affective functions of the insensible in the foregoing discussion, the choice between "affirmative" and "critical" seems both too large and too constrained. The idiom in the period acts like a spacer in discourse, a little tool, precise in its way, used to keep an interval open in seminal arguments about sensation in the history of philosophy and in the emotional transformations undergone by fictional heroines. It opens new possibilities to mediate between incompatible affective states in historiography and political economy. The ideological consequences of the addition of unfelt space to these stories and arguments are both apparent and varied. If literature in the long eighteenth century consistently depicts individuals and groups, in the past and in the present, as moved and moving insensibly, the idiom is designed to maintain an openness as to where they might go.

Notes

Introduction

1. Frances Burney, *Evelina: or, A Young Lady's Entrance into the World, in a Series of Letters*, 2nd ed. (London, 1779), 3:49.

2. Henry Brooke, *The Fool of Quality, or The History of Henry Earl of Moreland, in Four Volumes* (Dublin, 1766), 2:224. The novel would be complete in five volumes by 1770. Here Brooke's Mr. Fenton is retelling the story from Xenophon of Panthea and Araspes.

3. My discussion contrasts in this respect with two classic studies (themselves very different): William Empson, *Structure of Complex Words* (1951, Harmondsworth, England: Penguin, 1995); and Raymond Williams, *Keywords: A Vocabulary of Culture and Society* (Oxford: Oxford University Press, 1976). Empson's book explores the words *sense* and *sensible* in various combinations in chapters 12–15, including "Sense and Sensibility" (chap. 12); these chapters have influenced my treatment of *insensibly*, which includes, by negation, Empson's target term.

4. Samuel Johnson, *A Dictionary of the English Language* (London, 1755), vol. 1, s.v. "insensibly," definition 2. (Definition 1 is "Imperceptibly; in such a manner as is not discoverable by the senses.")

5. Brooke, *The Fool of Quality*, 1:187.

6. Samuel Richardson, *Clarissa. Or the History of a Young Lady*, 3rd ed. (London, 1751), 4:319; emphasis in the original.

7. Preeminent among them now is the excellent study by Wendy Anne Lee, *Failures of Feeling: Insensibility and the Novel* (Stanford, CA: Stanford University Press, 2018). Though Lee's book appeared a matter of days before the final draft of the present volume went to press, my discussion has benefited from Lee's argument, as presented in her article "The Scandal of Insensibility: The Bartleby Problem," *PMLA* 130, no. 5 (2015): 1406–19. Lee treats what I call the privative senses of *insensible* and *insensibility*, as distinguished from my interest in additive, adverbial processes. (While the words *insensibility* and *insensible*, the latter a noun, occur hundreds of times in her book, *insensibly* appears not once.) Lee tracks the personage of "the insensible" through literature of the (very) long eighteenth century, epitomized by Herman Melville's Bartleby, who is exceptionally impassive, sits stolidly as the "other" of feeling, and exerts a "non-narrative" force ("The Scandal of Insensibility," 1406b). In contrast, my book describes the successes of unfeeling, its ways of abetting sentiment, and asserts the unexceptional nature of insensible processes, as common property of all. For an earlier example of a theoretical interest in affective lack, see Lauren Gail Berlant, "Unfeeling Kerry," *Theory & Event* 8, no. 2 (2005), https://muse.jhu.edu/article/187843. Berlant

focuses on the "insensate political emotions" of the 2004 US presidential election, a numbness that had come over the public sphere.

8. Fredric Jameson, *Postmodernism, or, The Cultural Logic of Late Capitalism* (Durham, NC: Duke University Press, 1991), 15 (and throughout).

9. As Brian Massumi, *Parables for the Virtual: Movement, Affect, Sensation* (Durham, NC: Duke University Press, 2002), 16, puts it, "The vast majority of the world's sensations are certainly nonconscious. Nonconscious is a very different concept from the Freudian unconscious (although it is doubtless not unrelated to it). The differences are that repression does not apply to nonconscious perception and that nonconscious perception may, with a certain amount of ingenuity, be argued to apply to nonorganic matter."

10. See Adrian Johnston and Catherine Malabou, *Self and Emotional Life: Philosophy, Psychoanalysis, and Neuroscience* (New York: Columbia University Press, 2013), and especially Johnston's half of the book, for a critical account of this exegetical tradition, taking up Lacan's rejection of unfelt feelings in Freud at 118–49. Conversely, Johnston argues that Freud's texts indicate that "there can be, so to speak, unfelt (or, more accurately, misfelt) feelings" (79)—as when a patient misfeels his guilt as anxiety.

11. Gregory J. Seigworth and Melissa Gregg, "An Inventory of Shimmers," in *The Affect Theory Reader*, ed. Melissa Gregg and Gregory J. Seigworth (Durham, NC: Duke University Press, 2010), 2.

12. The spike of *imperceptibly* is even more dramatic, rising from nowhere in 1700 and peaking in 1784, after which, again, comes a steep drop.

13. Matthew L. Jockers, *Macroanalysis: Digital Methods and Literary History* (Urbana: University of Illinois Press, 2013), 120. For a homegrown methodology, much richer than mere Ngram searches and resulting in a diachronic, digital analysis of the concept of rights in the eighteenth century, see Peter de Bolla, *The Architecture of Concepts: The Historical Formation of Human Rights* (New York: Fordham University Press, 2013).

14. Edward Gibbon, *The History of the Decline and Fall of the Roman Empire*, ed. David Womersley (London: Penguin, 1994), 1:1040.

15. Here I quote from the final (1778) edition of David Hume, *The History of England* (Indianapolis: Liberty Fund, 1983), 5:18. There are small verbal differences between the passage quoted and its original form in *The History of Great Britain* (Edinburgh, 1754), 1:15.

16. Adam Smith, *An Inquiry into the Nature and Causes of the Wealth of Nations* (Indianapolis: Liberty Fund, 1981), vol. 1, bk. 3, 422.

17. Ibid., vol. 1, bk. 3, 418.

18. Paraphrased from Brooke, *The Fool of Quality*, 2:224. Even if we add "which fell on his soul," the privative sense modifying *him* still powerfully suggests that his soul did not receive the effects of these things.

19. Gibbon, *Decline and Fall*, 1:1028.

20. See Nathalie M. Phillips, *Distraction: Problems of Attention in Eighteenth-Century Literature* (Baltimore: Johns Hopkins University Press, 2016). Phillips's study raises questions that pertain to the insensible in some important respects—especially its role in Condillac's account of attention discussed in chapter I, section 3 of the present volume.

21. For a readily available account in English of Koselleck's approach see Reinhart Koselleck, *The Practice of Conceptual History: Timing History, Spacing Concepts*, trans. Todd Samuel Presner (Stanford, CA: Stanford University Press, 2002).

22. In this I maintain a Wittgensteinian impulse to recognize real differences between everyday and philosophical languages. The famous quotation runs: "When philosophers use a word—'knowledge,' 'being,' 'object,' 'I,' 'proposition,' 'name'—and try to grasp the *essence* of the thing, one must always ask oneself: is the word ever actually used this way in the language-game which is its original home?—What we do is to bring words back from their metaphysical to their everyday use." Ludwig Wittgenstein, *Philosophical Investigations*, trans. G. E. M. Anscombe, New York: Blackwell, 1958, 48e, sec. 116; emphasis in the original.

23. Joseph Addison, "No. 409: Thursday, June 19, 1712," in *The Spectator*, ed. Donald F. Bond (Oxford: Oxford University Press, 1965), 3:527.

24. Gibbon, *Decline and Fall*, 1:65.

25. See, e.g., the classic text by Henri F. Ellenberger, *The Discovery of the Unconscious: The History and Evolution of Dynamic Psychiatry* (1970; repr., New York: Basic Books, 1981), and especially chap. 2, "The Emergence of Dynamic Psychiatry," 53–109, which discusses Mesmer's role as the originator of modern psychiatry. Frank Tallis, *Hidden Minds: A History of the Unconscious* (New York: Arcade, 2012), 1–4, begins with G. W. Leibniz and his *New Essays on Human Understanding*, a response to Locke's *Essay* that links "insensible perceptions" to the insensible corpuscles treated by Boyle and Locke, though Leibniz's *New Essays* was not published until 1765, too late to influence English usage treated in my study. For the distinction between Leibniz and Locke on this point, see chapter I of the present volume.

26. Peter Sloterdijk, *Critique of Cynical Reason*, trans. Michael Eldred (Minneapolis: University of Minnesota Press, 1987), 49.

27. Benjamin Franklin et al., *Report of Dr. Benjamin Franklin, and other Commissioners, Charged by the King of France, with the Examination of the Animal Magnetism* (London, 1785), 2.

28. For a helpful study of Mesmerism, see Patricia Fara, *Sympathetic Attractions: Magnetic Practices, Beliefs, and Symbolism in Eighteenth-Century England* (Princeton, NJ: Princeton University Press, 1996).

29. In addition to Franklin, *Report of Dr. Benjamin Franklin*, see Franz Anton Mesmer, *Mesmer's Aphorisms and Instructions, by M. Caullet de Veaumore, Physician to the Household of Monsieur, his Most Christian Majesty's Brother* (London, 1785).

30. As demonstrated by Jean H. Hagstrum, "Towards a Profile of the Word *Conscious* in Eighteenth-Century Literature," in *Psychology and Literature in the Eighteenth Century*, ed. Christopher Fox (New York: AMS, 1987), 23–50, the term *conscious* had a vital and multivalent existence in eighteenth-century writing, with roots in the literature of antiquity (especially Virgil), and implications that evoked something like the unconscious long before the invention of depth psychology; see especially 38–46.

31. A principal text is Gilles Deleuze, *Spinoza: Practical Philosophy*, trans. Robert Hurley (San Francisco: City Lights, 1988), which offers, in the form of a critical dictionary, an "Index of the Main Concepts of the *Ethics*," 44–109. Deleuze also treats Spinozan thinking in many other works and numerous lectures, including *Expressionism in Philosophy: Spinoza*, trans. Martin Joughin (New York: Zone, 1990). See also Gilles Deleuze and Félix Guattari, *A Thousand Plateaus: Capitalism and Schizophrenia*, trans. Brian Massumi (Minneapolis: University of Minnesota Press, 1987), 153: "After all, is not Spinoza's *Ethics* the great book of the BwO [body without organs]?"

32. Seigworth and Gregg, "An Inventory," 3.

33. Brian Massumi, "Notes on the Translation and Acknowledgements," in Deleuze and Guattari, *A Thousand Plateaus*, xvi.

34. Deleuze, *Spinoza: Practical Philosophy*, 123.

35. As Deleuze contrasts them in *Practical Philosophy*, 49, "The *affectio* refers to a state of the affected body and implies the presence of the affecting body, whereas the *affectus* refers to the passage from one state to another."

36. Gilles Deleuze, "Cours Vincennes," January 24, 1978, trans. Timothy S. Murphy, Les Cours de Gilles Deleuze (website), https://www.webdeleuze.com/textes/14.

37. This is a literal translation of "En un sens la durée c'est toujours derrière notre dos, c'est dans notre dos qu'elle se passe." Gilles Deleuze, "Cours Vincennes," January 20, 1981, Les Cours de Gilles Deleuze (website), https://www.webdeleuze.com/textes/35.

38. Massumi, "Notes on the Translation," xvi.

39. See, e.g., the first of Jonathan I. Israel's monumental volumes on Spinoza's influence on Enlightenment thought, *Radical Enlightenment: Philosophy and the Making of Modernity 1650–1750* (Oxford: Oxford University Press, 2001), which devotes its only section on Britain's positive reception of Spinozan ideas (599–627) to Collins, Mandeville, Tindal, and Toland, though it identifies "a pervasive, even at times obsessive preoccupation with Spinoza" from the 1670s through the "early Enlightenment" (599). See also Wayne Hudson, *The English Deists: Studies in Early Enlightenment* (London: Pickering and Chatto, 2009), which gives a fuller account of the Deists' ideas, including their debts to Spinoza.

40. John Trenchard, *The Natural History of Superstition* (London, 1709), 24–26; my ellipsis omits a series of instances of the "secret Magick" that Trenchard offers.

41. See David Berman, *Berkeley and Irish Philosophy* (London: Continuum, 2005), 164, for a claim that "there is much in Trenchard which may be traced to Spinoza," including an "unwillingness to limit the power of matter."

42. Trenchard, *Natural History*, 26.

43. Eighteenth-century British readers and writers encountered Spinoza's ideas mostly in translations of Pierre Bayle's *Historical and Critical Dictionary*, in which the article on Spinoza is by far the longest. In a relatively rare edition, *An Historical and Critical Dictionary, by Monsieur Bayle* (London, 1710), the article on Spinoza runs from p. 2781 to p. 2804. Two rival editions appeared in 1734: *The Dictionary Historical and Critical of Mr Peter Bayle* (London, 1734–38), a "Second Edition" of the 1710 version, is substantially the same translation; *A General Dictionary, Historical and Critical*, trans. Thomas Birch et al. (London, 1734), is a new translation.

44. Jonathan I. Israel, *Enlightenment Contested: Philosophy, Modernity, and the Emancipation of Man* (Oxford: Oxford University Press, 2009), 51. This has been a consistent theme of Israel's voluminous project. Other scholarship, however, continues to unearth radical religious currents in Newton's unpublished papers. See, e.g., Rob Iliffe, *Priest of Nature: The Religious Worlds of Isaac Newton* (Oxford: Oxford University Press, 2017), 11: "If they had been unveiled to the Republic of Letters when he wrote them, and his authorship revealed, he would now be part of an elite pantheon of original thinkers who are lauded as part of a Radical Reformation or Radical Enlightenment."

45. For a suggestive treatment, see Paul Russell, *The Riddle of Hume's Treatise: Skepticism, Naturalism, and Irreligion* (Oxford: Oxford University Press, 2010), especially 70–82, though Russell focuses on the influence of Spinoza's *Theological-Political Treatise*, not the *Ethics*. Earlier explorations of affinities between Hume's thought and Spinoza's *Ethics* include Wim Klever, "Hume contra Spinoza?," *Hume Studies* 16, no. 2 (1990): 89–106; Wim Klever, "More about Hume's Debt to Spinoza," *Hume Studies* 19, no. 1 (1993): 55–74; and Annette C. Baier, "David Hume, Spinozist," *Hume Studies* 19, no. 2 (1993): 237–52.

46. Seigworth and Gregg, "An Inventory," 8.

47. Massumi, *Parables*, 20.

48. Brian Massumi, "Sensing the Virtual, Building the Insensible," in *Hypersurface Architecture*, ed. Stephen Perrella (New York: Wiley, 1998), 20.

49. Massumi, *Parables*, 26.

50. For examples in literary studies, see Adam Potkay, *The Passion for Happiness: Samuel Johnson and David Hume* (Ithaca, NY: Cornell University Press, 2000), which traces Hellenistic and Ciceronian models of happiness to Hume and Johnson; and his comprehensive history, *The Story of Joy: From the Bible to Late Romanticism* (Cambridge: Cambridge University Press, 2007). See also Vivasvan Soni, *Mourning Happiness: Narrative and the Politics of Modernity* (Ithaca, NY: Cornell University Press, 2012), which focuses on "an affective and domestic conception of sentimental happiness" (274) in the novel form as an earmark of its modernity.

51. For an illuminating survey of literature's range of affective modes in the eighteenth century and beyond, see Deidre Shauna Lynch, *Loving Literature: A Cultural History* (Chicago: University of Chicago Press, 2015). For an account of the surprisingly diverse affective engagements generated by a beloved literary figure, see Helen Deutsch, *Loving Dr. Johnson* (Chicago: University of Chicago Press, 2005).

52. See, e.g., Ildiko Csengei, *Sympathy, Sensibility and the Literature of Feeling in the Eighteenth Century* (Basingstoke, England: Palgrave Macmillan, 2012).

53. For a useful survey, see Aleksondra Hultquist, "New Directions in History of Emotion and Affect Theory in Eighteenth-Century Studies," *Literature Compass* 13, no. 12 (2016): 762–70. Hultquist has also edited "Emotion, Affect, and the Eighteenth Century," special issue, *The Eighteenth Century* 58, no. 3 (2017). Within that issue, Stephen Ahern, "Nothing More Than Feelings? Affect Theory Reads the Age of Sensibility," 281–95, is exceptional in its interest in the virtual character of affect, though Ahern tends to see virtuality as evident in "a surfeit of emotion" (287) that defeats expression, not in insensible intensities. See also Stephen Ahern, ed., *Affect Theory and Literary Critical Practice: A Feel for the Text* (Cham, Switzerland: Palgrave Macmillan, 2019), which surveys affect in literature from the medieval to the modern.

54. My own essay "Unfelt Affect," an initial step into the terrain explored in this book, is, of course, an exception; see James Noggle, "Unfelt Affect," in *Beyond Sense and Sensibility*, ed. Peggy Thompson (Lewisburg, PA: Bucknell University Press, 2015), 125–44.

55. Grossberg is complaining, in fact, that in too many accounts, affect has "become everything that is non-representational or non-semantic—that's what we now call affect"; and this seems too broad a definition to him. See Lawrence Grossberg, "Affect's Future: Rediscovering the Virtual in the Actual," interview by Gregory J. Seigworth

and Melissa Gregg, in Gregg and Seigworth, eds., *The Affect Theory Reader*, 316. Grossberg himself does, however, invoke the distinction in "Another Boring Day in Paradise: Rock and Roll and the Empowerment of Everyday Life," *Popular Music* 4 (1984): 227, which notes that the material context of rock and roll music is "defined by affective investments rather than by semantic representations."

56. Seigworth and Gregg, "An Inventory," 8.

57. Massumi, *Parables*, 25. Yet see also his discussion of the affective nature of the body's reception of signs, as he finds in the semiotics of C. S. Peirce a way to discuss a "performance" that "takes place wholly between the sign and the 'instinctively' activated body whose feeling is 'broken' by the sign's command to transition to a new feeling"; Massumi, "The Future Birth of the Affective Fact: The Political Ontology of Threat," in Gregg and Seigworth, eds., *The Affect Theory Reader*, 64.

58. See Eve Kosofsky Sedgwick, *Touching Feeling: Affect, Pedagogy, Performativity* (Durham, NC: Duke University Press, 2003), especially chap. 3, "Shame in the Cybernetic Fold: Reading Silvan Tomkins," 93–122, cowritten with Adam Frank, which attacks the view that affect is "discursively constructed" (109). This essay was originally published in 1995, the same year as Brian Massumi, "The Autonomy of Affect," *Cultural Critique* 31 (1995): 83–109. Massumi's essay would become the first chapter of his *Parables*. See William Egginton, "Affective Disorder," *Diacritics* 40, no. 4 (2012): 26, for a characterization of the Deleuzean strand of affect theory as a promise "to reorient a turn to the body that ended up not being about the body back to the body, and not just as an effect of cultural mediations of one sort or another." The preponderance of Leys's critique is focused on Massumi's applications of contemporary neuroscience.

59. Ruth Leys, "The Turn to Affect: A Critique," *Critical Inquiry* 37, no. 3 (2011): 469. As Leys notes, "In this regard, Massumi's attitude toward the sciences is scarcely to be differentiated from that of non-Deleuzean affect scholars, such as Sedgwick and [Daniel Lord] Smail" (468).

60. See Massumi, *Parables*, 29–31.

61. For accounts of affect in the humanities that invoke Damasio, see, e.g., Malabou's half of Johnston and Malabou, *Self and Emotional Life*, especially 26–34, 50–55; and N. Katherine Hayles, *Unthought: The Power of the Cognitive Nonconscious* (Chicago: University of Chicago Press, 2017), 42–43, 45–46. Hayles focuses on nonconscious cognition, not nonconscious affect, but her definitions of the former sometimes bleed into the latter, as when she includes "internal body systems and emotional and affectual nonconscious processes" (64) in what she generally calls nonconscious cognition.

62. For his account of the proto-self, see Antonio Damasio, *The Feeling of What Happens* (New York: Houghton Mifflin Harcourt, 1999), 133–67, and Antonio Damasio, *Self Comes to Mind* (New York: Random House, 2010), 201–2, 217–19.

63. Damasio, *Self Comes to Mind*, 201; emphasis in original.

64. Massumi, *Parables*, 37. Leys lists a number of Massumi's statements about affect that seem incompatible with any capacity it may have to be realized in actual brain states; see Leys, "The Turn," 468n62.

65. Richard Cantillon, *Essai sur la nature du commerce en général*, trans. Henry Higgs, 2nd ed. (London: Cass, 1959), 64.

66. For an argument that seeks to hold a larger concept of Enlightenment together, see John Robertson, *The Case for the Enlightenment: Scotland and Naples, 1680–1760* (Cambridge: Cambridge University Press, 2007).

67. See, among many others, G. J. Barker-Benfield, *The Culture of Sensibility: Sex and Society in Eighteenth-Century Britain* (Chicago: University of Chicago Press, 1996); and John Mullan, *Sentiment and Sociability: The Language of Feeling in the Eighteenth Century* (Oxford: Oxford University Press, 1984).

68. See, e.g., Emily Hodgson Anderson, "Forgetting the Self: Frances Burney and Staged Insensibility," in *Eighteenth-Century Authorship and the Play of Fiction: Novels and the Theater, Haywood to Austen* (London: Routledge, 2009), 46–76; and Lee, *Failures of Feeling*, chap. 1, "A Brief History of the Prude," 29–57.

69. See Margaret Koehler, *Poetry of Attention in the Eighteenth Century* (London: Palgrave Macmillan, 2012), 18, for the claim that "an approach that foregrounds the eighteenth-century fascination with attention proves especially congenial to the period's poetry. Eighteenth-century poems enact these historical and theoretical accounts of attention and share a commitment to *cultivate* readers' attention" (emphasis in the original).

70. For a particularly brilliant discussion of the challenges posed to literary representation by these figures, see Scott Dykstra, "Wordsworth's 'Solitaries' and the Problem of Literary Reference," *ELH* 63, no. 4 (1996): 893–928.

71. William Wordsworth, "Old Man Travelling: Animal Tranquillity and Decay," in William Wordsworth and Samuel Taylor Coleridge, *Lyrical Ballads, with a Few Other Poems* (London, 1798), 189, lines 3–12.

Chapter I. Philosophy

1. Richard Rorty, *Philosophy and the Mirror of Nature* (Princeton, NJ: Princeton University Press, 1979), 143, takes the term from Gilbert Ryle to describe the double-sidedness of Locke's term of art, *impression*.

2. As Charles Taylor, *Sources of the Self: The Making of Modern Identity* (Cambridge, MA: Harvard University Press, 1989), 49, characterizes the Lockean (and Humean) view of personal identity, "For Locke [personal identity] has this peculiarity that it essentially appears to itself. Its being is inseparable from self-awareness. Personal identity is then a matter of self-consciousness. . . . Self-perception is the crucial defining characteristic of the person for Locke."

3. I do not suggest that philosophers' attention in the period to consciousness, self-consciousness, and personal identity has ceased to interest scholars. For a detailed survey in British, French, and German intellectual history to around 1760, see Udo Thiel, *The Early Modern Subject: Self-Consciousness and Personal Identity from Descartes to Hume* (Oxford: Oxford University Press, 2011).

4. For instance, Jerrold Seigel, *The Idea of the Self: Thought and Experience in Western Europe since the Seventeenth Century* (Cambridge: Cambridge University Press, 2005), discerns three foci of theories of the self in the modern era—the bodily, the social, and the self-reflective or self in consciousness—and insists that emphasizing only the last of these is inadequate. He credits those philosophers, among whom he numbers Hume, Locke, and Smith, who draw on all three types in their conception of selfhood.

5. See Dror Wahrman, *The Making of the Modern Self: Identity and Culture in Eighteenth-Century England* (New Haven, CT: Yale University Press, 2004), which proposes an "*Ancien Régime*" (xi–xviii, emphasis in the original) of the self before "an essential core

of selfhood characterized by psychological depth, or interiority" (xi) took over after 1780.

6. For an account of the will understood as "external" in some writers of the period, see Jonathan Kramnick, *Actions and Objects from Hobbes to Richardson* (Stanford, CA: Stanford University Press, 2010); for an account of how novels conceive morality not as executed by internal intentions but as an artifact of sociolegal obligations, see Sandra Macpherson, *Harm's Way: Tragic Responsibility and the Novel Form* (Baltimore: Johns Hopkins University Press, 2010).

7. See Brian Massumi, "Notes on the Translation and Acknowledgements," in Gilles Deleuze and Félix Guattari, *A Thousand Plateaus: Capitalism and Schizophrenia*, trans. Brian Massumi (Minneapolis: University of Minnesota Press, 1987), xvi, which defines the term *affect* in Deleuze and Guattari as a "prepersonal intensity" different from "personal feeling."

8. Thus Deleuze glosses Spinoza in *Spinoza: Practical Philosophy*, trans. Robert Hurley (San Francisco: City Lights, 1988), 73.

9. Gilles Deleuze, "Cours Vincennes," January 24, 1978, trans. Timothy S. Murphy, Les Cours de Gilles Deleuze (website), https://www.webdeleuze.com/textes/14.

10. John Locke, *An Essay concerning Human Understanding*, ed. Peter Nidditch (Oxford: Oxford University Press, 1975), 525.

11. John Locke, *An Essay concerning Human Understanding*, ed. Peter Nidditch (Oxford: Oxford University Press, 1975), 335. Hereafter, page numbers will be cited parenthetically; all emphasis is in the original. The *Essay* first appeared in 1689, and went through four substantially revised editions during Locke's lifetime; the fourth of which was published in 1700.

12. Laurence Sterne, *The Life and Opinions of Tristram Shandy, Gentleman*, in *The Florida Edition of the Works of Laurence Sterne*, ed. Melvyn New and Joan New (Gainesville: University Presses of Florida, 1978–2009), 1:98.

13. The confusion arises partly because Locke's use of the terms *power, quality, sensation*, and *idea* here and throughout the *Essay* is somewhat slippery. A clarifying moment, a version of the sentences in 2.8.8, occurs in the following (unpunctuated) definition from his manuscript "Epitome" of the *Essay*: "Thus whitenesse coldnesse roundnesse as they are sensations or perceptions in the understanding I call Ideas as they are in a snow ball which has the power to produce these Ideas in the understanding I call them Qualitys"; quoted in James Hill and J. R. Milton, "The Epitome (*Abrégé*) of Locke's *Essay*," in *The Philosophy of John Locke: New Perspectives*, ed. Peter R. Anstey (London: Routledge, 2003), 19. In short, qualities are what reside in objects, and ideas (of them) are what reside in our minds.

14. On this view, see, e.g., Georges Dicker, *Berkeley's Idealism: A Critical Examination* (Oxford: Oxford University Press, 2011), 9–26.

15. Edwin McCann, "Locke's Distinction between Primary Primary Qualities and Secondary Primary Qualities," in *Primary and Secondary Qualities: The Historical and Ongoing Debate*, ed. Lawrence Nolan (Oxford: Oxford University Press, 2011), 169.

16. Lisa Downing, "Locke: The Primary and Secondary Quality Distinction," in *The Routledge Companion to Metaphysics*, ed. Robin Le Poidevin, Peter Simons, Andrew McGonigal, and Ross Cameron (Abingdon, England: Routledge, 2009), 101.

17. Ibid., 104.

18. For a classic discussion of problems with this doctrine, see Jonathan Bennett, *Locke, Berkeley, Hume: Central Themes* (Oxford: Clarendon, 1971), especially 106.

19. They do not come directly, of course, from "primary primary qualities," but we must assume that the "Bulk, Figure, Texture, and Motion" of insensible parts are more or less similar to those at the higher (secondary primary) level, which in turn pattern our ideas of them. See McCann, "Locke's Distinction," 176–79.

20. See Michael Ayers, *Locke*, vol. 1, *Epistemology* (London: Routledge, 1991), 61–62. For a discussion of primary qualities as resemblances and secondary qualities as "blank effects," see Michael Jacovides, "Locke's Distinctions between Primary and Secondary Qualities," in *The Cambridge Companion to Locke's "Essay concerning Human Understanding,"* ed. Lex Newman (Cambridge: Cambridge University Press, 2007), 106–10.

21. For an argument that such statements equate Locke's primary qualities to the scholastic concept of real essence, see Downing, "Locke: The Primary and Secondary Quality Distinction," 103–5.

22. A search for the phrase "insensible parts" in Eighteenth-Century Collections Online (https://www.gale.com/primary-sources/eighteenth-century-collections-online) turns up appearances in some 283 texts (many, of course, different editions of the same text, especially of the *Essay*) on theology and religion, mathematics, music, agriculture, and so on, in addition to natural history, anatomy, medicine, and physiology.

23. The phrases occur so frequently in Boyle that particular citations would be misleading in their limitation to single instances: "insensible parts" frequently appears, for instance, in *The History of Fluidity and Firmness* (1661), in *The Works of the Honourable Robert Boyle* (London, 1744), 1:248, among other places; "insensible particles" appears in *Some Considerations Touching on the Usefulness of Experimental Natural Philosophy* (1663), in *Works*, 1:452; and "insensible corpuscles" appears in *Experiments and Considerations Touching Colours* (1664), retitled *The Experimental History of Colours* in *Works*, 2:10). For a discussion of Boyle's corpuscularianism as a coherent philosophy, and specifically a comparison of the scholastic doctrine of "occult qualities" to the insensible, see Peter R. Anstey, *The Philosophy of Robert Boyle* (London: Routledge: 2000), 23–30.

24. See Peter R. Anstey, *John Locke and Natural Philosophy* (Oxford: Oxford University Press, 2011), 10–30, for an account of natural philosophy in the *Essay* as influenced by Boyle and others, and especially the problem of "epistemic access to the inner nature of things" (30), which Locke feared insurmountable and which Anstey calls "Corpuscular Pessimism," discussed in a chapter with that title (31–45).

25. Paragraphs 1–6 of the chapter discuss the positive ideas produced in us by privations such as darkness.

26. There is no question, of course, of its functioning as an inherent adjective in these contexts. With the phrase "insensible Parts," Locke is pointing out not that the parts themselves cannot feel, but that they cannot be perceived.

27. G. W. Leibniz, *Nouveaux essais sur l'entendement humain* (Paris: Ernest Flammarion, 1921), 17. Leibniz composed the *Nouveaux essais* in French and Latin.

28. G. W. Leibniz, *New Essays on Human Understanding*, trans. Peter Remnant and Jonathan Bennett (Cambridge: Cambridge University Press, 1996), 56. For the role of Leibniz's insensible perceptions in a long history of the philosophy of apperception, see Daniel Heller-Roazen, *The Inner Touch: Archaeology of a Sensation* (New York: Zone Books, 2007), 179–209.

29. Ibid., 55–56.

30. See Rosemarie Sponner Sand, *The Unconscious without Freud* (Lanham, MD: Rowman and Littlefield, 2013), which begins with a chapter devoted to Leibniz (1–20).

31. So Sand will remark, addressing Locke's doctrine of the association of ideas, that "associations are automatic; they are not mental actions; they happen; no thought is required. What Locke has given us is an explanation of unconsciously determined events which can be accepted by opponents of unconscious thought"; Sand, *Unconscious without Freud*, 70–71. This distinction between "unconscious thought" (of Leibniz) and the nonmental "unconsciously determined events" of Locke seems to me exactly right.

32. Brian Massumi, "Sensing the Virtual, Building the Insensible," in *Hypersurface Architecture*, ed. Stephen Perrella (New York: Wiley, 1998), 20.

33. As Michael Ayers remarks in "Primary and Secondary Qualities in Locke's *Essay*," in *Primary and Secondary Qualities: The Historical and Ongoing Debate*, ed. Lawrence Nolan (Oxford: Oxford University Press, 2011), 137, Locke's distinction "may still deserve the interest of philosophers as a classic, early case of a scientific ontology coming apart from the ontology of everyday life or 'common sense.' Locke's discussion may be admired by some as an early step towards an appreciation of how radically modern physics should change our view of the world and what is in it, even if it does not correspondingly change everyday ways of talking about it."

34. See Ayers, "Primary and Secondary Qualities," 142. The complications are also traced in McCann, "Locke's Distinction." For a literary assessment of the productive tension between Locke's empiricism and his skepticism, see Fred Parker, *Scepticism and Literature: An Essay on Pope, Hume, Sterne, and Johnson* (Oxford: Oxford University Press, 2003), 54–85.

35. Robert J. Fogelin, "The Tendency of Hume's Skepticism," in *The Skeptical Tradition*, ed. Myles Burnyeat (Berkeley: University of California Press, 1983), 410; emphasis in original. Fogelin is describing Hume in particular, but identifies the attitude as common throughout the long eighteenth century.

36. John Locke, quoted in Anstey, *John Locke and Natural Philosophy*, 40. Anstey offers numerous other instances in which Locke's understanding of the insensible nature of corpuscles gives rise to such totalizing skepticism (31–45).

37. Locke's vehemence in this passage, added to the second edition of 1694, is in response to critics who took him (or affected to take him) to be arguing that the soul ceases to exist during sleep.

38. The philosophical literature on personal identity in Locke is, of course, vast. For a classic analytic discussion of the problem at large, including detailed distinctions and comparisons between physical and psychological criteria for personal identity, see Derek Parfit, *Reasons and Persons* (Oxford: Oxford University Press, 1984), 204–9.

39. Jonathan Kramnick, *Actions and Objects from Hobbes to Richardson* (Stanford, CA: Stanford University Press, 2010), also sees a connection between organic and personal identity in Locke's *Essay* and recognizes how care about our future lives ties them together: "This imagining of future states of the same person and care for the person's happiness would seem to stitch ideas of the self to some sort of physical system" (93). Kramnick views this connection as a motive for Locke's meditations later in the *Essay* on "a relation between consciousness and matter" (94), although "Of Identity and Diversity" insists that neither personal nor organic identity subsists in identity of substance (material or otherwise).

NOTES TO PAGES 40–44

40. Galen Strawson, *Locke on Personal Identity: Consciousness and Concernment* (Princeton, NJ: Princeton University Press, 2011), 96.

41. Marya Schechtman, *The Constitution of Selves* (Ithaca, NY: Cornell University Press, 1996), 108.

42. Margaret Anne Doody once declared, "Nowadays, I look in the index of books on either sensibility or sentiment, and if there is no reference to David Hartley I close the volume"; see Doody, "Vibrations," *London Review of Books* 15, no. 15 (1993): 11.

43. David Hartley, *Observations on Man, His Frame, His Duty, and His Expectations* (London, 1749), 1:5. Hereafter, page numbers will be cited parenthetically, and are from vol. 1; all emphasis is in the original.

44. This is not to say that Newton's *Opticks* entirely neglects the philosophical definitions of Locke and Boyle regarding qualities, just that Hartley did not take up this aspect of the question. For Newton's subtle reliance on the doctrine of qualities, see Philippe Hamou, "Vision, Color, and Method in Newton's *Opticks*," in *Newton and Empiricism*, ed. Zvi Biener and Eric Schliesser (Oxford: Oxford University Press, 2014), 74–75.

45. The passage in Isaac Newton, *The Mathematical Principles of Natural Philosophy*, trans. Andrew Motte (London, 1729), 2:393, reads,

> And now we might add something concerning a certain most subtle Spirit, which pervades and lies hid in all gross bodies; by the force and action of which Spirit, the particles of bodies mutually attract one another at near distances, and cohere, if contiguous; and electric bodies operate to greater distances, as well repelling and attracting the neighbouring corpuscles; and light is emitted, reflected, refracted, inflected, and heats bodies; and all sensation is excited, and the members of animal bodies moved at the command of the will, namely, by the vibrations of this Spirit, mutually propagated along the solid filaments of the nerves, from the outward organs of sense to the brain, and from the brain into the muscles. But these are things that cannot be explain'd in few words, nor are we furnish'd with that sufficiency of experiments which is required to an accurate determination and demonstration of the laws by which this electric and elastic spirit operates.

46. Isaac Newton, *Opticks: or, A Treatise of the Reflections, Refractions, Inflections and Colours of Light*, 2nd ed. (London, 1718), 327–28. See also Hamou, "Vision, Color, and Method," especially 84–87.

47. For a view of the use of Newton in biological enquiries by Hartley and others, see Charles Wolfe, "On the Role of Newtonian Analogies in Eighteenth-Century Life Sciences: Vitalism and Provisionally Inexplicable Explicative Devices," in Biener and Schliesser, eds., *Newton and Empiricism*, 223–61, especially 232–36. See also C. U. M. Smith, "David Hartley's Newtonian Neuropsychology," *Journal of the History of the Behavioral Sciences* 23, no. 2 (1987): 123–36, which discusses Newton's influence, though without connecting the "infinitesimal" character of medullary particles to fluxions.

48. Newton does discuss fluxions in the *Quadratura Curvarum* appended to the 1704 *Opticks*, but this is a separate tract and does not appear in the 1718 and 1730 editions. Translations of the *Quadratura* appeared in 1710 (by John Harris) and 1745 (by John Stewart). As Augustus de Morgan, "The Early History of Infinitesimals in England" in the *Philosophical Magazine and Journal of Science*, 4th ser., 4, no. 6 (1852): 328, declares,

"In 1704 Newton in the *Quadratura curvarum* renounced and abjured the infinitely small quantity."

49. For instance, Jerome Christensen, "Philosophy/Literature: The Associationist Precedent for Coleridge's Late Poems," in *Philosophical Approaches to Literature: New Essays on Nineteenth- and Twentieth-Century Texts*, ed. William E. Cain (Cranbury, NJ: Associated University Presses, 1984), 32, dismisses the notions of the "infinitesimal elementary Body" and vibrations themselves in Hartley as invented, "speculative entities."

50. Cf. Newton, *Opticks*, 2nd ed. (London, 1718), 370, where Newton contrasts the small particles of light to chemicals and colors: "Now the smallest Particles of Matter may cohere by the strongest Attractions, and compose bigger Particles of weaker Virtue; and many of these may cohere and compose bigger Particles whose Virtue is still weaker, and so on for divers Successions, until the Progression end in the biggest Particles on which the Operations in Chymistry, and the Colours of natural Bodies depend, and which by cohering compose Bodies of a sensible Magnitude."

51. Newton, for his part, asserts in queries 29–31 of the *Opticks* that "Rays of Light [are] very small Bodies emitted from shining Substances" (345).

52. For an account of another application of calculus in the *Observations*, 339–42, which Hartley uses as an example of "arguing from Experiments and Observations, by Induction and Analogy" (339), see the standard work on Hartley, Richard C. Allen, *David Hartley on Human Nature* (Albany: State University of New York Press, 1999), 244–46. Allen does not discuss Hartley's recourse to calculus to conceptualize the "infinitely smaller."

53. See John L. Bell, "Continuity and Infinitesimals," in *The Stanford Encyclopedia of Philosophy*, fall 2013 ed., ed. Edward N. Zalta, http://plato.stanford.edu/archives/fall2013/entries/continuity/, which notes that "Newton later became discontented with the undeniable presence of infinitesimals in his calculus, and dissatisfied with the dubious procedure of 'neglecting' them. In the preface to the *De quadratura curvarum* he remarks that there is no necessity to introduce into the method of fluxions any argument about infinitely small quantities."

54. Isaac Newton, *The Method of Fluxions and Infinite Series; with its Application to the Geometry of Curve-lines*, ed. John Colson (London, 1736), xii.

55. George Berkeley, *The Analyst; or, A Discourse Addressed to an Infidel Mathematician* (London, 1734), 58–59.

56. Hartley does seem to equivocate somewhat in finally observing that "the Immateriality of the Soul has little or no Connexion with its Immortality" (512). That is, we may still believe in the Resurrection and eternal life, the truly important things, even if we are materialists. For Priestley's later dispute with this contention, see Simon Schaffer, "States of Mind: Enlightenment and Natural Philosophy," in *The Languages of Psyche: Mind and Body in Enlightenment Thought*, ed. G. S. Rousseau (Berkeley: University of California Press, 1991), 284.

57. See Jonathan Bennett, "Locke's Philosophy of Mind," in *The Cambridge Companion to John Locke*, ed. Vere Chappell (Cambridge: Cambridge University Press, 1994), which stresses that Locke was definitely a property dualist (89–90)—he subscribed to the view that mind and matter have radically different properties—and at least gestures toward embracing substance dualism (98–100). Bennett takes a hint from Michael

Ayers in suggesting that Locke's additions of the word *immaterial* to the fourth edition of the *Essay* "may have been a nervous response to Bishop Stillingfleet's accusation, a year earlier, that Locke was a materialist" (98). Boyle, for his part, is unequivocally a substance dualist, and his account of mind-body relations is based on "there being but two sorts of substances—material and immaterial"; see Robert Boyle, *Origin of Forms and Qualities According to the Corpuscular Philosophy* (1666), quoted in Peter Anstey, *The Philosophy of Robert Boyle* (London: Routledge: 2000), 188.

58. For Priestley's use of Hartley, see Schaffer, "States of Mind," 273–85.

59. Thomas Reid, *Essays on the Intellectual Powers of Man* (Edinburgh, 1785), 86, 84–85.

60. For Cheyne in this development, see G. J. Barker-Benfield, *The Culture of Sensibility: Sex and Society* (Chicago: University of Chicago Press, 1996), especially 6–16. For an influential literary discussion of Cheyne and Richardson, see John Mullan, *Sentiment and Sociability: The Language of Feeling in the Eighteenth Century* (Oxford: Oxford University Press, 1988), chap. 5, 201–40.

61. See George Cheyne, *Philosophical Principles of Religion, Natural and Reveal'd* (London, 1715), part 2, 8, where *"Relative Nothing"* is defined. This is a substantial revision of his *Philosophical Principles of Natural Religion* (1705).

62. See Anita Guerrini, *Obesity and Depression in the Enlightenment: The Life and Times of George Cheyne* (Norman: University of Oklahoma Press, 2000), 86–87, who notes that "in the second section of his work, he coupled the arithmetic of infinites with the '*Philosophick Principles of Reveal'd Religion.*' Here he recast his mathematical work from the first edition, not to rehabilitate his reputation as a mathematician, but to prove, by means of the mathematics of infinitesimals, the continuum between matter and spirit."

63. George Cheyne, *The Natural Method of Cureing the Diseases of the Body, and the Disorders of the Mind Depending on the Body* (London, 1742), 35.

64. Gilles Deleuze, *Francis Bacon: The Logic of Sensation*, trans. Daniel W. Smith (New York: Continuum, 2003), 39. Deleuze, discussing the British painter, elaborates on his notion of "the body without organs" (45) and notes how painting "make[s] visible the original unity of the senses" (37). For "'vibrations or oscillations'" (228) at the material roots of sensation in Leibniz, see Gilles Deleuze, "The Fold," trans. Jonathan Strauss, *Yale French Studies* 80 (1991): 227–47.

65. Brian Massumi, *Parables for the Virtual: Movement, Affect, Sensation* (Durham, NC: Duke University Press, 2002), 26, 27.

66. Massumi, *Parables*, 21.

67. For Condillac's relation to Locke, see Jerrold Seigel, *The Idea of the Self: Thought and Experience in Western Europe since the Seventeenth Century* (Cambridge: Cambridge University Press, 2005), 171–74.

68. Étienne Bonnot de Condillac, *An Essay on the Origin of Human Knowledge. Being a supplement to Mr. Locke's Essay on the Human Understanding*, trans. Thomas Nugent (London, 1756), 28. Hereafter, page numbers will be cited parenthetically.

69. The topic of attention has been taken up in newer studies of eighteenth-century literature, including Margaret Koehler, *Poetry of Attention in the Eighteenth Century* (London: Palgrave Macmillan, 2012); and Nathalie M. Phillips, *Distraction: Problems of Attention in Eighteenth-Century Literature* (Baltimore: Johns Hopkins University Press, 2016). Phillips refers in passing to Condillac (108–9), though to his *Grammaire*

(1775), not the *Essay*. As we shall see, the insensible can be a feature of distraction, but extends well beyond it to a vast range of unfelt phenomena from particles of matter to historical processes and socioeconomic cycles.

70. Étienne Bonnot de Condillac, *Essai sur l'origine des connaissances humaines* (Paris, 1746), 27.

71. Suzanne Gearhart, *The Open Boundary of History and Fiction: A Critical Approach to the French Enlightenment* (Princeton, NJ: Princeton University Press, 1984), 175.

72. Ibid., 172.

73. For an argument that such primary attributes of consciousness for Condillac as attention make use of linguistic elements, see Suzanne Roos, "Consciousness and the Linguistic in Condillac," *MLN* 114, no. 4 (1999): 667–90.

74. For the latter, see, e.g., John Jervis, *Sympathetic Sentiments: Affect, Emotion and Spectacle in the Modern World* (London: Bloomsbury, 2015), 85–110.

75. David Hume, *An Abstract of a Book Lately Published; Entituled, A Treatise of Human Nature* (London, 1740), 31.

76. James A. Harris, *Hume: An Intellectual Biography* (Cambridge: Cambridge University Press, 2015), 96.

77. Gilles Deleuze, *Empiricism and Subjectivity: An Essay on Hume's Theory of Human Nature*, trans. Constantin V. Boundas (New York: Columbia University Press, 1991), 103. Here Deleuze is characterizing "circumstance," which makes an association happen when it does: "if the principles of association explain that ideas are associated, only the principles of the passions can explain that a particular idea, rather than another, is associated at a given moment" (103).

78. Hume, *An Abstract*, 24.

79. David Hume, *A Treatise of Human Nature* (London, 1738–40), 1:175, 176. Hereafter, page numbers will be cited parenthetically, and are from vol. 1; all emphasis is in the original.

80. While Deleuze, in *Empiricism and Subjectivity*, 25, does not identify the insensible as part of the "affectivity" of association, he notes how it results from "the mind's easy passage from one idea to another, so that the essence of relations precisely becomes this easy transition."

81. For Hume's retreat in the *Philosophical Essays concerning Human Understanding* (London, 1748) from asserting that association is his primary achievement, see Harris, *Hume*, 224. The *Philosophical Essays* will, of course, come to be commonly called the *Enquiry concerning Human Understanding*.

82. Hume, *Philosophical Essays*, 84.

83. Annette C. Baier, *A Progress of Sentiments: Reflections on Hume's Treatise* (Cambridge, MA: Harvard University Press, 1991), 41, 42. For Baier's overall discussion of viewing association as "unconscious," see 41–44.

84. See especially Donald W. Livingston, *Hume's Philosophy of Common Life* (Chicago: University of Chicago Press, 1984).

85. David Hume, *Essays Moral, Political, and Literary*, ed. Eugene Miller (Indianapolis: Liberty Fund, 1985), 171.

86. See Rebecca Tierney-Hynes, "Haywood, Reading, and the Passions," in *The Eighteenth Century* 51, nos. 1–2 (2010): 153–72. Tierney-Hynes identifies Haywood—not only in *The Female Spectator* but in her novels and their prefaces—as "heir to a tradition

of theorizing about the passions that had reconstituted philosophy as a discipline in the seventeenth century" (155).

87. Eliza Haywood, *The Female Spectator* (London, 1745–46), 1:4, 3. Hereafter, volume and page numbers will be cited parenthetically.

88. For accounts of the feminist project of the *Female Spectator*, see the essays in Lynn Marie Wright and Donald J. Newman, eds., *Fair Philosopher: Eliza Haywood and the Female Spectator* (Lewisburg, PA: Bucknell University Press, 2006), and especially Juliette Merritt, "Reforming the Coquet? Eliza Haywood's Vision of a Female Epistemology," 176–92, which suggests that Haywood's persona as a "reformed coquette" who both knows passion and can reason as a result of it offers a "model for female knowledge" (178).

89. The larger message here is that we gravitate toward a contemplation of what is attractive in nature and tend to neglect less appealing creatures like caterpillars and snails, objects of interest to the party Haywood is describing. For an account of this episode in terms of its implicit expansion of women's gender role, see Kristin M. Girten, "Unsexed Souls: Natural Philosophy as Transformation in Eliza Haywood's *Female Spectator*," *Eighteenth-Century Studies* 43, no. 1 (2009): 55–74, especially 60–63.

90. Adam Smith, *The Theory of Moral Sentiments*, ed. D. D. Raphael and A. L. Macfie (Indianapolis: Liberty Fund, 1984), 320. Hereafter, volume and page numbers will be cited parenthetically.

91. Thomas Reid, *The Correspondence of Thomas Reid*, ed. Paul Wood (Edinburgh: Edinburgh University Press, 2002), 104.

92. For a discussion of Smith's response to this interpretation expressed in the (now lost) letter from Elliot, see Nicholas Phillipson, *Adam Smith: An Enlightened Life* (New Haven, CT: Yale University Press, 2010), 163.

93. As Raphael and Macfie point out in Smith, *The Theory of Moral Sentiments*, 135n3, Smith borrows the analogy of morality to the sizing of visual images from Hume's *Enquiry concerning the Principles of Morals* (London, 1751), though Hume does not remark on the automatic, insensible character of the process as Smith does. (Hume instead emphasizes "Judgment": "The Judgment here corrects the Inequalities of our internal Emotions and Perceptions; in like Manner, as it preserves us from Error, in the several Variations of Images, presented to our external Senses," 97.)

94. Eric Schliesser, review of D. D. Raphael, *The Impartial Spectator: Adam Smith's Moral Philosophy*, and Leonidas Montes, *Adam Smith in Context: A Critical Reassessment of Some Central Components of His Thought*, *Ethics* 118, no. 3 (2008): 574.

95. Charles L. Griswold Jr., *Adam Smith and the Virtues of Enlightenment* (Cambridge: Cambridge University Press, 1999), 186–93, finds both lawlike and sentimentally formed and applied "general rules" present in Smith, but (as here) emphasizes the latter as Smith's distinctive focus.

96. Robert Shaver, "Virtue, Utility, and Rules," in *The Cambridge Companion to Adam Smith*, ed. Knud Haakonssen (Cambridge: Cambridge University Press, 2006), 204, uses the phrase "formulated by induction" to describe how Smith thinks rules are formed.

97. As Samuel Fleischacker, "Philosophy in Moral Practice: Kant and Adam Smith," *Kant-Studien* 82, no. 3 (1991): 261, notes, "Duty, the regard for rules, thus forms the apex of Smith's system of moral judgment, directing 'reason' or 'conscience,' which in turn encourages or restrains our immediate selfish and benevolent passions." For

Fleischacker, this feature of Smith brings him "startlingly close" (261) to Immanuel Kant.

98. The word *reflection* means both "the action or process of thinking carefully or deeply about a particular subject" and "intelligent self-awareness, introspection," among other things; *Oxford English Dictionary*. s.v. "reflection." Smith seems to mean more the latter, a habitual thoughtfulness, than a process of theoretical construction.

99. Maria Alejandra Carrasco, "Adam Smith's Reconstruction of Practical Reason," *Review of Metaphysics* 58, no. 1 (2004): 91. Griswold, *Adam Smith and the Virtues of Enlightenment*, similarly refers to the impartial spectator himself as "a *phronimos* (person of practical wisdom)" (190).

Chapter II. Fiction

1. Henry Fielding, *The History of Tom Jones, a Foundling*, ed. John Bender and Simon Stern (Oxford: Oxford University Press, 1996), 171.

2. Jane Austen, *Jane Austen's "Sir Charles Grandison,"* ed. Brian Southam (Oxford: Oxford University Press, 1980), 55.

3. See, e.g., the 1826 letter by Lady Louisa Stewart to Sir Walter Scott in *The Private Letter-Books of Sir Walter Scott*, ed. Wilfred Partington (London: Hodder and Stoughton, 1930), 271–73, in which she recalls worrying as "a girl of fourteen not yet versed in sentiment," while reading Henry Mackenzie's *The Man of Feeling*, that "I should not cry enough to gain the credit of proper sensibility" (273). For a discussion of this and other examples of the demand for performative reading, see Paul Goring, *The Rhetoric of Sensibility* (Cambridge: Cambridge University Press, 2004), especially the section "Reading as Performance," 142–47.

4. See, e.g., David Marshall, "Adam Smith and the Theatricality of Moral Sentiments," *Critical Inquiry* 10, no. 4 (1984): 592–613; and Robert Markley, "Sentimentality as Performance: Shaftesbury, Sterne, and the Theatrics of Virtue," in *The New Eighteenth Century: Theory, Politics, English Literature*, ed. Felicity Nussbaum and Laura Brown (London: Methuen, 1987), 210–30.

5. I refer to Jonathan Kramnick, *Objects and Events from Hobbes to Richardson* (Stanford, CA: Stanford University Press, 2010), discussed in section 1 of chapter II; and Sandra Macpherson, *Harm's Way: Tragic Responsibility and the Novel Form* (Baltimore: Johns Hopkins University Press, 2010), discussed in section 2.

6. In the case of *Clarissa*, for instance, Watt describes Richardson's efforts at a "more exact transcription of psychological processes" and says (in an often-quoted formula) that the novel's letters offer "a short-cut, as it were, to the heart"; Ian Watt, *The Rise of the Novel* (Berkeley: University of California Press, 2001), 194–95.

7. See Deidre Shauna Lynch, *The Economy of Character: Novels, Market Culture, and the Business of Inner Meaning* (Chicago: University of Chicago Press, 1998), which recognizes an inward turn at midcentury but recognizes its function in market culture.

8. See Ildiko Csengei, *Sympathy, Sensibility and the Literature of Feeling in the Eighteenth Century* (Houndmills, England: Palgrave Macmillan, 2012), especially the chapter "Women and the Negative: The Sentimental Swoon in Eighteenth-Century Fiction," 140–68, which examines swooning's place in the medical discourse of the period and, later, in psychoanalysis. For an emphasis on the theatrical dimensions of swooning,

see Emily Hodgson Anderson, *Eighteenth-Century Authorship and the Play of Fiction* (New York: Routledge, 2009), especially the chapter "Forgetting the Self: Frances Burney and Staged Insensibility," 46–76.

9. See Michael Fried, *Absorption and Theatricality: Painting and the Beholder in the Age of Diderot* (Chicago: University of Chicago Press, 1988), which comments on the depiction of absorptive states in "French literary pictorialism in the 1760s" (199) as well as in French painting.

10. Fredric Jameson, *The Antinomies of Realism* (London: Verso, 2013), 83.

11. A Lacanian installment in this tradition is David Sigler, *Sexual Enjoyment in British Romanticism: Gender and Psychoanalysis, 1753–1835* (Montreal and Kingston, ON: McGill-Queen's University Press, 2015).

12. See, e.g., John Richetti, *The English Novel in History, 1700–1780* (London: Routledge, 1998), 24, which describes the characteristic style of part 1 of Behn's *Love-Letters Between a Nobleman and His Sister* as indulging "amatory rhetoric of the most flatulent sort, as the lovers claim to be overwhelmed by their emotions, swept away by volcanic passions."

13. Many libraries and electronic collections still attribute *Almahide* to Georges's sister Madeleine de Scudéry, like other works signed by him, but in this case scholars consider it to be principally Georges's work. See William Roberts, "New Light on the Authorship of *Almahide*," *French Studies* 25, no. 3 (1971): 271–80, which adds support to the attribution to Georges found in Jerome W. Schweitzer, *Georges de Scudery's Almahide: Authorship, Analysis, Sources and Structure* (Baltimore: Johns Hopkins University Press, 1939).

14. For Phillips's authorship of books 2–3 of part 3 of his English translation of *Almahide*, which was left unfinished by Scudéry, see Jerome W. Schweitzer, "Dryden's Use of Scudéry's *Almahide*," *Modern Language Notes*, 54, no. 3 (1939), 190–92.

15. Georges de Scudéry, *Almahide, or The Captive Lovers*, trans. J. Phillips (London, 1677), pt. 2, bk. 1, 29a.

16. Ibid.

17. The French original reads, "la soûmission qui paroist foible, est la plus forte de toutes les Machines que l'Amour employe contre un cœur; elle s'y insinuë insensiblement; elle s'en rend Maistresse sans qu'il s'en apperçoiue; & long-temps aprés qu'il est vaincu, il croit encore estre le victorieux." Georges de Scudéry, *Almahide, ou L'esclave Reine* (Paris, 1661), pt. 2, bk. 1, 205–6.

18. See, e.g., Scudéry, *Almahide, or The Captive Lovers*, pt. 1, bk. 1, 23b.

19. Scudéry, *Almahide, or The Captive Lovers*, pt. 3, bk. 1, 38a.

20. Ibid. For the French original, see Scudéry, *Almahide, ou L'esclave Reine*, pt. 3, bk. 1, 257–59.

21. See, e.g., Brian Massumi, *Parables for the Virtual: Movement, Affect, Sensation* (Durham, NC: Duke University Press, 2002), 276, which claims that "no rigid distinction between the living body and inorganic matter is sustainable . . . the difference between the sensitive capacities of organic and inorganic matter is of transductive mode and degree. There is no difference in kind."

22. Erica Harth, *Cartesian Women: Versions and Subversions of Rational Discourse in the Old Regime* (Ithaca, NY: Cornell University Press, 1992), 98.

23. Harth, *Cartesian Women*, 102.

24. See John Conley, "Madeleine de Scudéry," *Stanford Encyclopedia of Philosophy*, spring 2016 ed., ed. Edward N. Zalta, https://plato.stanford.edu/archives/spr2016/entries/madeleine-scudery/, which describes her Christian distrust of Epicureanism and her remark in *La Morale du Monde* (1686) that "one can never reasonably think that these alleged Atoms—which they are called in order to gain reverence for them—could create the eternal principles of the universe."

25. For an account of the generic affiliations of Behn's *Love-Letters*, see Ros Ballaster, *Seductive Forms: Women's Amatory Fiction from 1684 to 1740* (Oxford: Oxford University Press, 1992), 100–113. For an argument that *Love-Letters* is best described as a "courtesan narrative," see Alison Conway, "The Protestant Cause and a Protestant Whore: Aphra Behn's *Love-Letters*," *Eighteenth-Century Life*, 25, no. 3 (2001), 1–19.

26. Aphra Behn, *Love-Letters Between a Noble-Man and His Sister* (London, 1684), 91–92; emphasis in the original. The remaining two volumes were published as *Love Letters from a Noble Man to His Sister* (London, 1685) and *The Amours of Philander and Silvia* (London, 1687).

27. Michael McKeon, *The Secret History of Domesticity: Public, Private, and the Division of Knowledge* (Baltimore: Johns Hopkins University Press, 2006), 510.

28. See Boileau's translation of Longinus, *Traité du Sublime*, in *Oeuvres de Nicolas Boileau Despréaux, avec des éclaircissemens historiques* (Amsterdam, 1718), 2:24, with Longinus's famous commentary on the rhetorical effectiveness of Sappho's depiction of her own fragmented body: "N'admirez-vous point comment elle ramasse toutes ces choses, l'âme, le corps, l'ouïe, la langue, la vuë, la couleur, comme si c'étoient autant de personnes différentes, et prêtes à expirer?" See also chapter 18, "Des Hyperbates," 2:43–44.

29. For a discussion of this and other passages that reveal Behn's interest in both "the erotic possibilities of language and the power of the well-crafted letter to enact its own 'real,'" see Bradford K. Mudge, *The Whore's Story: Women, Pornography, and the British Novel, 1684–1830* (Oxford: Oxford University Press, 2000), 130.

30. It is not entirely clear which lute Behn has in mind, since a lute shows up more than once in Abraham Cowley's poetry. "The Garden," which appeared in *Verses Written on Several Occasions*, in *The Works of Mr. Abraham Cowley* (London, 1668), describes how the wooden lute of Orpheus can make trees understand its song "By Sympathy the Voice of Wood" (117). Another intriguing occurrence appears in the pastoral comedy *Love's Riddle* (London, 1638), written when Cowley was only sixteen, in which Bellula, at the center of a compulsive triangle in which love is not reciprocated, says, "We are three strings on *Venus* dainty'st Lute, / Where all three hinder one another's musick, / Yet all three joyne and make one harmony" (act 4, scene 1, n.p.). In another, even earlier published poem, "Constantia and Philetus," in *Poetical Blossomes by A.C.*, 2d ed. (London, 1636), sec. 24, n.p., we read, "Whilst thoughts 'gainst thoughts rise up in mutinie, / She tooke a Lute (being farre from any eares) / And tun'd this Song, posing that harmony / Which Poets wit attributes to the Spheares." In all these instances the lute produces a harmony arising despite will or intention.

31. Behn, *Love-Letters*, 92.

32. Her epistolary present tense can only recognize, as it unfolds, its unintentional betrayal of just-past intent. See Alexander Pope, "Eloisa to Abelard," in *The Twickenham Edition of the Poetry of Alexander Pope*, vol. 2, *The Rape of the Lock and Other Poems*,

ed. Geoffrey Tilloston (New Haven, CT: Yale University Press, 1962), 319, lines 13–14: "O write it not, my hand—the name appears / Already written—wash it out, my tears!"

33. Patricia Meyer Spacks, "Ev'ry Woman Is at Heart a Rake," *Eighteenth-Century Studies* 8, no. 1 (1974): 33. See also Ballaster, *Seductive Forms*, 34–35.

34. Spacks, "Ev'ry Woman," 46.

35. The term was, of course, popularized by Ballaster in *Seductive Forms*.

36. In the small canon composed in *Popular Fiction by Women, 1660–1730: An Anthology*, ed. Paula R. Backscheider and John J. Richetti (Oxford: Oxford University Press, 1996), representing eight works by seven authors, the usage of "insensibly" to characterize the action of desire appears (arguably) only once (in Haywood's *The British Recluse*), though the notion that desire overcomes heroines "by degrees" occurs more often. For instance, in *The Secret History of Queen Zarah* (1705), whose attribution to Delarivier Manley has been disputed in J. A. Downie, "What If Delarivier Manley Did Not Write *The Secret History of Queen Zarah*?," *Library: The Transactions of the Bibliographical Society* 5, no. 3 (2004), 247–64), we read that "Zarah was more and more love sick, which by degrees grew so upon her that it altered her quite." *The Secret History of Queen Zarah*, in Backscheider and Richetti, eds., *Popular Fiction*, 53.

37. Jonathan Kramnick, *Actions and Objects from Hobbes to Richardson* (Stanford, CA: Stanford University Press, 2010), 182.

38. Kramnick, *Actions and Objects*, 185, also contends that the external does not so much overtake the internal as render the distinction between them at times unstable, as he remarks of a passage in Haywood's *Fantomina*: "Terms of mind splatter only to become the actions they represent or consider."

39. For an account of the place of *The Mercenary Lover* in Haywood's career, and particularly its function as one of her "revenge fantasies" aimed at Richard Savage, see Kathryn R. King, *A Political Biography of Eliza Haywood* (London: Routledge, 2016), 32–33.

40. Eliza Haywood, *The Mercenary Lover: or, The Unfortunate Heiresses* (London, 1726), 17.

41. Ibid.

42. Michael B. Prince, "A Preliminary Discourse on Philosophy and Literature," in *The Cambridge History of English Literature, 1660–1780*, ed. John Richetti (Cambridge: Cambridge University Press, 2005), 420.

43. Clara Reeve, *The Progress of Romance, through Times, Countries, and Manners* (Colchester, England, 1785), 1:133.

44. For an account of how the rivalry shaped readers' responses to their works, see Allen Michie, *Richardson and Fielding: The Dynamics of a Critical Rivalry* (Lewisburg, PA: Bucknell University Press, 1999).

45. The remarks are quoted in James Boswell, *Life of Samuel Johnson*, ed. David Womersley (London: Penguin, 2008), 288.

46. Boswell, *Life of Samuel Johnson*, 353.

47. Reeve, *The Progress of Romance*, 1:135.

48. Henry Fielding, *The History of Tom Jones, a Foundling*, ed. John Bender and Simon Stern (Oxford: Oxford University Press, 1996), 171. Hereafter, page numbers will be cited parenthetically.

49. For both of these kinds of omission, see Stephen B. Dobranski, "What Fielding Doesn't Say in *Tom Jones*," *Modern Philology* 107, no. 4 (2010): 643–46.

50. Jill Campbell, "Fielding's Style," *ELH* 72, no. 2 (2005): 421.

51. Ibid.

52. Brian Massumi, *Parables for the Virtual: Movement, Affect, Sensation* (Durham, NC: Duke University Press, 2002), 30.

53. See Robert L. Chibka, "Henry Fielding, Mentalist: The Ins and Outs of Narration in *Tom Jones*," in *Henry Fielding in Our Time: Papers Presented at the Tercentenary Conference*, ed. J. A. Downie (Newcastle upon Tyne, England: Cambridge Scholars, 2008), 81–112.

54. John Locke, *An Essay concerning Human Understanding*, ed. Peter Nidditch (Oxford: Oxford University Press, 1975), 335.

55. Antonio Damasio, *The Feeling of What Happens: Body and Emotion in the Making of Consciousness* (New York: Houghton Mifflin Harcourt, 1999), 22; emphasis in the original.

56. Antonio Damasio, *Self Comes to Mind: Constructing the Conscious Brain* (New York: Random House, 2010), 22; emphasis in the original.

57. Ibid., 22–23. In a footnote to this passage, Damasio indicates that this "primordial self," which did not appear in his earlier work, is a low-level, conscious product of the mostly nonconscious proto-self, not a feature of the conscious "core self" (341n17).

58. Among the most cited treatments are G. J. Barker-Benfield, *The Culture of Sensibility: Sex and Society in Eighteenth-Century Britain* (Chicago: University of Chicago Press, 1996), 6–16; and John Mullan, *Sentiment and Sociability: The Language of Feeling in the Eighteenth Century* (Oxford: Oxford University Press, 1984), 201–40.

59. See D. A. Miller, *Jane Austen, or The Secret of Style* (Princeton, NJ: Princeton University Press, 2005), which thinks of style as the personhood, or nonpersonhood, of the author in respect to the characters and world she describes, as well as to the reader. Thus Miller defines Austen's style early on "as a truly out-of-body voice, so stirringly free of what it abhorred as 'particularity' or 'singularity' that it seemed to come from no enunciator at all" (1).

60. This confirms, though not quite in the sense she means, the observation in Campbell, "Fielding's Style," 422, that "Fielding's prose thus makes us feel, sentence-to-sentence as well as chapter-to-chapter and book-to-book, our embodiment as readers," as well as Fielding's own form of embodiment as narrator. Yet his perspective on what is insensible to others has a way distancing him from the social world he depicts.

61. John Bender, *Ends of Enlightenment* (Stanford, CA: Stanford University Press, 2012), 130.

62. For another intriguing instance of this position from Fielding's drama, see Henry Fielding, *Pasquin*, in *The Works of Henry Fielding* (London, 1762), 2:71, in which Trapwit describes to Fustian how the plot has hitherto advanced by "imperceptible degrees." Crucially, Trapwit is in the plot, not above it like an omniscient narrator.

63. Henry Fielding, *Amelia* (London, 1752), 4:207. For a consideration of this passage and *Amelia* as a whole as an acknowledgment of the world of chance that Fielding's narrator teaches his readers to confront, see Jesse Molesworth, *Chance and the Eighteenth-Century Novel* (Cambridge: Cambridge University Press, 2010), 175–89.

64. As Ann Jesse Van Sant, *Eighteenth-Century Sensibility and the Novel: The Senses in Social Context* (Cambridge: Cambridge University Press, 1993), 81–82, notes, "As used in *Clarissa*, the vocabulary of sensibility—*sensibility, sensible, insensible; delicacy; niceness*—shows the expected range of meanings from awareness or perception to physical and psychological delicacy, to refined generous feeling, to romantic susceptibility," but she concludes that "Richardson's use of trial as a means of revelation" is what really "marks *Clarissa* as a novel of sensibility."

65. Ian Watt, *The Rise of the Novel* (Berkeley: University of California Press, 2001), 175, 176.

66. See Tom Keymer, *Richardson's* Clarissa *and the Eighteenth-Century Reader* (Cambridge: Cambridge University Press, 1992), xvi.

67. Samuel Richardson, *Clarissa. Or, the History of a Young Lady*, 3rd ed. (London, 1751), 1:15. Hereafter, volume and page numbers will be cited parenthetically; all emphasis is in the original.

68. As Jonathan Kramnick, *Actions and Objects from Hobbes to Richardson* (Stanford, CA: Stanford University Press, 2010), 193, has it, "One way of describing Clarissa's own account of agency is to say that she holds fast to intentions. She believes that actions may be explained by an agent's reason for acting, and that reasons for acting have no dependence on external circumstance."

69. John Dussinger, *The Discourse of the Mind in Eighteenth-Century Fiction* (The Hague: De Gruyter, 1974), 94. Such motives include not only Clarissa's desire for Lovelace but her veiled aggression toward her family. Dussinger points to another moment in the famous letter 10 in volume 1 in which Anna considers Clarissa's "beginning love" as a "demon" possessing her, which she does not herself recognize.

70. *Oxford English Dictionary*, s.v. "own."

71. See also Michael McKeon, *The Secret History of Domesticity: Public, Private, and the Division of Knowledge* (Baltimore: Johns Hopkins University Press, 2005), 148, for the connection between the "relative absolutes" (after the "devolution" of political absolutism) of "the family freed from its serviceable signification of the state" and the "interior realms of autonomy and privacy, the secret precincts of the self," especially relevant to secret history and, at a subsequent dialectical stage, the domestic novel.

72. In a letter to Anna, she picks up her phrase "perverse fate": "Don't you see, my dear, that we seem all to be *impelled*, as it were, by a perverse fate, which none of us are able to resist?—And yet all arising (with a strong appearance of self-punishment) from ourselves?" Richardson, *Clarissa*, 2:246.

73. For a claim that Anna's appeal to custom and fate here mobilizes a coercive heteronormativity by forcing Clarissa's famous phrase "a conditional liking" into meaning love, see Sarah Nicolazzo, "Reading *Clarissa*'s 'Conditional Liking': A Queer Philology," *Modern Philology* 112, no. 1 (2014): 205–25, especially 224–25.

74. Samuel Richardson, *The History of Sir Charles Grandison* (London, 1753–54), 1:vi.

75. See Mark Kinkead-Weekes, *Samuel Richardson: Dramatic Novelist* (Ithaca, NY: Cornell University Press, 1973), 395. For a summation and questioning of the critical tradition of claiming that Richardson strove above all for "dramatic immediacy," see Keymer, *Richardson's* Clarissa *and the Eighteenth-Century Reader*, xvi.

76. Sandra Macpherson, *Harm's Way: Tragic Responsibility and the Novel Form* (Baltimore: Johns Hopkins University Press, 2010), 76.

77. See, e.g., Macpherson's contention in *Harm's Way*, 49, that the plague in Daniel Defoe's *Journal of the Plague Year* shows "we are responsible for what we 'insensibly' do" (quoting Defoe's use of the word).

78. Macpherson, *Harm's Way*, 95.

79. As Katherine Binhammer, "Knowing Love: The Epistemology of *Clarissa*," *ELH* 74, no. 4 (2007): 861, puts it, "the epistemological model that paints Clarissa's heart as betraying a truth that the owner does not consent to positions the critic as Lovelace, since both claim to know what she does not—her hidden desire for the rake."

80. William Beatty Warner, *Reading "Clarissa": The Struggles of Interpretation* (New Haven, CT: Yale University Press, 1979).

81. Lady Bradshaigh to Samuel Richardson, November 1748, in Samuel Richardson, *The Cambridge Edition of the Correspondence of Samuel Richardson*, vol. 5, *Correspondence with Lady Bradshaigh and Lady Echlion*, ed. Peter Sabor (Cambridge: Cambridge University Press, 2016), 19.

82. For an argument that wishes of readers like Lady Bradshaigh for a happy ending represent an evasion of Richardson's moral purposes (an evasion abetted, in my view, by a tendency of terms like *insensibly* to put the sources of our sensibility's satisfactions out of sight), see Adam Budd, "Why Clarissa Must Die: Richardson's Tragedy and Editorial Heroism," *Eighteenth-Century Life* 31, no. 3 (2007): 1–28.

83. Bradshaigh to Richardson, November 1748, in Richardson, *Correspondence*, 19.

84. One interesting index to Richardson's growing acceptance of the word appears in his application of it in *A Collection of the Moral and Instructive Sentiments, Maxims, Cautions, and Reflexions, Contained in the Histories of Pamela, Clarissa, and Sir Charles Grandison* (London, 1755) to passages in *Clarissa* in which it does not originally appear. He remarks, "Persons of Humility and Affability, by their sweetness of manners, insensibly draw people into their sentiments, iii. 276 [iv. 62]," 138. In Richardson, *Clarissa*, 4:62, the passage simply reads, "your sweetness of manners, your humility and affability, caused the subscription every one made to your sentiments."

85. Richardson, *The History of Sir Charles Grandison*, 2:30. Hereafter, volume and page numbers will be cited parenthetically.

86. Dorrit Cohn, *Transparent Minds: Narrative Modes for Presenting Consciousness in Fiction* (Princeton, NJ: Princeton University Press, 1978), remains a classic account of the literary dimensions of (among other modes) the free indirect style, which Cohn calls "narrated monologue"; see especially 99–140. See also Frances Ferguson, "Jane Austen, *Emma*, and the Impact of Form," *MLQ: Modern Language Quarterly* 61, no. 1 (2000): 157–80, which stresses the way free indirect discourse enacts a community's influence on individual consciousness, claiming, e.g., that Austen's style "recognizes what we might want to think of as a communal contribution to individuals" (164). Ferguson adds, "Austen uses a community to foreshadow an individual's actions" (164), especially in the "future perfect tense" (165), as the community anticipates how an individual will turn out.

87. For the function of Harriet as a narrator whose stories build "affective communities," see Tita Chico, "Details and Frankness: Affective Relations in 'Sir Charles Grandison,'" *Studies in Eighteenth-Century Culture* 38 (2009): 48–50.

88. For a development of the suggestion in Margaret Anne Doody, "Identity and Character in *Sir Charles Grandison*," in *Samuel Richardson: Tercentenary Essays*, ed.

Margaret Anne Doody and Peter Sabor (Cambridge: Cambridge University Press, 1989), 114, that Sir Charles embodies an "almost totalitarian" authority, see Rebecca Anne Barr, "Richardson's 'Sir Charles Grandison' and the Symptoms of Subjectivity," *The Eighteenth Century* 51, no. 4 (2010): 391–411.

89. John Richetti, *The English Novel in History, 1700–1780* (London: Routledge, 1999), 218.

90. Ibid., 216.

91. See, e.g., Julia Epstein, *The Iron Pen: Frances Burney and the Politics of Women's Writing* (Madison: University of Wisconsin Press, 1989), 117.

92. Frances Burney, *Evelina, or The History of a Young Lady's Entrance into the World*, ed. Edward A. Bloom (Oxford: Oxford University Press, 2002), 84. Hereafter, page numbers will be cited parenthetically.

93. Michael McKeon, *The Secret History of Domesticity: Public, Private, and the Division of Knowledge* (Baltimore: Johns Hopkins University Press, 2005), 703.

94. See the anonymous review of *Evelina, Critical Review* 46 (1778): 202–4.

95. See Vivien Jones, "The Seductions of Conduct: Pleasure and Conduct Literature," in *Pleasure in the Eighteenth Century*, ed. Roy Porter and Marie Mulvey Roberts (New York: New York University Press, 1996), 108–32, for a discussion of the variety of writing that scholars now tend to group under the heading "conduct books," including "sermons, letters, histories, fictions" (109), as well as their multiform, equivocal effects.

96. Wetenhall Wilkes, *A Letter of Genteel and Moral Advice to a Young Lady* (Dublin, 1740), 105. A little earlier Wilkes recommends a very deliberate practice of taking notes on one's readings, though he also remarks, "By thus digesting what you read, you will insensibly arrive at proper Notions of Virtue, Honour, and Justice" (100).

97. Frances Burney, *The Early Journals and Letters of Fanny Burney*, vol. 1, *1768–1773*, ed. Lars E. Troide (Kingston, ON: McGill-Queens University Press, 1988), 229.

98. James Fordyce, *Sermons to Young Women* (London, 1766), 1:94.

99. Fordyce, *Sermons*, 1:106.

100. Hester Chapone, *Letters on the Improvement of the Mind, Addressed to a Young Lady* (London, 1773), 1:134.

101. Frances Burney to Susanna Burney Phillips, November 29, 1783, in Frances Burney, *The Early Journals and Letters of Fanny Burney*, vol. 5, *1782–1783*, ed. Lars E. Troide and Stewart J. Cooke (Kingston, ON: McGill-Queens University Press, 2012), 421. For a persuasive argument that Burney's fiction exceeds the context of conduct literature often assigned to it, see Margaret Anne Doody, *Frances Burney: The Life in the Works* (New Brunswick, NJ: Rutgers University Press, 1988), especially 206–7.

102. Chapone, *Letters*, 2:36.

103. See, e.g., John Wesley, *Sermons on Several Occasions: In Three Volumes* (London, 1750), which asserts that the holy spirit "may insensibly open our Mind to receive Conviction, and fix that Conviction upon our Heart" (3:148–49).

104. After the moment of crisis, Evelina gives "free vent to the feelings I had most painfully stifled, in a violent burst of tears" (184). Sentiment's strong associations with Scottishness came in the persons of Henry Mackenzie, whose *Man of Feeling* appeared in 1771, and Adam Smith, whose *Theory of Moral Sentiments* appeared in 1759.

105. Earlier, soon after receiving the letter, Evelina seems to accept Mr. Villars's theory that Orville "must certainly been intoxicated when he wrote it." Burney, *Evelina*, 267.

106. Fredric Jameson, *The Antinomies of Realism* (London: Verso, 2013), 40. He here discusses an analogy between Gustave Flaubert's and Richard Wagner's compositional styles, which at times sacrifice plot or a "narrative" sonata structure for a "chromaticism of the body itself" (42).

107. Ibid., 42.

108. Ibid., 44–77.

109. Frances Burney, *The Early Journals and Letters of Fanny Burney*, vol. 4, *The Streatham Years, Part 2, 1780–1781*, ed. Betty Rizzo (Montreal and Kingston, ON: McGill-Queens University Press, 2003), 144.

110. Burney, *Early Journals*, 4:145; emphasis in the original.

111. Frances Burney, *Cecilia, or The Memoirs of an Heiress*, ed. Peter Sabor and Margaret Anne Doody (Oxford: Oxford University Press, 1988), 251. Hereafter, page numbers will be cited parenthetically.

112. For an account of the ambition of Burney's *Camilla* to represent the mental realm as distinct from the bodily or otherwise external realm, see Doody, *Frances Burney*, 256, where she remarks, "Edgar's blush [in *Camilla*] is not at all sufficient to indicate the process; the author has to give us the process itself by reflecting Edgar's mind."

113. This is the thesis put forth in Dror Wahrman, *The Making of the Modern Self: Identity and Culture in Eighteenth-Century England* (New Haven, CT: Yale University Press, 2006).

114. Word searches of Burney's last novel *The Wanderer* (1814), however, show *insensibly*, used additively, making a comeback, though forms of *involuntary* also appear, along with (intriguingly) *unconscious* and *unconsciously*.

115. See, e.g., Claudia L. Johnson, *Jane Austen: Women, Politics and the Novel* (Chicago: University of Chicago Press, 1988), which portrays *Sense and Sensibility*'s "character as a nineties novel" in its hewing to (though also critiquing) conventions of sentimental fiction: "Women abused in love are expected to die. This is what conventionally happens in sentimental novels, and this is what everyone, with stunning matter-of-factness, expects from Marianne" (64–65). See also Clara Tuite, *Romantic Austen: Sexual Politics and the Literary Canon* (Cambridge: Cambridge University Press, 2008), 58–62, which considers the "interimplication" (59) of sentimental and antisentimental fiction by the time Austen addressed them in *Sense and Sensibility*.

116. For an essay that critiques this schematism to illuminating effect, see Robert Garis, "Learning Experience and Change," in *Critical Essays on Jane Austen*, ed. B. C. Southam (London: Routledge and Kegan Paul, 1968), 60–82.

117. See Christopher C. Nagle, *Sexuality and the Culture of Sensibility in the British Romantic Era* (New York: Palgrave Macmillan, 2007), 101, which notes that "proper acknowledgment of Austen's investment in feeling would uncover layered traces of Sensibility"; later Nagle asserts that "the Dashwood sisters are not allegorical embodiments, respectively, of Sense and Sensibility; rather, as critics have come to see, the siblings share important elements of their putative opposites, challenging the notion that these qualities are antinomies" (113).

118. Jane Austen, *Sense and Sensibility*, ed. Ros Ballaster (London: Penguin, 1995), 57. Hereafter, page numbers will be cited parenthetically.

Chapter III. Historiography

1. Gilbert Burnet, *Bishop Burnet's History of his Own Time* (London, 1724–31), 1:455.
2. Rapin occasionally employs the term in his *History of England*, trans. Nicolas Tindal (London, 1725–31), though mostly to notice not historical processes but slow effects on individuals. For example, discussing the arrangements for marrying the future Charles I to the infanta of Spain, he remarks, "Others affirm, *Buckingham's* Aim was to induce the Prince insensibly to change his Religion, by exposing him to all the Temptations which of course he would meet with at the Court of *Madrid*" (9:533; emphasis in the original). Thomas Carte's infrequent appeals to the term recognize its potential to depict more general historical processes, as when he remarks, in *A General History of England* (London, 1747–55), 1:315, in the midst of a discussion of Alfred's reign, "For in all states, there will be in time some deviations from their original constitution, creeping in insensibly."
3. Dugald Stewart, "Account of the Life and Writings of Adam Smith," ed. I. S. Ross, in Adam Smith, *Essays on Philosophical Subjects*, ed. J. C. Bryce and William P. D. Wightman (Indianapolis: Liberty Fund, 1982), 217.
4. Hence the 1748 treatise *Les Moeurs* by François-Vincent Toussaint, which taxonomizes various moral and affective attitudes, appeared in English as *Manners: Translated from the French* (London, 1749).
5. J. G. A. Pocock, *Barbarism and Religion*, vol. 2, *Narratives of Civil Government* (Cambridge: Cambridge University Press, 1999), 72.
6. Edward Gibbon, *The History of the Decline and Fall of the Roman Empire*, ed. David Womersley (London: Penguin, 1994), 1:62.
7. For comment on nonconscious "cognitive assemblages" that include but extend beyond individually embodied and conscious cognition, see N. Katherine Hayles, *Unthought: The Power of the Cognitive Nonconscious* (Chicago: University of Chicago Press, 2017), especially 115–216.
8. Gibbon, *The Decline and Fall*, 1:102.
9. Joseph Addison, "No. 420: Wednesday, July 2, 1712," in *The Spectator*, ed. Donald F. Bond (Oxford: Oxford University Press, 1965), 2:574.
10. Mark Salber Phillips, *Society and Sentiment: Genres of Historical Writing in Britain, 1740–1820* (Princeton, NJ: Princeton University Press, 2000), 142.
11. For an account of Montesquieu's influence in England to the mid-eighteenth century, see Ursula Haskins Gonthier, *Montesquieu and England: Enlightened Exchanges, 1689–1755*, 2nd ed. (Abingdon, England: Routledge, 2016), which contends that "it is apposite to read the *Political Discourses* alongside Montesquieu's work as in several essays Hume responds specifically to issues raised in *L'Esprit des lois* and the *Considérations* [*sur les causes de la grandeur des Romains et de leur decadence*, 1734]" (103).
12. For Hume's introduction of himself to Montesquieu, with substantial comments on details of *L'esprit des lois*, see *The Letters of David Hume*, ed. J. Y. T. Greig (Oxford: Clarendon, 1932), 1:133–38. See also Cecil Patrick Courtney, "Morals and Manners in Montesquieu's Analysis of the British System of Liberty," in *Montesquieu and*

His Legacy, ed. Rebecca E. Kingston (Albany: State University of New York Press, 2008), 31.

13. Charles de Secondat, Baron de Montesquieu, *The Spirit of Laws*, trans. Thomas Nugent (London, 1750), 1:418. Hereafter, volume and page numbers will be cited parenthetically. For the possibility of Montesquieu's influence on Hume's *History of England* (and even on "Of National Characters"), see David Wootton, "David Hume: 'The Historian,'" in *The Cambridge Companion to Hume*, ed. David Fate Norton and Jacqueline Taylor, 2nd ed. (Cambridge: Cambridge University Press, 2008), 462–64.

14. For an assessment, see J. G. A. Pocock, *Barbarism and Religion*, vol. 1, *The Enlightenments of Edward Gibbon, 1737–1764* (Cambridge: Cambridge University Press, 1999), 82–93.

15. Edward Gibbon, *Essai sur l'étude de la littérature* (London, 1761), 105.

16. Among several examples, his reference in chapter 17 to Montesquieu as "an ingenious philosopher" seems delicately pejorative, as he goes on to argue that the view in *The Spirit of Laws* about rates of taxation relative to the public's "degrees of servitude and freedom" (1:632) is not borne out by the situation of the empire under Constantine. For discussion of the more positive attitudes toward Montesquieu also evinced by *The Decline and Fall*, see David Carrithers, "Montesquieu's Philosophy of History," *Journal of the History of Ideas* 47, no. 1 (1986): 64.

17. Edward Gibbon, *Miscellaneous Works of Edward Gibbon, Esquire, with Memoirs of His Life and Writings*, ed. John Lord Sheffield (London, 1796), 1:91. Sheffield assembled the memoirs from six separate autobiographical manuscripts by Gibbon.

18. Charles de Secondat, Baron de Montesquieu, *De la politique*, in *Oeuvres completes de Montesquieu*, edited by Roger Caillois (Paris, 1949–51), 1:112.

19. See Carrithers, "Montesquieu's Philosophy of History," 69.

20. Isaiah Berlin, *Against the Current: Essays in the History of Ideas*, 2nd ed. (Princeton, NJ: Princeton University Press, 2013), 202.

21. In Charles de Secondat, Baron de Montesquieu, *Reflections on the Causes of the Grandeur and Declension of the Romans*, translator unidentified (London, 1734), "peu à peu" sometimes gets rendered "by insensible Degrees" (see, e.g., 76), though the French original also uses the term *insensiblement*; see Charles de Secondat, Baron de Montesquieu, *Considerations sur les causes de la grandeur des Romains et de leur decadence* (Edinburgh, 1736), 74.

22. Brian Singer, *Montesquieu and the Discovery of the Social* (Houndmills, England: Palgrave Macmillan, 2013), 158.

23. Ibid., 161–62.

24. The translator, Nugent, is following the English convention of translating *moeurs* as "manners" and *manières* as "customs"; I include the original French for clarity's sake. Nugent's practice is shared by all eighteenth-century English translations of the terms I have seen.

25. For a brief but useful contrast of the two rivals, see Robert Darnton, "Voltaire, Historian," *Raritan* 35, no. 2 (2015), 23–24.

26. Voltaire, *The Age of Lewis XIV* (London, 1752), does not name a translator. J. G. A. Pocock, *Barbarism and Religion*, vol. 2, *Narratives of Civil Government* (Cambridge: Cambridge University Press, 1999), xiii, attributes it to Nugent, though this remains uncertain. We know that the printer Dodsley was looking for a translator for it, and that

Samuel Richardson let Charlotte Lennox, who was looking for work, know about it. See Samuel Richardson to Charlotte Lennox, April 6, 1752, in Samuel Richardson, *The Cambridge Edition of the Correspondence of Samuel Richardson*, vol. 10, *Correspondence Primarily on Sir Charles Grandison (1750–1754)*, ed. Betty A. Schellenberg (Cambridge: Cambridge University Press, 2015), 66. But no confirmation that she took it on is available, and as Norbert Schürer remarks in Charlotte Lennox, *Correspondence and Miscellaneous Documents*, ed. Norbert Schürer (Lewisburg, PA: Bucknell University Press, 2012), 35, the task of translating 728 pages in four months was not a "small Thing," though not impossible.

27. Voltaire, *The Age of Lewis XIV*, 1:2. Hereafter, volume and page numbers will be cited parenthetically.

28. The bracketed French is from Voltaire, *Le siècle de Louis XIV*, 2nd ed. (London, 1752), 1:470.

29. Pocock, *Barbarism and Religion*, 1:138.

30. Karen O'Brien, *Narratives of Enlightenment: Cosmopolitan History from Voltaire to Gibbon* (Cambridge: Cambridge University Press, 1997), 44.

31. Voltaire, *Le siècle de Louis XIV*, 2:242, 193.

32. Voltaire, *The Age of Lewis XIV* (Glasgow, 1753), 1:iii.

33. Voltaire, *Le siècle de Louis XIV*, 2:242.

34. Voltaire, *An Essay on Universal History, the Manners, and Spirit of Nations, from the Reign of Charlemaign to the Age of Lewis XIV*, trans. Thomas Nugent (London 1759), 2:129.

35. Voltaire, "A Recapitulation of the Whole of the Foregoing History, with the Point of Light in Which It Ought to be Considered," trans. Tobias Smollett et al., in *The Works of M. de Voltaire* (London, 1761), 9:144. The complete edition (1761–81) of the *Works* would eventually include thirty-five volumes.

36. See Pocock, *Barbarism and Religion*, 2:121: "The new *histoire des moeurs*, then, is not to substitute itself for the neo-classical narrative of deeds worthy of memory; it is in fact to restore that narrative; but renaissance, enlightenment and the transforming though not faultless monarchy of Louis XIV exist to perform the restitution of *moeurs* which is necessary before deeds are worth narrating again. The history Voltaire is now to write is in a sense a metahistory; it is about loss and recovery of history in the neo-classical meaning of the term."

37. Voltaire, "A Recapitulation," 9:149–50.

38. O'Brien, *Narratives of Enlightenment*, 46. For his use of the phrase, see, e.g., Voltaire, *Essay sur l'histoire générale et sur les moeurs et l'esprit des nations, depuis Charlemagne jusqu'à nos jours* (Amsterdam, 1758), 4:227: "Avec quelle lenteur, avec quelle difficulté le Genre humain se civilise."

39. James Moore, "Natural Rights and the Scottish Enlightenment," in *The Cambridge History of Eighteenth-Century Political Thought*, ed. Mark Goldie and Robert Wokler (Cambridge: Cambridge University Press, 2006), 311. John Dalrymple himself appeals to the unfelt at crucial, "philosophical" moments of his account, as when he remarks on multiple small factors that changed feudalism's character in *An Essay towards a General History of Feudal Property in Great Britain* (London, 1757), 197: "these imperceptible causes in the circumstances of mankind more powerful than any publick law[,] and no publick law itself, brought about this alteration." For the claim that Adam Smith

originated the concept and influenced other Scots in their applications of it, see Thierry C. Pauchant, "Adam Smith's Four-Stages Theory of Socio-Cultural Evolution: New Insights from His 1749 Lecture," *Adam Smith Review* 9 (2017): 49–74.

40. For an account of English historiography built on neoclassical models, see Philip Hicks, *Neoclassical History and English Culture: From Clarendon to Hume* (London: Palgrave Macmillan, 1998).

41. David Hume to Abbé Jean Bernard le Blanc, November 5, 1755, in David Hume, *The Letters of David Hume*, ed. J. Y. T. Greig (Oxford: Clarendon, 1932), 1:226.

42. David Hume to Gilbert Elliot (Lord Minto), May 1, 1760, in Hume, *Letters*, 1:325–26.

43. See Mark Salber Phillips, *On Historical Distance* (New Haven, CT: Yale University Press, 2013), for an account of the "abstract and disembodied" (70) mode of representation to which Hume had to resort in describing what the next century would call public opinion.

44. For a survey of some of these ironies, see James Noggle, *The Temporality of Taste in Eighteenth-Century British Writing* (Oxford: Oxford University Press, 2012), 96–123.

45. See, e.g., Craig Smith, "The Scottish Enlightenment, Unintended Consequences, and the Science of Man," *Journal of Scottish Philosophy* 7, no. 1 (2009): 9–28; Jonathan Sheehan and Dror Wahrman, *Invisible Hands: Self-Organization in the Eighteenth Century* (Chicago: University of Chicago Press, 2015); and Ronald Hamowy, *The Scottish Enlightenment and the Theory of Spontaneous Order* (Carbondale: Southern Illinois University Press, 1987).

46. This characteristic phrase appears in David Hume, *The History of Great Britain* (London, 1757), 2:140, the second Stuart volume that also includes the history of the Commonwealth, when Hume denies that Scottish resistance to monarchy had anything much to do with lofty libertarian principles and "proceeded more from the turbulency of their aristocracy and the bigotry of their ecclesiastics, than from any fixed passion towards civil liberty" (140).

47. David Hume, *The History of England* (Indianapolis: Liberty Fund, 1983), 5:18. Hereafter, volume and page numbers will be cited parenthetically. There are small verbal differences between the passage quoted and its original form in *The History of Great Britain* (Edinburgh, 1754), 1:15.

48. See James A. Harris, *David Hume: An Intellectual Biography* (Cambridge: Cambridge University Press, 2015), which takes as its primary theme the observation that "as a man of letters, [Hume] did not write as a specialist only for fellow specialists. He sought, and found, a very large readership among educated men and women of his day, in Britain, and in Europe more widely. . . . His task as a man of letters was to be part of the effort to bring that conversation, the conversation that we call the Enlightenment, into existence" (23–24).

49. David Hume, "Of the Rise and Progress of the Arts and Sciences," in *Essays Moral, Political, and Literary*, ed. Eugene F. Miller (Indianapolis: Liberty Fund, 1985), 114.

50. David Hume, "Of Luxury," in *Essays*, 271. (Hume changed the essay's title from "Of Luxury" to "Of Refinement in the Arts" in the 1760 edition.)

51. David Hume, *The History of England under the House of Tudor* (London, 1759), 1:67.

52. Ibid., 5:124.

53. David Hume, "Of the Standard of Taste," in *Essays*, 243.

54. David Hume to Michael Ramsay, undated, c. 1730, in Hume, *Letters*, 2:337. Though Greig designates the letter as undatable, James A. Harris, *David Hume*, 43, dates it to 1730 and identifies the books as "presumably Paul Pellisson-Fontanier's *Histoire de l'Académie Françoise*" and "presumably the final volume of Rapin's *Histoire d'Angleterre.*"

55. See Harris, *David Hume*, 78–81.

56. David Hume to Michael Ramsay, September 12, 1734, in Hume, *Letters*, 1:20.

57. Catharine Macaulay, *The History of England from the Ascension of James I to that of the Brunswick Line* (London, 1763–83), 1:275.

58. Ibid., 5:381.

59. Karen O'Brien, *Women and Enlightenment in Eighteenth-Century Britain* (Cambridge: Cambridge University Press, 2009), 155. O'Brien adds, "not for Macaulay the Gothic idea of female affective patriotism" (155).

60. For instance, in the introduction to Catharine Macaulay, *The History of England, from the Revolution to the Present Time, in a Series of Letters to the Reverend Doctor Wilson* (Bath, England, 1778), a side project undertaken before her completion of her historical magnum opus, she describes her intention to detail "those causes and circumstances, which have insensibly led us from the airy height of imaginary security, prosperity, and elevation, to our present state of danger and depravity" (2).

61. Macaulay, *History of England*, 5:383.

62. William Robertson, *The History of the Reign of the Emperor Charles V*, vol. 1, *View of the Progress of Society in Europe, from the Subversion of the Roman Empire, to the Beginning of the Sixteenth Century* (London, 1769), 290. Hereafter, page numbers will be cited parenthetically.

63. William Robertson, *The History of Scotland* (London, 1759), 1:110.

64. Karen O'Brien, *Narratives of Enlightenment: Cosmopolitan History from Voltaire to Gibbon* (Cambridge: Cambridge University Press, 1997), 102–4, has persuasively emphasized, however, the cosmopolitan impulses of *The History of Scotland* as well.

65. From the 1774 edition on, Robertson dropped "stupidity."

66. Daniele Francesconi, "William Robertson on Historical Causation and Unintended Consequences," *Cromohs* 4 (1999), http://www.fupress.net/index.php/cromohs/article/view/15745/14631, n49.

67. He will note, for instance, that "the Princes and statesmen of Italy," responding to the incursion of Charles VIII, "now extended to the affairs of Europe, the maxims of that political science which had hitherto been applied only to regulate the operations of the petty states in their own country . . . and had manifested the importance of attending to that great secret in modern policy, the preservation of a proper distribution of power among all the members of the system into which the states of Europe are formed." Robertson, *View of the Progress of Society in Europe*, 112.

68. William Robertson, *The History of America* (London, 1777), 1:28. This rather awkward sentence goes unrevised through the nine eighteenth-century editions of the *History*.

69. Robertson, *The History of America*, 1:360.

70. Adam Ferguson, *An Essay on the History of Civil Society* (Edinburgh, 1767), 419.

71. Frank E. Manuel, "Edward Gibbon: Historien-Philosophe," in *Edward Gibbon and the Decline and Fall of the Roman Empire*, ed. G. W. Bowersock, John Clive, and Stephen R. Graubard (Cambridge, MA: Harvard University Press, 1977), 169.

72. It appears, for instance, when Gibbon writes of the effects of Virgil's *Georgics* on the veterans of the Augustan era; see Edward Gibbon, *Essai sur l'étude de la littérature* (London, 1761), 43. Pocock, *Barbarism and Religion*, vol. 1, *The Enlightenments of Edward Gibbon, 1737–1764* (Cambridge: Cambridge University Press, 1999), 224, translates the passage thus: "His songs worked this marvel. The veterans grew insensibly accustomed to repose."

73. Leo Braudy, *Narrative Form in History and Fiction: Hume, Fielding, and Gibbon* (Princeton, NJ: Princeton University Press, 1970), 228.

74. David P. Jordan, *Gibbon and His Roman Empire* (Urbana: University of Illinois Press, 1971), 104.

75. David Womersley, *The Transformation of* The Decline and Fall of the Roman Empire (Cambridge: Cambridge University Press, 1987), 97.

76. Edward Gibbon, *Miscellaneous Works of Edward Gibbon, Esquire, with Memoirs of His Life and Writings* (London, 1796), 1:24.

77. Gibbon, *Miscellaneous Works*, 75.

78. See David Womersley, *Gibbon and the "Watchmen of the Holy City": The Historian and His Reputation, 1776–1815* (Oxford: Oxford University Press, 2002), 309–13.

79. Gibbon, *Miscellaneous Works*, 44–45.

80. Arnaldo Momigliano, "Gibbon's Contribution to Historical Method," in *Historia: Zeitschrift für Alte Geschichte* 2, no. 4 (1954): 454. The connection between Gibbon's identities as an *érudit* and a *philosophe* is a primary theme in Pocock, *Barbarism and Religion*, vol. 1; see especially 1:135–238.

81. Gibbon, *Miscellaneous Works*, 139–40.

82. Ibid., 140.

83. Edward Gibbon, *The History of the Decline and Fall of the Roman Empire*, ed. David Womersley (London: Penguin, 1994), 1:473–74.

84. See J. G. A. Pocock, *Barbarism and Religion*, vol. 5, *The First Triumph* (Cambridge: Cambridge University Press, 2010), 6, for the claim that Gibbon does not explicitly present himself as a religious skeptic in chapters 15 and 16 of *The Decline and Fall*: "The portrait of Gibbon as an irreligious scoffer, formed and condemned by his Christian and clerical readers in 1776–81, has been upheld and applauded by his Enlightened and agnostic readers from that day to this. It may well be correct; but how far does it describe his intentions or his performance?"

85. Ruth Mack, *Literary Historicity: Literature and Historical Experience in Eighteenth-Century Britain* (Stanford, CA: Stanford University Press, 2009), 165.

86. See F. R. Ankersmit, *Sublime Historical Experience* (Stanford, CA: Stanford University Press, 2005).

87. F. R. Ankersmit, quoted in Mack, *Literary Historicity*, 166; emphasis in the original Ankersmit.

88. Mack, *Literary Historicity*, 167.

89. Ibid., 162, 165.

90. Jonathan Israel, *Radical Enlightenment: Philosophy and the Making of Modernity, 1650–1750* (Oxford: Oxford University Press, 2001), 599.

91. In George Travis, *Letters to Edward Gibbon, Esq., Author of the History of the Decline and Fall of the Roman Empire* (Chester, England, 1784), 122, Travis goads Gibbon to declare his irreligion: "Walk no more forth with your Stiletto in the Twilight. Seek your adversary honorably, with your naked sword, in the face of day. Aspire to the credit of *Toland*, and *Tindal*,—of *Chubb*, and *Morgan*,—of *Vanini*, and *Spinoza*, by a direct attempt to break this *'Yoke of the Gospel'*"; emphasis in the original.

92. Gibbon also mentions "Spinozisme" in his *Essai sur l'étude de la littérature*, 125: "Mais les Stoiciens, dans leur mélange bizarre du Théisme le plus pur, du Spinosisme, et de l'idolatrie populaire, rapportoient ce paganism, dont ils étoient les zélateurs au culte de la nature brisée en autant de Dieux qu'elle a de faces différentes." Commenting on this passage, Pocock, *Barbarism and Religion*, 1:236, argues that at this point in Gibbon's career "he was proceeding deeper into skepticism, but not into either deism or non-theism of a Spinozistic kind."

93. Edward Gibbon, *Critical Observations on the Sixth Book of the Aeneid* (London, 1770), 25.

94. Ibid., 25–26; capitalization in the original.

95. Gibbon, *Critical Observations*, 26; capitalization in the original. He will go on, nonetheless, to imply that Warburton is wrong to exonerate Virgil of "Spinozism" (27).

96. Gibbon, *Critical Observations*, 26.

97. Pocock, *Barbarism and Religion*, 1:68.

98. Ibid., 69.

99. Catharine Macaulay, *Observations on the Reflections of the Right Hon. Edmund Burke, on the Revolution in France* (London, 1790), 54; emphasis in the original.

100. Edmund Burke, *Reflections on the Revolution in France*, in *Writings and Speeches of Edmund Burke*, vol. 8, *The French Revolution: 1790–1794*, ed. L. G. Mitchell (Oxford: Clarendon, 1989),108.

101. Lord Acton, quoted in Seamus F. Deane, "Lord Acton and Edmund Burke," *Journal of the History of Ideas* 33, no. 2 (1972): 330.

102. Edmund Burke, *An Essay Towards an Abridgment of the English History*, in *Writings and Speeches of Edmund Burke*, vol. 1, *The Early Writings*, ed. T. O. McLoughlin and James T. Boulton (Oxford: Clarendon, 1981), 445.

103. The principal work on this influence is C. P. Courtney, *Montesquieu and Burke* (Oxford: Blackwell, 1963), which contends that Montesquieu shaped Burke's historical perspectives in the *Abridgment* (46–57). See also F. P. Lock, *Edmund Burke*, vol. 1, *1730–1784* (Oxford: Clarendon, 1999), which asserts that "Montesquieu was [Burke's] master" (151) in his eclectic, multimethod approach to history. In the fullest account of Burke's historical thinking, Sora Sato, *Edmund Burke as Historian: War, Order, and Civilisation* (Houndmills, England: Palgrave Macmillan, 2018), 10, notes that "the writings of Montesquieu were particularly significant in shaping Burke's thought . . . even though Burke did not uncritically receive his mentor's ideas."

104. For an emphasis on the role of manners in Burke's view of history, see Sora Sato, "Edmund Burke's Ideas on Historical Change," *History of European Ideas* 40, no. 5 (2014): 675–92, especially 682–87.

105. See Daniel I. O'Neill, *The Burke-Wollstonecraft Debate: Savagery, Civilization, and Democracy* (State College: Pennsylvania State University Press, 2012), 53, for a presentation of the case for "Burke's close connection to the Scottish Enlightenment's

dominant intellectual concerns, specifically questions of epistemology in philosophy and moral theory and the attempt to develop a broadly systematic scientific study of history."

106. Burke, *Abridgment*, 368.

107. Ibid., 456.

108. Ibid., 443. For the importance of such gradualism in Burke's theory of the constitution, see John C. Weston Jr., "Edmund Burke's View of History," *Review of Politics* 23, no. 2 (1961): 203–29. Weston remarks that Burke "added his own idea of a gradual and developing realization" (220) of the idea of the English separation of powers to Montesquieu's theory of it, though as we have seen, Montesquieu does argue that manners operate "peu à peu."

109. T. O. McLoughlin, "Edmund Burke's *Abridgment of English History*," *Eighteenth-Century Ireland / Iris an dá chultúr* 5 (1990): 54. McLoughlin contrasts what he calls Hume's "Tory" views with Burke's, particularly on the constitutional importance of Magna Carta (53–57).

110. On this point, see Neil McArthur, "David Hume and the Common Law of England," *Journal of Scottish Philosophy* 3, no. 1 (2005): 67–82, especially 70–74.

111. For this emphasis, see O'Neill, *The Burke-Wollstonecraft Debate*, 73–77.

112. Burke, *Abridgment*, 540.

113. Ibid.

114. Edmund Burke, "The History of England, from the Invasion of Julius Cæsar to the Accession of Henry VII. In 2 vols. By David Hume. Printed for A. Millar" (review), in Edmund Burke et al., *The Annual Register, or A View of the History, Politicks, and Literature, of the Year 1761* (London, 1762), 301a, 301b.

115. Ibid., 301b–302a.

116. For his discussion of the Witenagemot (which he spells different ways), see David Hume, *The History of England* (Indianapolis: Liberty Fund, 1983), 1:143–47.

117. Burke, *Reflections*, 82.

118. Lock, *Edmund Burke*, 97.

119. Tom Furniss, *Edmund Burke's Aesthetic Ideology* (Cambridge: Cambridge University Press, 1993), 21.

120. Thus Frances Ferguson, *Solitude and the Sublime: Romanticism and the Aesthetics of Individuation* (New York: Routledge, 1992), 52, remarks that "if the beautiful insidiously induces a dangerous relaxation . . . the sublime acts as the antidote to the dissolution produced by the beautiful. All its strainings follow the dictates of the work ethic."

121. Ferguson, *Solitude and the Sublime*, 52, quotes the *Enquiry*: "the best remedy for all these evils (produced by the beautiful) is exercise or *labour*; and labour is a surmounting of *difficulties*, an exertion of the contracting power of the muscles." The parenthetical comment is Ferguson's own interpolation.

122. Edmund Burke, *A Philosophical Enquiry into the Origin of our Ideas of the Sublime and Beautiful*, ed. James T. Boulton (Notre Dame, IN: University of Notre Dame Press, 1958), 150, 155.

123. Hogarth, too, discusses the line of beauty in the idiom of the insensible: "You will see how *gradually* the changes in its shape are produced; how imperceptibly the different curvatures run into each other; and how easily the eye glides along the varied

wavings of its sweep." William Hogarth, *The Analysis of Beauty, Written with a View of Fixing the Fluctuating Ideas of Taste*, (London, 1753), 61. Hogarth's preferred terms for the variations of the line of beauty are "gradually" and "by degrees," and he too describes the "more or less-pleasing vibrations of the optic nerves" (95).

124. Burke, *Enquiry*, remarks on the "insensible swell" of a beautiful woman's body and concludes, "It gives me no small pleasure to find that I can strengthen my theory in this point, by the opinion of the very ingenious Mr. Hogarth; whose idea of the line of beauty I take in general to be extremely just" (115).

125. David Bromwich, *The Intellectual Life of Edmund Burke: From the Sublime and Beautiful to American Independence* (Cambridge, MA: Harvard University Press, 2014) is thus right, I think, to insist that the "continuity" (95) that literary scholars have tended to find between the *Enquiry* and Burke's later political writings should be recognized but not exaggerated.

126. Burke, *Enquiry*, 40.

127. Ibid., 103. For a discussion of the incompatibility of beauty in the *Enquiry* with immemorial custom as described in the later writings, see Bromwich, *Intellectual Life*, 81–84.

128. Burke, *Reflections*, 216, 217.

129. Ibid., 217.

130. Ibid.

131. Edmund Burke, *A Letter from Mr. Burke, to a Member of the National Assembly*, in *Writings and Speeches of Edmund Burke*, vol. 8, *The French Revolution: 1790–1794*, ed. L. G. Mitchell (Oxford: Clarendon, 1989), 331.

132. Edmund Burke, *Letter from the Right Hon. Edmund Burke, M. P. in the Kingdom of Great Britain, to Sir Hercules Langrishe, Bart. M.P. on the subject of Roman Catholics of Ireland . . .* (London, 1792), 81.

133. Edmund Burke, *Two Letters Addressed to a Member of the Present Parliament, On the Proposals for Peace with the Regicide Directory of France* (London, 1796), 99–100.

134. Burke, *Reflections*, 58. For commentary on Burke's relation to Priestley as a scientist and supporter of the revolution, see Jessica Riskin, *Science in the Age of Sensibility: The Sentimental Empiricists of the French Enlightenment* (Chicago: University of Chicago Press, 2002), 275–81. Air has been a popular topic in recent criticism and history of science. Steven Connor, *The Matter of Air: Science and Art of the Ethereal* (London: Reaktion, 2010), 65, discusses Burke's remarks on "wild *gas*"; and Jayne Elizabeth Lewis, *Air's Appearance: Literary Atmosphere in British Fiction, 1660–1794* (Chicago: University of Chicago Press, 2012), 197, discusses Burke and Priestley.

Chapter IV. Political Economy

1. James Steuart, *An Inquiry into the Principles of Political Oeconomy* (London, 1767), 2:560.

2. For an often-cited discussion, see Emma Rothschild, *Economic Sentiments: Adam Smith, Condorcet, and the Enlightenment* (Cambridge, MA: Harvard University Press, 2001), which remarks that Smith and Condorcet "have become emblems of the cold, hard, and rational Enlightenment. They are opposite emblems in many respects" (2).

3. For the relation in the eighteenth century between commercial writing and natural philosophy, see Margaret Schabas, *The Natural Origins of Economics* (Chicago: University of Chicago Press, 2005), especially the extended attention paid to Hume (58–78) and Smith (79–101).

4. Karl Marx, *Capital*, vol. 1, trans. Samuel Moore and Edward Aveling, ed. Frederick Engels, in Karl Marx and Friedrich Engels, *The Marx-Engels Reader*, ed. Robert C. Tucker (New York: Norton, 1978), 322; emphasis added.

5. See Jonathan Sheehan and Dror Wahrman, *Invisible Hands: Self-Organization and the Eighteenth Century* (Chicago: University of Chicago Press, 2015), which stresses throughout how thinkers across various areas of inquiry came to see that "complex systems, left to their own devices, generated order immanently, without external direction, through *self-organization*" (xi; emphasis in the original). See also Craig Smith, "The Scottish Enlightenment, Unintended Consequences and the Science of Man," *Journal of Scottish Philosophy* 7, no. 1 (2009): 9–28, for an overview of the "fascination" (10) with the notion in Scottish thought. A helpful older survey of the notion of unintended consequences and its political ramifications in the eighteenth century (and after) appears in J. W. Burrow, *Whigs and Liberals* (Oxford: Oxford University Press, 1988), 50–76.

6. Sheehan and Wahrman, *Invisible Hands*, 238.

7. Sheehan and Wahrman, *Invisible Hands*, 240, remark on "that key if not always comfortable element in conceptualizing self-organization: *God*."

8. Gilles Deleuze, *Spinoza: Practical Philosophy*, trans. Robert Hurley (San Francisco: City Lights, 1988), 123.

9. For the relation of "intensity" to "qualified" affect, see Brian Massumi, *Parables for the Virtual: Movement, Sensation, Affect* (Durham, NC: Duke University Press, 2002), 24–27; for feedback and resonation, see 34–39. Massumi concludes the introduction of *Parables* with his notion (quoting Giordano Bruno) that "only 'an insensible body is a truly continuous body'" (21), arguing that the virtual—potential—feeling, when transformed or "qualified" into felt feelings, becomes "discontinuous."

10. Dudley North, *Discourses Upon Trade: Principally Directed to the Cases of the Interest, Coynage, Clipping, Increase of Money* (London, 1691), 14.

11. Bernard Mandeville, *The Fable of the Bees*, 2 vols., ed. F. B. Kaye (Indianapolis: Liberty Fund, 1988), 1:9–40. Hereafter, volume and page numbers will be cited parenthetically; all emphasis is in the original.

12. Such is the general argument, announced in its title, of E. J. Hundert, *The Enlightenment's Fable: Bernard Mandeville and the Discovery of Society* (Cambridge: Cambridge University Press, 1994).

13. Mandeville would add a couple of paragraphs responding to critics in the third edition.

14. For this contrast, see Vivasvan Soni, *Mourning Happiness: Narrative and the Politics of Modernity* (Ithaca, NY: Cornell University Press, 2010), 263, though he also remarks in a footnote, "The coexistence of a sentimentalized conception of happiness with one that still refers to an outward condition is widespread" in the eighteenth century (263n37). For a general history of happiness from antiquity to modernity, see Darrin M. McMahon, *Happiness: A History* (New York: Grove, 2006).

15. For this point, and an excellent discussion in general of classical conceptions of (objective) happiness and the modern, nonmoralized and subjectivized happiness that

contrasts with it, see Adam Potkay, "Happiness, Unhappiness, and Joy," *Social Research* 77, no. 2 (2010): 523–44.

16. Aristotle, *Aristotle's Nicomachean Ethics, a New Translation*, trans. Robert C Bartlett and Susan D. Collins (Chicago: University of Chicago Press, 2011), 203.

17. See McMahon, *Happiness*, 68–70, which describes how "Felicity," as a goddess, "united public power and private prosperity under the aegis of the Roman state" (69). See also Federico D'Onofrio, "On the Concept of 'Felicitas Publica' in Eighteenth-Century Political Economy," *Journal of the History of Economic Thought* 37, no. 3 (2015): 449–71, for an account of the Italian context, which also provides a survey of uses of the idea of Felicitas Publica in Europe from the early modern period into the Enlightenment. D'Onofrio stresses that European political economy connected the notion to the success of the monarch, not necessarily to the eudaemonistic happiness of individuals or to the flourishing of a commercial state: Felicitas Publica "was obviously not meant as the individual happiness of the members of the community, but rather as the final goal of the monarch and his duty toward the society" (451), in this differing also from the motives of "the great thinkers of the Scottish Enlightenment, who lived in a parliamentary system" (467).

18. Bernard Mandeville, *Free Thoughts on Religion, the Church, and National Happiness* (London, 1720), 330. An enlarged and corrected version would appear in 1729, after volume 2 of the *Fable*.

19. Mandeville, *Free Thoughts*, 330; emphasis in the original.

20. Ibid., 331, 332.

21. Ibid., 333; emphasis in the original.

22. Ibid., 334.

23. Ibid.

24. Bernard Mandeville, *A Treatise of the Hypochondriack and Hysterick Passions, Vulgarly Call'd the Hypo in Men and Vapours in Women* (London, 1711), 151.

25. Joseph Butler, "Sermon 1: Upon Humane Nature, the Social Nature of Man," in *Fifteen Sermons Preached at the Rolls Chapel upon the following subjects . . .* (London, 1726), 5.

26. Ibid., 18.

27. Francis Hutcheson, *Reflections upon Laughter, and Remarks upon the Fable of the Bees* (Glasgow, 1750), 45, 53.

28. See Hundert, *The Enlightenment's Fable*, 134, which cites E. D. James, *Pierre Nicole: Jansenist and Humanist* (The Hague: Nijhoff, 1972), 38–43 and 124–25, and James's discussion of *pensées imperceptibles* in Nicole to place Mandeville in "the line of Jansenist moral psychology" (134). James defines these unfelt thoughts thus: "Nicole's conception of the *pensée imperceptible*, then, is essentially that of a maxim or principle which guides our judgment but of which we are unaware"; James, *Pierre Nicole*, 40).

29. Cleomenes is commonly seen as speaking for Mandeville against Horatio through the first four dialogues, with Horatio taking up more Mandevillean positions in the fifth and sixth, though John Robertson, *The Case for Enlightenment: Scotland and Naples, 1680–1760* (Cambridge: Cambridge University Press, 2005), 273–80, argues that the situation is more complicated.

30. Hundert, *The Enlightenment's Fable*, 51.

31. As Hundert, *The Enlightenment's Fable*, 51, remarks, "But when Mandeville intends to show what men have accomplished for themselves, he figures society as the creation of political cunning." See also F. B. Kaye, "Introduction," in Mandeville, *The Fable of the Bees*, 1:lxiv–lxvi, which stresses that Mandeville, especially in part 2, seeks to correct the impression conveyed at many places in part 1 that morality arose at any particular moment of manipulation of the populace by cunning.

32. Mandeville will occasionally distinguish, e.g., between the developments of European and American societies (see 2:319–20), but even there he tends to insist on the influence of a general "human Nature" (2:321).

33. For a classic account, see John Brewer, *The Sinews of Power: War, Money and the English State, 1688–1793* (Cambridge, MA: Harvard University Press, 1988), especially 88–95, 116–119, and 191–218.

34. Theoretically speaking, the incidence of taxation raises bigger questions and can be difficult to pin down; even "direct" taxes may not best be understood as falling on those who pay them. Does a land tax fall on landlords, or is it at least partially passed on to tenants in the form of raised rents? For a consideration of tax incidence in the period, see Donald N. McCloskey, "A Mismeasurement of the Incidence of Taxation in Britain and France, 1715–1810," *Journal of European Economic History* 7, no. 1 (1978): 209–10. This brief piece critiques Peter Mathias and Patrick O'Brien, "Taxation in Britain and France, 1715–1810: A Comparison of the Social and Economic Incidence of Taxes Collected for the Central Governments," *Journal of European Economic History* 5, no. 3 (1976): 601–50. For their response to McCloskey, see Peter Mathias and Patrick O'Brien, "The Incidence of Taxes and the Burden of Proof," *Journal of European Economic History* 7, no. 1 (1978): 211–13.

35. Patrick K. O'Brien, "The Political Economy of British Taxation, 1660–1815," *The Economic History Review* 41, no. 1 (1988): 10.

36. William Petty, *A Treatise of Taxes and Contributions* (London, 1662), 72.

37. Petty, *A Treatise of Taxes*, 20. For a discussion of Petty and his "pet proposal," what he calls "Accumulative Excize" (73) in the *Treatise*'s final chapter, "Of Excize" (71–75), see Ted McCormick, *William Petty and the Ambitions of Political Arithmetic* (Oxford: Oxford University Press, 2010), 142–44. See also D'Maris Coffman, *Excise Taxation and the Origins of Public Debt* (London: Palgrave Macmillan, 2013), 189, for excise as an "'insensible' imposition," indifferent to the political loyalties of the taxpayer.

38. William Petty, *The Political Anatomy of Ireland with the Establishment for that Kingdom when the late Duke of Ormond was Lord Lieutenant . . .* (London, 1691), 1. Internal evidence suggests that the tract was written much earlier, in 1665.

39. Asgill is best remembered now for the furor caused by his 1700 theological tract claiming people may be directly "translated" into Heaven without dying. See John Asgill, *An Argument Proving, that According to the Covenant of Eternal Life revealed in the Scriptures, Man may be Translated from Hence into that Eternal Life, without Passing through Death, altho the Human Nature of Christ himself could not be thus translated till he had passed through Death* (London, 1700).

40. John Asgill, *An Abstract of the Publick Funds*, 2nd ed. (London, 1715), 24–25; emphasis in the original. The quotation is from Gaius Valerius Catullus, Catallus 22 ("sed non videmus manticae quod tergo est").

41. Asgill, *An Abstract*, 24.

42. For a consideration of the regressive nature of some indirect taxes, see J. V. Beckett and Michael Turner, "Taxation and Economic Growth in Eighteenth-Century England," *Economic History Review* 43, no. 3 (1990): 377–403, especially 391–396. Of course, customs on imported luxuries mostly hit the rich, but excises—taxes on domestic trade—on things deemed necessities or near necessities in eighteenth-century society shifted the burden down the social ladder. Rich families often brewed their own beer, for instance, so an excise on it fell on those who had to get their beer in alehouses; Beckett and Turner, "Taxation and Economic Growth," 394.

43. Andrew Marvell, *Last Instructions to a Painter*, in *The Poems of Andrew Marvell*, ed. Nigel Smith (Abingdon, England: Routledge, 2013), 373, lines 131–32.

44. Henry Roseveare, *The Treasury: The Evolution of a British Institution* (New York: Columbia University Press, 1969), 55.

45. Charles Davenant, *An Essay upon Ways and Means of Supplying the War*, 3d ed. (London, 1702), 144, 145.

46. A standard work on the topic is Paul Langford, *The Excise Crisis: Society and Politics in the Age of Walpole* (Oxford: Clarendon, 1975).

47. See, e.g., such ballads as the anonymous *The City Triumphant: or, The Burning of the Excise-Monster, A new ballad* (London, 1733); and Philalethes, *Excise Elegy: or, The Dragon Demolish'd, A new ballad* (London, 1733).

48. Caleb D'Anvers [Nicholas Amhurst], *An Argument Against Excises, in Several Essays, lately published in the Craftsman, and now collected together* (London, 1733), 46. For the court perspective on the furor, see John, Lord Hervey's comments in his *Memoirs of the Reign of George II, from his Accession to the Death of Queen Caroline*, ed. John Wilson Croker, 2nd ed. (London, 1855), 1:159–205, and especially, for his portrayal of the opposition to the excise as an "epidemic madness," 161.

49. D'Anvers, *An Argument*, 23.

50. See, e.g., James A. Harris, *Hume: An Intellectual Biography* (Cambridge: Cambridge University Press, 2015), 269.

51. David Hume, "Of Taxes," in *Essays Moral, Political and Literary*, ed. Eugene F. Miller (Indianapolis: Liberty Fund, 1985), 345.

52. Ibid., 347.

53. Ibid., 348, 347.

54. James Steuart, *An Inquiry into the Principles of Political Oeconomy* (London, 1767), 2:520.

55. See Adam Smith, *Lectures on Jurisprudence*, ed. R. L. Meek, D. D. Raphael, and P. G. Stein (Indianapolis: Liberty Fund, 1982), 583, where Smith notes that taxes on consumption "are insensibly paid by the people" and (with a certain irony) therefore "*seem* most to favor liberty" (emphasis added).

56. Cantillon's colorful life and mysterious death have remained fascinating to scholars. The standard biographical account is Antoin E. Murphy, *Richard Cantillon: Entrepreneur and Economist* (Oxford: Clarendon, 1986).

57. Richard Cantillon, *Essai sur la nature du commerce en général*, trans. Henry Higgs, 2nd ed. (London: Cass, 1959). All citations here are from this second, 1959, edition. The French text that I will cite throughout is from the original French edition, *Essai sur la nature du commerce en général. Traduit de l'anglois* (London, 1755).

58. As Higgs declares in Cantillon, *Essai*, 388, "it is this analytical mode of approach to economic problems which is the most strikingly original characteristic of Cantillon. He brushes Ethics and Politics aside as imperiously as a referee orders the seconds out of the ring before a prize fight. The isolation of the conception of material wealth which is claimed as one of the original merits of Adam Smith, is strikingly true of Cantillon."

59. In the essay largely responsible for rediscovering Cantillon after a century or more of neglect, W. Stanley Jevons, "Richard Cantillon and the Nationality of Political Economy" (1881), in Cantillon, *Essai*, 333–60, calls the chapter "one of the most marvellous things in the book" (348).

60. Cantillon, *Essai*, 161–63.

61. Ibid., 163.

62. Ibid., 185.

63. Terence Hutchison, *Before Adam Smith: The Emergence of Political Economy, 1662–1776* (Oxford: Blackwell, 1988), 172.

64. Cantillon, *Essai*, 235–37.

65. Ibid., 185.

66. Postlethwayt articulates antiracist views in his *Britain's Commercial Interest Explained and Improved* (London, 1757), 2:217: "Are not the rational faculties of the negro people in the general equal to those of any other of the human species?" Yet he also accepts chattel slavery as a fact of his times: "For my own part, I cannot help expressing my dislike to the slave-trade, and wish an end could be put to it; and I am inclined to believe that practicable without injury to our plantations. At present, however, we shall take things as they are, and reason from them in their present state, and not from that wherein we could hope them to be" (2:217).

67. Peter Groenewegen recognizes the "lengthy quotations" from Cantillon in Postlethwayt's work but considers the common accusation of plagiarism "greatly exaggerated." See Peter Groenewegen, "Postlethwayt, Malachy," *Oxford Dictionary of National Biography*, online ed., http://www.oxforddnb.com/view/10.1093/ref:odnb/9780198614128.001.0001/odnb-9780198614128-e-22599.

68. Postlethwayt, *Britain's Commercial Interest*, 1:162–63.

69. For a discussion of Hume's theory of money and the specie-flow mechanism in particular, see Carl Wennerlind, "An Artificial Virtue and the Oil of Commerce: A Synthetic View of Hume's Theory of Money," in *David Hume's Political Economy*, ed. Carl Wennerlind and Margaret Schabas (Abingdon, England: Routledge, 2008), 110–13.

70. David Hume, "Of the Balance of Trade," in *Essays Moral, Political, and Literary*, ed. Eugene F. Miller (Indianapolis: Liberty Fund, 1985), 326; capitalization in the original.

71. Hume, "Of the Balance of Trade," 326.

72. Ibid., 309.

73. Ibid., 312. For a discussion of Hume's knowledge of the science of hydrostatics, see Margaret Schabas, "David Hume on Experimental Natural Philosophy, Money, and Fluids," *History of Political Economy* 33, no. 3 (2001): 411–35. Schabas plausibly (though speculatively) argues that Hume's probable acquaintance with theories of subtle electric fluids, in vogue especially in the late 1740s, informed his account of money's properties (though she admits he refers explicitly only to water).

For a groundbreaking discussion of Hume's knowledge of science, learned as a student at the University of Edinburgh in Robert Steuart's Physiological Library, see Michael Barfoot, "Hume and the Culture of Science in the Early Eighteenth Century," in *Studies in the Philosophy of the Scottish Enlightenment*, ed. M. A. Stewart (Oxford: Oxford University Press, 1989), 151–90. In the catalog of the library, "Mechanics and Hydrostatics" is its own category; see Barfoot, "Hume and the Culture of Science," 155–56; 160–65 comment on Hume's use of Boylean hydrostatics in particular.

74. Hume, "Of the Balance of Trade," 312.

75. Gilles Deleuze, *Spinoza: Practical Philosophy*, trans. Robert Hurley (San Francisco: City Lights, 1988), 123.

76. For a discussion of similarities between Hume's and Spinoza's accounts of the passions, however, see Wim Klever, "More about Hume's Debt to Spinoza," *Hume Studies* 19, no. 1 (1993): 55–74. Klever's evidence is more convincing as a demonstration of affinities between the two philosophers than as a demonstration of influence. A classic discussion comparing their views on reason and religion is Richard H. Popkin, "Hume and Spinoza," *Hume Studies* 5, no. 2 (1979), 65–93. As Popkin notes, "Spinoza and Hume part company on a very basic point. They agree on the critique of vulgar thought. But Hume's solution of making people aware of the role of order in the world goes contrary to Spinoza's insistence that order, in this teleological sense, is a man-made concept, and has nothing to do with the real nature of God" (83).

77. David Hume to President de Montesquieu, April 10, 1749, in *The Letters of David Hume*, ed. J. Y. T. Greig (Oxford: Oxford University Press, 1931), 1:37: "Il semble que l'argent, non plus que l'eau, ne peut être élevé ni abaissé aucune part beaucoup au delà du niveau auquel il est dans les endroits où la communication est ouverte, mais qu'il doit toujours s'élever ou s'abaisser en proportion des marchandises et du travail qui sont dans chaque Etat." (It seems that money, no more than water, cannot rise or sink below its level where communication is open; it must always rise or sink in proportion to the level of commodities and labor in each state.)

78. The possibility is raised in Istvan Hont, "The 'Rich Country–Poor Country' Debate Revisited: The Irish Origins and French Reception of the Hume Paradox," in Schabas and Wennerlind, eds., *David Hume's Political Economy*, 319n16, though Hont, here discussing the possible influence of Cantillon's ideas about the effect of the money supply on trade and industry, insists on the multiplicity of international influences on such questions.

79. William Petty, *A Treatise of Taxes and Contributions* (London, 1662), 87.

80. In *Della Moneta* (1751) Galiani (quoted in Hutchison, *Before Adam Smith*, 259–60) remarks:

> It is not necessary to consider the first developments in a case, but the permanent and fixed conditions, and in this there is always order and equality; just as water in a vessel, if disturbed, returns to the due level after a confused and irregular fluctuation. Second, that no accident can occur in nature which will carry things to infinite extremity; but a certain moral gravity, existing in everything, always draws them back from the straight line of infinity. . . . Nothing corresponds more closely to the laws of commerce. What gravity is in physics,

the desire for gain or for happiness is in man; and, this being assumed, all the physical laws of bodies can be verified perfectly in the morality of our life.

For Hume's acquaintance with Galiani in Paris, see Ernst Mossner, *The Life of David Hume* (Oxford: Clarendon, 1980), 480–81; see also Paola Zanardi, "Italian Responses to David Hume," in *The Reception of David Hume in Europe*, ed. Peter Jones (London: Bloomsbury Academic, 2005), 172, which notes that "Galiani had met Hume in Paris, and had argued with him over the theory of money, but he does not refer to him in his writings, and Hume in his turn did not find him at all congenial."

81. Hume, "Of the Balance of Trade," 313.

82. For another comparison by Hume of the passions to hydrostatics, see the concluding paragraph of "A Dissertation on the Passions" (1757): "I pretend not to have here exhausted this subject. It is sufficient for my purpose, if I have made it appear, that, in the production and conduct of the passions, there is a certain regular mechanism, which is susceptible of as accurate a disquisition, as the laws of motion, optics, hydrostatics, or any part of natural philosophy." David Hume, "A Dissertation on the Passions," in *A Dissertation on the Passions; The Natural History of Religion*, ed. Tom L. Beauchamp (Oxford: Clarendon, 2007), 29.

83. Hume, "Of the Balance of Trade," 314–15.

84. Money's communicative properties lead Schabas, in "David Hume on Experimental Natural Philosophy, Money, and Fluids," to develop the thesis that it is even more like electricity than water: "The sudden arrival of new money works its first effect almost instantaneously, as though the causal chain was strictly physical without any conscious reflection on the part of the people concerned. In this case, everyone is stimulated, not just the merchants, to intensify their work effort, almost as though they were charged by some physical force" (429).

85. Adam Smith, *An Inquiry into the Nature and Causes of the Wealth of Nations*, ed. R. H. Campbell and A. S. Skinner (Indianapolis: Liberty Fund, 1981), 2:687. Hereafter, page numbers will be cited parenthetically; all subsequent citations are for vol. 1.

86. See Warren J. Samuels, Marianne F. Johnson, and William F. Perry, *Erasing the Invisible Hand: Essays on an Elusive and Misused Concept in Economics* (Cambridge: Cambridge University Press, 2011), 77–82, which canvasses these and other possibilities. Samuels died in the process of preparing this book, which was finished by his collaborators, but it uses the first person singular throughout, so I refer to it herein as his work.

87. See Jonathan Sheehan and Dror Wahrman, *Invisible Hands: Self-Organization and the Eighteenth Century* (Chicago: University of Chicago Press, 2015), 238.

88. Samuels, Johnson, and Perry, *Erasing the Invisible Hand*, 60.

89. See, e.g., Anthony Brewer, "On the Other (Invisible) Hand . . . ," *History of Political Economy* 41, no. 3 (2009): 519–43, which treats the invisible hand in *The Theory of Moral Sentiments* as a real argument but "concede[s] immediately that Smith was indeed using (perhaps rather heavyhanded) irony as a literary device to make his point" (536). Samuels remarks, "The notion of an invisible hand seems to be used as a rhetorical device, as a means of capturing attention, by authors and others who believe they have something original and/or important to say"; Samuels, Johnson, and Perry, *Erasing the Invisible Hand*, 61.

90. William D. Grampp, "What Did Smith Mean by the Invisible Hand?," *Journal of Political Economy* 108, no. 3 (2000), 441, notes that Smith's use of the phrase "discloses how his rhetorical sallies could disfigure his economics."

91. Emma Rothschild, *Economic Sentiments: Adam Smith, Condorcet, and the Enlightenment* (Cambridge, MA: Harvard University Press, 2001), 116, claims that in *The Wealth of Nations*, "the invisible hand is best understood as a mildly ironic joke."

92. See Stefan Andriopoulos, "The Invisible Hand: Supernatural Agency in Political Economy and the Gothic Novel," *ELH* 66, no. 3 (1999): 739–58.

93. For an illuminating overview of tensions between the literary and the economic in the (now not so) "new economic criticism," see the review article by Elizabeth Hewitt, "The Vexed Story of Economic Criticism," *American Literary History* 21, no. 3 (2009): 618–32, and especially 621–23 for economists' suspicion of "poetic . . . flights of fancy" (622) in economic writing.

94. See Sheehan and Wahrman, *Invisible Hands*, which recurs to "self-organization" throughout; Craig Smith, *Adam Smith's Political Philosophy: The Invisible Hand and Spontaneous Order* (London: Routledge, 2006); and Ronald Hamowy, *The Scottish Enlightenment and the Theory of Spontaneous Order* (Carbondale: Southern Illinois University Press, 1987).

95. For the origin of this idea, see William Robert Scott, *Adam Smith, as Student and Professor* (Glasgow: Jackson, 1937), 14, which claims that "wherever the word 'opulence' occurs, we may be sure that we are reading some of Adam Smith's earliest work." In Adam Smith, *Lectures on Jurisprudence*, ed. R. L. Meek, D. D. Raphael, and P. G. Stein (Indianapolis: Liberty Fund, 1982), the phrase "the progress of opulence" frequently appears both in the section "Of Police" (1766) and "Early Draft of *The Wealth of Nations*" (early 1760s), which anticipates, e.g., comments on British North American colonies in *The Wealth of Nations* by noting their "rapid progress of opulence" (633).

96. The scholarly literature on Smith's approach to stadial theory is vast. For a review of it, and a claim that Smith himself originated the four-stages theory in a 1749 lecture and conveyed it to other contributors to the Scottish Enlightenment, see Thierry C. Pauchant, "Adam Smith's Four-Stages Theory of Socio-Cultural Evolution: New Insights from his 1749 Lecture," *Adam Smith Review* 9 (2017): 49–74.

97. For the argument that Smith's denunciation of the unnatural and retrograde order of European development is not as denunciatory as it seems, see Anthony Brewer, "Luxury and Economic Development: David Hume and Adam Smith," *Scottish Journal of Political Economy* 45 (1998): 78–98. See also Istvan Hont, *Jealousy of Trade: International Competition and the Nation-State in Historical Perspective* (Cambridge, MA: Harvard University Press, 2005), chap. 5, "Adam Smith and the Political Economy of the 'Unnatural and Retrograde' Order," especially 374–88, where Hont argues that book 3 is a polemic against François Quesnay and the Physiocrats, who contended that the proper priority of agriculture must be imposed by planners on modern commercial society.

98. For instance, Smith, *The Wealth of Nations*, 384, calls entails, especially in modern times, "completely absurd."

99. For discussion of these passages in the context of the idea of the invisible hand, see Smith, *Adam Smith's Political Philosophy*, 80–81.

100. For Smith's nostalgia for aspects of feudal social relations, see Maureen Harkin, "Adam Smith's Missing History: Primitives, Progress, and the Problem of Genre,"

ELH 72, no. 2 (2005): 435. For Smith's ambivalence toward luxury spending by the rich, see Brewer, "Luxury and Economic Development," 97: "In Smith's system, by contrast [with Hume's], luxury spending is double edged. In so far as it drives out feudal 'hospitality' it can have all the desirable incentive and political effects that Hume described, but in so far as it displaces saving, it slows growth."

101. See Sheehan and Wahrman, *Invisible Hands*, 267; and Smith, *Adam Smith's Political Philosophy*, 94. Neither discuss the passage's place in an "unnatural and retrograde" historical development or as anything other than optimal.

102. Adam Smith, *Essays on Philosophical Subjects*, ed. W. P. D. Wrightman and J. C. Bryce (Indianapolis: Liberty Fund, 1982), 54.

103. The passage in full notes that the rich "are led by an invisible hand to make nearly the same distribution of the necessaries of life, which would have been made, had the earth been divided into equal portions among all its inhabitants, and thus without intending it, without knowing it, advance the interest of the society, and afford means to the multiplication of the species"; Adam Smith, *The Theory of Moral Sentiments*, ed.. D. D. Raphael and A. L. Macfie (Indianapolis: Liberty Fund, 1984), 184–85.

104. Jack Russell Weinstein, *Adam Smith's Pluralism: Rationality, Education, and the Moral Sentiments* (New Haven, CT: Yale University Press, 2013), 228. Weinstein adds that, for Smith, "ambiguous laws may be constant" (229).

105. See Christopher J. Berry, *The Idea of Commercial Society in the Scottish Enlightenment* (Edinburgh: Edinburgh University Press, 2015), 51. Berry's comment here directly reflects on the "insensible operation" described in book 3, which he sees as emblematic of the role of chance in causal explanation in Scottish Enlightenment thinkers.

Epilogue

1. William Godwin, *Enquiry concerning Political Justice, and its Influence on Morals and Happiness*, 2nd ed. (London, 1796), 1:2. The first edition, whose introduction was substantially revised for the second edition quoted here, appeared in 1793.

2. Godwin, *Enquiry concerning Political Justice*, 1:2.

3. Ibid., 1:400–401.

4. Ibid., 1:414.

5. Ibid., 1:415. For a claim that Godwin's account of the mind in the *Enquiry* "anticipates post-Freudian theory" on the subject of the unconscious, see Thomas Pfau, *Romantic Moods: Paranoia, Trauma, and Melancholy, 1790–1840* (Baltimore: Johns Hopkins University Press, 2005), 121.

6. Godwin, *Enquiry concerning Political Justice*, 1:415.

7. Dudley North, *Discourses Upon Trade: Principally Directed to the Cases of the Interest, Coynage, Clipping, Increase of Money* (London, 1691), 14.

8. Karl Marx, *Capital*, trans. Samuel Moore and Edward Aveling, ed. Frederick Engels, in Karl Marx and Friedrich Engels, *The Marx-Engels Reader*, ed. Robert C. Tucker (New York: Norton, 1978), 322.

9. The formula—"we are not aware of this, nevertheless we do it"—has served as a starting point, often revisited, for Slavoj Žižek's efforts to shift the traditional epistemological focus of ideology, its emphasis on ideology as false beliefs, to a more fundamental dimension based on practices. In *The Sublime Object of Ideology* (New York:

Verso, 1989), 27, he asks, "Where is the place of ideological illusion, in the *'knowing'* or in the *'doing'* in reality itself?" The answer, the doing, permits people to subscribe to ideology by their actions even if they do not believe in it.

10. Godwin, *Enquiry concerning Political Justice*, 2:445–46.

11. Lawrence Grossberg, "Affect's Future: Rediscovering the Virtual in the Actual," in *The Affect Theory Reader*, ed. Melissa Gregg and Gregory J. Seigworth (Durham, NC: Duke University Press, 2010), 316.

12. The phrase appears in Stephen Ahern, "Nothing More Than Feelings? Affect Theory Reads the Age of Sensibility," *The Eighteenth Century* 58, no. 3 (2017), 288. Toward the end of his essay (288–91) Ahern surveys both writers who embrace the radical promise of affect and those who have their doubts.

13. Clive Barnett, "Political Affects in Public Space: Normative Blind-Spots in Non-Representational Ontologies," *Transactions of the Institute of British Geographers*, n.s., 33, no. 2 (2008): 198a; emphasis in the original.

Bibliography

Primary Sources

Anonymous. *The City Triumphant: or, The Burning of the Excise-Monster. A new ballad.* London, 1733.
Anonymous. Review of Frances Burney's *Evelina*. *Critical Review* 46 (1778): 202–4.
Aristotle. *Aristotle's Nicomachean Ethics, a New Translation.* Translated by Robert C. Bartlett and Susan D. Collins. Chicago: University of Chicago Press, 2011.
Asgill, John. *An Argument Proving, that According to the Covenant of Eternal Life revealed in the Scriptures, Man may be Translated from Hence into that Eternal Life, without Passing through Death, altho the Human Nature of Christ himself could not be thus translated till he had passed through Death.* London, 1700.
——. *An Abstract of the Publick Funds.* 2nd ed. London, 1715.
Austen, Jane. *Jane Austen's "Sir Charles Grandison."* Edited by Brian Southam. Oxford: Oxford University Press, 1980.
——. *Sense and Sensibility.* Edited by Ros Ballaster. London: Penguin, 1995.
Backscheider, Paula R., and John J. Richetti, eds. *Popular Fiction by Women, 1660–1730: An Anthology.* Oxford: Oxford University Press, 1996.
Bayle, Pierre. *The Dictionary Historical and Critical of Mr Peter Bayle.* 5 vols. London, 1734–38.
——. *A General Dictionary, Historical and Critical.* 10 vols. Translated by Thomas Birch et al. London, 1734.
——. *An Historical and Critical Dictionary, by Monsieur Bayle.* 4 vols. London, 1710.
Behn, Aphra. *The Amours of Philander and Silvia.* London, 1687.
——. *Love-Letters Between a Noble-Man and His Sister.* London, 1684.
——. *Love Letters From a Noble Man to His Sister.* London, 1685.
Berkeley, George. *The Analyst; or, A Discourse Addressed to an Infidel Mathematician.* London, 1734.
Boileau Despréaux, Nicolas. *Oeuvres de Nicolas Boileau Despréaux, avec des éclaircissemens historiques.* 4 vols. Amsterdam, 1718.
Bond, Donald F., ed. *The Spectator.* 5 vols. Oxford: Oxford University Press, 1965.
Boswell, James. *The Life of Samuel Johnson.* Edited by David Womersley. London: Penguin, 2008.
Boyle, Robert. *The Works of the Honourable Robert Boyle.* 5 vols. London, 1744.
Brooke, Henry. *The Fool of Quality, or The History of Henry Earl of Moreland, in Four Volumes.* Dublin, 1766.
Burke, Edmund. *Letter from the Right Hon. Edmund Burke, M. P. in the Kingdom of Great Britain, to Sir Hercules Langrishe, Bart. M.P. on the subject of Roman Catholics of*

Ireland, and the propriety of admitting them to the elective franchise, consistently with the principles of the constitution as established at the Revolution. London, 1792.

———. *A Philosophical Enquiry into the Origin of our Ideas of the Sublime and Beautiful.* Edited by James T. Boulton. Notre Dame, IN: University of Notre Dame Press, 1958.

———. *Two Letters Addressed to a Member of the Present Parliament, On the Proposals for Peace with the Regicide Directory of France.* London, 1796.

———. *Writings and Speeches of Edmund Burke.* 9 vols. Edited by Paul Langford. Oxford: Clarendon, 1981–2015.

Burke, Edmund, et al. *The Annual Register, or A View of the History, Politicks, and Literature, of the Year 1761.* London, 1762.

Burnet, Gilbert. *Bishop Burnet's History of his Own Time.* 2 vols. London, 1724–31.

Burney, Frances. *Cecilia, or The Memoirs of an Heiress.* Edited by Peter Sabor and Margaret Anne Doody. Oxford: Oxford University Press, 1988.

———. *The Early Letters and Journals of Fanny Burney.* 5 vols. Edited by Lars E. Troide et al. Kingston, ON: McGill-Queens University Press, 1988.

———. *Evelina: or, A Young Lady's Entrance into the World, in a Series of Letters.* 2nd ed. 3 vols. London, 1779.

———. *Evelina, or The History of a Young Lady's Entrance into the World.* Edited by Edward A. Bloom. Oxford: Oxford University Press, 2002.

Butler, Joseph. *Fifteen Sermons Preached at the Rolls Chapel upon the following subjects: Upon humane nature. Upon the Government of the Tongue. Upon Compassion. Upon the Character of Balaam. Upon Resentment. Upon Forgiveness of Injuries. Upon Self-Deceit. Upon the Love of our Neighbour. Upon the Love of God. Upon the Ignorance of Man. . . .* London, 1726.

Cantillon, Richard. *Essai sur la nature du commerce en général.* Translated by Henry Higgs. 2nd ed. London: Frank Cass, 1959.

———. *Essai sur la nature du commerce en général. Traduit de l'anglois.* London, 1755.

Carte, Thomas. *A General History of England.* 4 vols. London, 1747–55.

Chapone, Hester. *Letters on the Improvement of the Mind, Addressed to a Young Lady.* 2 vols. London, 1773.

Cheyne, George. *The Natural Method of Cureing the Diseases of the Body, and the Disorders of the Mind Depending on the Body.* London, 1742.

———. *Philosophical Principles of Religion, Natural and Reveal'd.* London, 1715.

Condillac, Étienne Bonnot de. *Essai sur l'origine des connaissances humaines.* Paris, 1746.

———. *An Essay on the Origin of Human Knowledge. Being a supplement to Mr. Locke's Essay on the Human Understanding.* Translated by Thomas Nugent. London, 1756.

Cowley, Abraham. *Love's Riddle.* London, 1638.

———. *Poetical Blossomes by A.C.* 2nd ed. London, 1636.

———. *The Works of Mr. Abraham Cowley.* London, 1668.

Dalrymple, John. *An Essay towards a General History of Feudal Property in Great Britain.* London, 1757.

D'Anvers, Caleb [Nicholas Amhurst]. *An Argument Against Excises, in Several Essays, lately published in the Craftsman, and now collected together.* London, 1733.

Davenant, Charles. *An Essay upon Ways and Means of Supplying the War.* 3rd ed. London. 1702.
Ferguson, Adam. *An Essay on the History of Civil Society.* Edinburgh, 1767.
Fielding, Henry. *Amelia.* 4 vols. London, 1752.
———. *The History of Tom Jones, a Foundling.* Edited by John Bender and Simon Stern. Oxford: Oxford University Press, 1996.
———. *The Works of Henry Fielding.* 4 vols. London, 1762.
Fordyce, James. *Sermons to Young Women.* 2 vols. London, 1766.
Franklin, Benjamin, et al. *Report of Dr. Benjamin Franklin, and other Commissioners, Charged by the King of France, with the Examination of the Animal Magnetism.* London, 1785.
Gibbon, Edward. *Critical Observations on the Sixth Book of the Aeneid.* London, 1770.
———. *Essai sur l'étude de la littérature.* London, 1761.
———. *The History of the Decline and Fall of the Roman Empire.* 3 vols. Edited by David Womersley. London: Penguin, 1994.
———. *Miscellaneous Works of Edward Gibbon, Esquire, with Memoirs of His Life and Writings.* 2 vols. Edited by John Lord Sheffield. London, 1796.
Godwin, William. *Enquiry concerning Political Justice, and its Influence on Morals and Happiness.* 2nd ed. 2 vols. London, 1796.
Hartley, David. *Observations on Man, His Frame, His Duty, and His Expectations.* 2 vols. London, 1749.
Haywood, Eliza. *The Female Spectator.* 4 vols. London, 1745–46.
———. *The Mercenary Lover: or, The Unfortunate Heiresses.* London, 1726.
Hervey, John. *Memoirs of the Reign of George II, from his Accession to the Death of Queen Caroline.* 2nd ed. 2 vols. Edited by John Wilson Croker. London, 1855.
Hogarth, William. *The Analysis of Beauty, Written with a View of Fixing the Fluctuating Ideas of Taste.* London, 1753.
Hume, David. *An Abstract of a Book Lately Published; entituled, A Treatise of Human Nature.* London, 1740.
———. *A Dissertation on the Passions; The Natural History of Religion.* Edited by Tom L. Beauchamp. Oxford: Clarendon, 2007.
———. *Enquiry concerning the Principles of Morals.* London, 1751.
———. *Essays Moral, Political, and Literary.* Edited by Eugene F. Miller. Indianapolis: Liberty Fund, 1985.
———. *The History of England.* 6 vols. Indianapolis: Liberty Fund, 1983. Originally published in 1778.
———. *The History of England Under the House of Tudor.* 2 vols. London, 1759.
———. *The History of Great Britain.* 2 vols. Edinburgh, 1754.
———. *The Letters of David Hume.* Edited by J. Y. T. Greig. 2 vols. Oxford: Clarendon, 1932.
———. *Philosophical Essays concerning Human Understanding.* London, 1748.
———. *Political Discourses.* London, 1752.
———. *A Treatise of Human Nature.* 3 vols. London, 1738–40.
Hutcheson, Francis. *Reflections upon Laughter, and Remarks upon The Fable of the Bees.* Glasgow, 1750.
Johnson, Samuel. *A Dictionary of the English Language.* 2 vols. London, 1755.

Leibniz, G. W. *New Essays on Human Understanding.* Translated by Peter Remnant and Jonathan Bennett. Cambridge: Cambridge University Press, 1996.

———. *Nouveaux essais sur l'entendement humain.* Paris: Flammarion, 1921.

Lennox, Charlotte. *Correspondence and Miscellaneous Documents.* Edited by Norbert Schürer. Lewisburg, PA: Bucknell University Press, 2012.

Locke, John. *An Essay concerning Human Understanding.* Edited by Peter Nidditch. Oxford: Oxford University Press, 1975.

Macaulay, Catharine. *The History of England from the Ascension of James I to that of the Brunswick Line.* 8 vols. London, 1763–83.

———. *The History of England, from the Revolution to the Present Time, in a Series of Letters to the Reverend Doctor Wilson.* Bath, England, 1778.

———. *Observations on the Reflections of the Right Hon. Edmund Burke, on the Revolution in France.* London, 1790.

Mandeville, Bernard. *The Fable of the Bees.* 2 vols. Edited by F. B. Kaye. Indianapolis: Liberty Fund, 1988.

———. *Free Thoughts on Religion, the Church, and National Happiness.* London, 1720.

———. *A Treatise of the Hypochondriack and Hysterick Passions, Vulgarly Call'd the Hypo in Men and Vapours in Women.* London, 1711.

Marvell, Andrew. *The Poems of Andrew Marvell.* Edited by Nigel Smith. Abingdon, England: Routledge, 2013.

Marx, Karl, and Friedrich Engels. *The Marx-Engels Reader.* Edited by Robert C. Tucker. New York: Norton, 1978.

Mesmer, Franz Anton. *Mesmer's Aphorisms and Instructions, by M. Caullet de Veaumore, Physician to the Household of Monsieur, his Most Christian Majesty's Brother.* London, 1785.

Montesquieu, Charles de Secondat, Baron de. *Considerations sur les causes de la grandeur des Romains et de leur decadence.* Edinburgh, 1736.

———. *Oeuvres completes de Montesquieu.* Edited by Roger Caillois. 2 vols. Paris, 1949–51.

———. *Reflections on the Causes of the Grandeur and Declension of the Romans.* London, 1734.

———. *The Spirit of Laws.* 2 vols. Translated by Thomas Nugent. London, 1750.

Newton, Isaac. *The Mathematical Principles of Natural Philosophy.* 2 vols. Translated by Andrew Motte. London, 1729.

———. *The Method of Fluxions and Infinite Series; with its Application to the Geometry of Curve-lines.* Edited by John Colson. London, 1736.

———. *Opticks: or, A Treatise of the Reflections, Refractions, Inflections and Colours of Light.* 2nd ed. London, 1718.

North, Dudley. *Discourses Upon Trade: Principally Directed to the Cases of the Interest, Coynage, Clipping, Increase of Money.* London, 1691.

Petty, William. *The Political Anatomy of Ireland with the Establishment for that Kingdom when the late Duke of Ormond was Lord Lieutenant . . . : to which is added Verbum Sapienti, or, An Account of the Wealth and Expences of England, and the Method of Raising Taxes in the Most Equal Manner.* London, 1691.

———. *A Treatise of Taxes and Contributions.* London, 1662.

Philalethes. *An Excise Elegy: or, The Dragon Demolish'd, A new ballad.* London, 1733.

Pope, Alexander. *The Twickenham Edition of the Poetry of Alexander Pope*. 11 vols. Edited by John Butt et al. London: Methuen, 1938–68.

Postlethwayt, Malachy. *Britain's Commercial Interest Explained and Improved*. 2 vols. London, 1757.

Rapin de Thoyras, Paul. *History of England*. 14 vols. Translated by Nicolas Tindal. London, 1725–31.

Reeve, Clara. *The Progress of Romance, through Times, Countries, and Manners*. 2 vols. Colchester, England, 1785.

Reid, Thomas. *The Correspondence of Thomas Reid*. Edited by Paul Wood. Edinburgh: Edinburgh University Press, 2002.

———. *Essays on the Intellectual Powers of Man*. Edinburgh, 1785.

Richardson, Samuel. *The Cambridge Edition of the Correspondence of Samuel Richardson*. 12 vols. (projected). Edited by Peter Sabor et al. Cambridge: Cambridge University Press, 2013–.

———. *Clarissa. Or, the History of a Young Lady*. 3rd ed. 8 vols. London, 1751.

———. *A Collection of the Moral and Instructive Sentiments, Maxims, Cautions, and Reflexions, Contained in the Histories of Pamela, Clarissa, and Sir Charles Grandison*. London, 1755.

———. *The History of Sir Charles Grandison*. 7 vols. London, 1753–54.

Robertson, William. *The History of America*. 2 vols. London, 1777.

———. *The History of Scotland*. 2 vols. London, 1759.

———. *The History of the Reign of the Emperor Charles V*. 3 vols. London, 1769.

Scott, Walter. *The Private Letter-Books of Sir Walter Scott*. Edited by Wilfred Partington. London: Hodder and Stoughton, 1930.

Scudéry, Georges de. *Almahide, or The Captive Lovers*. Translated by J. Phillips. London, 1677.

———. *Almahide, ou L'esclave Reine*. 3 vols. Paris, 1661–63.

Smith, Adam. *Essays on Philosophical Subjects*. Edited by W. P. D. Wrightman and J. C. Bryce. Indianapolis: Liberty Fund, 1982.

———. *An Inquiry into the Causes of the Wealth of Nations*. 2 vols. Edited by R. H. Campbell and A. S. Skinner. Indianapolis: Liberty Fund, 1981.

———. *Lectures on Jurisprudence*. Edited by R. L. Meek, D. D. Raphael, and P. G. Stein. Indianapolis: Liberty Fund, 1982.

———. *The Theory of Moral Sentiments*. Edited by D. D. Raphael and A. L. Macfie. Indianapolis: Liberty Fund, 1984.

Sterne, Laurence. *The Florida Edition of the Works of Laurence Sterne*. Edited by Melvyn New and Joan New. 9 vols. Gainesville: University Presses of Florida, 1978–2009.

Steuart, James. *An Inquiry into the Principles of Political Oeconomy*. 2 vols. London, 1767.

Stewart, Dugald. "Account of the Life and Writings of Adam Smith." Edited by I. S. Ross. In Adam Smith, *Essays on Philosophical Subjects*. Edited by J. C. Bryce and William P. D. Wightman. Indianapolis: Liberty Fund, 1982.

Toussaint, François-Vincent. *Manners: Translated from the French*. London, 1749.

———. *Les Moeurs*. Amsterdam, 1748.

Travis, George. *Letters to Edward Gibbon, Esq., Author of the History of the Decline and Fall of the Roman Empire*. Chester, England, 1784.

Trenchard, John. *The Natural History of Superstition*. London, 1709.
Voltaire [François-Marie Arouet]. *The Age of Lewis XIV*. 2 vols. London, 1752.
———. *The Age of Lewis XIV*. 2 vols. Glasgow, 1753.
———. *An Essay on Universal History, the Manners, and Spirit of Nations, from the Reign of Charlemaign to the Age of Lewis XIV*. 4 vols. Translated by Thomas Nugent. London 1759.
———. *Essay sur l'histoire générale et sur les moeurs et l'esprit des nations, depuis Charlemagne jusqu'à nos jours*. 7 vols. Amsterdam, 1758.
———. *Le siècle de Louis XIV*. 2nd ed. 2 vols. London, 1752.
———. *The Works of M. de Voltaire*. 25 vols. Translated by Tobias Smollett, T. Francklin, et al. London, 1761.
Wesley, John. *Sermons on Several Occasions: In Three Volumes*. London, 1750.
Wilkes, Wetenhall. *A Letter of Genteel and Moral Advice to a Young Lady*. Dublin, 1740.
Wordsworth, William, and Samuel Taylor Coleridge. *Lyrical Ballads, with a Few Other Poems*. London, 1798.

Secondary Sources

Ahern, Stephen, ed. *Affect Theory and Literary Critical Practice: A Feel for the Text*. Cham, Switzerland: Palgrave Macmillan, 2019.
———. "Nothing More than Feelings? Affect Theory Reads the Age of Sensibility." *The Eighteenth Century* 58, no. 3 (2017): 281–95.
Allen, Richard C. *David Hartley on Human Nature*. Albany: State University of New York Press, 1999.
Anderson, Emily Hodgson. *Eighteenth-Century Authorship and the Play of Fiction: Novels and the Theater, Haywood to Austen*. London: Routledge, 2009.
Andriopoulos, Stefan. "The Invisible Hand: Supernatural Agency in Political Economy and the Gothic Novel." *ELH* 66, no. 3 (1999): 739–58.
Ankersmit, F. R. *Sublime Historical Experience*. Stanford, CA: Stanford University Press, 2005.
Anstey, Peter R. *John Locke and Natural Philosophy*. Oxford: Oxford University Press, 2011.
———. *The Philosophy of Robert Boyle*. London: Routledge, 2000.
Ayers, Michael. *Locke*. 2 vols. London: Routledge, 1991.
———. "Primary and Secondary Qualities in Locke's *Essay*." In *Primary and Secondary Qualities: The Historical and Ongoing Debate*, edited by Lawrence Nolan, 136–57. Oxford: Oxford University Press, 2011.
Baier, Annette C. "David Hume, Spinozist." *Hume Studies* 19, no. 2 (1993): 237–52.
———. *A Progress of Sentiments: Reflections on Hume's* Treatise. Cambridge, MA: Harvard University Press, 1991.
Ballaster, Ros. *Seductive Forms: Women's Amatory Fiction from 1684 to 1740*. Oxford: Oxford University Press, 1992.
Barfoot, Michael. "Hume and the Culture of Science in the Early Eighteenth Century." In *Studies in the Philosophy of the Scottish Enlightenment*, edited by M. A. Stewart, 151–90. Oxford: Oxford University Press, 1989.

Barker-Benfield, G. J. *The Culture of Sensibility: Sex and Society in Eighteenth-Century Britain.* Chicago: University of Chicago Press, 1996.
Barnett, Clive. "Political Affects in Public Space: Normative Blind-Spots in Non-Representational Ontologies." *Transactions of the Institute of British Geographers*, n.s., 33, no. 2 (2008): 186–200.
Barr, Rebecca Anne. "Richardson's 'Sir Charles Grandison' and the Symptoms of Subjectivity." *The Eighteenth Century* 51, no. 4 (2010): 391–411.
Beckett, J. V., and Michael Turner. "Taxation and Economic Growth in Eighteenth-Century England." *Economic History Review* 43, no. 3 (1990): 377–403.
Bell, John L. "Continuity and Infinitesimals." *The Stanford Encyclopedia of Philosophy*, fall 2013 ed., edited by Edward N. Zalta. http://plato.stanford.edu/archives/fall2013/entries/continuity.
Bender, John. *Ends of Enlightenment.* Stanford, CA: Stanford University Press, 2012.
Bennett, Jonathan. *Locke, Berkeley, Hume: Central Themes.* Oxford: Clarendon, 1971.
———. "Locke's Philosophy of Mind." In *The Cambridge Companion to John Locke*, edited by Vere Chappell, 89–114. Cambridge: Cambridge University Press, 1994.
Berlant, Lauren Gail. "Unfeeling Kerry." *Theory & Event* 8, no. 2 (2005). https://muse.jhu.edu/article/187843.
Berlin, Isaiah. *Against the Current: Essays in the History of Ideas.* 2nd ed. Princeton, NJ: Princeton University Press, 2013.
Berman, David. *Berkeley and Irish Philosophy.* London: Continuum, 2005.
Berry, Christopher J. *The Idea of Commercial Society in the Scottish Enlightenment.* Edinburgh: Edinburgh University Press, 2015.
Binhammer, Katherine. "Knowing Love: The Epistemology of *Clarissa*." *ELH* 74, no. 4 (2007): 859–79.
Braudy, Leo. *Narrative Form in History and Fiction: Hume, Fielding, and Gibbon.* Princeton, NJ: Princeton University Press, 1970.
Brewer, Anthony. "Luxury and Economic Development: David Hume and Adam Smith." *Scottish Journal of Political Economy* 45 (1998): 78–98.
———. "On the Other (Invisible) Hand . . ." *History of Political Economy* 41, no. 3 (2009): 519–43.
Brewer, John. *The Sinews of Power: War, Money and the English State, 1688–1793.* Cambridge, MA: Harvard University Press, 1988.
Bromwich, David. *The Intellectual Life of Edmund Burke: From the Sublime and Beautiful to American Independence.* Cambridge, MA: Harvard University Press, 2014.
Budd, Adam. "Why Clarissa Must Die: Richardson's Tragedy and Editorial Heroism." *Eighteenth-Century Life* 31, no. 3 (2007): 1–28.
Burrow, J. W. *Whigs and Liberals.* Oxford: Oxford University Press, 1988.
Campbell, Jill. "Fielding's Style." *ELH* 72, no. 2 (2005): 407–28.
Carrasco, Maria Alejandra. "Adam Smith's Reconstruction of Practical Reason." *Review of Metaphysics* 58, no. 1 (2004): 81–116.
Carrithers, David. "Montesquieu's Philosophy of History." *Journal of the History of Ideas* 47, no. 1 (1986): 61–80.
Chibka, Robert L. "Henry Fielding, Mentalist: The Ins and Outs of Narration in *Tom Jones*." In *Henry Fielding in Our Time: Papers Presented at the Tercentenary*

Conference, edited by J. A. Downie, 81–112. Newcastle upon Tyne, England: Cambridge Scholars, 2008.

Chico, Tita. "Details and Frankness: Affective Relations in 'Sir Charles Grandison.'" *Studies in Eighteenth-Century Culture* 38 (2009): 45–68.

Christensen, Jerome. "Philosophy/Literature: The Associationist Precedent for Coleridge's Late Poems." In *Philosophical Approaches to Literature: New Essays on Nineteenth- and Twentieth-Century Texts*, edited by William E. Cain, 27–50. Cranbury, NJ: Associated University Presses, 1984.

Coffman, D'Maris. *Excise Taxation and the Origins of Public Debt*. London: Palgrave Macmillan, 2013.

Cohn, Dorrit. *Transparent Minds: Narrative Modes for Presenting Consciousness in Fiction*. Princeton, NJ: Princeton University Press, 1978.

Conley, John. "Madeleine de Scudéry." In *The Stanford Encyclopedia of Philosophy*, spring 2016 ed, edited by Edward N. Zalta. https://plato.stanford.edu/archives/spr2016/entries/madeleine-scudery/.

Connor, Steven. *The Matter of Air: Science and Art of the Ethereal*. London: Reaktion, 2010.

Conway, Alison. "The Protestant Cause and a Protestant Whore: Aphra Behn's *Love-Letters*." *Eighteenth-Century Life* 25, no. 3 (2001): 1–19.

Courtney, Cecil Patrick. *Montesquieu and Burke*. Oxford: Blackwell, 1963.

———. "Morals and Manners in Montesquieu's Analysis of the British System of Liberty." In *Montesquieu and His Legacy*, edited by Rebecca E. Kingston, 31–48. Albany: State University of New York Press, 2008.

Csengei, Ildiko. *Sympathy, Sensibility and the Literature of Feeling in the Eighteenth Century*. Basingstoke, England: Palgrave Macmillan, 2012.

Damasio, Antonio. *The Feeling of What Happens: Body and Emotion in the Making of Consciousness*. New York: Houghton Mifflin Harcourt, 1999.

———. *Self Comes to Mind: Constructing the Conscious Brain*. New York: Random House, 2010.

Darnton, Robert. "Voltaire, Historian." *Raritan* 35, no. 2 (2015): 20–28.

Deane, Seamus F. "Lord Acton and Edmund Burke." *Journal of the History of Ideas* 33, no. 2 (1972): 325–35.

De Bolla, Peter. *The Architecture of Concepts: The Historical Formation of Human Rights*. New York: Fordham University Press, 2013.

Deleuze, Gilles. "Cours Vincennes," January 20, 1981. Les Cours de Gilles Deleuze (website), https://www.webdeleuze.com/textes/35.

———. "Cours Vincennes," January 24, 1978. Translated by Timothy S. Murphy. Les Cours de Gilles Deleuze (website). https://www.webdeleuze.com/textes/14.

———. *Empiricism and Subjectivity: An Essay on Hume's Theory of Human Nature*. Translated by Constantin V. Boundas. New York: Columbia University Press, 1991.

———. *Expressionism in Philosophy: Spinoza*. Translated by Martin Joughin. New York: Zone, 1990.

———. "The Fold." Translated by Jonathan Strauss. *Yale French Studies* 80 (1991): 227–47.

———. *Francis Bacon: The Logic of Sensation*. Translated by Daniel W. Smith. New York: Continuum, 2003.

———. *Spinoza: Practical Philosophy.* Translated by Robert Hurley. San Francisco: City Lights Books, 1988.
Deleuze, Gilles, and Félix Guattari. *A Thousand Plateaus: Capitalism and Schizophrenia.* Translated by Brian Massumi. Minneapolis: University of Minnesota Press, 1987.
De Morgan, Augustus. "The Early History of Infinitesimals in England." *Philosophical Magazine and Journal of Science,* 4th ser., 4, no. 6 (1852): 321–30.
Deutsch, Helen. *Loving Dr. Johnson.* Chicago: University of Chicago Press, 2005.
Dicker, Georges. *Berkeley's Idealism: A Critical Examination.* Oxford: Oxford University Press, 2011.
Dobranski, Stephen B. "What Fielding Doesn't Say in *Tom Jones.*" *Modern Philology* 107, no. 4 (2010): 632–53.
D'Onofrio, Federico. "On the Concept of 'Felicitas Publica' in Eighteenth-Century Political Economy." *Journal of the History of Economic Thought* 37, no. 3 (2015): 449–71.
Doody, Margaret Anne. *Frances Burney: The Life in the Works.* New Brunswick, NJ: Rutgers University Press, 1988.
———. "Identity and Character in *Sir Charles Grandison.*" In *Samuel Richardson: Tercentenary Essays,* edited by Margaret Anne Doody and Peter Sabor, 110–32. Cambridge: Cambridge University Press, 1989.
———. "Vibrations." *London Review of Books* 15, no. 15 (1993): 11–13.
Downie, J. A. "What If Delarivier Manley Did *Not* Write *The Secret History of Queen Zarah?*" *Library: The Transactions of the Bibliographical Society* 5, no. 3 (2004): 247–64.
Downing, Lisa. "Locke: The Primary and Secondary Quality Distinction." In *The Routledge Companion to Metaphysics,* edited by Robin Le Poidevin, Peter Simons, Andrew McGonigal, and Ross Cameron, 98–109. Abingdon, England: Routledge, 2009.
Dussinger, John. *The Discourse of the Mind in Eighteenth-Century Fiction.* The Hague: De Gruyter, 1974.
Dykstra, Scott. "Wordsworth's 'Solitaries' and the Problem of Literary Reference." *ELH* 63, no. 4 (1996): 893–928.
Egginton, William. "Affective Disorder." *Diacritics* 40, no. 4 (2012): 25–43.
Ellenberger, Henri F. *The Discovery of the Unconscious: The History and Evolution of Dynamic Psychiatry.* New York: Basic Books, 1970.
Empson, William. *The Structure of Complex Words.* Harmondsworth, England: Penguin, 1995.
Epstein, Julia. *The Iron Pen: Frances Burney and the Politics of Women's Writing.* Madison: University of Wisconsin Press, 1989.
Fara, Patricia. *Sympathetic Attractions: Magnetic Practices, Beliefs, and Symbolism in Eighteenth-Century England.* Princeton, NJ: Princeton University Press, 1996.
Ferguson, Frances. "Jane Austen, *Emma,* and the Impact of Form." *MLQ: Modern Language Quarterly* 61, no. 1 (2000): 157–80.
———. *Solitude and the Sublime: Romanticism and the Aesthetics of Individuation.* New York: Routledge, 1992.
Fleischacker, Samuel. "Philosophy in Moral Practice: Kant and Adam Smith." *Kant-Studien* 82, no. 3 (1991): 249–69.

Fogelin, Robert J. "The Tendency of Hume's Skepticism." In *The Skeptical Tradition*, edited by Myles Burnyeat, 397–412. Berkeley: University of California Press, 1983.

Francesconi, Daniele. "William Robertson on Historical Causation and Unintended Consequences." *Cromohs* 4 (1999). http://www.fupress.net/index.php/cromohs/article/view/15745/14631.

Fried, Michael. *Absorption and Theatricality: Painting and the Beholder in the Age of Diderot*. Chicago: University of Chicago Press, 1988.

Furniss, Tom. *Edmund Burke's Aesthetic Ideology*. Cambridge: Cambridge University Press, 1993.

Garis, Robert. "Learning Experience and Change." In *Critical Essays on Jane Austen*, edited by B. C. Southam, 60–82. London: Routledge and Kegan Paul, 1968.

Gearhart, Suzanne. *The Open Boundary of History and Fiction: A Critical Approach to the French Enlightenment*. Princeton, NJ: Princeton University Press, 1984.

Girten, Kristin M. "Unsexed Souls: Natural Philosophy as Transformation in Eliza Haywood's *Female Spectator*." *Eighteenth-Century Studies* 43, no. 1 (2009): 55–74.

Gonthier, Ursula Haskins. *Montesquieu and England: Enlightened Exchanges, 1689–1755*. 2nd ed. Abingdon, England: Routledge, 2016.

Goring, Paul. *The Rhetoric of Sensibility*. Cambridge: Cambridge University Press, 2004.

Grampp, William D. "What Did Smith Mean by the Invisible Hand?" *Journal of Political Economy* 108, no. 3 (2000): 441–65.

Gregg, Melissa, and Gregory J. Seigworth, eds. *The Affect Theory Reader*. Durham, NC: Duke University Press, 2010.

Griswold, Charles L., Jr. *Adam Smith and the Virtues of Enlightenment*. Cambridge: Cambridge University Press, 1999.

Groenewegen, Peter. "Postlethwayt, Malachy." *Oxford Dictionary of National Biography*, online ed. http://www.oxforddnb.com/view/10.1093/ref:odnb/9780198614128.001.0001/odnb-9780198614128-e-22599.

Grossberg, Lawrence. "Affect's Future: Rediscovering the Virtual in the Actual," interview by Gregory J. Seigworth and Melissa Gregg. In *The Affect Theory Reader*, edited by Melissa Gregg and Gregory J. Seigworth, 309–88. Durham, NC: Duke University Press, 2010.

———. "Another Boring Day in Paradise: Rock and Roll and the Empowerment of Everyday Life." *Popular Music* 4 (1984): 225–58.

Guerrini, Anita. *Obesity and Depression in the Enlightenment: The Life and Times of George Cheyne*. Norman: University of Oklahoma Press, 2000.

Hagstrum, Jean H. "Towards a Profile of the Word *Conscious* in Eighteenth-Century Literature." In *Psychology and Literature in the Eighteenth Century*, edited by Christopher Fox, 23–50. New York: AMS, 1987.

Hamou, Philippe. "Vision, Color, and Method in Newton's *Opticks*." In *Newton and Empiricism*, edited by Zvi Biener and Eric Schliesser, 66–93. Oxford: Oxford University Press, 2014.

Hamowy, Ronald. *The Scottish Enlightenment and the Theory of Spontaneous Order.* Carbondale: Southern Illinois University Press, 1987.

Harkin, Maureen. "Adam Smith's Missing History: Primitives, Progress, and the Problem of Genre." *ELH* 72, no. 2 (2005): 429–51.

Harris, James A. *Hume: An Intellectual Biography.* Cambridge: Cambridge University Press, 2015.

Harth, Erica. *Cartesian Women: Versions and Subversions of Rational Discourse in the Old Regime.* Ithaca, NY: Cornell University Press, 1992.

Hayles, N. Katherine. *Unthought: The Power of the Cognitive Nonconscious.* Chicago: University of Chicago Press, 2017.

Heller-Roazen, Daniel. *The Inner Touch: Archaeology of a Sensation.* New York: Zone Books, 2007.

Hewitt, Elizabeth. "The Vexed Story of Economic Criticism." *American Literary History* 21, no. 3 (2009): 618–32.

Hicks, Philip. *Neoclassical History and English Culture: From Clarendon to Hume.* London: Palgrave Macmillan, 1998.

Hill, James, and J. R. Milton. "The Epitome (*Abrégé*) of Locke's Essay." In *The Philosophy of John Locke: New Perspectives*, edited by Peter R. Anstey, 3–25. London: Routledge, 2003.

Hont, Istvan. *Jealousy of Trade: International Competition and the Nation-State in Historical Perspective.* Cambridge, MA: Harvard University Press, 2005.

———. "The 'Rich Country–Poor Country' Debate Revisited: The Irish Origins and French Reception of the Hume Paradox." In *David Hume's Political Economy*, edited by Margaret Schabas and Carl Wennerlind, 243–323. Abingdon, England: Routledge, 2008.

Hudson, Wayne. *The English Deists: Studies in Early Enlightenment.* London: Pickering and Chatto, 2009.

Hultquist, Aleksondra, ed. "Emotion, Affect, and the Eighteenth Century." Special issue, *The Eighteenth Century* 58, no. 3 (2017).

———. "New Directions in History of Emotion and Affect Theory in Eighteenth-Century Studies." *Literature Compass* 13, no. 12 (2016): 762–70.

Hundert, E. J. *The Enlightenment's Fable: Bernard Mandeville and the Discovery of Society.* Cambridge: Cambridge University Press, 1994.

Hutchison, Terence. *Before Adam Smith: The Emergence of Political Economy, 1662–1776.* Oxford: Blackwell, 1988.

Iliffe, Rob. *Priest of Nature: The Religious Worlds of Isaac Newton.* Oxford: Oxford University Press, 2017.

Israel, Jonathan I. *Enlightenment Contested: Philosophy, Modernity, and the Emancipation of Man.* Oxford: Oxford University Press, 2009.

———. *Radical Enlightenment: Philosophy and the Making of Modernity 1650–1750.* Oxford: Oxford University Press, 2001.

Jacovides, Michael. "Locke's Distinctions between Primary and Secondary Qualities." In *The Cambridge Companion to Locke's "Essay concerning Human Understanding,"* edited by Lex Newman, 101–29. Cambridge: Cambridge University Press, 2007.

James, E. D. *Pierre Nicole: Jansenist and Humanist.* The Hague: Nijhoff, 1972.

Jameson, Fredric. *The Antinomies of Realism.* London: Verso, 2013.

———. *Postmodernism, or, The Cultural Logic of Late Capitalism*. Durham, NC: Duke University Press, 1991.
Jervis, John. *Sympathetic Sentiments: Affect, Emotion and Spectacle in the Modern World*. London: Bloomsbury, 2015.
Jevons, W. Stanley. "Richard Cantillon and the Nationality of Political Economy." In *Essai sur la nature du commerce en général*, by Richard Cantillon, 2nd ed., translated by Henry Higgs, 333–60. London: Frank Cass, 1959.
Jockers, Matthew L. *Macroanalysis: Digital Methods and Literary History*. Urbana: University of Illinois Press, 2013.
Johnson, Claudia L. *Jane Austen: Women, Politics and the Novel*. Chicago: University of Chicago Press, 1988.
Johnston, Adrian, and Catherine Malabou. *Self and Emotional Life: Philosophy, Psychoanalysis, and Neuroscience*. New York: Columbia University Press, 2013.
Jones, Vivien. "The Seductions of Conduct: Pleasure and Conduct Literature." In *Pleasure in the Eighteenth Century*, edited by Roy Porter and Marie Mulvey Roberts, 108–32. New York: New York University Press, 1996.
Jordan, David P. *Gibbon and His Roman Empire*. Urbana: University of Illinois Press, 1971.
Keymer, Tom. *Richardson's Clarissa and the Eighteenth-Century Reader*. Cambridge: Cambridge University Press, 1992.
King, Kathryn R. *A Political Biography of Eliza Haywood*. London: Routledge, 2016.
Kinkead-Weekes, Mark. *Samuel Richardson: Dramatic Novelist*. Ithaca, NY: Cornell University Press, 1973.
Klever, Wim. "Hume contra Spinoza?" *Hume Studies* 16, no. 2 (1990): 89–106.
———. "More about Hume's Debt to Spinoza." *Hume Studies* 19, no. 1 (1993): 55–74.
Koehler, Margaret. *Poetry of Attention in the Eighteenth Century*. London: Palgrave Macmillan, 2012.
Koselleck, Reinhart. *The Practice of Conceptual History: Timing History, Spacing Concepts*. Translated by Todd Samuel Presner. Stanford, CA: Stanford University Press, 2002.
Kramnick, Jonathan. *Actions and Objects from Hobbes to Richardson*. Stanford, CA: Stanford University Press, 2010.
Langford, Paul. *The Excise Crisis: Society and Politics in the Age of Walpole*. Oxford: Clarendon, 1975.
Lee, Wendy Anne. *Failures of Feeling: Insensibility and the Novel*. Stanford, CA: Stanford University Press, 2018.
———. "The Scandal of Insensibility: The Bartleby Problem." *PMLA* 130, no. 5 (2015): 1406–19.
Lewis, Jayne Elizabeth. *Air's Appearance: Literary Atmosphere in British Fiction, 1660–1794*. Chicago: University of Chicago Press, 2012.
Leys, Ruth. "The Turn to Affect: A Critique." *Critical Inquiry* 37, no. 3 (2011): 434–72.
Livingston, Donald W. *Hume's Philosophy of Common Life*. Chicago: University of Chicago Press, 1984.
Lock, F. P. *Edmund Burke*. Vol. 1, *1730–1784*. Oxford: Clarendon, 1999.
Lynch, Deidre Shauna. *The Economy of Character: Novels, Market Culture, and the Business of Inner Meaning*. Chicago: University of Chicago Press, 1998.

———. *Loving Literature: A Cultural History.* Chicago: University of Chicago Press, 2015.
Mack, Ruth. *Literary Historicity: Literature and Historical Experience in Eighteenth-Century Britain.* Stanford, CA: Stanford University Press, 2009.
Macpherson, Sandra. *Harm's Way: Tragic Responsibility and the Novel Form.* Baltimore: Johns Hopkins University Press, 2010.
Manuel, Frank E. "Edward Gibbon: Historien-Philosophe." In *Edward Gibbon and the Decline and Fall of the Roman Empire*, edited by G. W. Bowersock, John Clive, and Stephen R. Graubard, 167–81. Cambridge, MA: Harvard University Press, 1977.
Markley, Robert. "Sentimentality as Performance: Shaftesbury, Sterne, and the Theatrics of Virtue." In *The New Eighteenth Century: Theory, Politics, English Literature*, edited by Felicity Nussbaum and Laura Brown, 210–30. London: Methuen, 1987.
Marshall, David. "Adam Smith and the Theatricality of Moral Sentiments." *Critical Inquiry* 10, no. 4 (1984): 592–613.
Massumi, Brian. "The Autonomy of Affect." *Cultural Critique* 31 (1995): 83–109.
———. "The Future Birth of the Affective Fact: The Political Ontology of Threat." In *The Affect Theory Reader*, edited by Melissa Gregg and Gregory J. Seigworth, 52–70. Durham, NC: Duke University Press, 2010.
———. "Notes on the Translation and Acknowledgements." In *A Thousand Plateaus: Capitalism and Schizophrenia*, by Gilles Deleuze and Félix Guattari, xvi–xix. Translated by Brian Massumi. Minneapolis: University of Minnesota Press, 1987.
———. *Parables for the Virtual: Movement, Affect, Sensation.* Durham, NC: Duke University Press, 2002.
———. "Sensing the Virtual, Building the Insensible." In *Hypersurface Architecture*, edited by Stephen Perrella, 16–25. New York: Wiley, 1998.
Mathias, Peter, and Patrick O'Brien. "The Incidence of Taxes and the Burden of Proof." *Journal of European Economic History* 7, no. 1 (1978): 211–13.
———. "Taxation in Britain and France, 1715–1810: A Comparison of the Social and Economic Incidence of Taxes Collected for the Central Governments." *Journal of European Economic History* 5, no. 3 (1976): 601–50.
McArthur, Neil. "David Hume and the Common Law of England." *Journal of Scottish Philosophy* 3, no. 1 (2005): 67–82.
McCann, Edwin. "Locke's Distinction between Primary Primary Qualities and Secondary Primary Qualities." In *Primary and Secondary Qualities: The Historical and Ongoing Debate*, edited by Lawrence Nolan, 158–89. Oxford: Oxford University Press, 2011.
McCloskey, Donald N. "A Mismeasurement of the Incidence of Taxation in Britain and France, 1715–1810." *Journal of European Economic History* 7, no. 1 (1978): 209–10.
McCormick, Ted. *William Petty and the Ambitions of Political Arithmetic.* Oxford: Oxford University Press, 2010.
McKeon, Michael. *The Secret History of Domesticity: Public, Private, and the Division of Knowledge.* Baltimore: Johns Hopkins University Press, 2006.
McLoughlin, T. O. "Edmund Burke's *Abridgment of English History*." *Eighteenth-Century Ireland / Iris an dá chultúr* 5 (1990): 45–59.

McMahon, Darrin M. *Happiness: A History.* New York: Grove, 2006.
Merritt, Juliette. "Reforming the Coquet? Eliza Haywood's Vision of a Female Epistemology." In *Fair Philosopher: Eliza Haywood and the Female Spectator,* edited by Lynn Marie Wright and Donald J. Newman, 176–92. Lewisburg, PA: Bucknell University Press, 2006.
Michel, Jean-Baptiste et al. "Quantitative Analysis of Culture Using Millions of Digitized Books." *Science* 331.6014 (2011): 176–82.
Michie, Allen. *Richardson and Fielding: The Dynamics of a Critical Rivalry.* Lewisburg, PA: Bucknell University Press, 1999.
Miller, D. A. *Jane Austen, or The Secret of Style.* Princeton, NJ: Princeton University Press, 2005.
Molesworth, Jesse. *Chance and the Eighteenth-Century Novel.* Cambridge: Cambridge University Press, 2010.
Momigliano, Arnaldo. "Gibbon's Contribution to Historical Method." *Historia: Zeitschrift für Alte Geschichte* 2, no. 4 (1954): 450–63.
Moore, James. "Natural Rights and the Scottish Enlightenment." In *The Cambridge History of Eighteenth-Century Political Thought,* edited by Mark Goldie and Robert Wokler, 291–316. Cambridge: Cambridge University Press, 2006.
Mossner, Ernst. *The Life of David Hume.* Oxford: Clarendon, 1980.
Mudge, Bradford K. *The Whore's Story: Women, Pornography, and the British Novel, 1684–1830.* Oxford: Oxford University Press, 2000.
Mullan, John. *Sentiment and Sociability: The Language of Feeling in the Eighteenth Century.* Oxford: Oxford University Press, 1984.
Murphy, Antoin E. *Richard Cantillon: Entrepreneur and Economist.* Oxford: Clarendon, 1986.
Nagle, Christopher C. *Sexuality and the Culture of Sensibility in the British Romantic Era.* New York: Palgrave Macmillan, 2007.
Nicolazzo, Sarah. "Reading *Clarissa*'s 'Conditional Liking': A Queer Philology." *Modern Philology* 112, no. 1 (2014): 205–25.
Noggle, James. *The Temporality of Taste in Eighteenth-Century British Writing.* Oxford: Oxford University Press, 2012.
———. "Unfelt Affect." In *Beyond Sense and Sensibility: Moral Formation and the Literary Imagination from Johnson to Wordsworth,* edited by Peggy Thompson, 125–44. Lewisburg, PA: Bucknell University Press, 2015.
O'Brien, Karen. *Narratives of Enlightenment: Cosmopolitan History from Voltaire to Gibbon.* Cambridge: Cambridge University Press, 1997.
———. *Women and Enlightenment in Eighteenth-Century Britain.* Cambridge: Cambridge University Press, 2009.
O'Brien, Patrick K. "The Political Economy of British Taxation, 1660–1815." *Economic History Review* 41, no. 1 (1988): 1–32.
O'Neill, Daniel I. *The Burke-Wollstonecraft Debate: Savagery, Civilization, and Democracy.* State College: Pennsylvania State University Press, 2012.
Parfit, Derek. *Reasons and Persons.* Oxford: Oxford University Press, 1984.
Parker, Fred. *Scepticism and Literature: An Essay on Pope, Hume, Sterne, and Johnson.* Oxford: Oxford University Press, 2003.

Pauchant, Thierry C. "Adam Smith's Four-Stages Theory of Socio-Cultural Evolution: New Insights from His 1749 Lecture." *Adam Smith Review* 9 (2017): 49–74.
Pfau, Thomas. *Romantic Moods: Paranoia, Trauma, and Melancholy, 1790–1840*. Baltimore: Johns Hopkins University Press, 2005.
Phillips, Mark Salber. *On Historical Distance*. New Haven, CT: Yale University Press, 2013.
———. *Society and Sentiment: Genres of Historical Writing in Britain, 1740–1820*. Princeton, NJ: Princeton University Press, 2000.
Phillips, Natalie M. *Distraction: Problems of Attention in Eighteenth-Century Literature*. Baltimore: Johns Hopkins University Press, 2016.
Phillipson, Nicholas. *Adam Smith: An Enlightened Life*. New Haven, CT: Yale University Press, 2010.
Pocock, J. G. A. *Barbarism and Religion*. 6 vols. Cambridge: Cambridge University Press, 1999–2015.
Popkin, Richard H. "Hume and Spinoza." *Hume Studies* 5, no. 2 (1979): 65–93.
Potkay, Adam. "Happiness, Unhappiness, and Joy." *Social Research* 77, no. 2 (2010): 523–44.
———. *The Passion for Happiness: Samuel Johnson and David Hume*. Ithaca, NY: Cornell University Press, 2000.
———. *The Story of Joy: From the Bible to Late Romanticism*. Cambridge: Cambridge University Press, 2007.
Prince, Michael B. "A Preliminary Discourse on Philosophy and Literature." In *The Cambridge History of English Literature, 1660–1780*, edited by John Richetti, 391–422. Cambridge: Cambridge University Press, 2005.
Richetti, John. *The English Novel in History, 1700–1780*. London: Routledge, 1998.
Riskin, Jessica. *Science in the Age of Sensibility: The Sentimental Empiricists of the French Enlightenment*. Chicago: University of Chicago Press, 2002.
Roberts, William. "New Light on the Authorship of *Almahide*." *French Studies* 25, no. 3 (1971): 271–80.
Robertson, John. *The Case for the Enlightenment: Scotland and Naples, 1680–1760*. Cambridge: Cambridge University Press, 2007.
Roos, Suzanne. "Consciousness and the Linguistic in Condillac." *MLN* 114, no. 4 (1999): 667–90.
Rorty, Richard. *Philosophy and the Mirror of Nature*. Princeton, NJ: Princeton University Press, 1979.
Roseveare, Henry. *The Treasury: The Evolution of a British Institution*. New York: Columbia University Press, 1969.
Rothschild, Emma. *Economic Sentiments: Adam Smith, Condorcet, and the Enlightenment*. Cambridge, MA: Harvard University Press, 2001.
Russell, Paul. *The Riddle of Hume's Treatise: Skepticism, Naturalism, and Irreligion*. Oxford: Oxford University Press, 2010.
Samuels, Warren J., Marianne F. Johnson, and William F. Perry. *Erasing the Invisible Hand: Essays on an Elusive and Misused Concept in Economics*. Cambridge: Cambridge University Press, 2011.

Sand, Rosemarie Sponner. *The Unconscious without Freud.* Lanham, MD: Rowman and Littlefield, 2013.

Sato, Sora. *Edmund Burke as Historian: War, Order, and Civilisation.* Houndmills, England: Palgrave Macmillan, 2018.

———. "Edmund Burke's Ideas on Historical Change." *History of European Ideas* 40, no. 5 (2014): 675–92.

Schabas, Margaret. "David Hume on Experimental Natural Philosophy, Money, and Fluids." *History of Political Economy* 33, no. 3 (2001): 411–35.

———. *The Natural Origins of Economics.* Chicago: University of Chicago Press, 2005.

Schaffer, Simon. "States of Mind: Enlightenment and Natural Philosophy." In *The Languages of Psyche: Mind and Body in Enlightenment Thought*, edited by G. S. Rousseau, 233–90. Berkeley: University of California Press, 1991.

Schechtman, Marya. *The Constitution of Selves.* Ithaca, NY: Cornell University Press, 1996.

Schliesser, Eric. Review of D. D. Raphael, *The Impartial Spectator: Adam Smith's Moral Philosophy* and Leonidas Montes, *Adam Smith in Context: A Critical Reassessment of Some Central Components of His Thought. Ethics* 118, no. 3 (2008): 569–75.

Schweitzer, Jerome W. "Dryden's Use of Scudéry's *Almahide*," *Modern Language Notes* 54, no. 3 (1939): 190–92.

———. *Georges de Scudery's Almahide: Authorship, Analysis, Sources and Structure.* Baltimore: Johns Hopkins University Press, 1939.

Scott, William Robert. *Adam Smith, as Student and Professor.* Glasgow: Jackson, 1937.

Sedgwick, Eve Kosofsky. *Touching Feeling: Affect, Pedagogy, Performativity.* Durham, NC: Duke University Press, 2003.

Sedgwick, Eve Kosofsky, and Adam Frank. "Shame in the Cybernetic Fold: Reading Silvan Tomkins." In *Touching Feeling: Affect, Pedagogy, Performativity*, by Eve Kosofsky Sedgwick, 93–122. Durham, NC: Duke University Press, 2003.

Seigel, Jerrold. *The Idea of the Self: Thought and Experience in Western Europe since the Seventeenth Century.* Cambridge: Cambridge University Press, 2005.

Shaver, Robert. "Virtue, Utility, and Rules." In *The Cambridge Companion to Adam Smith*, edited by Knud Haakonssen, 189–213. Cambridge: Cambridge University Press, 2006.

Sheehan, Jonathan, and Dror Wahrman. *Invisible Hands: Self-Organization and the Eighteenth Century.* Chicago: University of Chicago Press, 2015.

Sigler, David. *Sexual Enjoyment in British Romanticism: Gender and Psychoanalysis, 1753–1835.* Montreal and Kingston, ON: McGill-Queen's University Press, 2015.

Singer, Brian. *Montesquieu and the Discovery of the Social.* Houndmills, England: Palgrave Macmillan, 2013.

Sloterdijk, Peter. *Critique of Cynical Reason.* Translated by Michael Eldred. Minneapolis: University of Minnesota Press, 1987.

Smith, C. U. M. "David Hartley's Newtonian Neuropsychology." *Journal of the History of the Behavioral Sciences* 23, no. 2 (1987): 123–36.

Smith, Craig. *Adam Smith's Political Philosophy: The Invisible Hand and Spontaneous Order.* London: Routledge, 2006.
——. "The Scottish Enlightenment, Unintended Consequences, and the Science of Man." *Journal of Scottish Philosophy* 7, no. 1 (2009): 9–28.
Soni, Vivasvan. *Mourning Happiness: Narrative and the Politics of Modernity.* Ithaca, NY: Cornell University Press, 2012.
Spacks, Patricia Meyer. "Ev'ry Woman is at Heart a Rake." *Eighteenth-Century Studies* 8, no. 1 (1974): 27–46.
Strawson, Galen. *Locke on Personal Identity: Consciousness and Concernment.* Princeton, NJ: Princeton University Press, 2011.
Tallis, Frank. *Hidden Minds: A History of the Unconscious.* New York: Arcade, 2012.
Taylor, Charles. *Sources of the Self: The Making of Modern Identity.* Cambridge, MA: Harvard University Press, 1989.
Thiel, Udo. *The Early Modern Subject: Self-Consciousness and Personal Identity from Descartes to Hume.* Oxford: Oxford University Press, 2011.
Tierney-Hynes, Rebecca. "Haywood, Reading, and the Passions." *The Eighteenth Century* 51, nos. 1–2 (2010): 153–72.
Tuite, Clara. *Romantic Austen: Sexual Politics and the Literary Canon.* Cambridge: Cambridge University Press, 2008.
Van Sant, Ann Jesse. *Eighteenth-Century Sensibility and the Novel: The Senses in Social Context.* Cambridge: Cambridge University Press, 1993.
Wahrman, Dror. *The Making of the Modern Self: Identity and Culture in Eighteenth-Century England.* New Haven, CT: Yale University Press, 2004.
Warner, William Beatty. *Reading "Clarissa": The Struggles of Interpretation.* New Haven, CT: Yale University Press, 1979.
Watt, Ian. *The Rise of the Novel.* Berkeley: University of California Press, 2001.
Weinstein, Jack Russell. *Adam Smith's Pluralism: Rationality, Education, and the Moral Sentiments.* New Haven, CT: Yale University Press, 2013.
Wennerlind, Carl. "An Artificial Virtue and the Oil of Commerce: A Synthetic View of Hume's Theory of Money." In *David Hume's Political Economy*, edited by Carl Wennerlind and Margaret Schabas, 105–26. Abingdon, England: Routledge, 2008.
Weston, John C., Jr. "Edmund Burke's View of History." *Review of Politics* 23, no. 2 (1961): 203–29.
Williams, Raymond. *Keywords: A Vocabulary of Culture and Society.* New York: Oxford University Press, 1976.
Wittgenstein, Ludwig. *Philosophical Investigations.* 2nd ed. Translated by G. E. M. Anscombe. New York: Blackwell, 1958.
Wolfe, Charles. "On the Role of Newtonian Analogies in Eighteenth-Century Life Sciences: Vitalism and Provisionally Inexplicable Explicative Devices." In *Newton and Empiricism*, edited by Zvi Biener and Eric Schliesser, 223–61. Oxford: Oxford University Press, 2014.
Womersley, David. *Gibbon and the "Watchmen of the Holy City": The Historian and His Reputation, 1776–1815.* Oxford: Oxford University Press, 2002.
——. *The Transformation of* The Decline and Fall of the Roman Empire. Cambridge: Cambridge University Press, 1987.

Wootton, David. "David Hume: 'The Historian.'" In *The Cambridge Companion to Hume*, 2nd ed., edited by David Fate Norton and Jacqueline Taylor, 447–79. Cambridge: Cambridge University Press, 2008.

Wright, Lynn Marie, and Donald J. Newman, eds. *Fair Philosopher: Eliza Haywood and the Female Spectator.* Lewisburg, PA: Bucknell University Press, 2006.

Zanardi, Paola. "Italian Responses to David Hume." In *The Reception of David Hume in Europe*, edited by Peter Jones, 161–81. London: Bloomsbury Academic, 2005.

Žižek, Slavoj. *The Sublime Object of Ideology.* New York: Verso, 1989.

Index

Addison, Joseph, 9, 115–16
additive unfeeling, 2, 5–6, 8, 15, 22, 69, 102, 107, 109–10, 138, 149, 152, 177, 194, 197n7, 220n114. *See also* privative unfeeling
affectio, affectus, 13–14, 26, 142, 200n35.
affect theory, 3, 8, 11, 13–18, 26, 33, 49, 75, 99–100, 115, 142–43, 157, 161, 180–81, 191, 195–96, 197–98n7, 202nn58–59, 202n61, 204n7, 213n21, 230n9, 239n12
Agricola, Gnaeus Julius, 146
Ahern, Stephen, 201n53, 239n12
Alexander the Great, 122
Allen, Richard C., 208n52
amatory fiction, 73, 78–79, 80, 81, 94, 213n12
Amhurst, Nicholas, 172
Anderson, Emily Hodgson, 212–13n8
animal magnetism, 10–11
animal spirits, 14, 32, 49
Ankersmit, F. R., 141–42
Anstey, Peter R., 205nn23–24, 206n36
Aristotle, Aristotelianism, 67, 161
Asgill, John, 171, 232nn39–40
association of ideas, 19–21, 26, 42, 47–49, 50–58, 67, 206n31, 210n77, 210nn80–81, 210n83
attention and inattention, 8–9, 39, 51–53, 55, 60, 152, 198n21, 203n69, 210n73. *See also* distraction
Augustus, Caesar, 122
Austen, Jane, 20, 69, 86, 108–11, 216n59, 218n86, 220n115
autonomic activity, 48, 142, 162
Ayers, Michael, 31, 34, 206n33, 208–209n57

Baier, Annette C., 56, 201n45, 210n83
Ballaster, Ros, 214n25, 215n35
Barbon, Nicholas, 171
Barfoot, Michael, 234–35n73
Barker-Benfield, G. J., 209n60

Barnett, Clive, 195
Barr, Rebecca Anne, 218–219n88
Bayle, Pierre, 200n43
Beckett, J. V., 233n42
Behn, Aphra, 20, 73, 76–80, 213n12, 214nn25–26, 214nn29–30
Bell, John L., 208n53
Bender, John, 86
Bennett, Jonathan, 205n18, 208–209n57
Berington, Joseph, 116
Berkeley, George, 29, 45
Berlant, Lauren Gail, 197–98n7
Berlin, Isaiah, 118
Berman, David, 200n41
Berry, Christopher J., 190, 238n105
Binhammer, Katherine, 218n79
blank narrative, 7, 18, 71, 77, 89, 91, 93–94, 96–97, 99–100, 110–11, 135–36
Boileau Despréaux, Nicolas, 77, 214n28
Bolingbroke, Henry St. John, viscount, 127, 172
Boswell, James, 215n45
Boyle, Robert, 10, 27, 32, 43, 199n25, 205nn23–24, 207n44, 208–209n57, 234–35n73
Bradshaigh, Lady Dorothy, 91–92, 110, 218n82
Braudy, Leo, 137
Brewer, Anthony, 236n89, 237n97, 237–38n100
Brewer, John, 232n33
Bromwich, David, 229n125, 229n127
Brooke, Henry, 1, 2, 7, 15, 197n2
Bruno, Giordano, 230n9
Budd, Adam, 218n82
Burke, Edmund, 145–46; *Abridgment of the English History*, 146–48, 227nn102–3, 228n109; *Letter . . . to a Member of the National Assembly*, 151; *Letter . . . to Sir Hercules Langrishe*, 151; *Letters on a Regicide Peace*, 152; *Philosophical*

259

INDEX

Burke, Edmund (*continued*)
  Enquiry into the Origin of Our Ideas of the Sublime and Beautiful, 148–50; *Reflections on the Revolution in France*, 145, 148, 150–51, 153; review of Hume's *History of England*, 147–48
Burnet, Gilbert, 113
Burney, Frances, 78, 192, 194; *Camilla*, 107; *Cecilia*, 11, 104–107; *Evelina*, 1, 7, 9, 11, 19, 94, 95–103, 105–6, 110, 220n105; *Letters and Journals*, 96–97, 104, 194; *The Wanderer*, 220n114
Burrow, J. W., 230n5
Butler, Joseph, 40, 164–65

Campbell, Jill, 82–83, 85–86, 216n60
Cantillon, Richard, 19, 20, 176–81, 183, 234n56, 235n78
Carrasco, Maria Alejandra, 67
Carrithers, David, 118, 222n16
Carte, Thomas, 113, 221n2
Catullus, Gaius Valerius, 232n40
civilization of the passions, 6, 18, 62, 92, 117, 125, 134–36, 166, 192
Chapone, Hester, 97
Charlemagne, 146
Charles I of England, 130
Charles II of England, 113, 171
Cheyne, George, 46–47, 85, 209nn60–62
Chico, Tita, 218n87
Christensen, Jerome, 208n49
Cicero, 143, 201n50
Clarendon, Edward Hyde, first earl of, 113
Coffman, D'Maris, 233n37
cognition, 8, 16, 83, 143, 115, 202n61, 221n7
Cohn, Dorrit, 218n86
Colbert, Jean-Baptiste, 180
Collins, Anthony, 13, 200n39
Colson, John, 45
Condillac, Étienne Bonnot de, 19, 20, 27, 50–54, 56,192, 198n20, 209n67, 210n73
Condorcet, Marie Jean Antoine Nicolas de Caritat, Marquis of, 229n2
conduct books, 95–98, 219n95, 219n101
conjectural history, 113–14, 133, 137–39
Conley, John, 214n24
Connor, Steven, 229n134
Constantine the Great, 222n16
Conway, Alison, 214n25
corpuscles, corpuscularianism, 10, 14, 32–35, 194, 199n25, 205n23, 206n36, 207n45
Courtney, Cecil Patrick, 221–22n12, 227n103

Cowley, Abraham, 76–77, 214n30
Critical Review, 96
Csengei, Ildiko, 212n8
culture, 18, 22, 47, 70, 126, 130, 135
Curchod, Suzanne, 138

Dalberg-Acton, John, 1st Baron Acton, 146
Dalrymple, John, 126, 223n39
Damasio, Antonio, 17, 84, 202nn61–62, 216n57
Darnton, Robert, 222n25
Davenant, Charles, 171–72
Davenant, William, 171
de Bolla, Peter, 198n13
Defoe, Daniel, 218n77
degrees (slow, imperceptible), 2, 5–6, 21, 49, 60–61, 71, 79, 88, 96–97, 105, 110, 115, 138, 141, 146, 152, 169, 173, 176, 178, 215n36, 216n62, 228–29n123
de Morgan, Augustus, 207–208n48
Deleuze, Gilles, 3, 11, 13, 16, 26, 33, 49, 55, 143, 157, 180, 199n31, 200n35, 202n58, 204n7, 209n64; 210n77, 210n80
Descartes, René, and Cartesianism, 36, 51, 75
Deutsch, Helen, 201n51
distraction, 8, 40, 51, 60, 198n20, 209–10n69. *See also* attention and inattention
Dobranski, Stephen, 216n49
Dodsley, Robert, 122–23, 147, 222–23n26
D'Onofrio, Federico, 231n17
Doody, Margaret Anne, 207n42, 218–19n88, 219n101, 220n112
Downie, J. A., 215n36
Downing, Lisa, 30, 205n21
Dryden, John, 74
dualism, 13–14,16, 45–46, 48, 51, 142, 208–209n57
Dussinger, John, 88, 217n69
Dykstra, Scott, 203n70

Edward III of England, 124
Egginton, William, 202n58
Ellenberger, Henri F., 199n25
Elliot, Gilbert, 62, 127, 211n92
Empson, William, 197n3
Enlightenment, 1, 5, 20, 49, 124–25, 128, 132, 138, 140, 143, 145, 202n66, 229n2; British, 20–21, 116, 118; English, 14, 20; French, 20, 114, 117–25; moderate mainstream, 14, 20; radical, 14, 20, 200n44; Utrecht, 122–23; Scottish, 18, 20, 116, 126, 128, 146, 157, 184, 190,

INDEX 261

227–28n105, 230n5, 231n17, 237n96, 238n105

Fara, Patricia, 199n28
feedback, 3, 15, 85, 157, 160–61, 165, 230n9
Ferguson, Adam, 114, 136
Ferguson, Frances, 218n86, 228nn120–21
feudalism, 6, 136, 148, 158, 185–87, 190, 194, 223n39, 237–38n100
Fielding, Henry, 20, 73, 81, 93, 111, 192; *Amelia*, 86–87; *Pasquin*, 216n62; *Tom Jones*, 69, 81–87, 89, 94
Flaubert, Gustave, 220n106
Fleischacker, Samuel, 211–12n97
Fleury, André-Hercule de, 122–23
flow, 3, 15, 42, 85, 97, 176–82
Fogelin, Robert J., 35, 206n35
Fordyce, James, 96–97
four-stages theory, 18, 20, 126, 145, 185–86, 237n96
Francesconi, Daniele, 134
Frank, Adam, 202n58
Franklin, Benjamin, 10
free indirect discourse, 71, 93, 106, 111, 218n86
French Revolution, 145, 153, 170
Freud, Sigmund, Freudianism, 3, 36, 72, 78, 198nn9–10, 238n5
Fried, Michael, 71, 213n9
Furniss, Tom, 148–49

Galiani, Fernando, 181, 235–36n80
Garis, Robert, 220n116
Gearhart, Suzanne, 52
Gibbon, Edward, 20, 116, 140, 145, 155, 193; *Critical Observations on the Sixth Book of the Aeneid*, 143; *Decline and Fall of the Roman Empire*, 6, 8–9, 23, 57, 115, 118, 127, 137–44, 226n84, 227n91; *Essai sur l'étude de la littérature*, 118, 137, 226n72, 227n92; *Memoirs*, 118, 137, 138–40, 153, 222n17
Girten, Kristin M., 211n89
Glorious Revolution of 1688, 127, 147
Godwin, William, 18, 191–92, 195, 238n1
Gonthier, Ursula Haskins, 221n11
Goring, Paul, 212n3
Grampp, William D., 237n90
Gregg, Melissa, 11, 14–16, 201–202n55
Greig, J. Y. T., 225n54
Griswold, Jr, Charles L., 211n95, 212n99
Groenewegen, Peter, 234n67
Grossberg, Lawrence, 16, 195, 201–202n55

group or collective affect, 6–7, 16, 19, 114, 125, 127–29, 133, 152, 155, 159, 161–68, 169
Guattari, Félix, 13, 199n31, 204n7
Guerrini, Anita, 209n62

Hagstrum, Jean H., 199n30
Hamou, Philippe, 207n44
Harkin, Maureen, 237–38n100
Harris, James A., 55, 210n81, 224n48, 225n54
Harth, Erica, 75
Hartley, David, 7, 10, 17, 19, 20, 26, 27, 42–49, 50, 51, 192
Hayles, N. Katherine, 202n61, 221n7
Haywood, Eliza, 18, 19, 20, 27, 78, 210–11n86; *British Recluse*, 215n36; *Fantomina*, 215n38; *Female Spectator*, 59–61, 109, 138, 192–93, 211nn88–89; *Love in Excess*, 79; *Mercenary Lover*, 73, 79–80, 215n39
Heller-Roazen, Daniel. 205n28
Henry VII of England, 127, 130, 132
Hervey, John, Lord, 233n48
Hewitt, Elizabeth, 237n93
Hicks, Philip, 224n40
Higgs, Henry, 176, 234n58
Hogarth, William, 149, 228–29n123, 229n124
Home, Henry, Lord Kames, 126
Hont, Istvan, 235n78, 237n97
Hudson, Wayne, 200n39
Hultquist, Aleksondra, 201n53
Hume, David, 14, 19–20, 27, 50, 60, 63, 67, 114, 116, 133, 134, 143–44, 146–47, 155, 166, 178, 191–92, 194, 201n45, 201n50, 203n2, 203n4, 206n35, 221n12, 224n48, 228n109, 230n3, 235n76, 235–36n80, 237–38n100; *An Abstract of . . . a Treatise of Human Nature*, 54–55; "Dissertation on the Passions," 236n82; *Enquiry concerning the Principles of Morals*, 211n93; *History of England*, 6, 126–32, 134, 138, 146–48, 153, 193, 222n13, 224n43; *History of Great Britain*, 128, 198n15, 222n13, 224nn46–47; *Letters*, 118, 126–27, 131–32, 181, 221n12, 225n54, 235n77; "Of Luxury," 130, 224n50; "Of National Characters," 114, 118, 222n13; "Of Taxes," 173–74, 175, 179; "Of the Balance of Trade," 10, 179–82, 183–84, 234n69; "Of the Rise and Progress of the Arts and Sciences,"

INDEX

Hume, David (*continued*)
129; "Of the Standard of Taste," 131; *Philosophical Essays concerning Human Understanding*, 55–56, 210n81; *Political Discourses*, 173, 179, 221n11; *Treatise of Human Nature*, 54–57, 129, 131; "The Sceptic," 58, 60
Hundert, E. J, 166, 230n12, 231n28, 232n31
Hutcheson, Francis, 164–65
Hutchison, Terence, 178

ideology, 18, 148–49, 173, 192–96, 238–39n9
Iliffe, Rob, 200n44
infinitesimal, 17, 19, 21, 26, 42–49, 100, 155, 207–208nn47–49, 209n62
inherent adjectives, *see* noninherent and inherent adjectives
Innocent XI, 124
insensible, as civilizing, 6, 62, 117, 125, 134–35, 136, 166; as eclectic idiom, 3, 5, 10, 14, 18, 20–21 32, 67, 156, 192; as "lubricant," 6, 53, 56; political uses of, 18, 127–29, 146–48, 150–53, 156, 158, 166, 169–74, 191–92; as stylistic device, 2, 5, 9, 16, 20–21, 27, 54, 59, 66, 69, 73–74, 78, 81, 83, 85–87, 91, 108, 114, 116, 125, 135, 137–38, 145, 151, 153, 159, 169, 177, 184, 192, 195, 228–29n123; as revolutionary, 6, 128–30, 132, 134, 155, 187–88, 195
insensible perceptions, 27, 31, 33, 50, 51, 52, 55–56, 199n25, 206n31. *See also* unconscious mental contents
intensity, 3, 13, 15–16, 26, 49, 56, 74, 78, 100, 157, 186, 201n53, 204n7, 230n9
involuntariness, 11, 71–72, 77, 80, 85, 90, 101–7, 220n114
Israel, Jonathan I., 20, 143, 200n39, 220n44

Jacobites, 113
Jacovides, Michael, 205n20
James I of England, 130, 131
James, duke of York and James II of England, 113, 171
James, E. D., 231n28
Jameson, Fredric, 2, 71, 99–100, 220n106
Jevons, William Stanley, 20, 234n59
Jockers, Matthew L., 5
John, king of England, 146–47
Johnson, Claudia, L., 220n115
Johnson, Samuel, 81; *Dictionary*, 2, 8–9, 42, 114, 197n4, 201n50
Johnston, Adrian, 198n10

Jones, Vivien, 219n95
Jordan, David P., 137

Kant, Immanuel, Kantianism, 114, 211–212n97
Kaye, F. B., 232n31
Keymer, Tom, 87, 217n75
King, Kathryn R., 215n39
Klever, Wim, 201n45, 235n76
Koehler, Margaret, 203n69
Koselleck, Reinhart, 9
Kramnick, Jonathan, 79, 204n6, 206n39, 215n38, 217n68

Lacan, Jacques, and Lacanianism, 3, 72, 198n10, 213n11
Lavoisier, Antoine, 10
law, 96, 118, 120–21, 125, 127, 130, 134, 146–48, 151–53, 156, 163, 175–76, 181, 184, 186, 190, 211n95, 223n39, 236n82, 238n104
Le Blanc, Jean–Bernard, abbé 126
Lee, Wendy Anne, 7, 197n7
Leibniz, G. W., 27, 32–33, 36, 44, 49, 52, 199n25, 205n27, 206n31, 209n64
Lennox, Charlotte, 222–23n26
Lewis, Jayne Elizabeth, 229n134
Leys, Ruth, 16, 202nn58–59, 202n64
liberty, 122, 127–28, 132, 134, 145–48, 153, 163, 172–73, 183, 224n46, 233n55
Libet, Benjamin, 17
Lock, F. P., 148, 227n103
Locke, John, 14, 20; "Epitome" of the *Essay*, 204n13; *Essay concerning Human Understanding*, 6, 9–10, 19, 25–41, 42, 43, 46–48, 50–52, 57, 60, 83, 191–92, 194, 199n25, 203nn1–2, 203n4, 204n11, 204n13, 205nn20–21, 206n31, 206nn33–34, 206n36–39, 207n44, 208–209n57, 209n67
Longinus, 77, 214n28
Louis III of France, 123
Louis XIV of France, 117, 122–25
Louis XVI of France, 10
Lynch, Deidre Shauna, 201n51, 212n7

Macaulay, Catharine, 132, 145, 225n60
Macfie, A. L., 211n93
Mack, Ruth, 141–42
Mackenzie, Henry, 212n3, 219n104
Macpherson, Sandra, 90–91, 102, 204n6, 218n77
Magna Carta, 146–48, 228n109

INDEX

Malabou, Catherine, 202n61
Mandeville, Bernard, 20, 21, 156, 184, 187, 200n39; *Fable of the Bees*, 15, 18, 21, 62, 128, 155, 159–62, 164–68, 188, 190, 230n13, 232n31; *Free Thoughts on Religion, the Church, and National Happiness*, 162–64, 231n18; *The Grumbling Hive*, 18, 159, 162; *Treatise of the Hypochondriack and Hysterick Passions*, 163–64
Manley, Delariver, 215n36
Manuel, Frank E., 137
Marvell, Andrew, 171–72
Marx, Karl, 156, 180, 193–94
Massumi, Brian, 13, 15, 16–17, 33, 49, 83, 142, 198n9, 202nn57–59, 202n64, 204n7, 213n21, 230n9
materialism and material processes, 6–7, 10, 14, 26, 38, 42–43, 45–47, 51, 67, 70, 75–78, 84, 119, 142–43, 153, 156, 189, 208n56, 208–209n 57
Mathias, Peter, 233n34
McCann, Edwin, 30, 206n34
McCloskey, Donald N., 233n34
McCormick, Ted, 233n37
McKeon, Michael, 76–77, 96, 217n71
McLoughlin, T. O., 147, 228n109
McMahon, Darrin M., 230n14, 231n17
mechanism, mechanics, 10, 13–14, 27, 32, 34, 46, 75, 78
mediation, 6–7, 17, 26, 28, 37, 41, 47–48, 51, 58, 60–61, 63, 67, 95, 114, 125, 130, 144, 156, 188, 196
Medici family, 122
mercantilism, 175, 178, 180–81
Merritt, Juliette, 211n88
Mesmer, Franz Anton, Mesmerism, 10–11, 199n25, 199nn28–29
Methodism, 97
Michie, Allen, 215n44
Middleton, Conyers, 138–40
Miller, D. A., 85–86, 216n59
Milton, John, 74
Misraki, Paul, 1, 3
moeurs (manners), 6, 96–97, 114, 117, 119–25, 126, 130–34, 146–47, 150, 152–53, 185, 221n4 222n24, 223n36, 227n104, 228n108
Molesworth, Jesse, 216n63
Momigliano, Arnaldo, 139
Montesquieu, Charles-Louis de Secondat, Baron de, 20, 51, 117, 125–26, 133, 146, 152, 181, 222n26, 227n103, 228n108,

235n77; *De la Politique*, 118; *Reflections on the Causes of the Grandeur and Declension of the Romans*, 221n11, 222n21; *Spirit of Laws*, 114, 117–22, 153, 222n16
Moore, James, 126
morality and moral philosophy, 19, 25–26, 58, 59–67, 69–71, 74, 90, 92, 95–97, 102, 104,106–7, 111, 114, 119, 152, 162, 164–65, 168, 173, 176, 181–82, 194, 204n6, 211n93, 211–12n97, 227–28n105, 232n31, 235–236n80
Mossner, Ernst, 235–36n80
Mudge, Bradford K., 214n29
Mullan, John, 209n60
Murphy, Antoin E., 233n56

Nagle, Christopher C., 220n117
neuroscience, neurophysiology, 17, 43, 49, 50, 84, 202n58
Newton, Isaac, 10, 14, 20, 42–47, 200n44, 207nn44–45, 207nn47–48, 208nn50–53
Ngrams, 3–4, 11–12, 18, 23, 102–103, 198nn12–13
Nicolazzo, Sarah, 217n73
Nicole, Pierre, 231n28
Nietzsche, Friedrich, 168
nonconsciousness, 36, 38–39, 41, 48–49, 56, 82–85, 98, 101, 115, 121, 141–42, 175, 192, 202n61, 216n57, 221n7; vs. the unconscious, 3, 17, 27, 33, 99, 167–68, 198n9
noninherent and inherent adjectives, 7–8, 15, 22, 32, 205n26
North, Dudley, 159, 192
Nugent, Thomas, 20, 51–53, 118, 122, 222n24, 222–23n26

O'Brien, Karen, 123, 125, 132, 225n59, 225n64
O'Brien, Patrick K., 170, 233n34
O'Neill, Daniel I., 227–28n105
openness of affect to the world, 8, 11, 14, 17–18, 115, 196. *See also* unspecificity of unfeeling
Ovid, 80

panpsychism, 75–76, 143
Parfit, Derek, 206n38
Parker, Fred, 206n34
Parrault, Claude, 75
Pauchant, Thierry, 223–24n39, 237n96
Peirce, C. S., 202n57

Pellisson–Fontanier, Paul, 131, 225n54
personal identity, 9, 25–26, 33, 36–41, 57, 107, 203n2, 203n4, 203–204n5, 206nn38–39
Petty, William, 18, 170–71, 181, 232nn37–38
Pfau, Thomas, 238n5
Philip II of Macedon, 122
Philip IV of France, 124
Phillips, John, 74, 213n14
Phillips, Mark Salber, 116, 127, 224n43
Phillips, Natalie, 198n20, 209–10n69
Phillipson, Nicholas, 211n92
Physiocrats, 237n97
Pocock, J. G. A., 20, 114, 123, 141, 143, 222–23n26, 223n36, 226n72, 226n80, 226n84, 227n92
politeness, 6, 92, 98–99, 116–17, 131, 144, 145, 156, 165–68
Pope, Alexander, 35, 78, 214–15n32
Popkin, Richard H., 235n76
Postlethwayt, Malachy, 179, 234nn66–67
Potkay, Adam, 160, 201n50, 230–31n15
prepersonal affect, 7–8, 13, 19, 26, 74–75, 114–15, 125, 204n7
Priestley, Joseph, 14, 46, 152, 208n56, 209n58, 229n134
Prince, Michael, 80
privative unfeeling, 2, 5, 7–9, 22, 38, 62, 69, 70–71, 102, 109, 135, 149, 152, 177, 197–98n7, 198n18. *See also* additive unfeeling
progress, 8–9, 116, 121, 132–34, 136, 145, 148, 166–67, 185–87, 190–92, 237n96
proto-self, 17, 84, 202n62, 216n57

qualified affect, 15, 157, 230n9
Quesnay, François, 237n97

Raphael, D. D., 211n93
Ramsay, Andrew Michael (Chevalier Ramsay), 181
Ramsay, Michael, 131
Rapin de Thoyras, Paul, 113, 131, 221n2, 225n54
Reeve, Clara, 81
reflexivity, of author's activity in own account, 115–16, 193: Burke's, 148, 150–52; Condillac's, 54; Gibbon's, 57, 116, 137–44, 193; Haywood's, 59–60, 138; Hume's, 57–58, 116, 132, 128, 138, 193; Smith's, 186–87, 190
Reid, Thomas, 40, 46, 62
Reinhardt, Django, 1

resonation, 15–16, 49, 78, 157, 230n9
Richardson, Samuel, 20, 42, 46, 73, 81, 85, 111, 209n60, 222–23n26; *Collection of the Moral and Instructive Sentiments . . .* , 218n84; *Clarissa*, 2, 70, 71, 81, 87–92, 94, 107, 110, 212n6, 217n64, 218n84; *Sir Charles Grandison*, 69, 89, 92–4, 218n87, 218–19n88
Richetti, John, 95, 213n12
Riskin, Jessica, 229n134
Roberts, William, 213n13
Robertson, John, 202n66, 231n29
Robertson, William, 114, 132–35, 146–47, 166, 225n67
Rochester, John Wilmot, second earl of, 80
romance, 59, 73–76, 78, 81, 94, 99, 108, 111
Roos, Suzanne, 210n73
Rorty, Richard, 203n1
Roseveare, Henry, 171
Rothschild, Emma, 229n2, 237n91
Russell, Paul, 201n45
Ryle, Gilbert, 203n1

Samuels, Warren J., 184, 236n86, 236n89
Sand, Rosemarie Sponner, 206nn30–31
Sappho, 214n28
Sato, Sora, 227nn103–104
Savage, Richard, 215n39
scales of unfeeling, 18–19, 26, 50, 59, 71, 113–15, 127–28, 155–56
Schabas, Margaret, 230n3, 234–35n73, 236n84
Schaffer, Simon, 208n56, 209n58
Schechtman, Marya, 40
Schliesser, Eric, 63
Schürer, Norbert, 222–23n26
Schweitzer, Jerome W., 213nn13–14
Scott, Walter, 212n3
Scott, William Robert, 237n95
Scudéry, Georges de, 74–77, 194, 213n13, 213n17
Scudéry, Madeleine de, 75–76, 213n13, 214n24
secretness, 13, 17, 21, 60, 66, 69, 82–86, 124–25, 127, 133, 180, 182, 200n40
Sedgwick, Eve Kosofsky, 16, 202nn58–59
Seigel, Jerrold, 203n4, 209n67
Seigworth, Gregory J., 11, 14–16
sensibility, 1, 3, 6–9, 16, 18, 22, 27, 42, 47, 70, 87, 97–98, 107–11, 119, 127–28, 130, 134, 141, 146, 151, 197n3, 207n42, 217n64, 220n117

INDEX

sentiment, sentimentalism, 8, 13, 25–6, 42, 50, 55–6, 59, 62–67, 69–70, 73, 78, 81, 85, 98, 108–11, 113–14, 115–17, 119, 125, 127–34, 145, 149–54, 155, 181, 197n7, 201n50, 207n42, 212n3, 219n104, 220n115
Shaftesbury, Anthony Ashley Cooper, first earl of (Lord Ashley), 36
Shaver, Robert, 211n96
Sheehan, Jonathan, 230n5, 230n7, 237n94, 238n101
Sigler, David, 213n11
Singer, Brian, 119
skepticism, 17, 20, 27, 34–36, 85–86, 116, 119, 141–44, 206nn34–36, 226n84, 227n92
Sloterdijk, Peter, 10
Smith, Adam, 14, 203n4, 223–24n39; "History of Astronomy," 189; *Lectures on Jurisprudence*, 185, 233n55, 237n95; *Theory of Moral Sentiments*, 19–21, 26–27, 61–67, 69, 135, 189, 192, 203n4, 211nn91–92, 211–12nn96–99, 219n104, 236n89, 238n103; *Wealth of Nations*, 6, 18, 19–20, 128, 155–59, 174–75, 178, 183–90, 194, 229n2, 230n3, 234n58, 236n89, 237n90, 237–38nn95–105
Smith, C. U. M., 207n47
Smith, Craig, 230n5, 238n101
Soni, Vivasan, 201n50, 230n14
Spacks, Patricia Meyer, 78
Spinoza, Baruch, 11, 13–14, 20, 26, 143, 157, 180–81, 199n31, 200n39, 200n41, 200n43, 201n45, 204n8, 227nn91–92, 235n76
Sterne, Laurence, 28
Steuart, James, 155, 157, 174
Steuart, Robert, 234–35n73
Stewart, Lady Louisa, 212n3
Stillingfleet, Edward, 208–9n57
Strawson, Galen, 40
sublime, 9, 77, 141–42, 148–49, 214n28, 228n120

Tallis, Frank, 199n25
taste, 9, 61, 97, 109, 129, 131, 186
Taylor, Charles, 203n2
temporality, affective, 2, 26, 37–38, 42, 50, 70–71, 79, 89–90, 94, 96, 99–101, 104–7, 111, 123, 126–27, 132, 142, 157, 166–67, 177–78, 180, 194
Thiel, Udo, 203n3
Thomson, James, 22

Tierney-Hynes, Rebecca, 210–11n86
Tillemont, Louis Sébastien Le Nain de, 140
Tindal, Matthew, 13, 200n39
Toland, John, 13, 200n39
Tories, 228n109
Toussaint, François-Vincent, 221n4
Travis, George, 227n91
Trenchard, John, 13–14, 17, 200nn40–41
Tuite, Clara, 220n115
Turner, Michael, 233n42

unconscious, 2–3, 10–11, 33, 36, 52, 56, 70–72, 86, 88, 99, 165, 199n30, 206nn30–31, 210n83, 220n114, 238n5
unconscious, vs. nonconsciousness. See nonconsciousness, vs. the unconscious
unconscious mental contents, 3, 11, 27, 31, 33, 36–37, 50, 53, 55–56, 58, 60, 62–64, 66–67, 72, 167–68, 206n31, 231n28. See also insensible perceptions
unintended consequences, 90, 127–28, 132, 134, 147–48, 157–58, 184, 230n5
unspecificity of unfeeling, 8, 11, 15, 17, 38, 61, 115, 129, 138. See also prepersonal affect

Van Sant, Ann Jesse, 217n64
Virgil, 143, 199n30, 226n72
virtuality, 15–17, 33, 49, 83, 157, 161, 191–92, 201n53
vitalism, 14, 46
Voltaire (François-Marie Arouet), 20, 51, 117, 121, 126, 134, 222n26; *Age of Lewis XIV*, 122–124, 127; *Essay on Universal History*, 122, 124–25, 127

Wagner, Richard, 220n106
Wahrman, Dror, 203–4n5, 220n113, 230n5, 230n7, 237n94, 238n101
Walpole, Robert, 122–23, 172
Warburton, William, 143, 227n95
Warner, William, 91
Watt, Ian, 70, 87, 89, 212n6
Weinstein, Jack Russell, 190, 238n104
Wennerlind, Carl, 234n69
Wesley, John, 219n103
Weston, Jr., John C., 228n108
Whigs, 113, 147
Wilkes, Wetenhall, 96, 219n96
will, 25–26, 49, 63, 70, 79, 84, 90–91, 102, 104–6, 114, 173, 180
Witenagemot, 146–48, 228n116
Wittgenstein, Ludwig, 199n22

Wolfe, Charles, 207n47
Womersley, David, 137
Wootton, David, 222n13
Wordsworth, William, 22–23, 203n70

Xenophon, 197n2

Young, Edward, 22

Zanardi, Paola, 235–36n80
Žižek, Slavoj, 238–39n9
Zola, Émile, 100

Printed in the USA
CPSIA information can be obtained
at www.ICGtesting.com
LVHW041206150324
774517LV00035B/1321

9 781501 770128